Representations of China in Latin American Literature (1987–2016)

Liverpool Latin American Studies

Series Editor: Matthew Brown, University of Bristol
Emeritus Series Editor: Professor John Fisher

---

12 The Reinvention of Mexico: National Ideology in a Neoliberal Era
Gavin O'Toole

13 Armies, Politics and Revolution: Chile, 1808–1826
Juan Luis Ossa Santa Cruz

14 Andean Truths: Transitional Justice, Ethnicity, and Cultural Production in Post-Shining Path Peru
Anne Lambright

15 Positivism, Science, and 'The Scientists' in Porfirian Mexico: A Reappraisal
Natalia Priego

16 Argentine Cinema and National Identity (1966–1976)
Carolina Rocha

17 Decadent Modernity: Civilization and 'Latinidad' in Spanish America, 1880–1920
Michela Coletta

18 Borges, Desire, and Sex
Ariel de la Fuente

19 Contacts, Collisions and Relationships: Britons and Chileans in the Independence era, 1806–1831
Andrés Baeza Ruz

20 Writing and the Revolution: Venezuelan Metafiction 2004–2012
Katie Brown

21 Marvels of Medicine: Literature and Scientific Enquiry in Early Colonial Spanish America
Yarí Pérez Marín

22 Colonial Legacies and Contemporary Identities in Chile Revisiting Catalina de los Ríos y Lisperguer
Céire Broderick

23 Literary Reimaginings of Argentina's Independence: History, Fiction, Politics
Catriona McAllister

24 Football and Nation Building in Colombia (2010–2018): The Only Thing That Unites Us
Peter J. Watson

25 A World Without Hunger: Josué de Castro and the Geography of Survival
Archie Davies

26 Distortion and Subversion: Punk Rock Music and the Protests for Free Public Transportation in Brazil (1996–2011)
Rodrigo Lopes de Barros

27 The Woodbine Parish Report on the Revolutions in South America (1822): The Foreign Office and Early British Intelligence on Latin America
Mariano Schlez

28 A City Against Empire: Transnational Anti-Imperialism in Mexico City, 1920–1930
Thomas K. Lindner

Liverpool Latin American Studies, New Series 29

Representations of China in Latin American Literature (1987–2016)

Maria Montt Strabucchi

LIVERPOOL UNIVERSITY PRESS

First published 2023 by
Liverpool University Press
4 Cambridge Street
Liverpool
L69 7ZU

This paperback edition published 2025

British Library Cataloguing-in-Publication data
A British Library CIP record is available

ISBN 978-1-83764-427-8 (hardback)
ISBN 978-1-83624-558-2 (paperback)

Typeset by Carnegie Book Production, Lancaster
Printed and bound by CPI Group (UK) Ltd, Croydon CR0 4YY

Contents

Acknowledgements

This book was written with the support and encouragement of many colleagues, friends, and family. It is based on my Ph.D. in Latin American Cultural Studies at The University of Manchester, under the guidance of Hilary Owen and James Scorer. I would like to express my deepest thanks to Hilary for her invaluable kindness, patience, immense knowledge, and exceptional guidance; to James for his precise comments, and expert knowledge; and to Sarah Bowskill and Joseph McGonagle for their stimulating questions and encouragement. I would also like to thank Heather Inwood, Esther Gómez Sierra, Zheng Yangwen, and Chris Perriam for their generous help and recommendations. I would also like to thank the UoM Spanish, Portuguese, and Latin American Studies department members and the School of Arts, Languages and Cultures Graduate School staff, as they were always helpful and enthusiastic.

In different ways and at different moments, Carol Chan, Camila Gatica, and Ceire Broderick pushed me through to the completion of this book. Thanks to Claudio Rolle, Fernando Purcell, Olaya Sanfuentes, René Millar, Patricio Bernedo, Ximena Illanes, Joaquín Fermandois, Rafael Gaune, Pablo Whipple, Susana Gazmuri, Manuel Gárate, Daniela Serra, María José Cot, Alfredo Riquelme, José Ragas, Rafael Sagredo, Macarena Ponce de León, Jorge Rojas, Stephan Ruderer, Sol Serrano, Nancy Nicholls, Carolina Odone, Javier Correa, Rosario Rodríguez, Bárbara Silva, Johannes Rehner, Roberto Durán, Agustín Letelier, María Elvira Ríos, José Miguel Vidal, Claudia Labarca, Rosario Hubert, Carla Rivera, Amelia Sáiz-López, Rosario Hubert, Nicole Jenne, Francisco Urdinez and Valeria Palanza for their continuous encouragement. Thanks to Daphné Richet-Cooper, Ana Allamand, Patricia Palma, Magdalena Besser, Martin Cassassus, Catalina Carrasco, Gabriela Zapata, Fernando Pérez, Mariana Perry, Denise Misleh, Darinka Radovic, Gorica Majstorovic, Marisol Verdugo, Denisse Sepúlveda, Anita Morales, Harriet Lamb and Joel Anicama for their advice and friendship along the way. Thanks to all the friends at the UoM Graduate School for their encouragement and company when most needed. Throughout the PhD: Eleanor K. Jones, Jan Gryta, Kaya Davies Hayon, Nicola Tomlinson, Mary Farrelly,

Joseph Twist, Alistair Dickins, Jeremy John Gunson, Elena Anna Spagnuolo, Jessica Coatesworth, Thomas Wroblewski, Katarzyna Nowak and Davide Porzio, Kathleen Easlick, Paulina Kolata, Luke Kelly, Carole Myers, Nicola Runciman, Nicola Jones, Lew Ryder, Vitaly Kazakov, Gwynne George, Ben Wilcock, Michael Smith, Helen Kilburn and so many others. Special thanks to Lucía Stecher, Héctor Hoyos and Ignacio López-Calvo, and to Beatrice Glow and Julia Wong for their inspiration.

Special acknowledgments to the editorial board and the anonymous readers at Liverpool University Press. I would particularly like to thank Chloé Johnson for her kind support throughout the production and publication process—especially under the challenging conditions during the Covid-19 pandemic.

I am extremely grateful that my Ph.D. work was made possible by Becas Chile Scholarship of the Chilean Government and la Pontificia Universidad Católica de Chile, as well as the following funding and grants: ANID Fondecyt de Iniciación 11200151 and ANID Iniciativa Científica Núcleo Milenio NCS2022_053 on the Impacts of China in Latin America (ICLAC). The Pontificia Universidad Católica de Chile and The University of Manchester, the Centro de Estudios Asiáticos UC, the Grupo de Estudios Transpacíficos (GETS) and the Asia and the Americas section at the Latin American Studies Association (LASA) are the institutions and organizations which stimulated conversations and research on China, discussions central to this book. Parts of this book were presented at different conferences and seminars, and some sections were published in journal articles and edited collections. I thank the organizers, participants and reviewers for their comments and suggestions.

Special thanks to Rodney Strabucchi, Joan Ewer and Giselle Gibbons for their key support completing this manuscript. Thanks to Nuria Alsina, whose inspiring mentorship and friendship I miss so much.

All these persons and many others not mentioned have been my village. They have helped me raise the children and finish this book. Thanks to my whole family and, in particular, to my parents, to Joaquín, Lucía and Ana for their unwavering support and love. I dedicate this book to them.

All errors remain my own.

Introduction

In May of 2016, I unexpectedly came across an art installation by the artist Beatrice Glow. Her work explored the relationship between Asia and the Americas, focusing on the case of Chinese migration to Peru. Together with a Chinese fan and an extract of a Peruvian coolie agreement document, Glow's installation included a dictionary prepared by her of the meaning of the term 'china-o'.[1] Indeed, in Spanish, 'el chino' or 'la china' is an expression used to refer to an Asian/Chinese person, someone that *looks* 'Chinese'. In her 'chino/a' dictionary, Glow explores how the term has been used in different parts of Latin America,[2] exploring its racist uses beyond ethnic definitions. Glow's selection includes examples from television advertisements, such as the Brahma beer advertisement 'la china paga', which aired in Peru, to politicians' nicknames, notably Alberto 'el chino' Fujimori. Many of the uses she observes in Peru are also present in other Latin American countries. For example, beyond its links to ethnicity and racism, the term is sometimes used for those who have expressed sympathy for Maoism, such as Argentine politician Carlos 'el chino' Zannini, and is used for people who are perceived to 'look' 'Chinese' or Asian.[3] While Glow's art adds to the growing list of exhibits that explore the relationship between Asia and the Americas and suggests the importance that this relationship has today, her 'dictionary' is incredibly insightful in hinting towards the histories which inform the presence of 'China' in Latin America and which underpin this book. Glow's project suggests ways to think about how and why 'China' is

1 Beatrice Glow, *Taparaco Myth* 塔琶拉古傳說 *Mito Taparaco* (Lima: B. Glow, 2009); *What Is Chino? Memories and Imaginaries of Asian Latin America*, 2014 <http://post.at.moma.org/content_items/500-what-is-chino-memories-and-imaginaries-of-asian-latin-america> [accessed 1 August 2021]. Throughout this book, I have kept quotes in the original Spanish.

2 Here, I use the term Latin America as a useful concept, aware of its complexity and malleability.

3 Maria Montt Strabucchi, Carol Chan, and María Elvira Ríos, *Chineseness in Chile: Shifting Representations during the Twenty-First Century*, Studies of the Americas (Cham: Palgrave Macmillan, 2022) <https://doi.org/10.1007/978-3-030-83966-6>.

represented in Latin America, which is my project: my focus, however, is on how 'China' is represented in late twentieth- and early twenty-first-century Latin American literature. Glow's 'dictionary' is an especially useful way to introduce this book, as her work recalls how 'China' is put to play within specific and arbitrary classification systems.

As Glow's work signalled in the first years of the 2000s, Asia has appeared as an ever more relevant topic of study in Latin America, and China has played a central role in these investigations. Its position in Latin America has been approached in different cultural forms. For example, the Argentinean Sebastián Borensztein explored issues of communication and cultural differences in the film *Un cuento chino* (*Chinese Take-Away*).[4] The film was a high-grossing movie in Argentina and went on to win several prizes internationally. Earlier, the Chilean artist Bruna Truffa had explored the presence of Chinese industrial, cultural, and aesthetic objects in her individual exposition *Hecho en China* (Made in China, 2007). Her work was exhibited in a famous art gallery (Sala Gasco de Arte Contemporáneo) and was discussed by the mainstream press.[5] Although the growing weight of China is also felt in its symbolical-cultural dimension, despite some studies on Orientalism in Latin America, and some studies of fiction and its authors, it is surprising how little scholarship has been devoted to the study of the representations of China in Latin America. China's role in Latin America remains an under-researched area, notwithstanding the growing corpus of literature on the topic. However, this seems to have been changing fast since the second decade of the twenty-first century.[6] Current research has focused on case studies by

4 In English, it was known as *Chinese Take-Away*; Sebastián Borensztein, *Un cuento chino*, 2011.

5 In 2022 she opened an exhibition "Sellos de ocio" at MAVI UC in Chile, where China is also present through the inclusion of Chinese landscapes and imagery, including a stamp which represents her name.

6 Among others, Monica DeHart, *Transpacific Developments: The Politics of Multiple Chinas in Central America* (Ithaca and London: Cornell University Press, 2021); Carol Chan, 'Imagining and Linking Latin America: Chinese Regional Mobilities and Social Networks in Chile', *Journal of Latin American Geography*, 17.2 (2018), pp. 23–45; Maria Montt Strabucchi and Carol Chan, 'Questioning the Conditional Visibility of the Chinese: (Non)Normative Representations of China and Chineseness in Chilean Cultural Productions', *Journal of Chinese Overseas*, 16.1 (2020), pp. 90–116 <https://doi.org/10.1163/17932548-12341414>; Montt Strabucchi, Chan, and Ríos; Carol Wise, *Dragonomics: How Latin America is Maximizing (or Missing out on) China's International Development Strategy* (New Haven: Yale University Press, 2020); *The Political Economy of China–Latin America Relations in the New Millennium: Brave New World*, ed. by Margaret Myers and Carol Wise (New York: Routledge, 2017); *China en América Latina. Lecciones para la Cooperación Sur-Sur y el Desarrollo Sostenible*, ed. by Rebecca Ray and others (Lima: Universidad del Pacífico; Boston University, 2016); *Cultural and Literary Dialogues Between Asia and Latin America*, ed. by Axel Gasquet and Gorica Majstorovic (Cham: Springer International Publishing, 2021)

country that study the economic and historical links between regions, the assimilation of Asian cultures in Latin America, Spain, and Portugal, how Asians in Latin America represent themselves in literature, or how Asia is seen and represented by Latin American travellers, among others. Regarding China's specific case, most scholarly research has focused on economic relations, especially the growing economic and geopolitical influence of the People's Republic of China (PRC) in the region. In recent years, scholarship on Chinese–Latin American relations has grown, responding to newly opened archives, new memoirs, revisionist research, and the rising economic and political exchange between both regions. This has led to a re-evaluation of the role and presence of the Chinese diaspora in Latin America and the cultural relationship between China and Latin America.

While representations of China in Latin American film are present historically in the region,[7] it is in literature that a significant corpus can be found. Since the 1990s, preceded by the country's reforms in the 1980s and its rapid integration into the world market,[8] the PRC and Latin America have engaged in a qualitatively and quantitatively new relationship. Since then, the presence of China in

<https://doi.org/10.1007/978-3-030-52571-2>; *Trans-Pacific Encounters: Asia and the Hispanic World*, ed. by Koichi Hagimoto (Newcastle upon Tyne: Cambridge Scholars Publishing, 2016); Kim Beauchesne, Koichi Hagimoto, and Ineke Phaf-Rheinberger, 'Interrogantes asiáticos y miradas latinoamericanas: Una introducción', *Revista de crítica literaria latinoamericana*, 44.87 (2018), pp. 9–17; Laura J. Torres-Rodríguez, *Orientaciones Transpacíficas. La modernidad mexicana y el espectro de Asia* (Chapel Hill: The University of North Carolina Press, 2019).

7 Among others, Ignacio López-Calvo, *Dragons in the Land of the Condor: Writing Tusán in Peru* (Tucson: The University of Arizona Press, 2014); Ana Paulina Lee, *Mandarin Brazil: Race, Representation, and Memory* (Stanford: Stanford University Press, 2018); María Elvira Ríos, María Montt, and Carol Chan, 'El imaginario de lo chino en las revistas magazinescas chilenas de principios del siglo XX', *Revista Rumbos TS. Un espacio crítico para la reflexión en Ciencias Sociales*, 24 (2021), pp. 129–150 <https://doi.org/10.51188/rrts.num24.434>; Daisy Saravia, *Migración china y orientalismo modernista. Análisis en la revista Variedades (1909-1919)* (Lima: Ediciones MyL, 2020); *Narrativas de "lo chino" en la las Américas y la Peninsula Ibérica*, ed. by Maria Montt Strabucchi and Amelia Saiz-López (Barcelona: Edicions Bellaterra, 2020); *Representaciones de China en las Américas y la Península Ibérica*, ed. by Joaquín Beltrán Antolín, Francisco Javier Haro, and Amelia Sáiz, Biblioteca de China Contemporánea (Barcelona: Edicions Bellaterra, 2016).

8 Robert Evan Ellis, *China in Latin America: The Whats and Wherefores* (Boulder: Lynne Rienner Publishers, 2009); Robert Evan Ellis, *China on the Ground in Latin America: Challenges for the Chinese and Impacts on the Region* (New York: Palgrave Macmillan, 2014); Enrique Dussel Peters, 'Latin America and the Caribbean and China: Socioeconomic Debates on Trade and Investment and the Case of CELAC', in *China and Latin America in Transition*, ed. by Shoujun Cui and Manuel Pérez García (New York: Palgrave Macmillan, 2016), pp. 157–173; Johannes Rehner, Sebastián Baeza, and Jonathan Barton, *En Hombros de Gigantes. Una Geografía Económica del Comercio Chile-Asia* (Santiago: GEOlibros, 2015); Myers and Wise; Wise; *China in Argentina:*

Latin American literature has increased. Starting in 1987 with the publication of the Argentinean César Aira's *Una novela china* (A Chinese Novel) and accelerating through the 2000s, there has been a steady production of Latin American narrative fiction dealing with China and the Chinese in Latin America. More than twenty novels written by Latin American authors in Spanish, which revolve around China, were published between 1987 and 2016. Through an analysis of a selection of these texts, this book explores how 'China' and 'chinos/as' have been imagined and represented in Latin American novels.

The word 'China' usually denotes China as a country, but the use of the term 'chino' in Latin America is far from stable.[9] As anthropologist Lok Siu shows, the word 'chino' often refers to 'Asian' as a racial category rather than as an ethnic Chinese identity.[10] According to Siu, with regard to the Mexican context, the term 'chino/a' is explicitly noted and used matter-of-factly for racial difference, and yet there is little connection made between discourses of racial difference and the power of racialization with its consequent production of social and cultural marginalization.[11] 'Chino/a' also recalls the hegemonic imperialism embodied by identity constructions in the Spanish colonial period in Latin America, where all Asians were collected together under the category of 'chinos'.[12] The term is sometimes also used with no specific relation to any Asian origin, as in the eighteenth-century caste system, where 'chino' was used to describe the mixture of 'Morisco con Española';[13] or as derived from the Quechua word *čína* meaning female or servant.[14] These

Ethnographies of a Global Expansion, ed. by Máximo Badaró (Cham: Springer International Publishing, 2022) <https://doi.org/10.1007/978-3-030-92422-5>.

9 DeHart, *Transpacific Developments: The Politics of Multiple Chinas in Central America*; Montt Strabucchi, Chan, and Ríos; Torres-Rodríguez.

10 Lok Siu, *Memories of a Future Home: Diasporic Citizenship of Chinese in Panama* (Stanford: Stanford University Press, 2007), p. 202; Lok Siu, 'Hemispheric Raciality: Yellowface and the Challenge of Transnational Critique', *Asian Diasporic Visual Cultures and the Americas*, 2.1–2 (2016), pp. 163–179; Lok Siu, 'Diasporic Cultural Citizenship: Chineseness and Belonging in Central America', *Social Text*, 19.4 (2001), pp. 7–28.

11 Lok Siu, 'Chino Latino Restaurants: Converging Communities, Identities, and Cultures', *Afro-Hispanic Review*, 27.1 (2008), pp. 161–71; Lok Siu, 'Hemispheric Raciality'; See also, for Chile, Wonjung Min, 'Mis Chinos, Tus Chinos: The Orientalism of Chilean K-Pop Fans', *International Communication Gazette*, 83.8 (2021), pp. 799–817 <https://doi.org/10.1177/1748048520928254>.

12 Tatiana Seijas, *Asian Slaves in Colonial Mexico* (New York: Cambridge University Press, 2015); Diego Luis, 'The Armed Chino: Licensing Fear in New Spain', *Journal of Colonialism and Colonial History*, 20.1 (2019), pp. 1–24 <https://doi.org/10.1353/cch.2019.0000>.

13 Anonymous, *Las castas*, 18th century, Museo Nacional del Virreinato, Tepotzotlán, Mexico.

14 Real Academia Española, 'chino3,na', *Diccionario de la Lengua Española*, 2017 <http://dle.rae.es/?id=8ppm97c> [accessed 1 July 2021].

different understandings of the term 'chino/a' suggest the various ways one can think about how China is represented in Latin America.

'China' usually does refer to a generic Asia, the sovereign country, or an exotic imaginary about it, similar to Edward Said's understanding of the 'Orient' in a European context,[15] whereas I use 'China' principally as a multidimensional term whereby both the sovereign country (such as the PRC or the Republic of China — Taiwan) and the exotic imaginary of it, at least partially converge. More specifically, as a corollary of this exotic imaginary, this book proposes that in the novels studied here, the term 'China' is used to interrupt certain discourses of 'otherness' based on essentialist understandings of differences within Latin America. As the novels studied here reflect upon homogenizing assumptions of both China and Latin America, they also expose the ways in which Latin America has regularly failed to engage with China itself and not with its stereotyped image. Moreover, they reveal how complex cultural heritage can be reduced to empty signifiers, becoming a pastiche of culture devoid of meaning and significance. Thus, I use 'China' as a hybrid term that has a flexible discursive matrix that embodies both geopolitical China and the mythical 'China', without necessarily prioritizing one or the other, thus constantly expanding its range of meanings.

By revealing the exoticized and racist assumptions about China that have long shaped Latin America's 'China' since the arrival of the Spanish in 1492, the novels studied here expose how 'China' continues to be shaped by set ideas of an exotic, distant, and faraway imaginary. Disclosing how China can embody 'otherness' in Latin America, the novels engage with China in previous terms of exoticizing discursive formations, challenging that 'otherness' to varying degrees, engaging with that which has traditionally placed 'China' as distant and different. Thus, my main argument is that the novels studied here deconstruct the very idea of Latin American identities through the figure of 'China'. My analysis hence reveals a potentially more inclusive concept of China and the Chinese in Latin American imaginaries. In this sense, 'China' functions as a space that allows the Latin American author to question essentialist historical notions of identity and difference and to suggest new ways of thinking about community in the region, arguably taking a more cosmopolitan stance.

And yet, while many novels studied here disclose and interrupt 'China' as fetish for otherness in Latin America, stereotypes seem to endure, as occurred during the COVID-19 pandemic, where racist and xenophobic expressions towards the Chinese became present in Chile.[16] The 'rise of China' has indeed brought more attention to China in Latin America, thus increasing the number of novels on China being published in the region and

15 Edward Said, *Orientalism* (London: Penguin, 2003).

16 Carol Chan and Maria Montt Strabucchi, 'Many-Faced Orientalism: Racism and Xenophobia in a Time of the Novel Coronavirus in Chile', *Asian Ethnicity*, 22.2 (2021), pp. 374–94 <https://doi.org/10.1080/14631369.2020.1795618>.

made available in bookshops and libraries. One can now find entire sections of Chinese authors' works translated into Spanish in bookshops in Buenos Aires or Santiago, and many more books and articles on China are being published in Spanish. However, it is not necessarily a contemporary China as an economic power that is primarily recalled in the novels' paratextual aspects – their titles, covers, and marketing processes - but rather the evocation of a traditional and exoticized 'China'. Whilst this is arguably performative, and the novels themselves subvert it within their texts, it also runs the risk of reinstating essentialist differences.

Before the 1980s, most texts linked to China published in Latin America were framed by political commitments and within a Cold War context – marked by the Communist Revolution of 1949, the Sino-Soviet Split, *rapprochement* with the United States, and its 'opening up' in the 1980s. Those novels that were not invested in party-politics were, while significant, sporadic. In this sense, only after the late 1980s and more so in the early 2000s did narrative fiction start being published. Before this, China and the Orient in Latin American literature go back to the works of Rubén Darío (1867–1916), especially his poem collection, *Azul* (1888), and are also present in the works of the Mexican José Juan Tablada (1871–1945) and the Chilean Vicente Huidobro (1893–1948).[17] Efrén Rebolledo (1877–1929), Salvador Elizondo (1932–2006), José Lezama Lima (1910–1976), Octavio Paz (1914–1998), and Pablo Neruda (1904–1973) also include the so-called 'Orient' in some of their works.[18] It is also possible to find 'China' throughout Jorge Luis Borges's work[19] and in José Donoso's short story *China*.[20] Texts published by travellers in the 1950s and 1960s gave differing voices to revolutionary China. Many of them included testimonies of travel to other Asian countries; many texts were published throughout the 1950s and up to the 1980s regarding travel to China.[21] Most were published as travel accounts, but novels and poems were

17 Marcela Labraña, 'Poesía oriental y visualidad en Darío, Tablada y Huidobro', *Estudios Avanzados*, 22 (2014), pp. 1–12.

18 Octavio Paz, *Vislumbres de la India* (Barcelona: Seix Barral, 1995); Pablo Neruda, *Oriente* (Barcelona: Littera, 2004); Pablo Neruda, *Confieso que he vivido: memorias* (Barcelona: Editorial Seix Barral, 2011); Edmundo Olivares Briones, *Pablo Neruda, los caminos de oriente* (Santiago: LOM Ediciones, 2000); Gabriela Jauregui, 'Apuntes on Orientalism in/and Latin American Literature: Darío, Tablada, Borges, Paz and Sarduy', *Canadian Review of Comparative Literature/Revue Canadienne de Littérature Comparée*, 35.1–2 (2008), p. 70.

19 Jorge Luis Borges, *Otras Inquisiciones (1937–1952)* (Buenos Aires: Sur, 1952); Jorge Luis Borges, *Historia Universal de la Infamia* (Buenos Aires: Vintage Español, 2012); Jorge Luis Borges, *Ficciones* (Madrid: Alianza, 1997).

20 José Donoso, *Los mejores cuentos de José Donoso* (Santiago de Chile: Zig-Zag, 1966).

21 Jorge J. Locane and María Montt Strabucchi, 'El Viaje América Latina-China. Una Interacción Sur-Sur Sui Generis', *TRANSMODERNITY: Journal of Peripheral Cultural Production of the Luso-Hispanic World*, 9.3 (2020), pp. 1–5; Rosario Hubert, 'Intellectual Cartographies of the Cold War: Argentinean Visitors to the People's

also published. In most of them, essentialist views of China prevail not only within the texts themselves but also within their paratextual aspects.

Thinking of the paratext as a 'threshold',[22] to use Gérard Genette's term—as the means through which a text makes a book of itself for the readers and public—the corpus of novels selected here display an exoticized imaginary of 'China', further disclosing the mutual tropes and themes which are established and subverted within the texts themselves. Regarding the paratextual aspects of these novels, we can see how, on one level, 'China' is presented through racialized stereotypes as the 'racialized oriental', embodied by the figure of the 'chino' across different texts. On another level, a gendered representation of 'China' is another major theme across these texts, contrasting overt representations of hegemonic and public expressions of masculinity with domestic and private spaces usually occupied by the 'chino'. Another pattern that emerges in these representations of 'China' is the notion of spatial distance, which tends to locate 'China' on the *other* (geographical and cultural) side of the world.

Indeed, we find a visually encoded construction of difference and exoticism throughout the paratextual aspects of novels on China published in Latin America (in this book, I do not analyse novels published by ethnic Chinese or their descendants). A mysterious 'China', which blends into an indistinct 'orient', appears on the books' back covers, in quotes, and in their marketing. For example, *El ombligo del dragón*'s (The Dragon's Bellybutton)[23] back matter description not only evokes China's mysteriousness but also describes an aspect of the book as being part of the 'oriental mythology'. In *Los impostores* (The Impostors),[24] the recommendation on the back cover tells us that the story occurs in 'el corazón de la remota China'; on *Un chino en bicicleta*'s (A Chinese on a Bicycle)[25] back cover, the recommendation states that the protagonist will see himself immersed in the 'desconocida cultura china de las calles de Buenos Aires'; and the recommendation of *La mujer en la Muralla* (The Woman on the Wall)[26] suggests that the novel is about, among other things, the 'distintas corrientes eróticas, religiosas y filosóficas que bullían en la China altiva y fascinante de aquella época'. The recommendation of *Hotel Pekín* (Peking Hotel)[27] describes how the novel is set within

Republic of China 1952-1958', in *Handbook of Literature and Space*, ed. by Robert Tally (London: Routledge, 2016), pp. 337–48.

22 Gérard Genette and Marie Maclean, 'Introduction to the Paratext', *New Literary History*, 22.2 (1991), pp. 261–72 (p. 261).

23 Ximena Sánchez Echenique, *El ombligo del dragón* (Mexico City: Tusquets, 2007). For the titles of books, I have included translations the first time I mention them and then use Spanish.

24 Santiago Gamboa, *Los impostores* (Barcelona: Seix Barral, 2002).

25 Ariel Magnus, *Un chino en bicicleta* (Bogota: Grupo Editorial Norma, 2007).

26 Alberto Laiseca, *La mujer en la Muralla* (Buenos Aires: Planeta, 1990).

27 Santiago Gamboa, *Hotel Pekín* (Bogota: Editorial Planeta Colombiana, 2008).

the 'complejas relaciones entre China y Occidente', recalling a binary East/West division of the world. This is something that is also echoed in the ways the books are marketed and commented upon. For example, in the online literary blog Lecturalia, *Una novela china*[28] is described as a 'fábula erótica, intemporal y eternal aunque ineludiblemente china' which calls China 'Imperio de la Porcelana'.

The covers of the novels show how the literary market continues to appeal to stereotypical images of China, with mostly figurative covers that depict iconic Chinese objects, using ochre and red tones. Another element that repeats itself is the use of Chinese characters; we can find them on the covers of *Una novela china*, *La mujer en la Muralla*, *Un chino en bicicleta*, *Los impostores*, *Hotel Pekín*, *Verde Shanghai*[29] and *El mármol*.[30] In the case of *El mármol*, the book was published with three different covers online: one had an extract of the book, another had drawings of frogs, and the third had a collage that included a picture of Mao, a maneki-neko cat, and different objects that recall 'China', suggestive of the multiplicity of objects and ideas related to it. Another aspect that is striking on these books' covers is the somewhat limited relevance given to particular places: they depict a suspended place, evoking a broad notion of a mysterious and faraway 'China' represented by pictures of the Great Wall, as in the case of *La mujer en la Muralla*; the representation of a road, in the case of *El ombligo del dragón*; or a door in semidarkness, in the case of *Un chino en bicicleta*. We also find repeated images of 'Chinese' women whose faces are partly covered or hidden from us. For example, in *Verde Shanghai*, a 'Chinese' couple is seated at a table, but the scene is occluded by a Chinese style carved window or door. The marketization of *Verde Shanghai* presents the novel as one that is to be recognized as 'Chinese' by the Latin American public. And in the edition of *El país imaginado* published by Impedimenta,[31] the cover shows two Chinese girls in qipaos, originally a poster of Kwong Sang Hong Ltd.

Aside from their paratextual elements the texts themselves may seem to reinforce otherness and difference as central to the articulation of identity. From this perspective, some of these novels could be seen to reinforce a Latin American 'Westernized' narrative and the construction of Chinese 'otherness'. The novels could arguably be accused of essentializing 'China'. Moreover, while the novels have been published by major publishing houses, some of their features seem to be clues aimed at local readers, such as the use of slang, obscuring their ironic reworking of 'China' for a broader public. As Graham Huggan reminds us, 'strategic essentialism' runs the risk of

28 César Aira, *Una novela china* (Buenos Aires: Javier Vergara, 1987).

29 Cristina Rivera Garza, *Verde Shanghai*, Kindle (Mexico City: Tusquets, 2011).

30 César Aira, *El mármol*, Kindle 2012 (Buenos Aires: La Bestia Equilátera, 2011).

31 Eduardo Berti, *El país imaginado* (Madrid: Impedimenta, 2012), originally published in Buenos Aires by Planeta in 2011.

reinstating the same differences it aims to challenge.[32] Indeed, the paratextual in these novels hints at the ways through which 'China' continues to be produced, exchanged and consumed in Latin America; how 'China' is branded through specific colours, figures, images, and objects.[33] And beyond this, how the paratextual itself is being altered in relation to new technologies, and their effect on readership and distribution, as well as the intensification of the links between China and Latin America. Against this background, this book proposes that the imaginary fictionalization of 'China' allows these authors to reflect on essentialist understandings of difference, identity, and community in Latin America.

This book thus focuses on how and why Latin American writers have represented 'China' in their texts. Among other readings, novels in which 'China' is central to the main story have already been valued as an escape from immediate reality.[34] They have also explored the distance between cultures, revealing localized conditions of otherness[35] and the anxieties related to the uncertainties of cultural globalization,[36] while other novels have been expressions of interest in the meeting of Hispanic and Chinese cultures.[37] Along these lines, it is possible to outline further axes along which we can understand a novelist's decision to write about 'China'. While the ideas presented above inform my understanding of the choice to depict 'China' in the novels studied here, my research reveals the multidimensional role of 'China' as metonym of Asia and as a symbol of 'otherness'.

On one level, we see these novels engaging with discourses of an imagined China as itself 'exotic' and 'other'. On another level, 'China' in these novels is informed by the rise of the PRC as an economic world power,[38] which no doubt informs the commercial appeal of China as a theme in the Latin American publication market. Related to this, we need to take into consideration demographic changes. Since the 1980s, the Chinese population in Argentina, Venezuela, Panama, Ecuador, and Mexico has increased dramatically,[39] a fact also linked to the opening-up of the PRC. On a

32 Graham Huggan, *The Postcolonial Exotic: Marketing the Margins* (London: Routledge, 2001), p. 14.

33 Montt Strabucchi, Chan, and Ríos.

34 María Laura de Arriba, 'Raras ficciones nuevas', *Revista del CELEHIS*, 5.6-7-8 (1996), pp. 213–53 (p. 244).

35 Francine Masiello, 'Bodies in Transit: Travel, Translation and Gender', in *Voice-Overs, Translation and Latin American Studies*, ed. by Daniel Balderston and Schwartz (New York: State University of New York Press, 2002), pp. 213–23 (p. 216).

36 Héctor Hoyos, 'Orientalismo, globalización e imaginarios transpacíficos en la novela latinoamericana actual', *Cuadernos de Literatura*, 17.34 (2013), pp. 82–105 (p. 83).

37 Jennifer Prince, 'Ella, Yo y El Yotro: Orientalisms and Identities in Cristina Rivera Garza's "Verde Shanghai"', in *Orientalism of the Hispanic and Luso-Brazilian World*, ed. by Araceli Tinajero (New York: Escribana Books, 2014), pp. 118–36 (pp. 118–19).

38 Myers and Wise.

39 For the analysis, I have included all data termed as China, Continental China,

further level, 'China' allows Latin American authors to adopt an external standpoint from which to explore Latin American identity, marked by the significance of the 'chino' standing historically outside the traditional Latin American racial and cultural axes of *mestizaje*.[40] The case of China is representative then, not only because it is linked to the country's growing economic power and migrant community, but also because, arguably, the figure of the 'chino' has progressively grown in visibility in recent years.

From this perspective, 'China' seems to serve as a concept through which to critique the exclusion of the Chinese in discourses of *mestizaje* and national identity while simultaneously critiquing the construction of 'Chineseness'. In this sense, and following Sean Metzger, I understand "Chineseness" to be produced contingently;[41] it can also be created, used, or dismantled in multiple ways.[42] On one level, the understanding of *mestizaje* as a historical mixing of populations, a cultural phenomenon, and a political endeavour, endures in Latin America. Its specific meaning and deployment have changed over time, and vary from country to country within the region.[43] Despite changes in its nuances over time and place, *mestizaje* in Latin America can be defined as a term which emphasizes cultural and racial mixing, homogenizing and reducing difference, even though, in reality, racial distinctions along essentialist physiological lines remain prevalent.[44] Indeed, there is no single definition of *mestizaje* in Latin America, and the term itself contains tensions between sameness and difference, and between inclusion and exclusion.

For the purposes of this book, I define *mestizaje* as a cultural and racial mixture along the axes of 'whiteness' and 'blackness'. However, it is a term used throughout Latin America whose meaning is nuanced according to the local context that emphasizes mixing and homogenization yet allows for

People's Republic of China, Taiwan and Nationalist China. Department of Economic and Social Affairs United Nations Population Division, 'World Population Prospects' (United Nations, 2015); CELADE, 'Investigación de la Migración Internacional en Latinoamérica - IMILA' (CELADE, Population Division, ECLAC, 2016) <http://celade.cepal.org/bdcelade/imila/> [accessed 1 September 2021].

40 Peter Wade, 'Repensando el mestizaje', *Revista Colombiana de Antropología*, 39 (2003), pp. 273–96; Peter Wade, 'Racismos latinoamericanos desde una perspectiva global', *Nueva Sociedad*, 13 April 2021, pp. 25–41.

41 Sean Metzger, 'Oriental Sensitivity: Towards a Poetics of Global Studies', *New Global Studies*, 14.3 (2020), pp. 287–305 <https://doi.org/10.1515/ngs-2020-0040>.

42 Montt Strabucchi, Chan, and Ríos, p. 12.

43 *Mestizaje and Globalization: Transformations of Identity and Power*, ed. by Stefanie Wickstrom and Philip D. Young (Tucson: University of Arizona Press, 2014); Paul K. Eiss, 'Introduction: Mestizo Acts', *Latin American and Caribbean Ethnic Studies*, 11.3 (2016), pp. 213–21.

44 Lok Siu, 'Hemispheric Raciality', p. 176; Peter Wade, 'Mestizaje, Multiculturalism, Liberalism, and Violence', *Latin American and Caribbean Ethnic Studies*, 11.3 (2016), pp. 323–43 (p. 323).

essentialist physiological distinctions to remain. As such it is a word that needs to be considered in intersectional terms, as *mestizaje* interacts with gender, ethnicity, class, and other factors.[45] Expressions of *mestizo* identity harbour within themselves a tension that inherently implies a permanent dimension of national differentiation, and yet also allows for processes of inclusion.

While traditionally the term includes a discourse of mixture, mestizo can be subjected to hierarchical ordering through which they are made to occupy inferior locations, can be discriminated against, and/or rendered exotic.[46] Indeed, while Latin America's ethnoracial classification can be quite fluid, skin colour is a predictor of inequality.[47] Wade demonstrates that while *mestizaje* in itself can challenge the idea of identity via notions of hybridity, the elements that constitute the mosaic of *mestizaje* can retain their essentialist definition, reinforcing racial hierarchies and stereotypes.[48]

As a forcible eradication of difference, or as a continuous construction of difference, *mestizaje*, like multiculturalism, can mask difference and fetishize that 'other' that does not fit. Indeed, although *mestizaje* is constructed upon notions of mixture, structures of difference remain in place. Building on Wade, I see *mestizaje* as holding the potential to be essentialist due to the production of difference found in its central structure: in relation to my argument, *mestizaje* can, on one level, be a celebration of the 'other' as the origin of difference. It can thus violently reproduce a 'we' discourse of community in the name of inclusion or multiculturalism.[49]

Indeed, Asians have remained absent from discussions of the processes of *mestizaje*. As Kathleen López states, the Asian component has often been 'absent in key anthologies on Latin American, Caribbean, and Latino literature, language, music, foodways, and culture'.[50] At the same time, however, López also notes that Asians, and particularly the Chinese, were paradoxically central to Latin American debates on national identity and culture due to the elements of anti-Asian racism to be found across the

45 I define race as a social construct based on differences, in particular physical features, and ethnicity on cultural differences, although both are intertwined; Edward Eric Telles and PERLA, *Pigmentocracies: Ethnicity, Race, and Color in Latin America* (Chapel Hill: University of North Carolina Press, 2014), p. 30.

46 Peter Wade, 'Rethinking "Mestizaje": Ideology and Lived Experience', *Journal of Latin American Studies*, 37.2 (2005), pp. 239–57 (p. 255).

47 Telles and PERLA, pp. 10–13.

48 Wade, 'Rethinking Mestizaje', p. 257.

49 Sara Ahmed, *Strange Encounters: Embodied Others in Post-Coloniality* (London: Routledge, 2000), p. 113.

50 Kathleen López, 'The Asian Presence in *Mestizo* Nations: A Response', in *Critical Terms in Caribbean and Latin American Thought*, ed. by Yolanda Martínez-San Miguel, Ben. Sifuentes-Jáuregui, and Marisa Belausteguigoitia (New York: Palgrave Macmillan, 2016), pp. 125–31 (p. 130).

Americas.[51] Indeed, from the late nineteenth and early twentieth century, *mestizo* discourses of racial inclusion were disrupted by immigration restrictions, anti-Asian sentiment, and the qualified portrayal of Asians as potential citizens.[52] Anti-Chinese movements have further played a role in generating *mestizo* nationalism.[53] In some cases these debates turned particularly violent for the Chinese, with the local Peruvian government

51 In the discourses of *mestizaje* formulated in the late nineteenth and early twentieth centuries, Asian bodies were excluded and viewed as being beyond incorporation, in contrast to the emphasis given to European and indigenous components. See Kathleen López, 'In Search of Legitimacy: Chinese Immigrants and Latin American Nation Building', in *Immigration and National Identities in Latin America*, ed. by Nicola Foote and Michael Goebel (Gainsville: University Press of Florida, 2014), pp. 182–204; López, 'The Asian Presence in *Mestizo* Nations: A Response', in *Critical Terms in Caribbean and Latin American Thought*, ed. by Yolanda Martínez-San Miguel, Ben. Sifuentes-Jáuregui, and Marisa Belausteguigoitia (New York: Palgrave Macmillan, 2016), pp. 125–31. See also Jason Oliver Chang, 'Comparative Orientalism in Latin American Revolutions: Antichinismo of Mexico and El Salvador', *Latin American Research Review*, 54.4 (2019), pp. 992–1006 <https://doi.org/10.25222/larr.615>; Robin M. DeLugan, '"Turcos" and "Chinos" in El Salvador: Orientalizing Ethno-Racialization and the Transforming Dynamics of National Belonging', *Latin American and Caribbean Ethnic Studies*, 11.2 (2016), pp. 142–62. López notes how Asians in particular have been viewed as 'temporary and fleeting migrant streams without a permanent imprint on society' (López, 'The Asian Presence in *Mestizo* Nations', p. 125).

52 López, 'The Asian Presence in *Mestizo* Nations', p. 128; Kanji Sato, 'Formation of La Raza and the Anti-Chinese Movement in Mexico', *Transforming Anthropology*, 14.2 (2006), pp. 181–86 (p. 181); Elliott Young, *Alien Nation: Chinese Migration in the Americas from the Coolie Era Through World War II* (University of North Carolina Press, 2014); Robert Chao Romero, *The Chinese in Mexico, 1882–1940* (Tucson: University of Arizona Press, 2010).

53 In the '*mestizo* nations' of Latin America, elite formulations of *mestizaje* viewed Asians as 'beyond incorporation, detrimental to the moral and physical well-being of the nation' (López, 'The Asian Presence in *Mestizo* Nations', p. 127. See, among others, Evelyn Hu-DeHart, 'From Area Studies to Ethnic Studies: The Study of the Chinese Diaspora in Latin America', in *Asian Americans: Comparative and Global Perspectives*, ed. by Shirley Hune, Stephen S. Fugita, and Amy Ling (Pullman: Washington State University Press, 1991), pp. 5–16; Erika Lee, 'Orientalisms in the Americas: A Hemispheric Approach to Asian American History', *Journal of Asian American Studies*, 8.3 (2005), pp. 235–56; Evelyn Hu-DeHart and Kathleen López, 'Asian Diasporas in Latin America and the Caribbean: An Historical Overview', *Afro-Hispanic Review*, 27.1 (2008), pp. 9–21; Elliott Young; Jason Oliver Chang, *Chino: Anti-Chinese Racism in Mexico, 1880–1940*, Kindle (Urbana, Chicago, and Springfield: University of Illinois Press, 2017); Fredy González, *Paisanos Chinos: Transpacific Politics among Chinese Immigrants in Mexico*, Philip E. Lilienthal Book in Asian Studies (University of California Press, 2017); Chan, 'Imagining and Linking Latin America: Chinese Regional Mobilities and Social Networks in Chile'; Heidi Tinsman, 'Rebel Coolies, Citizen Warriors, and Sworn Brothers: The Chinese

ordering the destruction of Chinese quarters in 1909,[54] or the slaughtering of hundreds of Chinese in Mexico in 1911.[55] Also in Mexico, discriminatory legislation led to the expulsion of the Chinese from Sonora in 1931.[56] From this perspective, it is necessary to take into account the different politics of national integration through which the Chinese are represented or whose image is constructed in Latin America.[57] The Chinese have been variously constructed in terms of race, ethnicity, gender, and class, depending upon the context, which has been influenced by diaspora-homeland ties, the imperialism and hegemony of the United States, and the differences within and between diasporas and in different countries.[58] And while experiences varied throughout different Latin American countries and cities, as the following chapters show, similar cases are to be found across the Americas.

This book analyses a broad sample of novels linked to China published by Latin American authors between 1987 and 2016, identifying the main themes and tropes they present. Each chapter elaborates a theme present within the broader corpus of novels. In the first chapter, I analyse *Una novela china* by the Argentine author César Aira (1987), *La mujer en la Muralla* by (also Argentine) Alberto Laiseca (1990), *La escuela del dolor humano de Sechuán* by Peruvian-Mexican Mario Bellatin (2001), and Argentine Eduardo Berti's *El país imaginado* (2011). In the second chapter I analyse *Un chino en bicicleta* (2007) by the Argentine Ariel Magnus, *El mármol* (2011) by César Aira, and *Verde Shanghai* (2011) by Mexican author Cristina

Loyalty Oath and Alliance with Chile in the War of the Pacific', *Hispanic American Historical Review*, 98.3 (2018), pp. 439–69.

54 Humberto Rodríguez Pastor, *Herederos del dragón: historia de la comunidad China en el Perú* (Lima: Fondo Editorial del Congreso del Perú, 2000).

55 Chao Romero.

56 López, 'The Asian Presence in *Mestizo* Nations'; Chang, *Chino*.

57 Chan, 'Imagining and Linking Latin America: Chinese Regional Mobilities and Social Networks in Chile'; Carol Chan, 'Permanent Migrants and Temporary Citizens: Multinational Chinese Mobilities in the Americas', *Global Networks*, 21.1 (2020), pp. 64–83 <https://doi.org/10.1111/glob.12279>; Monica DeHart, 'Chino Tico Routes and Repertoires: Cultivating Chineseness and Entrepreneurism for a New Era of Trans-Pacific Relations', *The Journal of Latin American and Caribbean Anthropology*, 23.1 (2018), pp. 74–93; Luciana Denardi, 'Chinese Migrations to Argentina: Diasporic Bureaucracy, Identifications and Rituals', in *Chinese Immigration in Latin America: Some Cultural Contributions*, ed. by Pablo Baisotti (Newcastle upon Tyne: Cambridge Scholars Publishing, 2020), pp. 69–88; Jorge Moraga Reyes, 'Reparto comunitario y gasto agonístico: diferenciaciones y hegemonías entre antiguos y nuevos migrantes chinos en Chile', *Rumbos TS*, 17 (2018), 133–52.

58 See, for example, Edith Wen-Chu Chen, '"You Are Like Us, You Eat Plátanos": Chinese Dominicans, Race, Ethnicity, and Identity', *Afro-Hispanic Review*, 27.1 (2008), pp. 23–40; Paula C. Park, 'Asian Latino Conflict and Solidarity in Díaz's The Brief and Wondrous Life of Oscar Wao', *CLCWeb: Comparative Literature and Culture*, 17.2 (2015), pp. 1–9; Lok Siu, *Memories of a Future Home*.

Rivera Garza. In this chapter I also refer to *Asesinato en una lavandería china* by Juan José Rodríguez (1996),[59] *Ojos de Lagarto* (2009) by the Mexican Bernardo Fernández, *El misterio del Barrio Chino* (2013) by the Peruvian José Güich Rodríguez, *Chinardos* (2014) by the Argentine Fernando del Río,[60] *La casa del dolor ajeno* by the Mexican author Julián Herbert (2015),[61] and *Tacos altos* (2016) by the Argentine author Federico Jeanmaire.[62] In the third and final chapter, I analyse *Los impostores* (2002)[63] and *Hotel Pekín* (2008),[64] both by the Colombian Santiago Gamboa; Mexican author Ximena Sánchez Echenique's *El ombligo del dragon* (2007);[65] and *Shanghai* (2011, 2013, 2014),[66] later published in a printed edition as *Los ojos de una ciudad china* (2016),[67] by the Uruguayan author Gabriel Peveroni.

During the research for this book, I managed to identify more and more texts where 'China' was a central or relevant feature in the plot, strengthening my idea that there is indeed a corpus of literature on Chinese topics in Latin America that are not (necessarily) linked to ethnicity, and that has continued to grow intensely in recent years. Although I mention them, I do not include a full analysis of them. For example, this book does not analyse in detail *Hija de la Fortuna*[68] by the Chilean Isabel Allende, where the Chilean protagonist falls in love with a Chinese man in California during the Gold Rush, and where multiple othernesses negotiate their agency in a context where Britain and Western powers are hegemonic. Other novels are the Peruvian Julio Heredia Martínez's *Libro de los muchachos chinos*,[69] a homoerotic text published after the author's stay in China; or the Peruvian Oswaldo Reynoso's *Los Eunucos Inmortales*,[70] where the plot centres around a young Peruvian man in Beijing in 1989. Indeed, these books can also be considered within the three different chapters in this book: *Hija de la Fortuna*, *Libro de los muchachos chinos* and *Los eunucos inmortales* can be considered as travel to China narratives, the topic of chapter 3. And the

59 Juan José Rodríguez, *Asesinato en una lavandería china* (Mexico D.F: Consejo Nacional para la Cultura y las Artes, 1996).

60 Fernando del Río, *Chinardos*, Kindle (Córdoba: Eduvim, 2014).

61 Julián Herbert, *La casa del dolor ajeno* (México, D.F: Literatura Random House, 2015).

62 Federico Jeanmaire, *Tacos altos* (Barcelona: Editorial Anagrama, 2016).

63 Gamboa, *Los impostores*.

64 Gamboa, *Hotel Pekín*.

65 Sánchez Echenique.

66 Gabriel Peveroni, *Shanghai #1. Enero 2010* (Alfaguara, 2013); *Shanghai #2. Febrero 2005* (Alfaguara, 2013); *Shanghai #3. Marzo 2007* (Alfaguara, 2014).

67 Gabriel Peveroni, *Los ojos de una ciudad china* (Montevideo: HUM, 2016).

68 Isabel Allende, *Hija de la fortuna* (Barcelona: Plaza & Janés, 1999).

69 Julio Heredia Martínez, *Libro de los muchachos chinos*, 1959th edn (Lima: Comité Killka, 1990).

70 Oswaldo Reynoso, *Los eunucos inmortales* (Lima: PEISA, 1995).

novel *La rosa de la China*[71] by Jaime Panqueva presents a fictional narration on the origins of Catarina San Juan and la China Poblana, and arguably could also be included in the third chapter of the book.[72] Furthermore, the novels *En qué piensa una cabeza recién cortada*[73] written by Juan Carlos Cabezas, where the story is set during the dynasty of Qin Shihuang, and *Contagio, La ruta del virus de la seda*[74] by Alberto Delgado, where different stories are set in China during the COVID-19 pandemic, could be included in chapter 1, where the plots occur in China.

As mentioned earlier, other novels, poetry, travelogues, or short stories about China can also be found earlier and during this period in Latin America. Among others, Rosalba Campra's *Los cuentos del cuchillo de Jade*[75] or the plays of Griselda Gambaro[76] could also fruitfully engage with my ideas here. We also find the above mentioned Isabel Allende's *Hija de la Fortuna*, Rafael Bernal's *El complot mongol*,[77] first published in 1969, and José Castro Urioste's ¿Y tú que has hecho?,[78] as well as the episode of Julio Cortázar's character, Wong, and his knowledge of Chinese torture in *Rayuela*.[79] Fernando De Trazegnies Granda's *En el país de las colinas de arena*,[80] Salvador Elizondo's *Farabeuf o la crónica de un instante*,[81] Daniel Guebel's *La perla del emperador*[82] (where a Chinese man visits a woman in Malaysia offering her a

71 Jaime Panqueva, *La rosa de la china: La increible historia de una princesa que llegó de Oriente para convertirse en la milagrosa Catarina San Juan, la China Poblana* (Mexico D.F: Planeta, 2011).

72 For a detailed analysis see the work of Francisco Y. Chen-López 'La historia "contrabandeada" del encuentro transpacífico en La rosa de la China (2011) de Jaime Panqueva', *TRANSMODERNITY: Journal of Peripheral Cultural Production of the Luso-Hispanic World*, 8.4 (2018), pp. 39–59.

73 Juan Carlos Quezadas, *En qué piensa una cabeza recién cortada* (Mexico City: Progreso, 2009).

74 Alberto Delgado, *Contagio. La ruta del virus de la seda* (Santiago: Trayecto Ediciones, 2021).

75 Raúl Brasca, 'Oriente en Occidente: Acerca de "Cuentos del cuchillo de jade" de Rosalba Campra', *Les Ateliers du SAL*, 5 (2014), pp. 111–20; Rosalba Campra, *Ella contaba cuentos chinos*, Libro-Objeto (later published as 'Cuentos del cuchillo de jade') (Madrid: Del Centro de Editores, 2008); *Cuentos del cuchillo de jade* (Buenos Aires: Ediciones Al Margen, 2009).

76 Griselda Gambaro, *Teatro* (Buenos Aires: Ediciones de la Flor, 1984).

77 Rafael Bernal, *El complot mongol* (Barcelona: Libros del Asteroide, 2013).

78 José Castro Urioste, *Y tú qué has hecho?* (Lima: Ediciones SM, 2011).

79 Julio Cortázar, *Rayuela* (Buenos Aires: Editorial Sudamericana, 1966).

80 Fernando de Trazegnies Granda, *En el país de las colinas de arena: Reflexiones sobre la inmigración china en el Perú del S. XIX desde la perspectiva del derecho* (Lima: Pontificia Universidad Católica del Perú, 1994).

81 Salvador Elizondo, *Farabeuf o la crónica de un instante* (Mexico City: Joaquín Mortiz, 1965).

82 Daniel Guebel, *La perla del emperador* (Buenos Aires: Emecé Editores, 1990).

mysterious pearl), Armando Guerrero Rodríguez' *Caen las hojas al viento*,[83] Miguel Gutiérrez's *Babel, el paraíso*,[84] Mirko Lauer's *Secretos Inútiles*,[85] and Mercedes Valdivieso's *Los ojos de bambú* can also be included on this list.[86] Novels written by (self-identified) members of the Chinese diaspora in Latin America, such as the works of Siu Kam Wen,[87] Julia Wong Kcomt,[88] or Gustavo Ng[89] have also not been included in this book. From this perspective, this book aims to offer a way of approaching and considering literary work published in Latin America linked to China overall.

The book builds on a small but growing body of studies on the representations of China in Latin American literature. While some of the novels chosen for my analysis have already been studied independently or in small groups, as of yet there is no overview that permits comparison, or the recognition of trends, themes, or tropes in the region. There has been no analysis that groups and examines these novels relationally from within broader literary discourses on China in Latin America, beyond national perspectives.[90] While

83 Armando Guerrero Rodríguez, *Caen las hojas al viento* (Pisco, 1998).

84 Miguel Gutiérrez, *Babel, el paraíso* (Lima: Colmillo Blanco Editorial, 1993).

85 Mirko Lauer, *Secretos inútiles: una novela* (Lima: Hueso Húmero Ediciones, 1991).

86 Mercedes Valdivieso, *Los ojos de bambú* (Santiago: Zig-Zag, 1964).

87 Kam Wen Siu, *El tramo final* (Lima: Lluvia Editores, 1985); Kam Wen Siu, *Viaje a Itaca: novela* (Morrisville: Lulu, Inc., 2004); Kam Wen Siu, *La vida no es una tómbola* (Lima: Universidad Nacional, Mayor de San Marcos, Ediciones del Vicerrectorado Académico, 2008); Kam Wen Siu, *El furor de mis ardores: novela* (Lima: Casatomada, 2009); Kam Wen Siu, *El verano largo: novela* (Lima: Casatomada, 2012); Kam Wen Siu, *La estatua en el jardín* (Lima: Universidad Ricardo Palma, Editorial Universitaria, 2013).

88 Julia Wong Kcomt, *Bocetos para un cuadro de familia* (Lima: Borrador Editores, 2008); Julia Wong Kcomt, *Doble felicidad* (Lima: Editatú, 2012); Julia Wong Kcomt, *Mongolia* (Lima: Animal de Invierno, 2015).

89 Gustavo Ng, *Mariposa de Otoño* (Buenos Aires: Chirimbote, 2017).

90 Academic literary studies have mostly chosen a national canon approach, while edited volumes adopt approaches to Asia but do not emphasize a comparative perspective. Among the pivotal works for the study of the representations of China and Asia in Latin America, and exclusion of the Chinese from national identities, we find, among others, the works of Julia Kushigian, such as *Orientalism in the Hispanic Literary Tradition: In Dialogue with Borges, Paz, and Sarduy* (Albuquerque: University of New Mexico Press, 1991). See also *Orientalisms of the Hispanic and Luso-Brazilian World*, ed. by Araceli Tinajero (New York: Escribana Books, 2014); Jauregui; Debbie Lee-DiStefano, *Three Asian-Hispanic Writers from Peru: Doris Moromisato, José Watanabe, Siu Kam Wen* (Lewiston: Edwin Mellen Press, 2008); Anne-Marie Lee-Loy, *Searching for Mr. Chin: Constructions of Nation and the Chinese in West Indian Literature* (Philadelphia: Temple University Press, 2010); Hoyos; Álvaro Fernández Bravo, 'Apropiaciones de la cultura china en la literatura sudamericana contemporánea: Contribución para un mapa tentativo a partir de obras de César Aira, Bernardo Carvalho y Siu Kam Wen', *452oF Revista de Teoría de la literatura y Literatura Comparada*,

my analysis exposes the differences between the novels that engage with the local, national, or urban context, as well as their temporal settings, my research demonstrates how elements which are common to the corpus of texts also become available. A broader approach that is both regional and thematic allows for the observation of common points and differences in the representations of China in Latin America, going beyond national or local politics and economic circumstances. This approach allows me to take into consideration the complexity of representations and their role in the persistence of dominant conceptions of, among other things, race and gender.[91] It also allows me to consider that, since the 1980s, and in a particularly accelerated fashion since the year 2000, a clearly identifiable corpus of narrative fiction on China has been published across the region.

The book is structured as follows: the following section is a theoretical proposal that aims to show how 'China' allows for an exploration of the construction of otherness in Latin America, which goes beyond the binary structures of West/non-West, East/West, and North/South. In other words, it explores how difference is used to challenge fixed views on otherness, and thus how 'China' becomes a lens to interrupt essentialist notions of

13 (2015), pp. 50–70; Jorge Locane, 'China en América Latina o los límites del cosmopolitismo (liberal): A propósito de La casa del dolor ajeno (2015)', *A Contracorriente: una revista de estudios latinoamericanos*, 16.3 (2019), pp. 302–16; Chang, *Chino*.2014 Among texts that take national approaches we find Axel Gasquet, *Oriente al sur: El orientalismo literario argentino de Esteban Echeverría a Roberto Arlt* (Buenos Aires: Eudeba, 2007); Chisu Teresa Ko, 'Between Foreigners and Heroes: Asian-Argentines in a Multicultural Nation', in *Rethinking Race in Modern Argentina*, ed. by Eduardo Elena and Paulina L. Alberto (New York: Cambridge University Press, 2016), pp. 268–88; Julián Vazeilles, 'Orientalismos "periféricos" en la narrativa contemporánea argentina: Breves notas sobre la novela María Domecq (2007), de Juan Forn' (Centro de Estudios Corea Argentina, Universidad de Buenos Aires, 2007); Amanda Holmes, 'China in Argentine Exotismo: Contemporary Inventions of the Orient', *Bulletin of Spanish Studies*, 85.1 (2008), pp. 71–83; Luis Pulido Ritter, 'Representación de los chinos en la literatura y la cultura de Panamá', in *TransPacífico. Conexiones y convivencias en AsiAmericas. Un simposio transareal* (Berlin: editorial tranvía, Verlag Walter Frey, 2013), pp. 79–101. A leading author in the field is Ignacio López-Calvo who has published, among other studies, *Imaging the Chinese in Cuban Literature and Culture* (Gainesville: University Press of Florida, 2008) and *Dragons in the Land of the Condor*. Most works are shaped or respond to Said's foundational ideas on Orientalism; see, for example, Robin Fiddian, '"El Oriente" by Jorge Luis Borges: A Poetic Boutique and Emblem of the East', *Romanic Review*, 98.2/3 (2007), pp. 189–203, 321; Shlomy Mualem, 'Imaginative Geography: Dialectical Orientalism in Borges', *TRANSMODERNITY: Journal of Peripheral Cultural Production of the Luso-Hispanic World*, 6.1 (2016), pp. 131–51; Masiello.

91 Elizabeth Hallam and Brian V. Street, 'Introduction', in *Cultural Encounters: Representing Otherness*, ed. by Elizabeth Hallam and Brian V. Street (London: Routledge, 2000), pp. 1–10 (p. 7).

identity. In chapter 1, where the novels' plots are set 'in China', I argue that through overtly constructed discourses, 'China' appears as a symbolic object endowed with its own meaning and value, where the act of narration itself becomes central to the retrieval and destabilization of the story being told. The book then analyses novels where Chinese topics or Chinese people in Latin America are at the centre of the text; in this chapter, I show how novels critique or criticize discourses that support a racially homogeneous Latin America by emphasizing its heterogeneity and hybridity beyond 'local' black and indigenous cultures. Then, in chapter 3, I continue to explore the way in which novels where the plot is set on travel to 'China' and where the 'East' becomes displaced disclose forms of contemporary othering by challenging Eurocentric structures and 'national' epistemologies. In the Epilogue, I explore the need to continue exploring the way in which 'China' and otherness are constructed, deployed, and challenged in different contexts, within and beyond Latin American contemporary fiction.

A Theoretical Proposal: 'China' as Supplement through Strangerness

This book dissects how novels challenge fixed views of otherness. I explore how 'China' allows for an exploration of the construction of otherness in Latin America, which goes beyond the binary structures of West/non-West, East/West, and North/South. This section explains the theoretical proposal further analysed in the coming pages. It attempts to understand how 'China' is present and what its role is in these novels. The novels here expose the binary structures through which 'China' has been constructed and how it has challenged essentialist notions of identity. On one level, a Latin American composite identity emerges in these novels as a way of countering *mestizaje*: interacting with, rather than replacing, national, ethnic, and regional identities. While there continues to be a particular ontology of the Chinese as the 'other', the narrative fiction studied here becomes a space from which Latin American authors demand that Latin America come to terms with its own composite identity.

Because the Chinese people have not formed part of the axes of *mestizaje* in Latin America, their historic articulation from 'the outside' paradoxically locates them at the centre of discussions on national identity. In other words, through their paradoxical absence in *mestizaje*, the 'Chinese' become central figures who enable the articulation of national identities in Latin America. Within this context and understanding of *mestizaje*, the Chinese are excluded from one of the prevailing ways of defining identity in the region. This helps explain why Latin American writers turn to China to explore 'otherness' in Latin America. The impossibility of situating the Chinese within a *mestizo* framework simultaneously problematizes it and questions the belonging of Chinese/Asian communities within Latin American identities. From this perspective, 'China' can be analysed as a 'supplement' to the discourses of *mestizaje* available in Latin America.

Jacques Derrida, building on Jean-Jacques Rousseau's theorizations on writing in relation to speech,[92] observes that the supplement is always an exterior addition, simultaneously adding on and substituting. When something is *lacking*, something else must be added. For him, 'the sign, the image, the representation, which come to supplement the absent presence are the illusions that sidetrack [...] us'.[93] In other words, Derrida analyses how the supplement can simultaneously be something that completes or may substitute another thing and can therefore be a threat. Supplements simultaneously complete and create an excess. In Gayatri Chakravorty Spivak's words, 'the supplement is dangerous because not only does it suggest that full presence can be added to, but it also suggests that presence has a lack which can be filled'.[94] It is precisely Derrida's logic of the supplement that I see regarding 'China' and its interruption of discourses surrounding *mestizaje*. 'China' disturbs the hierarchies at work within *mestizaje*, simultaneously supplementing it and revealing the lack of the presence of 'China' within the discourses of *mestizaje* available throughout Latin America. From this perspective, the use of 'China' in the novels analysed here can be considered a way of denouncing the exclusion of the Chinese while simultaneously revealing the racial and cultural politics involved in their construction as the 'other' and of 'otherness' itself in Latin America.

That the Chinese are represented (and challenged) in these novels mostly as a 'racial absolute', as one single racial and cultural identity, contributes significantly to how I view the occurrence of the texts' deconstruction of *mestizaje*. Because *mestizaje*, in its most common understanding in Latin America, refers to the racial and cultural mixing of the European and indigenous population of the Americas, the representation of 'China' in the novels as a racial absolute rather than itself a product of its own forms of *mestizaje*, points to the powers at play in the construction of difference. While *mestizaje* entails a struggle of what should be excluded or included, thus revealing how power hierarchies can be challenged and inclusion promoted,[95] it may simultaneously essentialize and exclude those who do not fit. By interrupting fixed assumptions of what entails the lineages of *mestizaje*, 'China' deconstructs otherness, challenging the active production and continued management of difference as contained in *mestizaje*.

In this sense, the novels selected here engage with a Latin American perspective that reveals how constructions of otherness transcend national

92 Jacques Derrida, *Of Grammatology* (Baltimore: The Johns Hopkins University Press, 2016), p. 158.

93 Derrida, p. 167.

94 Gayatri Spivak in Derrida, p. 355.

95 Wade, 'Repensando el mestizaje'; Wade, 'Mestizaje, Multiculturalism, Liberalism, and Violence'.

boundaries. Given the emphasis on openness and flexibility, Doreen Massey's theorizations of space, which see spatial relations as central to an understanding of politics and power, are especially relevant to my rationale in determining the corpus of novels studied here. All have been written by Latin American, Spanish-speaking authors since the 1980s and can be seen to challenge the 'closure of identity in a territorialised space of bounded places'.[96] Following Massey, I see places as unbounded, characterized by internal conflicts, 'created and recreated from interactions with other spaces which are characterised by unequal flows and exchanges'.[97] From this perspective, the novels studied here show the intersection between nationally defined differences in their particular understanding of 'China' and a simultaneous engagement in themes that are to be found across Latin America. In specific terms, novels were selected that encouraged a discussion of China's role and the Chinese in Latin American communities, which are both a part of, and go beyond, local, and national contexts.

I explore the use of 'China' through Ahmed's figure of the 'stranger' and 'strange encounters',[98] to go beyond Said's theorizations on *Orientalism*.[99] By offering an explanatory system for the historical, political, and cultural construction of 'otherness', *Orientalism* has proved itself useful to a wide variety of analytical approaches. However, there has been a well-rehearsed critique of Said's *Orientalism*. Said has been accused of ignoring class relations in the emergence of 'Orientalism' and of inconsistency in characterizing it as a system of representations or misrepresentations.[100] Some say he misappropriates Foucault by presenting no theory of resistance and offering no alternative to what it critiques,[101] which makes the book theoretically inconsistent,[102] and that he also fails to see women as active participants in power relations, ignoring gender positions within his texts.[103] Rather, he has

96 Doreen Massey, *For Space* (London: SAGE, 2005), p. 183.

97 Doreen Massey, *Space, Place and Gender* (Cambridge: Polity Press, 1994), pp. 1–9.

98 Ahmed, *Strange Encounters*.

99 Chisu Teresa Ko, 'Orientalism and De-Orientalism in Contemporary Latin America: Reading César Aira', *TRANSMODERNITY: Journal of Peripheral Cultural Production of the Luso-Hispanic World*, 8.3 (2018), pp. 149–67; Brett Levinson, 'The Death of the Critique of Eurocentrism: Latinamericanism as a Global Praxis/Poiesis', in *Orientalism and Identity in Latin America: Fashioning Self and Other from the (Post) Colonial Margin*, ed. by Erik Camayd-Freixas (Tucson: University of Arizona Press, 2013), pp. 19–34; Said.

100 Aijaz Ahmad, *In Theory: Classes, Nations, Literatures* (London: Verso, 1992).

101 Robert Young, *White Mythologies: Writing History and the West* (London: Routledge, 1990).

102 James Clifford, *The Predicament of Culture: Twentieth-Century Ethnography, Literature, and Art* (Cambridge: Harvard University Press, 1988).

103 Lisa Lowe, *Critical Terrains: French and British Orientalisms* (London: Cornell University Press, 1991); Sara Mills, *Discourses of Difference: An Analysis of Women's Travel Writing and Colonialism* (London: Routledge, 1991).

been said to emphasize dominance and power over cultural interaction,[104] not presenting an alternative to the reductive approaches he describes throughout his text.[105] While this does not undermine the fact that power determines which representations are accepted as 'true', which have emerged from a structure of imperial domination,[106] the dichotomy between 'Orient' and 'Occident' that emerges in *Orientalism* rests on stereotypes that ultimately essentialize and fetishize the 'Orient'.

Herself working through paradigms drawn from feminist theory and postcolonialism, Ahmed explores the tensions implicit in the use of 'strangerness', where postcolonialism has traditionally concerned itself with the 'other' in relation to the ontological status of the subject. Her notion of 'strange encounters' allows us to address how the meetings that produce the 'stranger' are 'determined, but not fully determined', and to understand '*how that figure is put to work, and made to work,* in particular times and places'.[107] Ahmed defines the 'stranger' as 'the one whom we have already identified in the event of being named as alien'.[108] She suggests that the figure of the 'stranger' is *produced* through knowledge *in* the encounter and that the recognition of the stranger is an affective judgment.[109] 'Strange encounters' reopen past encounters, determined by their historical relation, and involve difference, given that there is an asymmetry of power. Ahmed explains that subjects come into existence as entities only through encounters with others, and thus the subject's existence cannot be separated from the 'others' who are encountered.

Ahmed's ideas are relevant to my book because they highlight our 'need to pay attention to the *shifting conditions* in which encounters between others, and between other, others, take place'.[110] As Ahmed shows, we identify the other as a 'stranger' in recognizing them as such. The stranger can become a fetishized category (what she terms 'stranger fetishism'), as 'the stranger' is cut off from the histories which have led them to be determined as such. In this way, Ahmed signals the *complexity* of the relationship between histories of colonialism and contemporary modes of encounter. According to her, 'if we consider the production of "the stranger" through relationships of knowledge [...], we can draw attention to the processes of inclusion and exclusion, or incorporation and expulsion, that are concealed in stranger fetishism'.[111]

104 Bill Ashcroft and Pal Ahluwalia, *Edward Said* (London: Routledge, 2001).

105 Dag Hallvard Nestby, 'The Great Dialogue: Overcoming the Dichotomising Logic of Orientalism' (unpublished doctoral dissertation, Norges Teknisk-naturvitenskapelige Universitet, 2013).

106 Ashcroft and Ahluwalia, p. 75.

107 Ahmed, *Strange Encounters*, pp. 11–17.

108 Ahmed, *Strange Encounters*, p. 2.

109 Sara Ahmed, 'Making Strangers', *Feminist Killjoys*, (2014) <http://feministkilljoys.com/2014/08/04/making-strangers/> [accessed 1 July 2017].

110 Ahmed, *Strange Encounters*, p. 13.

111 Ahmed, *Strange Encounters*, p. 57.

Ahmed's statement brings our attention to the mechanisms involved in producing the 'fetishized stranger' and fixed otherness, using ideas I develop in the first chapter. While Ahmed states that 'we need to move our attention from the production of otherness to the (re)production of strangerness',[112] I build on her work to argue that we need to move our attention to the ways through which the (re)production of strangerness also continues to produce 'otherness'. The fetishized stranger, being constructed as the 'other', exposes the processes at play and through which 'otherness' is constituted, communicated, transformed, incorporated, resisted, and reinvented.[113] In other words, focusing on strangerness allows us to observe not only how strangerness continues to be (re)produced but also how it continues to (re) produce otherness. This process is as much national as it is transnational, informed by the histories that determine the encounter. This book questions the distinction between 'centre' and 'margin' and fixed notions of otherness, thus revealing what Berthold Schoene calls the 'anachronism of these [...] hegemonic distinctions between self and other'.[114]

It is precisely because of the anachronism inherent in hegemonic distinctions that I consider it necessary to explore the mechanisms at play in the relation between 'stranger' (and strangerness) and 'other' (and otherness). Otherness and strangerness are sometimes used interchangeably, and their differences generate no consensus. For example, Bianca Szytniewski explores unfamiliarity, otherness, and strangerness, showing how sometimes otherness is perceived as a universal social condition, in contradistinction to the otherness of another human being. In contrast, strangerness occurs only when the otherness of the other becomes irritating or disturbing.[115] For Ahmed, as Vince Marotta shows, 'the stranger as other is constituted through power relations that are embedded in the past as much as in the present',[116] and thus Ahmed does not distinguish the 'stranger' from the 'other'. In this book, I will consider otherness as an essentialist ontology and strangerness as unfixed and flexible, the latter's condition being due to the central importance of the process of encounter. The ontological status of the subject thus differs in my working definitions of strangerness and otherness. While in strangerness the process of recognition of the stranger is open-ended, as the process is dynamic and open, in otherness the subject is considered as an essential

112 Ahmed, *Strange Encounters*, p. 61.

113 Hallam and Street, pp. 1–5.

114 Berthold Schoene, *The Cosmopolitan Novel* (Edinburgh: Edinburgh University Press, 2011), p. 27.

115 Bianca Szytniewski, 'The Dynamics of Unfamiliriaty in the German-Polish Border Region 1970s, 1980s, and 1990s', in *Borders and Border Regions in Europe: Changes, Challenges and Chances*, ed. by Arnaud Lechevalier and Jan Wielgohs (Bielefeld: Transcript Verlag, 2013), pp. 183–99 (p. 185).

116 Vince P. Marotta, *Theories of the Stranger: Debates on Cosmopolitanism, Identity and Cross-Cultural Encounters*, Kindle (Abingdon: Routledge, 2017) loc. 557.

other distinct from the self. Through encounters, this ontological 'other' is simultaneously fixed and being recognized. Thus, by focusing on 'strange encounters', we can bring attention to the ways in which 'fetishized strangers' and 'otherness' are brought about, where fetishization fixes and essentializes subjects as 'others'.

Essentialist differentiations between people within Latin America have been most frequently studied regarding race and ethnicity, revealing how social stratification is linked to race.[117] Studies on race and ethnicity in Latin America have shown how they may structure inequalities, that skin colour is a consistent but overlooked dimension of inequality, and that ethnoracial discrimination is commonly experienced and witnessed.[118] In specific terms of 'otherness' in Latin America, we find the work of Tzvetan Todorov, who argues that the relation of the West to the other in Latin America during the conquest was multi-dimensional. He views it as a case in which the axes include value judgment, rapprochement, or distancing in relation to the other, and the knowledge or ignorance of the other's identity.[119] Siskind, in his analysis of literary *modernismo*, states that the foreign 'other' was the signifier of a cosmopolitan desire.[120] Elizabeth Sosa takes another perspective, using otherness as a category of analysis that allows Latin America's position on the periphery to be challenged by approaching the subject at the periphery from different perspectives.[121] And as Lesley Wylie has shown, otherness in the Americas has been parodied in literature through the *novela de la selva*,[122]

117 Edward Telles and Liza Steele, 'Pigmentocracia en las Américas: ¿cómo se relaciona el logro educativo con el color de piel?', *Proyecto Afrolatin@*, 2012.73 (2012) <http://afrolatinoproject.org/2012/06/28/pigmentocracia-en-las-americas-como-se-relaciona-el-logro-educativo-con-el-color-de-piel/> [accessed 5 January 2021]; Peter Wade and Mónica Moreno-Figueroa, 'Alternative Grammars of Anti-Racism in Latin America', *Interface: A Journal for and about Social Movements*, 13.2 (2022), pp. 20–50; Carol Chan, 'Chinese Migrants' Spatial Politics of Belonging, Identity, and Citizenship in Santiago de Chile', *Citizenship Studies*, 25.1 (2020), pp. 106–23; Macarena Bonhomme, '"We're a Bit Browner but We Still Belong to the White Race": Making Whiteness in the Context of South-South Migration in Chile', *Latin American and Caribbean Ethnic Studies*, 18.2 (2023), pp. 227–43 <https://doi.org/10.1080/17442222.2022.2099170>; Ignacio Aguiló, *The Darkening Nation: Race, Neoliberalism and Crisis in Argentina* (Cardiff: University of Wales Press, 2018).

118 Peter Wade, *Race and Ethnicity in Latin America* (London: Pluto Press, 1997); Peter Wade, 'Articulations of Eroticism and Race: Domestic Service in Latin America', *Feminist Theory*, 14.2 (2013), pp. 187–202; Telles and PERLA, pp. 219–29.

119 Tzvetan Todorov, *The Conquest of America: The Question of the Other* (Norman: University of Oklahoma Press, 1999), p. 185.

120 Mariano Siskind, *Cosmopolitan Desires: Global Modernity and World Literature in Latin America* (Evanston: Northwestern University Press, 2014), pp. 122–23.

121 Elizabeth Sosa, 'La otredad: Una visión del pensamiento latinoamericano contemporáneo', *Letras*, 51.80 (2009), pp. 349–72 (p. 369).

122 Lesley Wylie, 'Hearts of Darkness: The Celebration of Otherness in the Latin

removing any original essence of what it is trying to represent. Indeed, otherness has been central to many studies of Latin American literature and identity beyond the fact that otherness can still be further theorized in the region.

A useful approach to studying 'otherness' in Latin America is provided by using Kuan-Hsing Chen's ideas in his monograph *Asia as Method*. In it, Chen proposes positioning the West as 'bits and fragments that intervene in local social formations in a systematic, but never totalizing, way'.[123] The West can thus be viewed as one more cultural resource rather than on oppositional terms. Chen's rationale, which suggests the need for an 'Asia and the rest' worldview, in which there is a paradigm shift towards a deimperialized, decolonized, and de-Cold War mentality, informs my understanding of how China appears in the novels studied here. Through his logic of 'Asia as method', which implies the possibility of shifting points of reference, China enters Latin American history and becomes part of it, but not in a totalizing manner. From this stance, the novels may question the role that 'China', as well as the 'West', and 'otherness' in general, have in Latin America.[124]

American Novela de La Selva', *Romance Studies*, 23.2 (2005), pp. 105–16; Lesley Wylie, 'Colonial Tropes and Postcolonial Tricks: Rewriting the Tropics in the "Novela de La Selva"', *The Modern Language Review*, 101.3 (2006), pp. 728–42.

123 Kuan-Hsing Chen, *Asia as Method: Towards De-Imperialization* (Durham: Duke University Press, 2010), p. 223.

124 It is possible to find calls for a broadening of the approaches, perspectives, and frames of reference for Asian literary and cultural studies; the proposal to incorporate Latin America into Asian Studies, and for reflection on the development of historiography theoretically centred around the Pacific. Indeed, it is possible to find many publications from the last few years which call for the development of theoretical approaches to explore Asia and Latin America. These can be seen as responding to a series of publications in Latin America (and Asia) which explored the relationship, but were still evaluated within political and historical contexts, and traditional Orientalism. Indeed, as Verónica Junyoung Kim states, '[...] Asia-Latin America brings into contact differing forms of power-knowledge and elucidates the workings of the politics of knowledge and the politics of our lack of knowledge' Junyoung Verónica Kim, 'Asia–Latin America as Method: The Global South Project and the Dislocation of the West', *Verge: Studies in Global Asias*, 3.2 (2017), pp. 97–117 (p. 101). See, among others, 'Remapping the Transpacific: Critical Approaches between Asia and Latin America', ed. by Andrea Bachner and Pedro Erber, *Verge: Studies in Global Asias*, 3.2 (2017); Ko, 'Orientalism and De-Orientalism in Contemporary Latin America: Reading César Aira'; Jie Lu and Martin Camps, 'Constructing a New Field of Inquiry: Latin American in Asian Literary and Cultural Studies', in *Transpacific Literary and Cultural Connections: Historical and Cultural Interconnections between Latin America and Asia*, ed. by Jie Lu and Martin Camps, e-book (Cham: Palgrave Macmillan, 2020), pp. 1–18 <https://doi.org/10.1007/978-3-030-55773-7_1>; Pedro Iacobelli and Maria Montt Strabucchi, 'Encuentros con Asia: Una reflexión en torno a la historiografía latinoamericana desde la cuenca del océano Pacifico', *Historia 396*, 10.2 (2020), pp. 179–204.

By putting Chen's ideas into conversation with Ahmed's, we can see how 'China' allows Latin American authors to write beyond hegemonic knowledge systems, such as 'Western' or Eurocentric narratives. 'Strangerness' and 'Asia as method' thus disclose the mechanisms at play in the (de)construction of racialized and essentialist 'otherness' in these novels. Chen's demand for multiple frames of reference not only allows us to consider the various dimensions at play in recognition of the stranger but also calls for a specific understanding of the subject.

As I will explore in more detail later, Nancy's understanding of the subject as 'being-with', with its emphasis on the relationship between subjects reminds us to focus on the recognition process of the 'stranger' as such. This focus on process is a way of recalling that the 'strangerness' results from the encounter of subjects and is not intrinsic to one or the other. This Nancean perspective on the subject allows us to think of the encountering process and emphasizes the transnational aspects at work in constructing strangerness. Thus, Nancy's notion of the 'inoperative community' can be understood as a non-essentialist reading of cosmopolitanism, as developed by Schoene.[125]

Through 'strange encounters', Ahmed argues, we already recognize 'a stranger' as the one we do not know, where 'some bodies' are more recognizable as strangers than others. Ahmed argues that we must refuse to take for granted the status of any given subject as a potential 'stranger', what I term here as 'otherness', with regard to its essentialist and fetishized nature. According to Ahmed, using the figure of the stranger metaphorically unites different forms of displacement and power imbalance under one single label. Ahmed argues that 'we need to understand how identity is established through strange encounters without producing a universe of strangers', since to conclude that we are all strangers is to avoid dealing with the political process whereby some others are designated as *stranger than other others*.[126] Ahmed's articulation of the stranger allows us to question the frames of reference through which 'China' will be constructed as such. Therefore, an analysis of strange encounters 'allows us to address how the encounters that produce "the stranger" as a figure with linguistic and bodily integrity are determined'[127] and are simultaneously concealed by stranger fetishism. In other words, the fetishization of strangers fixes them as objects and as the 'other', thereby denying them any form of agency or subjectivity. In this sense, Ahmed's figure of the 'stranger' allows us to go beyond an 'ontological other'.

Reminding us of the frames of reference through which 'China' can be defined simultaneously as exotic and as the fetishized stranger, postcolonial scholar Graham Huggan usefully describes 'exoticism' as both a particular mode of aesthetic perception and a practice which renders 'people, objects

125 Schoene.

126 Ahmed, *Strange Encounters*, p. 6.

127 Ahmed, *Strange Encounters*, p. 17.

and places strange […] and which effectively manufactures otherness even as it claims to surrender to its immanent mystery'.[128] According to Ahmed, communities construct these figures of 'the beyond' to define themselves. For Ahmed, the 'alien' is not simply what we fail to identify in the encounter, but the one we have already identified as 'alien'. Insofar as the 'alien' gathers all that is beyond the human into the singularity of a given form, it becomes a fetish in psychoanalytical terms. Indeed, the figure of the 'stranger' and Ahmed's concept of 'strange encounters' allow us to go beyond 'our' familiar typologies in the analysis of Latin American novels that set their stories in China, allowing for a dialogue that does not simply hold the 'other' in a fixed place.[129]

From this perspective, Nancy's approaches to the subject as 'being with' and the community as 'inoperative' are central to my analysis of how 'China' is represented in Latin American novels. Because Nancy questions the (fetishistic) constructions of the subject, and of an essential community, his ideas reveal the ways in which it is possible to move beyond essentialist notions of existence and community. In other words, Nancy provides a way out of essentialist understandings of subjectivity. Like Ahmed, Nancy also moves away from the terminology of the 'other'.

Nancy proposes the concept of 'singular plural' or 'being-with', where each singularity exists in relation to other singularities.[130] According to him, the I is necessarily constituted in relation to a plurality. For Nancy, 'the singular plural means that there are singularities whose identity or selfhood can only be found in their "relation" to other singularities'.[131] Nancy emphasizes that people *are* in-common.[132] In relation to Ahmed, Nancy demonstrates how the recognition of 'strangers' is produced in the encounter, and that our relationship to others informs all encounters.

Building on the subject as 'being-in-common' Nancy proposes his idea of the 'inoperative community'. For Nancy, the 'community' remains unrepresentable. Nancy's thesis is that at the core of Western political thinking there exists a longing for an 'original community'. This longing contrasts with the current sense of disintegration. Arguing that there is no 'essential community', and yet that people are-in-common, Nancy outlines the 'inoperative community' as a 'collective human necessity without fixed teleological function', as Schoene aptly puts it.[133]

In this sense, then, both Nancy and Ahmed critique the celebration of otherness in ethical philosophy. Ahmed characterizes ethics as a kind of

128 Huggan, p. 13.

129 Ahmed, *Strange Encounters*, p. 9.

130 Jean-Luc Nancy, *Being Singular Plural* (Stanford: Stanford University Press, 2000).

131 Marie-Eve Morin, *Jean-Luc Nancy* (Cambridge: Polity, 2012), p. 2.

132 Christopher Watkin, 'A Different Alterity: Jean-Luc Nancy's "Singular Plural"', *Paragraph*, 30.2 (2007), pp. 1292–97.

133 Schoene, p. 17.

hospitality towards strangers, arguing that the 'ethical demand is to work with that which has already been assimilated, in order to work with that which fails to be assimilated'.[134] From this perspective, a focus on strangerness allows us to think about how a fetishized 'China' reveals the structures of differentiation at play in Latin America. Ahmed and Nancy thus facilitate our understanding of how the 'chino/a' has been excluded from articulations of *mestizaje*, notwithstanding the real presence of Chinese people in Latin America.

My reading of Ahmed and Nancy allows for a critical reflection on what enables, and determines, the encounter, instead of installing a 'mono-directional inclusion of the Other into hegemonic designs'.[135] The authors use China to disrupt discourses of otherness, challenging hegemonic racial and essentialist notions of identity in Latin America while evoking the being-in-common of the Latin American author at a personal, local, and global level. From a cosmopolitan perspective, the novels can be analysed through various interconnected local, national, transnational, and global levels to expose their critique of 'stranger fetishism'.

Cosmopolitanism calls for an understanding of the world that is committed to the liaison between the local and the global. Remaining aware of voices that denounce some of cosmopolitanism's Eurocentric and universalizing stances, I suggest that cosmopolitanism's transnational approach allows for a challenge to Western hegemony and Eurocentric worldviews. My argument is not that the cosmopolitan is to be equated with a loose definition of a universal global community in which everyone participates, which itself may simultaneously exercise and conceal inequalities, but rather that it challenges the positions related to a cosmopolitan perspective. Indeed, the 1990s were a watershed for 'cosmopolitanism' in scholarship;[136] within this view we find, for example, Kwame Anthony Appiah's vision of a cosmopolitan community, where individuals enter relationships founded on mutual respect, despite their differences.[137] Proponents of new understandings of cosmopolitanism attempt to disassociate it from prior universal, hegemonic definitions. Rather, they argue that cosmopolitanism is now a variety of provisional concrete practical stances that can lead to strategic alliances and networks that cross territorial and political

134 Ahmed, *Strange Encounters*, p. 16.

135 Johanna Leinius, 'Decolonizing Cosmopolitanism in Practice: From Universalizing Monologue to Intercultural Dialogue?', in *Cosmopolitanism and Transnationalism: Visions, Ethics and Practices* (Helsinki: Helsinki Collegium for Advanced Studies, 2014), pp. 39–65 (p. 41).

136 Juan Flores, *The Diaspora Strikes Back: Caribeño Tales of Learning and Turning* (Abingdon: Routledge, 2010); Pnina Werbner, *Anthropology and the New Cosmopolitanism: Rooted, Feminist and Vernacular Perspectives* (Oxford: Berg, 2008).

137 Kwame Anthony Appiah, *Cosmopolitanism: Ethics in a World of Strangers* (London: Penguin, 2007).

borders.[138] Also going beyond the above notions of 'traditional cosmopolitanism', Schoene draws on Nancy to propose a new understanding of cosmopolitanism, one in which the representation of worldwide human living and global community remains continually liable to affiliation and capable of dispersion.[139] While Nancy dismisses the term 'cosmopolitan' because of its associations with universalism and its ideological nature,[140] his theoretical reconceptualization does allow for a new, non-identitarian understanding of cosmopolitanism. According to Schoene, this kind of cosmopolitanism signals a 'departure from traditional internationalist perspectives while stressing the significance of local cultures [...]'.[141] According to Schoene, a novel's cosmopolitanism lies in its particular stance towards the world.[142] This stance is defined by him in terms of Nancy's 'inoperative community', that refuses to circumscribe community within a fixed or totalizing essence. As Schoene shows, Nancy's outline of community as inoperative and being-in-common 'imagin[es] global community beyond "the people" or (united) nations, and outside the utopian/dystopian framework of ideological modelling or transcendent meaning-making'.[143]

Of course, this movement towards a global community could be taken as much as an effect of globalization, as of cosmopolitanism. However, Nancy sees in globalization a chaotic agglomeration ruled by capitalism, that 'promotes the freedom and movement of singular beings'.[144] In contrast to globalization, I see this cosmopolitanism as aware of difference, more a sensibility than a set of rules or absolute notion of relationality. This cosmopolitanism allows us to focus on the relative difference, rather than on an essentialist understanding of differences. In this process, cosmopolitanism exposes the ways in which 'stranger fetishism' is constructed and deployed through a fetishized 'China' in these novels.

Throughout this book, I use the word fetish in different but interrelated ways to refer to the role that 'China' plays in Latin America through these novels. I follow both Bhabha's understanding of fetish, where the stereotype is fetishized,[145] and Ahmed's definition, where the stranger is cut off from the histories of their determination. Using stereotypical descriptions, the texts

138 Pheng Cheah, 'The Cosmopolitical', in *The Ashgate Research Companion to Cosmopolitanism*, ed. by Maria Rovisco and Magdalena Nowicka (Farnham: Ashgate, 2011), pp. 211–24 (p. 218).

139 Schoene, p. 17.

140 Nancy.

141 Schoene, p. 1.

142 Schoene, p. 16.

143 Schoene, p. 17.

144 Jane Hiddlestone, 'Globalisation', ed. by Peter Gratton and Marie-Eve Morin, *The Nancy Dictionary* (Edinburgh: Edinburgh University Press, 2015), pp. 101–3 (p. 103).

145 Homi K. Bhabha, *The Location of Culture* (Oxon: Routledge, 1994), p. 106.

themselves show the limits of fixed oppositions in terms of understanding the complexities of identity. In this sense, I also borrow from Anne McClintock, who going beyond Bhabha, shows how 'fetishes can involve triangulated contradictions, or more than three [contradictions]'.[146] For McClintock, the fetish 'embodies a crisis in social meaning', housing symbolic and material difference at both a personal and historical level. In her work, she repurposes the fetish as a theoretical tool to explore the ambiguities and complexities of the self within specific histories and contexts. The fetish, as viewed by McClintock, is a useful concept for theorizing about objects, places, people, and practices that are contradictory and ambiguous.[147] McClintock's ideas are central to my understanding of 'China' as a third term which involves contradictions and is multidimensional, informed by history and imaginaries. Building on McClintock, I see fetishism as exposing the hierarchies of social difference, as well as how these differences are articulated through other inequalities or alterities, such as gender or race. From this perspective, building on McClintock, I see the fetishistic construction of 'China' in the novels I review as involving contradictions and engaging multiple approaches, including historical narratives of cultural difference and diversity.

In this sense, the stereotype as fetish makes it possible for us to accept differences between the 'others' and among 'selves', while at the same time believing there is coherence between those same 'selves' and 'others'. The construction of the 'other' as a stereotype creates the fantasy of a coherent identity of the 'self', that simultaneously reveals the fantasy as being in fact beyond the control of the 'self'. It is from this perspective that the idea of the fetish is central to my analysis of novels that have a specific engagement with stereotypical images of 'China' and 'Chineseness'. The stereotype helps identify the formation of hegemonic structures, as well as the participation of subjects that have been made invisible in national and Latin American discourses, exposing the critical relations between different social structures and institutions, as well as revealing the structures of racial, ethnic, and class power that exist in Latin America.

By choosing a specific nation or nationality to write about, the novels studied here engage with previous fantasies and stereotypes, myths, and projections of places and nationalities. This imagined 'China' builds upon

146 Anne McClintock, *Imperial Leather: Race, Gender, and Sexuality in the Colonial Contest* (New York: Routledge, 1995), p. 202.

147 According to McClintock, fetishes inhabit 'the threshold of both personal and historical memory', marking a 'crisis in social meaning as the embodiment of an impossible irresolution' (p. 184). The individual thus gains symbolic control by displacing power onto the fetish, and then manipulating the fetish and its threat of (terrifying) ambiguity. McClintock thus calls for an opening up of the definition of fetishism to more theoretical and historically fruitful alleys that would include both psychoanalytic insights (such as disavowal or displacement) and historical narratives of cultural difference and diversity. See McClintock, pp. 184–85, 202.

inherited European views of the East, informed by geographical factors, conquest narratives, and an imaginary on China, which has been forged throughout history.[148] Indeed, as Robin Fiddian states,

> the discovery of a New World beyond the western horizon of Renaissance Europe brought about a realignment of relations between East and West, introducing a third term that effectively re-cast Europe as the Old World sandwiched between the "New World" of the Americas, [...] and the Ancient Worlds of the Middle and Far East [...].[149]

Fiddian's statement helps to explain the complex positioning of the Americas within an East–West binary. Following my understanding of the outlined fetish, it is possible that America's 'discovery', which fixes 'America' as 'non-Western', leads to a crisis which in turn fixes the 'Orient' beyond the Americas for the Americas. China thus becomes a fetishized metonym of 'Orient' and 'other' which lie beyond the geographical limits of the Americas. 'China' can hence be seen as a metonym of the exotic 'other'. The Latin American author posits themselves within the 'oriental', and the 'orientalist' Latin America. By showing 'China' as the 'other' through 'strangerness', the author reveals 'China' as an unstable and fetishized subject for Latin America. By noting the various novels' challenges regarding the 'otherness' of the Chinese, it is possible to see how they disclose how 'China' has ultimately become a fetish of otherness for Latin America.

As a 'fetishized other', the real China is simultaneously used to recall the discontinuities and changes it has experienced as the 'other'. It masks its imagined absence and difference in Latin America,[150] while simultaneously pointing to its lack of representation. In this process of metonymy, the novels strategically expose how 'China' is multidimensional and heterogeneous and should not be thought of from within an essentialist, fixed framework.

By acknowledging both China and Latin America as embodying the potential to be perceived as 'exotic', the novels can gain symbolic control, displacing power onto these fetishized exotic locations, exposing the constructedness of stereotypes, and thus manipulating the fetish. An analysis of China's role allows us to see how these Latin American authors engage with global issues while simultaneously emphasizing the local context in which the 'fetishized stranger' is constructed and through which 'China' is played out in different ways. This shifts the understandings of 'China' from representing a concrete presence as a country, to 'belonging' within Latin America, to a

148 See, for example, the imagined 'China' that Susan Sontag explores and reflects upon in her short story 'Project for a Trip to China'; in her words: 'Perhaps I will write the book about my trip to China before I go.' Susan Sontag, 'Project for a Trip to China', in *I, Etcetera* (London: Anchor Books, 1991), pp. 3–32.

149 Fiddian, p. 190.

150 See, among others, Montt Strabucchi and Chan; Montt Strabucchi, Chan, and Ríos; DeHart, *Transpacific Developments: The Politics of Multiple Chinas in Central America.*

'China' that becomes a concept through which philosophical considerations come to be articulated. Through the analyses of novels here, national and racial assemblages are deconstructed; by using 'China' rather than reinstating essentialism, essentialism itself is called into question. At a time when China becomes a ubiquitous and growing actor in the world, whose power and growth has become central to Latin America, both economically and socially, to think of how 'China' is thought of and represented allows us for a more nuanced understanding of how we think and relate to each other.

References

Aguiló, Ignacio, *The Darkening Nation: Race, Neoliberalism and Crisis in Argentina* (Cardiff: University of Wales Press, 2018)

Ahmad, Aijaz, *In Theory: Classes, Nations, Literatures* (London: Verso, 1992)

Ahmed, Sara, 'Making Strangers', *Feminist Killjoys*, (2014) <http://feministkilljoys.com/2014/08/04/making-strangers/> [accessed 1 July 2017]

———, *Strange Encounters: Embodied Others in Post-Coloniality* (London: Routledge, 2000)

Aira, César, *El mármol*, Kindle 2012 (Buenos Aires: La Bestia Equilátera, 2011)

———, *Una novela china* (Buenos Aires: Javier Vergara, 1987)

Allende, Isabel, *Hija de la fortuna* (Barcelona: Plaza & Janés, 1999)

Anonymous, *Las castas*, 18th century, oil on canvas, 4243 x 5962, Museo Nacional del Virreinato, Tepotzotlán, Mexico

Appiah, Kwame Anthony, *Cosmopolitanism: Ethics in a World of Strangers* (London: Penguin, 2007)

de Arriba, María Laura, 'Raras ficciones nuevas', *Revista del CELEHIS*, 5.6-7–8 (1996), pp. 213–53

Ashcroft, Bill, and Pal Ahluwalia, *Edward Said* (London: Routledge, 2001)

Bachner, Andrea, and Pedro Erber, eds, 'Remapping the Transpacific: Critical Approaches between Asia and Latin America', *Verge: Studies in Global Asias*, 3.2 (2017)

Badaró, Máximo, ed., *China in Argentina: Ethnographies of a Global Expansion* (Cham: Springer International Publishing, 2022) <https://doi.org/10.1007/978-3-030-92422-5>

Beauchesne, Kim, Koichi Hagimoto, and Ineke Phaf-Rheinberger, 'Interrogantes asiáticos y miradas latinoamericanas: Una Introducción', *Revista de crítica literaria latinoamericana*, 44.87 (2018), pp. 9–17

Beltrán Antolín, Joaquín, Francisco Javier Haro, and Amelia Sáiz, eds., *Representaciones de China en las Américas y la Península Ibérica*, Biblioteca de China Contemporánea (Barcelona: Edicions Bellaterra, 2016)

Bernal, Rafael, *El complot mongol* (Barcelona: Libros del Asteroide, 2013)

Berti, Eduardo, *El país imaginado* (Madrid: Impedimenta, 2012)

Bhabha, Homi K., *The Location of Culture* (Oxon: Routledge, 1994)

Bonhomme, Macarena, '"We're a Bit Browner but We Still Belong to the White Race": Making Whiteness in the Context of South-South Migration in Chile', *Latin American and Caribbean Ethnic Studies*, 18.2 (2023), pp. 227–43 <https://doi.org/10.1080/17442222.2022.2099170>

Borensztein, Sebastián, *Un Cuento Chino* (2011)
Borges, Jorge Luis, *Ficciones* (Madrid: Alianza, 1997)
———, *Historia Universal de la Infamia* (Buenos Aires: Vintage Español, 2012)
———, *Otras Inquisiciones (1937–1952)* (Buenos Aires: Sur, 1952)
Brasca, Raúl, 'Oriente en Occidente: Acerca de "Cuentos del cuchillo de jade" de Rosalba Campra', *Les Ateliers du SAL*, 5 (2014), pp. 111–20
Campra, Rosalba, *Cuentos del cuchillo de jade* (Buenos Aires: Ediciones Al Margen, 2009)
———, *Ella contaba cuentos chinos*, Libro-Objeto (later published as 'Cuentos del cuchillo de jade') (Madrid: Del Centro de Editores, 2008)
Castro Urioste, José, *Y tú qué has hecho?* (Lima: Ediciones SM, 2011)
CELADE, 'Investigación de la Migración Internacional en Latinoamérica - IMILA' (CELADE, Population Division, ECLAC, 2016) <http://celade.cepal.org/bdcelade/imila/> [accessed 1 September 2021]
Chan, Carol, 'Chinese Migrants' Spatial Politics of Belonging, Identity, and Citizenship in Santiago de Chile', *Citizenship Studies*, 25.1 (2020), pp. 106–23
———, 'Imagining and Linking Latin America: Chinese Regional Mobilities and Social Networks in Chile', *Journal of Latin American Geography*, 17.2 (2018), pp. 23–45
———, 'Permanent Migrants and Temporary Citizens: Multinational Chinese Mobilities in the Americas', *Global Networks*, 21.1 (2020), pp. 64–83 <https://doi.org/10.1111/glob.12279>
Chan, Carol, and Maria Montt Strabucchi, 'Many-Faced Orientalism: Racism and Xenophobia in a Time of the Novel Coronavirus in Chile', *Asian Ethnicity*, 22.2 (2021), pp. 374–94 <https://doi.org/10.1080/14631369.2020.1795618>
Chang, Jason Oliver, *Chino: Anti-Chinese Racism in Mexico, 1880–1940*, Kindle (Urbana, Chicago, and Springfield: University of Illinois Press, 2017)
———, 'Comparative Orientalism in Latin American Revolutions: Antichinismo of Mexico and El Salvador', *Latin American Research Review*, 54.4 (2019), pp. 992–1006 <https://doi.org/10.25222/larr.615>
Chao Romero, Robert, *The Chinese in Mexico, 1882–1940* (Tucson: University of Arizona Press, 2010)
Cheah, Pheng, 'The Cosmopolitical', in *The Ashgate Research Companion to Cosmopolitanism*, ed. by Maria Rovisco and Magdalena Nowicka (Farnham: Ashgate, 2011), pp. 211–24
Chen, Edith Wen-Chu, '"You Are Like Us, You Eat Plátanos": Chinese Dominicans, Race, Ethnicity, and Identity', *Afro-Hispanic Review*, 27.1 (2008), pp. 23–40
Chen, Kuan-Hsing, *Asia as Method: Towards De-Imperialization* (Durham: Duke University Press, 2010)
Chen-López, Francisco Y., 'La historia "contrabandeada" del encuentro transpacífico en La rosa de la China (2011) de Jaime Panqueva', *TRANSMODERNITY: Journal of Peripheral Cultural Production of the Luso-Hispanic World*, 8.4 (2018), pp. 39–59
Clifford, James, *The Predicament of Culture: Twentieth-Century Ethnography, Literature, and Art* (Cambridge: Harvard University Press, 1988)
Cortázar, Julio, *Rayuela* (Buenos Aires: Editorial Sudamericana, 1966)

DeHart, Monica, 'Chino Tico Routes and Repertoires: Cultivating Chineseness and Entrepreneurism for a New Era of Trans-Pacific Relations', *The Journal of Latin American and Caribbean Anthropology*, 23.1 (2018), pp. 74–93

———, *Transpacific Developments: The Politics of Multiple Chinas in Central America* (Ithaca and London: Cornell University Press, 2021)

Delgado, Alberto, *Contagio. La ruta del virus de la seda* (Santiago: Trayecto Ediciones, 2021)

Del Río, Fernando, *Chinardos*, Kindle (Córdoba: Eduvim, 2014)

DeLugan, Robin M., '"Turcos" and "Chinos" in El Salvador: Orientalizing Ethno-Racialization and the Transforming Dynamics of National Belonging', *Latin American and Caribbean Ethnic Studies*, 11.2 (2016), pp. 142–62

Denardi, Luciana, 'Chinese Migrations to Argentina: Diasporic Bureaucracy, Identifications and Rituals', in *Chinese Immigration in Latin America: Some Cultural Contributions*, ed. by Pablo Baisotti (Newcastle upon Tyne: Cambridge Scholars Publishing, 2020), pp. 69–88

Derrida, Jacques, *Of Grammatology* (Baltimore: The Johns Hopkins University Press, 2016)

Donoso, José, *Los mejores cuentos de José Donoso* (Santiago de Chile: Zig-Zag, 1966)

Dussel Peters, Enrique, 'Latin America and the Caribbean and China: Socioeconomic Debates on Trade and Investment and the Case of CELAC', in *China and Latin America in Transition*, ed. by Shoujun Cui and Manuel Pérez García (New York: Palgrave Macmillan, 2016), pp. 157–73

Eiss, Paul K., 'Introduction: Mestizo Acts', *Latin American and Caribbean Ethnic Studies*, 11.3 (2016), pp. 213–21

Elizondo, Salvador, *Farabeuf o la crónica de un instante* (Mexico City: Joaquín Mortiz, 1965)

Ellis, Robert Evan, *China in Latin America: The Whats and Wherefores* (Boulder: Lynne Rienner Publishers, 2009)

———, *China on the Ground in Latin America: Challenges for the Chinese and Impacts on the Region* (New York: Palgrave Macmillan, 2014)

Fernández Bravo, Álvaro, 'Apropiaciones de la cultura china en la literatura sudamericana contemporánea: Contribución para un mapa tentativo a partir de obras de César Aira, Bernardo Carvalho y Siu Kam Wen', *452oF Revista de Teoría de la literatura y Literatura Comparada*, 13 (2015), pp. 50–70

Fiddian, Robin, '"El Oriente" by Jorge Luis Borges: A Poetic Boutique and Emblem of the East', *Romanic Review*, 98.2/3 (2007), pp. 189–203, 321

Flores, Juan, *The Diaspora Strikes Back: Caribeño Tales of Learning and Turning* (Abingdon: Routledge, 2010)

Gambaro, Griselda, *Teatro* (Buenos Aires: Ediciones de la Flor, 1984)

Gamboa, Santiago, *Hotel Pekín* (Bogota: Editorial Planeta Colombiana, 2008)

———, *Los impostores* (Barcelona: Seix Barral, 2002)

Gasquet, Axel, *Oriente al sur: El orientalismo literario argentino de Esteban Echeverría a Roberto Arlt* (Buenos Aires: Eudeba, 2007)

Gasquet, Axel, and Gorica Majstorovic, eds. *Cultural and Literary Dialogues Between Asia and Latin America* (Cham: Springer International Publishing, 2021) <https://doi.org/10.1007/978-3-030-52571-2>

Genette, Gérard, and Marie Maclean, 'Introduction to the Paratext', *New Literary History*, 22.2 (1991), pp. 261–72

Glow, Beatrice, *Taparaco Myth 塔琶拉古傳說 Mito Taparaco* (Lima: B. Glow, 2009)

———, *What Is Chino? Memories and Imaginaries of Asian Latin America*, 2014 <http://post.at.moma.org/content_items/500-what-is-chino-memories-and-imaginaries-of-asian-latin-america> [accessed 1 August 2021]

González, Fredy, *Paisanos Chinos: Transpacific Politics among Chinese Immigrants in Mexico*, Philip E. Lilienthal Book in Asian Studies (University of California Press, 2017)

Guebel, Daniel, *La perla del emperador* (Buenos Aires: Emecé Editores, 1990)

Guerrero Rodríguez, Armando, *Caen las hojas al viento* (Pisco, 1998)

Gutiérrez, Miguel, *Babel, el paraíso* (Lima: Colmillo Blanco Editorial, 1993)

Hagimoto, Koichi, ed., *Trans-Pacific Encounters: Asia and the Hispanic World* (Newcastle upon Tyne: Cambridge Scholars Publishing, 2016)

Hallam, Elizabeth, and Brian V. Street, 'Introduction', in *Cultural Encounters: Representing Otherness*, ed. by Elizabeth Hallam and Brian V. Street (London: Routledge, 2000), pp. 1–10

Herbert, Julián, *La casa del dolor ajeno* (México, D.F: Literatura Random House, 2015)

Heredia Martínez, Julio, *Libro de los muchachos chinos* (Lima: Comité Killka, 1990)

Hiddlestone, Jane, 'Globalisation', ed. by Peter Gratton and Marie-Eve Morin, *The Nancy Dictionary* (Edinburgh: Edinburgh University Press, 2015), pp. 101–3

Holmes, Amanda, 'China in Argentine Exotismo: Contemporary Inventions of the Orient', *Bulletin of Spanish Studies*, 85.1 (2008), pp. 71–83

Hoyos, Héctor, 'Orientalismo, globalización e imaginarios transpacíficos en la novela latinoamericana actual', *Cuadernos de Literatura*, 17.34 (2013), pp. 82–105

Hubert, Rosario, 'Intellectual Cartographies of the Cold War: Argentinean Visitors to the People's Republic of China 1952-1958', in *Handbook of Literature and Space*, ed. by Robert Tally (London: Routledge, 2016), pp. 337–48

Hu-DeHart, Evelyn, 'From Area Studies to Ethnic Studies: The Study of the Chinese Diaspora in Latin America', in *Asian Americans: Comparative and Global Perspectives*, ed. by Shirley Hune, Stephen S. Fugita, and Amy Ling (Pullman: Washington State University Press, 1991), pp. 5–16

Hu-DeHart, Evelyn, and Kathleen López, 'Asian Diasporas in Latin America and the Caribbean: An Historical Overview', *Afro-Hispanic Review*, 27.1 (2008), pp. 9–21

Huggan, Graham, *The Postcolonial Exotic: Marketing the Margins* (London: Routledge, 2001)

Iacobelli, Pedro, and Maria Montt Strabucchi, 'Encuentros con Asia: Una reflexión en torno a la historiografía latinoamericana desde la cuenca del océano Pacifico', *Historia 396*, 10.2 (2020), pp. 179–204

Jauregui, Gabriela, 'Apuntes on Orientalism in/and Latin American Literature: Darío, Tablada, Borges, Paz and Sarduy', *The Canadian Review of Comparative Literature*, 35.1–2 (2008)

Jeanmaire, Federico, *Tacos altos* (Barcelona: Editorial Anagrama, 2016)

Kim, Junyoung Verónica, 'Asia–Latin America as Method: The Global South Project and the Dislocation of the West', *Verge: Studies in Global Asias*, 3.2 (2017), pp. 97–117

Ko, Chisu Teresa, 'Between Foreigners and Heroes: Asian-Argentines in a Multicultural Nation', in *Rethinking Race in Modern Argentina*, ed. by Eduardo Elena and Paulina L. Alberto (New York: Cambridge University Press, 2016), pp. 268–88

———, 'Orientalism and De-Orientalism in Contemporary Latin America: Reading César Aira', *TRANSMODERNITY: Journal of Peripheral Cultural Production of the Luso-Hispanic World*, 8.3 (2018), pp. 149–67

Kushigian, Julia, *Orientalism in the Hispanic Literary Tradition: In Dialogue with Borges, Paz, and Sarduy* (Albuquerque: University of New Mexico Press, 1991)

Labraña, Marcela, 'Poesía oriental y visualidad en Darío, Tablada y Huidobro', *Estudios Avanzados*, 22 (2014), pp. 1–12

Laiseca, Alberto, *La mujer en la Muralla* (Buenos Aires: Planeta, 1990)

Lauer, Mirko, *Secretos inútiles: una novela* (Lima: Hueso Húmero Ediciones, 1991)

Lee, Ana Paulina, *Mandarin Brazil: Race, Representation, and Memory* (Stanford: Stanford University Press, 2018)

Lee, Erika, 'Orientalisms in the Americas: A Hemispheric Approach to Asian American History', *Journal of Asian American Studies*, 8.3 (2005), pp. 235–56

Lee-DiStefano, Debbie, *Three Asian-Hispanic Writers from Peru: Doris Moromisato, José Watanabe, Siu Kam Wen* (Lewiston: Edwin Mellen Press, 2008)

Lee-Loy, Anne-Marie, *Searching for Mr. Chin: Constructions of Nation and the Chinese in West Indian Literature* (Philadelphia: Temple University Press, 2010)

Leinius, Johanna, 'Decolonizing Cosmopolitanism in Practice: From Universalizing Monologue to Intercultural Dialogue?', in *Cosmopolitanism and Transnationalism: Visions, Ethics and Practices* (Helsinki: Helsinki Collegium for Advanced Studies, 2014), pp. 39–65

Levinson, Brett, 'The Death of the Critique of Eurocentrism: Latinamericanism as a Global Praxis/Poiesis', in *Orientalism and Identity in Latin America: Fashioning Self and Other from the (Post)Colonial Margin*, ed. by Erik Camayd-Freixas (Tucson: University of Arizona Press, 2013), pp. 19–34

Locane, Jorge, 'China en América Latina o los límites del cosmopolitismo (liberal): A propósito de La casa del color ajeno (2015)', *A Contracorriente: una revista de estudios latinoamericanos*, 16.3 (2019), pp. 302–16

Locane, Jorge J., and María Montt Strabucchi, 'El Viaje América Latina-China. Una Interacción Sur-Sur Sui Generis', *TRANSMODERNITY: Journal of Peripheral Cultural Production of the Luso-Hispanic World*, 9.3 (2020), pp. 1–5

López, Kathleen, 'In Search of Legitimacy: Chinese Immigrants and Latin American Nation Building', in *Immigration and National Identities in Latin America*, ed. by Nicola Foote and Michael Goebel (Gainsville: University Press of Florida, 2014), pp. 182–204

———, 'The Asian Presence in *Mestizo* Nations: A Response', in *Critical Terms in Caribbean and Latin American Thought*, ed. by Yolanda Martínez-San Miguel, Ben. Sifuentes-Jáuregui, and Marisa Belausteguigoitia (New York: Palgrave Macmillan, 2016), pp. 125–31

López-Calvo, Ignacio, *Dragons in the Land of the Condor: Writing Tusán in Peru* (Tucson: The University of Arizona Press, 2014)
———, *Imaging the Chinese in Cuban Literature and Culture* (Gainesville: University Press of Florida, 2008)
Lowe, Lisa, *Critical Terrains: French and British Orientalisms* (London: Cornell University Press, 1991)
Lu, Jie, and Martin Camps, 'Constructing a New Field of Inquiry: Latin American in Asian Literary and Cultural Studies', in *Transpacific Literary and Cultural Connections: Historical and Cultural Interconnections between Latin America and Asia*, ed. by Jie Lu and Martin Camps, Historical and Cultural Interconnections between Latin America and Asia, e-book (Cham: Palgrave Macmillan, 2020), pp. 1–18 <https://doi.org/10.1007/978-3-030-55773-7_1>
Luis, Diego, 'The Armed Chino: Licensing Fear in New Spain', *Journal of Colonialism and Colonial History*, 20.1 (2019), pp. 1–24 <https://doi.org/10.1353/cch.2019.0000>
Magnus, Ariel, *Un chino en bicicleta* (Bogota: Grupo Editorial Norma, 2007)
Marotta, Vince P., *Theories of the Stranger: Debates on Cosmopolitanism, Identity and Cross-Cultural Encounters*, Kindle (Abingdon: Routledge, 2017)
Masiello, Francine, 'Bodies in Transit: Travel, Translation and Gender', in *Voice-Overs, Translation and Latin American Studies*, ed. by Daniel Balderston and Schwartz (New York: State University of New York Press, 2002), pp. 213–23
Massey, Doreen, *For Space* (London: SAGE, 2005)
———, *Space, Place and Gender* (Cambridge: Polity Press, 1994)
McClintock, Anne, *Imperial Leather: Race, Gender, and Sexuality in the Colonial Contest* (New York: Routledge, 1995)
Metzger, Sean, 'Oriental Sensitivity: Towards a Poetics of Global Studies', *New Global Studies*, 14.3 (2020), pp. 287–305 <https://doi.org/10.1515/ngs-2020-0040>
Mills, Sara, *Discourses of Difference: An Analysis of Women's Travel Writing and Colonialism* (London: Routledge, 1991)
Min, Wonjung, 'Mis Chinos, Tus Chinos: The Orientalism of Chilean K-Pop Fans', *International Communication Gazette*, 83.8 (2021), pp. 799–817 <https://doi.org/10.1177/1748048520928254>
Montt Strabucchi, Maria, and Carol Chan, 'Questioning the Conditional Visibility of the Chinese: (Non)Normative Representations of China and Chineseness in Chilean Cultural Productions', *Journal of Chinese Overseas*, 16.1 (2020), pp. 90–116 <https://doi.org/10.1163/17932548-12341414>
Montt Strabucchi, Maria, Carol Chan, and María Elvira Ríos, *Chineseness in Chile: Shifting Representations during the Twenty-First Century*, Studies of the Americas (Cham: Palgrave Macmillan, 2022) <https://doi.org/10.1007/978-3-030-83966-6>
Montt Strabucchi, Maria, and Amelia Saiz-López, eds, *Narrativas de "lo chino" en la las Américas y la Península Ibérica* (Barcelona: Edicions Bellaterra, 2020)
Moraga Reyes, Jorge, 'Reparto comunitario y gasto agonístico: diferenciaciones y hegemonías entre antiguos y nuevos migrantes chinos en Chile', *Rumbos TS*, 17 (2018), pp. 133–52

Morin, Marie-Eve, *Jean-Luc Nancy* (Cambridge: Polity, 2012)
Mualem, Shlomy, 'Imaginative Geography: Dialectical Orientalism in Borges', *TRANSMODERNITY: Journal of Peripheral Cultural Production of the Luso-Hispanic World*, 6.1 (2016), pp. 131–51
Myers, Margaret, and Carol Wise, eds., *The Political Economy of China–Latin America Relations in the New Millennium: Brave New World* (New York: Routledge, 2017)
Nancy, Jean-Luc, *Being Singular Plural* (Stanford: Stanford University Press, 2000)
Neruda, Pablo, *Confieso que he vivido: memorias* (Barcelona: Editorial Seix Barral, 2011)
———, *Oriente* (Barcelona: Littera, 2004)
Nestby, Dag Hallvard, 'The Great Dialogue: Overcoming the Dichotomising Logic of Orientalism' (unpublished doctoral dissertation, Norges Teknisk-naturvitenskapelige Universitet, 2013)
Ng, Gustavo, *Mariposa de Otoño* (Buenos Aires: Chirimbote, 2017)
Olivares Briones, Edmundo, *Pablo Neruda, los caminos de oriente* (Santiago: LOM Ediciones, 2000)
Panqueva, Jaime, *La rosa de la china: La increíble historia de una princesa que llegó de Oriente para convertirse en la milagrosa Catarina San Juan, la China Poblana* (Mexico D.F.: Planeta, 2011)
Park, Paula C., 'Asian Latino Conflict and Solidarity in Díaz's The Brief and Wondrous Life of Oscar Wao', *CLCWeb: Comparative Literature and Culture*, 17.2 (2015), pp. 1–9
Paz, Octavio, *Vislumbres de la India* (Barcelona: Seix Barral, 1995)
Peveroni, Gabriel, *Los ojos de una ciudad china* (Montevideo: HUM, 2016)
———, *Shanghai #1. Enero 2010* (Alfaguara, 2013)
———, *Shanghai #2. Febrero 2005* (Alfaguara, 2013)
———, *Shanghai #3. Marzo 2007* (Alfaguara, 2014)
Prince, Jennifer, 'Ella, Yo y El Yotro: Orientalisms and Identities in Cristina Rivera Garza's "Verde Shanghai"', in *Orientalism of the Hispanic and Luso-Brazilian World*, ed. by Araceli Tinajero (New York: Escribana Books, 2014), pp. 118–36
Pulido Ritter, Luis, 'Representación de los chinos en la literatura y la cultura de Panamá', in *TransPacífico. Conexiones y convivencias en AsiAmericas. Un simposio transareal* (Berlin: editorial tranvía, Verlag Walter Frey, 2013), pp. 79–101
Quezadas, Juan Carlos, *En qué piensa una cabeza recién cortada* (Mexico City: Progreso, 2009)
Ray, Rebecca, Kevin P. Gallagher, Andrés López, and Cynthia Sanborn, eds., *China en América Latina. Lecciones para la Cooperación Sur-Sur y el Desarrollo Sostenible* (Lima: Universidad del Pacífico; Boston University, 2016)
Real Academia Española, 'chino3,na', *Diccionario de la Lengua Española*, (2017) <http://dle.rae.es/?id=8ppm97c> [accessed 1 July 2021]
Rehner, Johannes, Sebastián Baeza, and Jonathan Barton, *En Hombros de Gigantes. Una Geografía Económica Del Comercio Chile-Asia* (Santiago: GEOlibros, 2015)
Reynoso, Oswaldo, *Los eunucos inmortales* (Lima: PEISA, 1995)

Ríos, María Elvira, María Montt, and Carol Chan, 'El imaginario de lo chino en las revistas magazinescas chilenas de principios del siglo XX', *Revista Rumbos TS. Un espacio crítico para la reflexión en Ciencias Sociales*, 24 (2021), pp. 129–50 <https://doi.org/10.51188/rrts.num24.434>

Rivera Garza, Cristina, *Verde Shanghai*, Kindle (Mexico City: Tusquets, 2011)

Rodríguez, Juan José, *Asesinato en una lavandería china* (Mexico D.F: Consejo Nacional para la Cultura y las Artes, 1996)

Rodríguez Pastor, Humberto, *Herederos del dragón: historia de la comunidad China en el Perú* (Lima: Fondo Editorial del Congreso del Perú, 2000)

Said, Edward, *Orientalism* (London: Penguin, 2003)

Sánchez Echenique, Ximena, *El ombligo del dragón* (Mexico City: Tusquets, 2007)

Saravia, Daisy, *Migración china y orientalismo modernista. Análisis en la revista Variedades (1909–1919)* (Lima: Ediciones MyL, 2020)

Sato, Kanji, 'Formation of La Raza and the Anti-Chinese Movement in Mexico', *Transforming Anthropology*, 14.2 (2006), pp. 181–86

Schoene, Berthold, *The Cosmopolitan Novel* (Edinburgh: Edinburgh University Press, 2011)

Seijas, Tatiana, *Asian Slaves in Colonial Mexico* (New York: Cambridge University Press, 2015)

Siskind, Mariano, *Cosmopolitan Desires: Global Modernity and World Literature in Latin America* (Evanston: Northwestern University Press, 2014)

Siu, Kam Wen, *El furor de mis ardores: novela* (Lima: Casatomada, 2009)

———, *El tramo final* (Lima: Lluvia Editores, 1985)

———, *El verano largo: novela* (Lima: Casatomada, 2012)

———, *La estatua en el jardín* (Lima: Universidad Ricardo Palma, Editorial Universitaria, 2013)

———, *La vida no es una tómbola* (Lima: Universidad Nacional, Mayor de San Marcos, Ediciones del Vicerrectorado Académico, 2008)

———, *Viaje a Itaca: novela* (Morrisville: Lulu, Inc., 2004)

Siu, Lok, 'Chino Latino Restaurants: Converging Communities, Identities, and Cultures', *Afro-Hispanic Review*, 27.1 (2008), pp. 161–71

———, 'Diasporic Cultural Citizenship: Chineseness and Belonging in Central America', *Social Text*, 19.4 (2001), pp. 7–28

———, 'Hemispheric Raciality: Yellowface and the Challenge of Transnational Critique', *Asian Diasporic Visual Cultures and the Americas*, 2.1–2 (2016), pp. 163–79

———, *Memories of a Future Home: Diasporic Citizenship of Chinese in Panama* (Stanford: Stanford University Press, 2007)

Sontag, Susan, 'Project for a Trip to China', in *I, Etcetera* (London: Anchor Books, 1991), pp. 3–32

Sosa, Elizabeth, 'La otredad: Una visión del pensamiento latinoamericano contemporáneo', *Letras*, 51.80 (2009), pp. 349–72

Szytniewski, Bianca, 'The Dynamics of Unfamiliriaty in the German-Polish Border Region 1970s, 1980s, and 1990s', in *Borders and Border Regions in Europe: Changes, Challenges and Chances*, ed. by Arnaud Lechevalier and Jan Wielgohs (Bielefeld: Transcript Verlag, 2013), pp. 183–99

Telles, Edward Eric and PERLA, *Pigmentocracies: Ethnicity, Race, and Color in Latin America* (Chapel Hill: University of North Carolina Press, 2014)

Telles, Edward, and Liza Steele, 'Pigmentocracia en las Américas: ¿cómo se relaciona el logro educativo con el color de piel?', *Proyecto Afrolatin@*, 2012.73 (2012) <http://afrolatinoproject.org/2012/06/28/pigmentocracia-en-las-americas-como-se-relaciona-el-logro-educativo-con-el-color-de-piel/> [accessed 5 January 2021]

Tinajero, Araceli, ed., *Orientalisms of the Hispanic and Luso-Brazilian World* (New York: Escribana Books, 2014)

Tinsman, Heidi, 'Rebel Coolies, Citizen Warriors, and Sworn Brothers: The Chinese Loyalty Oath and Alliance with Chile in the War of the Pacific', *Hispanic American Historical Review*, 98.3 (2018), pp. 439–69

Todorov, Tzvetan, *The Conquest of America: The Question of the Other* (Norman: University of Oklahoma Press, 1999)

Torres-Rodríguez, Laura J., *Orientaciones Transpacíficas. La modernidad mexicana y el espectro de Asia* (Chapel Hill: The University of North Carolina Press, 2019)

Trazegnies Granda, Fernando de, *En el país de las colinas de arena: Reflexiones sobre la inmigración china en el Perú del S. XIX desde la perspectiva del derecho* (Lima: Pontificia Universidad Católica del Perú, 1994)

United Nations, Department of Economic and Social Affairs, Population Division, 'World Population Prospects' (United Nations, 2015)

Valdivieso, Mercedes, *Los ojos de bambú* (Santiago: Zig-Zag, 1964)

Vazeilles, Julián, 'Orientalismos "periféricos" en la narrativa contemporánea argentina: Breves notas sobre la novela María Domecq (2007), de Juan Forn' (Centro de Estudios Corea Argentina, Universidad de Buenos Aires, 2007)

Wade, Peter, 'Articulations of Eroticism and Race: Domestic Service in Latin America', *Feminist Theory*, 14.2 (2013), pp. 187–202

———, 'Mestizaje, Multiculturalism, Liberalism, and Violence', *Latin American and Caribbean Ethnic Studies*, 11.3 (2016), pp. 323–43

———, *Race and Ethnicity in Latin America* (London: Pluto Press, 1997)

———, 'Racismos latinoamericanos desde una perspectiva global', *Nueva Sociedad*, (2021), pp. 25–41

———, 'Repensando el mestizaje', *Revista Colombiana de Antropología*, 39 (2003), pp. 273–96

———, 'Rethinking "Mestizaje": Ideology and Lived Experience', *Journal of Latin American Studies*, 37.2 (2005), pp. 239–57

Wade, Peter, and Mónica Moreno-Figueroa, 'Alternative Grammars of Anti-Racism in Latin America', *Interface: A Journal for and about Social Movements*, 13.2 (2022), pp. 20–50

Watkin, Christopher, 'A Different Alterity: Jean-Luc Nancy's "Singular Plural"', *Paragraph*, 30.2 (2007), pp. 1292–97

Werbner, Pnina, *Anthropology and the New Cosmopolitanism: Rooted, Feminist and Vernacular Perspectives* (Oxford: Berg, 2008)

Wickstrom, Stefanie, and Philip D. Young, eds., *Mestizaje and Globalization: Transformations of Identity and Power* (Tucson: University of Arizona Press, 2014)

Wise, Carol, *Dragonomics: How Latin America is Maximizing (or Missing out on) China's International Development Strategy* (New Haven: Yale University Press, 2020)

Wong Kcomt, Julia, *Bocetos para un cuadro de familia* (Lima: Borrador Editores, 2008)

———, *Doble felicidad* (Lima: Editatú, 2012)

———, *Mongolia* (Lima: Animal de Invierno, 2015)

Wylie, Lesley, 'Colonial Tropes and Postcolonial Tricks: Rewriting the Tropics in the "Novela de La Selva"', *The Modern Language Review*, 101.3 (2006), pp. 728–42

———, 'Hearts of Darkness: The Celebration of Otherness in the Latin American Novela de La Selva', *Romance Studies*, 23.2 (2005), pp. 105–16

Young, Elliott, *Alien Nation: Chinese Migration in the Americas from the Coolie Era Through World War II* (University of North Carolina Press, 2014)

Young, Robert, *White Mythologies: Writing History and the West* (London: Routledge, 1990)

CHAPTER ONE

In 'China'

Novels by Latin American Authors Set in China

Adrián Ferrero, in his review of the book *El país imaginado*[1] (2011) by Eduardo Berti (1964–)[2], posits it within a 'Western' 'chinoiserie' and an Argentine tradition of 'Chinese' works.[3] The novel, narrated in the first person, is set in the China of the 1930s and is about the relationship between two girls and the choices they can make within different loyalties, traditions, and power structures. However, the story challenges exoticism; it is set in China, though the events could have occurred anywhere. The novel thus leads the reader to reflect upon the significance of this 'imagined country' within a Latin American context. Through my analyses of *Una novela china* (A Chinese Novel) by César Aira,[4] *La mujer en la Muralla* (The Woman on the Wall) by Alberto Laiseca,[5] and *La escuela del dolor humano de Sechuán* (The School of Human Pain of Szechuan, from now *La escuela*) by Mario Bellatin,[6] and closing with a brief reflection on *El país imaginado* (The Imagined Country) by Eduardo Berti,[7] 'China' in these novels is revealed both as a physical space

1 Eduardo Berti, *El país imaginado* (Buenos Aires: Planeta, 2011).

2 Eduardo Berti, an Argentine author established in France and member of the literary group Oulipo. Oulipo (acronym for Ouvroir de Littérature Potentielle) is a literary experimental group founded in France in 1960 which seeks to create *littérature à contraintes*; Berti is the first Latin American to belong to Oulipo.

3 Adrián Ferrero, 'Review of *El país imaginado* by Eduardo Berti', *Chasqui*, 41.2 (2012), pp. 221–24 (p. 223).

4 Aira's novels are usually signed off with a year which does not correspond to the year in which the text was published. The novel, first published in 1987, is signed off with the date 15 January 1984. César Aira, *Una novela china* (Buenos Aires: Javier Vergara, 1987); César Aira, *Una novela china* (Buenos Aires: Debolsillo, 2005).

5 Alberto Laiseca, *La mujer en la Muralla* (Buenos Aires: Planeta, 1990).

6 Originally published in 2001, the later editions of *La escuela del dolor humano de Sechuán* differ in content and length. In this chapter, I use the 2005 edition as the central text for my analysis. Mario Bellatin, *La escuela del dolor humano de Sechuán* (Mexico City: Tusquets Editores, 2001); *La escuela del dolor humano de Sechuán* (Buenos Aires: Interzona, 2005).

7 Berti, *El país imaginado*.

and a discursive context that allows for self-reflexive explorations of narrative discourse, in ways that foreground the negotiation of power in the histories of both China and Latin America.

In post-dictatorship Argentina, according to Martín Caparrós, the choice of an exotic setting became a trend for the 'nueva narrativa'.[8] Caparrós differentiates between 'us', who 'nobody needs', and 'them', the 1960s generation, who thought that literature had a place within a discourse that sought to change the world.[9] These authors may be included in an Argentinean narrative trend that María Laura de Arriba calls 'the novel of alienation'.[10] She argues that what is at stake here is the very urgent necessity of reflecting on the defeat and horror of a recent past not yet laid to rest in Argentina itself. This type of novel seeks to escape from immediate reality, locating its stories in exotic places and alien times.[11] Building on this idea in the 1980s, a group of Argentinean authors founded a literary group, to which Aira and Laiseca were both linked at the time, and called it 'Shangai'.[12] Caparrós recalls that the group was created 'casi paródicamente', where the choice of a location acted as a symbol for that which is as far as possible from Argentina geographically and culturally. The group described itself as sharing a distrust of politics and a disengagement from literary programmes as narratives of 'the real'.

As presented by Caparrós and others, the 'Shangai' group can, on one level, be regarded as a response to Jorge Luis Borges's foundational essay 'El escritor argentino y la tradición' (The Argentine Writer and Tradition, 1953), which argued for freedom from 'local colour' in literary expression for the Argentinean author. Borges expressed the need to write 'sin los camellos por delante', because 'el culto argentino del color local es un reciente culto europeo que los nacionalistas debiesen rechazar por foráneo'.[13] Borges was referring to a literary tradition that did not need to resort to local clichés to be authentic, and which offered freedom from the restricting burden of portraying 'local colour'.[14] By conspicuously over-using and overstating the

8 Martín Caparrós, 'Nuevos avances y retrocesos de la nueva novela argentina en lo que va del mes de abril', *Babel*, 2.10 (1989), pp. 43–45.

9 Caparrós.

10 María Laura de Arriba, 'Raras ficciones nuevas', *Revista del CELEHIS*, 5.6–7–8 (1996), pp. 213–53 (p. 245).

11 de Arriba, p. 244.

12 In the spring of 1987, Shangai's manifesto circulated in Buenos Aires. It was published in the widely distributed newspaper *Página 12* and the magazine *El Periodista*. The members of that group would later establish the literary magazine *Babel, Revista de Libros* (1988–1991) Roxana Patiño, 'Revistas literarias y culturales argentina de los 80', *Ínsula*, 715–716 (2006), pp. 2–5.

13 Jorge Luis Borges, 'El escritor argentino y la tradición', in *Discusión*, essay originally published 1953 (Madrid: Alianza, 1976), pp. 128–37.

14 Silvia G. Kurlat Ares, 'Post-Utopian Imaginaries: Narrating Uncertainty', in *A Companion to Latin American Literature and Culture*, ed. by Sara Castro-Klaren

exotic, these writers parody 'official narratives' regarding tradition or culture. The nature of this act of disruption emerges through their explanation for using the name 'Shangai'.

In their manifesto, the group stated that 'Shangai' represented a form of temporal exoticism, the only utopia allowed in a city that already knew itself to be exotic.[15] Indeed, upon examination, 'la palabra Shangai, no existe, porque puede escribirse de tantas formas distintas que ni siquiera es necesario escribirla'.[16] The group also challenged the ideas associated with the word 'Shangai': 'Shangai suena a chino básico, y sólo lo incomprensible azuza la mirada.'[17] The 'Shangai' group was also aware of the English term 'to be Shanghaied', to be spirited away while asleep or drunk and press-ganged into work. And above all, the group played with the arbitrary nature of their choice of name, 'Shangai es, sobre todo, un mito, innecesario'.[18] Furthermore, the choice of a place linked with the nineteenth-century expansion of the British Empire evokes histories of colonialism, exploitation, and racism.

Caparrós, in keeping with the spirit of 'Shangai', downplays the manifesto and endorses an interest in fragmentation and digression. While the malleability of 'Shangai' as presented by Caparrós leads to the notion that the actual Chinese city itself is irrelevant, the choice of a city that conventionally embodies the 'exotic' and is linked to imperialism in the Western imagination may point to a location whose narratives have been continuously and strategically redefined.[19] It evokes a place whose history has been displaced, given to it, or imposed upon it by authors. It also evokes the liminal in ways that are particularly relevant to my interpretation of Ahmed's 'stranger' in this chapter.

Indeed, like the 'Shangai' group in Argentina, Latin American novels whose stories or main events are set in China offer a particular way to explore 'China'. This chapter argues that, through subjective, overtly constructed discourses, 'China' in these types of novels appears as a symbolic object endowed with its own meaning and value, perceived as having an inherent value that is separable from the historical referent symbolized here. In this

(Chichester: Wiley-Blackwell, 2013), pp. 620–35 (p. 626); Arthur Rose, *Literary Cynics: Borges, Beckett, Coetzee* (London: Bloomsbury, 2017), p. 44.

15 Caparrós.

16 While most texts refer to the group as 'Shangai' (without the 'h', different from the romanization of the city's name and how the group itself spells it) it is also possible to find it referred to as 'Shanghai', the official transcription of the Chinese characters into Spanish. This confusion regarding the way in which to spell the group's name engages with the manifesto's interest in digression from the traditional, by using the word without considering any spelling rules. Caparrós.

17 Caparrós.

18 Caparrós.

19 Xiaolan Chen, 'Primitive and Modern: Two Faces of Shanghai in Chinese and Western Literature', *Frontiers of Literary Studies in China*, 1.4 (2007), pp. 543–54.

context, narration becomes central to the retrieval and destabilization of the story being told.

The stories are all situated in China during different periods: *La mujer en la Muralla* is set during the Qin dynasty (221–207 BC), *Una novela china* is set during the first thirty years of Communist rule (1949–late-1970s), *La escuela* plays out across both 'imperial' and 'communist' periods in China, and *El país imaginado* occurs during the first half of the twentieth century. In contrast, Latin America's presence in these texts is subliminal, if it is present at all. These novels present their stories revealing the failure of an overarching plot to fully recover any 'real' history or histories, (re)inventing narrative discourses, and thus re-encoding power relations through the construction of a recognizable 'China'. The novels can, in different ways, be read as broad postmodern allegories for the asymmetrical distribution of power at different points in history.

Through specific narrative constructions, the novels challenge any specific ontology of China and the Chinese, instead opening up a 'space of encounter' with China. Indeed, specific historical and cultural imagery permits an evocation of China through the figure of the 'stranger', as proposed by Sara Ahmed's work of critical theory, *Strange Encounters*.[20] Following Ahmed, we can see how the novels expose the construction of the 'stranger' *in* the encounter. I suggest that the way in which these novels act as 'spaces of encounter' is problematized by the traces of asymmetrical power relations that outline people's positions within society. In this sense, the historical context in which they were written sheds significant light on why these writers turned to China to engage in their reflections on the distribution of power. I suggest they do this in their works because China, perceived as antipodal and unknown, embodies specific forms of grand narratives and autocratic power. Asymmetrical distributions of power will be shown to be associated with authoritarian or hegemonic rule and the embodiment of power, or lack of it, among different members of society.

Una novela china and *La mujer en la Muralla* were published a few years after the end of the *Proceso de Reorganización Nacional* (1976–1983) and during the implementation of neoliberal policies and processes of democratization in Argentina. *La escuela* was published after the fall of the *Partido Revolucionario Institutional* (PRI). Published as they were at a time of 'overabundance of information and discourses', as described by Reinaldo Laddaga, these novels conform very broadly to the postmodern trend of foregrounding the fictitious nature of 'master narratives'.[21] The novels can thus be seen to engage with a Latin American public whose idea of China is influenced by Orientalism and Cold War discourses on China as despotic and distant, while simultaneously

20 Sara Ahmed, *Strange Encounters: Embodied Others in Post-Coloniality* (London: Routledge, 2000).

21 Reinaldo Laddaga, *Espectáculos de realidad. Ensayo sobre la narrativa latinoamericana de las últimas dos décadas* (Buenos Aires: Beatriz Viterbo Editora, 2007), p. 20.

interrupting these discourses and the prior representations of that country.[22] Precisely because they reveal the complexities of the previous histories and discourses that those 'encounters' contain, these novels can also constructively be analysed through the framework of postcolonialism.

From this perspective, this chapter aims to show how these novels offer an 'attitude of resistance to cultural colonisation that is a vital characteristic of postcolonial discourse'.[23] Ignacio López-Calvo persuasively argues for the difficulty of taking a postcolonial approach to the representation of China in Latin American texts.[24] In his study, specifically on Sino-Peruvian (*tusán*) literature, he shows how this difficulty arises partly from the fact that China was never fully colonized by Western powers and that in the Peruvian context, the *tusán* discourse's other, the dominant *criollo*, is, in fact, a community formerly colonized by an imperial power and later by economic neo-colonialism. Unlike *tusán* literature, the novels studied here can also be considered part of a *criollo* discourse, informed by Western narratives on China that reproduce the exploitative relationship between the imperial Western metropolis and its colonies. From this angle, I deploy the term 'postcolonial' to revise assumptions that privilege certain narratives and as a strategy for reading cultural representations under the optic of power relations.

The novels studied in this chapter reveal themselves to be postmodern through the presence of unreliable narrators, fragmented narratives, and paradoxes, among other features.[25] In this sense, and using Doreen Massey's reconfigured understanding of space as situational and in constant change,[26]

22 Beyond literature, such as film and magazines, see María Elvira Ríos, María Montt, and Carol Chan, 'El imaginario de lo chino en las revistas magazinescas chilenas de principios del siglo XX', *Revista Rumbos TS. Un espacio crítico para la reflexión en Ciencias Sociales*, 24 (2021), pp. 129–50 <https://doi.org/10.51188/rrts.num24.434>; Maria Montt Strabucchi, Carol Chan, and Maria Elvira Ríos, *Chineseness in Chile: Shifting Representations during the Twenty-First Century*, Studies of the Americas (Cham: Palgrave Macmillan, 2022) <https://doi.org/10.1007/978-3-030-83966-6>.

23 Silvia Nagy-Zekmi, 'Relocation of Knowledge: The Postcolonial Debate in Latin America', *Phoebe: Gender and Cultural Critique*, 16.1 (2004), pp. 1–9 (p. 7).

24 Ignacio López-Calvo, *Dragons in the Land of the Condor: Writing Tusán in Peru* (Tucson: The University of Arizona Press, 2014).

25 Discussion of postmodernism grew to particular prominence in Latin America mainly during the 1990s. Nelly Richard, 'Latinoamérica y la posmodernidad', *Escritos. Revistas de Ciencias del Lenguaje*, (1996), pp. 271–80. As Diana Palaversich shows, the concept of postmodernism can be used for Latin America, when considering the interrelated cultural, political and economic phenomena which arise from the region's immersion in global and transnational capitalism; see Diana Palaversich, *De Macondo a McOndo. Senderos de la postmodernidad latinoamericana* (Barcelona: Plaza y Valdés, 2005). See also the idea of postmodernity as '*acentuación* de la modernidad', as proposed by Pablo Oyarzun, *La desazón de lo moderno. Problemas de la modernidad* (Santiago: Cuarto Propio / Arcis, 2001), p. 58.

26 Doreen Massey, *For Space* (London: SAGE, 2005).

it coincides with a moment within the establishment of transnational capital, characterized by immanence, the noting of dispersion, fragmentation, and a fading sense of history. From this perspective, I argue that the novels studied in this chapter engage with Hutcheon's concepts of narrative perspective to problematize self-consciousness, the 'real', and the incorporation of actual historical figures and texts. Moreover, they go beyond Eurocentric and North American frames of reference, allowing, in turn, an encounter with China as the 'stranger'. In this way, the novels studied here reflect on both their own 'locality' and their belonging to the global community, as well as to global experiences of power imbalance.

Within this context, the novels studied in this chapter can be defined on one level in the terms Hutcheon proposes in *A Poetics of Postmodernism*, as historiographic metafiction, in that they are 'intensely self-reflexive and yet paradoxically also lay claim to historical events and personages'.[27] Their 'theoretical self-awareness of history and fiction as human constructs [...] [allow] for [...] [their] rethinking and reworking of the forms and contents of the past', working '*within* conventions in order to subvert them'.[28] As Hutcheon claims, 'fiction is offered as another of the discourses by which we construct our versions of reality',[29] played out in terms of parody and metafiction. While these texts engage with a specific historical-political reality, they simultaneously question the construction of discourses that claim to establish any form of direct representational or mimetic correspondence with reality. The texts can be seen to engage with specific historical-political realities, both within China and Latin America, while they remain aware of history and fiction as human constructs. This disavowal of access to a 'real historical past' as an expression of counter-power, in which the recognition of mediated textual access through fiction is favoured, forms the basis for my analysis in this chapter. Given the doubt inherent in any guarantee of meaning, Ahmed's theoretical approach to 'strangerness' is useful for analysing the novels.

In this sense, these novels contest the discourses of otherness, drawing attention 'to the forms of authorisation and labour concealed by stranger fetishism'.[30] Read as 'strange encounters', in which strangerness, as discussed earlier, unfolds as people encounter each other, these novels reopen prior histories of encounter between China and Latin America. Past histories informed these encounters: the Cold War; histories of imperialism and colonialism; refusing a Eurocentric perspective on knowledge and worldviews; and denying the impact and persistence of these histories. In this way, they

27 Linda Hutcheon, *A Poetics of Postmodernism: History, Theory, Fiction* (New York: Routledge, 1988), p. 5.

28 Hutcheon, p. 5. On the question of truth in history and fiction see Carlo Ginzburg, *Threads and Traces: True False Fictive*, trans. by Anne C. Tedeschi and John Tedeschi (Berkeley: University of California Press, 2012).

29 Hutcheon, pp. 40, 45.

30 Ahmed, p. 74.

engage with a Latin American reader, and these encounters are embedded in multiple experiences. The potential openness and elasticity of these novels, made available through their fragmented narratives, may ultimately affect a reader's perspective on prior histories they are familiar with. These novels destabilize boundaries and create new spaces through which China can be 'encountered', all while being shaped by these histories.

To explore how the narrative aesthetic works (de)constructively in these novels, thus engaging with Hutcheon's 'historiographic metafiction' and Ahmed's 'strange encounters' as textual practices, I also use Bakhtin's theory of heteroglossia. Bakhtin suggests that the novel orchestrates its themes by 'means of the social diversity of speech types and by differing individual voices'.[31] Heteroglossia, therefore, enters the novel through 'authorial' speech, the speeches of narrators, inserted genres, and characters' speech. Heteroglossia, 'once incorporated into the novel [...] is *another's speech in another's language*, serving to express authorial intentions but in a refracted way'.[32] From this perspective, the novels appear to play with different languages and versions of reality, none of which may lay claim to an absolute 'truth'. For my purposes, heteroglossia makes available the various utterances through which the stranger is encountered as 'stranger'. Through 'hybrid construction', where one single speaker contains two languages, and through the ironizing of 'authorial authority', Bakhtin's techniques of incorporating heteroglossia into the novel may reveal the discourses through which power positions are (de)constructed. These discourses are studied here through Ahmed's terms as something that remakes '*what it is that we may yet have in common*',[33] while not holding the other in place. Indeed, given that an exploration of heteroglossia allows us to discern the complex interplay of power relations between subject positions in the novel, a final, further question must concern the allegorical relationship that this may have with the asymmetrical distribution of power in broader historical and political contexts.

To hone my allegorical reading, I draw on Jeremy Tambling's approach through Walter Benjamin. Tambling shows how Fredric Jameson's concept of 'national allegories' assumes that there is a continuous narrative to be retrieved. However, Benjamin's approach nears that of deconstruction, showing meaning to be discontinuous, drawing attention to its constructed nature, and rejecting any single and consistent meaning.[34] Tambling refers to this as a postmodern allegory, 'where fragments suggest the impossibility

31 Mikhail Bakhtin, *The Dialogic Imagination: Four Essays*, ed. by Michael Holquist (Austin: University of Texas Press, 1981), p. 263.

32 Bakhtin, p. 324.

33 Ahmed, p. 181.

34 Jeremy Tambling, *Wong Kar-Wai's Happy Together* (London: Hong Kong University Press, 2003), pp. 14–15. For Latin America, see also Doris Sommer, *Foundational Fictions: The National Romances of Latin America* (Berkeley: University of California Press, 1991).

of reading a text for a single isolatable truth'.[35] Thus, no supposition of an underlying, coherent meaning can be made. From this perspective, I read these novels as a broad, postmodern allegory for the asymmetrical distribution of power: the texts reveal the *constructedness* of their narrations. This position suggests the power imbalance that the ability to 'construct' embodies.

Indeed, Victoria Albornoz presents the use of parody and allegory, together with the 'fictionalisation of fiction', as distinctive features of Latin American literature in the 1990s. This literature, she suggests, arises from the need for release from historical reality and is characterized by the construction of diverse subjectivities, voices, and narrative configurations.[36] Indeed, a large body of literature dealt with the legacy of trauma. Argentinean literary production particularly saw itself immersed in privatization processes and the reduction of the state, the internationalizing of the economy, and an overall questioning of the institutional order.[37] Francine Masiello has suggested that Argentinean literature's journey through the 'Orient' during this time utilizes the distance between cultures to explore the construction of meaning, 'to explore their own conditions as "other" in the society in which they live'.[38] In this sense, one way Albornoz's 'release' can be seen in Argentina's literature is by choosing an 'exotic' setting.

In the novels studied here, 'Shangai' (thinking about the opening paragraphs of this chapter) appears to be 'produced' through knowledge: it is simultaneously known and unknown, yet recognizable as 'stranger'. Therefore, the novels studied here allow us to explore a necessary component of Ahmed's theory, namely: '*how bodies are differentiated through the metonymic association of some bodies (and not others) with the border that confounds identity*'.[39] The 'Shangai group' can be seen to question the exclusion of Shanghai from its own histories: the group's manifesto seems to call for a reopening of past encounters, exploring the different and fragmented approaches that the city/word allows. In this sense, the use of an exotic setting reopens prior histories, gives up any totalizing thesis, and casts doubt on any guarantee of meaning. This concept of a 'novel of alienation' appears on one level to act as a way of reconciling the escape from 'immediate' reality with a reflection

35 Jeremy Tambling, *Allegory* (London: Routledge, 2010), p. 159.

36 Carla Victoria Albornoz, 'La pedagogía del dolor en la escritura fragmentaria de Mario Bellatin', *Hipertexto*, 13 (2011), pp. 3–23 (pp. 3–4).

37 Graciela Montaldo, 'Aira, un arte basado en la incorrección. El cuestionamiento de las instituciones en una vanguardia finisecular', in *De Alfonsín al Menemato (1983-2001)*, ed. by Rocco Carbone and Ana Ojeda, Literatura Argentina siglo XX (Buenos Aires: Fundación Crónica General, 2010), VII, pp. 94–106 (p. 101).

38 Francine Masiello, 'Bodies in Transit: Travel, Translation and Gender', in *Voice-Overs, Translation and Latin American Studies*, ed. by Daniel Balderston and Marcy E. Schwartz (New York: State University of New York Press, 2002), pp. 213–23 (p. 216).

39 Ahmed, p. 52.

on Argentina's recent concrete horrors under the *Junta* of the *Proceso de Reorganización Nacional*, embodying the differing discourses at play in this post-dictatorship scenario.

Indeed, the 'Shangai' group established itself within a very specific historical context, where the narratives enforced by the authoritarian *Junta* were being examined. As described by Caparrós, the group was established in a country where bodies had been 'mutilados, corrompidos y, sobre todo, ocultados, desaparecidos'.[40] He states that they write in a 'desert of bodies', and he believes that in these authors' novels bodies are 'elididos, desenfocados, inhallables'.[41] Both *Una novela china* and *La mujer en la Muralla* reveal themselves to be heirs to the 'Shangai manifesto', and the relationship of both Aira and Laiseca to this movement is highly relevant to my following analysis.

A Recognizable China: *Una novela china*, by César Aira

Considered part of the 'Shangai group', César Aira (1949–) is a prolific author who has written over eighty short novels. He is considered an exponent of Argentinean literature, and has gained international recognition. His work has been described in terms of lessons about vital topics: the twists of fate; the demonic drive of youth; love; and its 'nightmarish version': marriage.[42] Aira's novels have often toyed with presentations of the 'East', as exemplified in *El volante*,[43] *El pequeño monje budista*,[44] and *El mármol*,[45] but *Una novela china* is the only one to use China solely and overtly as a setting.

Aira's work can be divided into a 'canonical corpus', formed by his novels published in the 1980s, which Jesús Montoya Juárez suggests can be read as national narratives, a rewriting of history, or travel writing; and the 'novelitas', a 'serie b', published in the 1990s, where the production of his texts is accompanied by extensive reference to mass culture.[46] His texts have

40 Caparrós.

41 Caparrós.

42 Sandra Contreras, *Las vueltas de César Aira* (Rosario: Beatriz Viterbo Editora, 2002), pp. 292–93.

43 César Aira, *El volante* (Rosario: Beatriz Viterbo Editora, 1992).

44 César Aira, *El pequeño monje budista* (Buenos Aires: Mansalva, 2005). See also Chisu Teresa Ko, 'Orientalism and De-Orientalism in Contemporary Latin America: Reading César Aira', *TRANSMODERNITY: Journal of Peripheral Cultural Production of the Luso-Hispanic World*, 8.3 (2018), pp. 149–67.

45 César Aira, *El mármol*, Kindle 2012 (Buenos Aires: La Bestia Equilátera, 2011).

46 Jesús Montoya Juárez, 'Dos sentidos del humor de fin de Siglo: César Aira y Leo Maslíah', in *Encuentro de Latinoamericanistas Españoles: Viejas y nuevas alianzas entre América Latina y España* (Santander: CEEIB, 2006), pp. 1668–84 (p. 1669); 'Aira y los aireanos. Literatura argentina y cultura masiva desde los noventa', in *Entre lo global y lo local: La narrativa latinoamericana en el cambio de siglo (1990-2006)*, ed. by Jesús Montoya Juárez and Esteban Ángel (Madrid: Vervuert, Iberoamericana, 2008), pp. 51–76 (p. 53).

been described as a literature based on continuity, a return to a beginning, and procedure.[47] Dierdra Reber also differentiates Aira's works of the 1980s as 'historical', albeit heavily parodic, novels.[48] Indeed, Aira's work as a whole is difficult to label. Graciela Montaldo points to Aira's radical features, situated as surrealist, something also noted by other authors.[49] Aira himself compares his work with surrealists such as Max Ernst or Joseph Ernst and says that 'respecto de los personajes, prefiero los estereotipos o marionetas, sin psicología o profundidad'.[50] His narrative fiction, including the 'Eastern' novels, can certainly be classed on one level as postmodern, questioning as these novels do both ontology and narrative fixity. Aira himself, however, has rejected this term for his work.[51] As Reinaldo Laddaga puts it, 'los libros de Aira se resisten al resumen'.[52]

In *Las vueltas de César Aira*, one of the first extensive studies on Aira's work, Sandra Contreras also rejects the term, and suggests the alternative: that his work is better considered as '*una singular vuelta a las vanguardias históricas en el fin de siglo*'.[53] She hypothesizes that Aira's 'vuelta al relato' is the result of the questions his work poses from the perspective as if it were of the literary 'vanguardia'.[54] Montaldo also reads Aira's literature as avant-garde.[55] Contreras describes Aira's writing as 'huida hacia adelante', which assumes a writing style that never returns to make corrections, thus disrespecting the coherence of the plot, and engaging with the questions that have underpinned Argentine narrative since the 1970s: how should a story be

47 Margarita Remón-Raillard, 'La narrativa de César Aira: Una sorpresa continua e ininterrumpida', *Foro Hispánico*, 24.1 (2003), pp. 53–64 (p. 59); Ana Porrúa, 'César Aira: Implosión y juventud', *Punto de Vista*, 81 (2005), pp. 24–29 (p. 25); Graciela Villanueva, 'El "enfrente del enfrente": Circuitos urbanos en las novelas de César Aira', in *Ciudades y el fin de siglo XX en América Latina: literaturas, culturas, representaciones*, ed. by Teresa Orecchia Havas (Bern: Peter Lang, 2007), pp. 369–81 (p. 369).

48 Dierdra Reber, 'Cure for the Capitalist Headache: Affect and Fantastic Consumption in César Aira's Argentine "Baghdad"', *MLN*, 122.2 (2007), pp. 371–99 (p. 371).

49 Graciela Montaldo, 'Una literatura que lo puede todo', in *Literatura Latino-Americana do século XXI*, ed. by Beatriz Resende (Rio de Janeiro: Aeroplano, 2005), pp. 127–39 (p. 127); Graciela Speranza, *Fuera de campo: Literatura y arte argentinos después de Duchamp* (Barcelona: Anagrama, 2006), pp. 289–315.

50 Ernesto Escobar Ulloa, 'Entrevista a César Aira', *The Barcelona Review*, 2004. <http://www.barcelonareview.com/44/s_ca.htm> [accessed 1 July 2021].

51 Carlos Alfieri, 'César Aira: El mejor Cortázar es un mal Borges', *Revista de Cultura Ñ, Clarín*, 2014 <http://www.elortiba.org/aira.html> [accessed 1 July 2021].

52 Reinaldo Laddaga, 'Espectáculos de realidad. Ensayo sobre la narrativa latinoamericana de las últimas dos décadas', *Comunicação & Política*, 24.3 (2006), pp. 159–78 (p. 159); *Espectáculos de realidad. Ensayo sobre la narrativa latinoamericana de las últimas dos décadas*, p. 7.

53 Contreras, p. 14.

54 Contreras, p. 21.

55 Montaldo, VII, p. 95.

told? What is its nature and function?[56] Nevertheless, following Hutcheon's notion of 'historiographic metafiction', and concurring with Montoya Juárez and other critics,[57] I suggest that Aira's work, and specifically *Una novela china*, can still be read as postmodern on account of its self-reflecting metafiction, and its problematization of mimetic representation.

Set in rural revolutionary China, *Una novela china* presents the story of Lu Hsin (Lu), whose romantic desire is fulfilled after he marries a native girl from the mountains surrounding his village. To achieve this, he adopts and raises a child from the mountains, whom he then marries. Parallel to his romance, the narrator introduces us to the various occupations held by Lu throughout his life, such as his literary and engineering works. The narrator introduces the story by reflecting on human life, events, histories, and history. He explains how every place is touched by events, within a wider, eternal circumstance and how, ultimately, everything passes and is forgotten.[58] The narrator informs us he has learned about the story of Lu, and decided to commit it to memory. He tells the reader that the story will be forgotten, and that he intends to remember it 'exclusivamente como parte del trabajo, mucho más amplio y abarcador, de olvidarla'.[59] His explicit choice to select certain passages from Lu's life, his use of ellipses, his comments, and his ambiguous presentations of the character's thoughts, all point to his being an unreliable narrator. The reader is addressed as if from a Chinese context, as if they were familiar with a Chinese cultural framework. The narrator thus leads the narratee towards a specific historical context that provides the time-frame in which the story develops.

One particularly significant aspect by which the narrator's reliability is called into question is his explicitly stated decision to tell Lu's story. While he presents elements that appear to be central to Lu's life, the exceptionality of these, and the reason the narrator calls him 'nuestro héroe' or 'hombre-orquesta', is not explained.[60] The narrator refers to Lu's 'fantástica inteligencia'. Still, his ambiguous presentation of him as having 'falso mandarinismo', without explaining what would constitute real mandarin, invites the reader to wonder whether Lu's story might just be 'nonsense'.[61] Lu's more developed perspectives which the narrator comments on act as marker of his exceptionality. Yet his fame is attributed to an editorial which portrayed him as one of the initiators of the Cultural Revolution, an event

56 Contreras, pp. 11–12.

57 Montoya Juárez, 'Dos sentidos del humor de fin de Siglo: César Aira y Leo Maslíah', p. 1673; Sylvia Saítta, 'En torno al 2001 en la narrativa argentina', *Literatura y Lingüística*, 29 (2013), pp. 131–48 (pp. 136–37).

58 Aira, *Una novela china*, p. 3.

59 Aira, *Una novela china*, p. 5.

60 Aira, *Una novela china*, pp. 30, 61.

61 Aira, *Una novela china*, p. 6.

described as 'la más fantástica confusión que hubiera reinado nunca sobre la faz de la tierra'.[62]

Overall, there is no clear justification of the narrator's choice. This allows us to contemplate the possibility of a narrator who only by mistake considers Lu's story to be worth telling. The narrator's unreliability is also underlined through the equivocal presentation of Lu. For example, he is presented as 'un mandarín, salvo que no lo era'.[63] Furthermore, while Lu is presented as a man of science, he is also given away as superstitious. This overtly controlling, yet subjective narrator reveals the inability to access any certainty.[64] The narrator's selection, concealment, and delay of the delivery of information also act as markers of unreliability. A bird's-eye view and presumably unlimited knowledge allow him to focus on certain scenes and situations. Likewise, the impression that the narrator is concealing information is indeed suggested by the narrator himself. The reader is left to wonder what the narrator has not said or may never say. As noted, the narrator has chosen to present the story of Lu, but also intrudes on the text with his own comments, continuously displacing the information presented. This displacement appears, for example, using expressions such as 'creyó entender' or 'creyó verlas'.[65] This indicates the uncertainty of the narrator's knowledge of Lu's thoughts or the interarticulations of the thoughts of both. At certain moments, the narrator's thoughts seem to coincide with Lu's, as occurs in phrases such as 'la frontera entre la salud mental y la demencia es imperceptible'.[66] In this case, free indirect speech is a marker for the ambiguity of the narrator-character relationship, while the utterance reveals a certain 'wisdom' on the narrator's part.

This leaves the authenticity of the events that occur open to question. For example, as is the case with Lu's quotation from 'miss Moore'.[67] If we assume that his intention is, in fact, to cite Marianne Moore's poem 'Silence', then Lu's completion of the verse would represent a misquotation of it. While Lu quotes 'My house is not an inn' in English, the poem states 'Make my house your inn',[68] leading the reader to reconsider Lu's knowledge. This forces us to ask whether Lu is actually a fool who has been mistaken for a hero. In revealing Lu's fallibility through the words of a mediating narrator who trusts him, the narrator's fallibility is emphasized. This fallibility, in turn, reveals a text that seems self-consciously aware of its subjectivity and partial representation of a 'truth'.

62 Aira, *Una novela china*, p. 75.
63 Aira, *Una novela china*, p. 5.
64 Hutcheon, p. 117.
65 Aira, *Una novela china*, pp. 35, 74.
66 Aira, *Una novela china*, p. 21.
67 Aira, *Una novela china*, p. 49.
68 Marianne Moore, 'Silence' <http://www.poets.org/poetsorg/poem/silence-2> [accessed 19 February 2021].

Furthermore, this unreliable narrator is also allegedly 'Chinese', and assumes that the narratee is familiar with what he is presenting, as he sets the story in a supposedly recognizable 'China'. The use of Chinese names for towns and people, or the mention of porcelain and dragons, contribute to establish a repertoire of imagery which 'instantly' refers the reader to China. This is reinforced through the mention of specific historical events, such as the Long March or the Cultural Revolution.[69] Vocabulary, such as 'li', a traditional unit of distance, and the continuous mention of tea drinking, also contribute to rendering a recognizable 'China'. Yet the search for 'gekorisen' [sic] or the mention of a plant called 'Hannokan' [sic],[70] both apparently invented words, also parody an 'oriental' setting, as their pronunciation in Spanish suggest an 'oriental' language. These 'invented words' reveal an utterance populated with social intentions,[71] serving the purpose of recreating a fetishized China through 'strangerness'. As Ahmed suggests, the recognition of the stranger is an affective judgement, here recalled through words which 'appear' as 'strange'. In this way, the 'China' represented in *Una novela china* corresponds, on one level, to the country China, while other more imprecise elements, which seem to belong to the realm of fiction due to their 'invented' nature, allow the reader to regard that depiction as fallible, illusory and deceptive.

Phrases which attribute certain traits to the Chinese and other ethnic groups in China contribute to the description of a particular 'China', such as 'los chinos tenemos distintos mundos superpuestos', the distinction between 'chinos de verdad' and otherwise, or the racist description of a character as with 'cara amarilla de mandarin'.[72] The world appears to be culturally divided between East and West: Lu is presented as knowledgeable about the Western world: he knows various Western languages, has a predilection for the work of the writer Jean Paul, knows by heart the works of Von Chamisso, venerates Kant, and reads Stendhal and other Western authors in their original languages.[73]

Nevertheless, Lu's interaction with the Western world is presented as partial, as can be seen in his preparation of ice-cream without knowing of its existence in the 'West'.[74] Furthermore, we also see a signalling to the Latin American canon through a reference to the day García Márquez's 'coronel Aureliano Buendía' was introduced to ice.[75] This reference to the Latin American canon thus shows how Lu's relationship with the 'West' is ambiguous and fragmented.

69 Aira, *Una novela china*, pp. 6, 75.

70 Aira, *Una novela china*, pp. 23, 94.

71 Bakhtin, pp. 277–78, 300.

72 Aira, *Una novela china*, pp. 93, 26, 77.

73 Aira, *Una novela china*, pp. 9, 16.

74 Aira, *Una novela china*, p. 8.

75 This signals towards the opening lines of Gabriel García Márquez's novel *Cien años de soledad*. Gabriel García Márquez, *Cien Años de Soledad* (Madrid: Espasa-Calpe,

On the one hand, his discovery of ice is presented as overdue. On the other, Lu seems to have known that the discovery had already been made but fails to admit it openly. Overall, Lu is presented as being specifically 'Chinese', with the text stressing his reflective attitude, presenting him as 'muy oriental' and 'de espíritu mandarin'.[76] These lies and falsities signal the postmodern concern for the 'truth(s) relative to the specificity of place and culture',[77] leading the reader to question the construction of discourses.

The 'Chineseness' of Lu is also played out in opposition to the mountain-dwellers, the ethnic group to which his adopted daughter and future wife Hin belongs. In the story, the mountaineers are presented as different: for example, his adopted daughter Hin turns out to be a 'typical' highland beauty, and she wears a 'different' hairstyle.[78] Incest is presented as a custom of the mountain-dwellers, but not of the Chinese. Moreover, his daughter and wife-to-be is part of a different race, 'preciosa y rara'.[79] While Lu is presented as a kind of hero who has rescued her, their relationship is based on a power imbalance stemming from race, age and class differences.

Lu's position of power is made available by the fact that the mountaineers are practically voiceless and indistinguishable from one another, which Lu depicted as dismissively hiring people to take care of his daughter or to help him run a newssheet. And yet, the narrator states,[80] Lu is aware of racial issues. Lu's conflation with the narrator conveys the latter's prejudice regarding race, and highlights his generalizations about Chinese culture, revealing layers of power asymmetry. This embodies Ahmed's theories as well as Tambling's notion of the postmodern allegory, as these 'encounters' show how the figure of the 'stranger' is put to work, via the asymmetry of power, that also involves difference, while the impossibility of a single isolatable truth is also suggested.[81] In this way, the narrator and Lu appear powerful, while the exercise of Lu's power limits Hin's agency. At the same time, the novel undermines Lu's power, as he is powerless in his submission to the narrator and is presented within an authoritarian context: while he contests power (through his publishing of a revisionist editorial), a stronger force (the Party) uses his voice (the 'most famous dazhibao') to put into motion a bigger process of change (the Cultural Revolution). As in postmodern fiction, the story instils power but then challenges it.

Against this backdrop, language creates an atmosphere of timelessness. The specific historical context introduces the reader to the Communist

1983), p. 59. It has also been noted by Ida Vitale, in 'Un vestido rosa y después: César Aira', *Vuelta*, 165 (1990), pp. 42–45 (p. 45).

76 Aira, *Una novela china*, pp. 67, 74.

77 Hutcheon, p. 108.

78 Aira, *Una novela china*, pp. 8, 60.

79 Aira, *Una novela china*, pp. 18, 60.

80 Aira, *Una novela china*, p. 15.

81 Tambling, *Allegory*, p. 159.

revolution, which has been a fundamental element in Latin America's imaginary of China since the 1950s, as noted by Amanda Holmes.[82] In the case of Argentina, many travellers had visited China and then published testimonies of their trip, while news of the Chinese revolution also appeared in the press.[83] As noted by both Megan Ferry[84] and Holmes,[85] the Cultural Revolution posters that circulated in Latin America featured an 'orientalized' exotic space; a revolutionary paradise associated with the promotion of China's socialist ideology. The revolution reframed China's representation in Latin American literature and culture by including aspects of its recent history while it also sought to maintain its exotic appeal.[86]

While addressing the narratee from the context of Revolutionary China, the narrator also recalls a timeless and static China, a stereotypical trope of the country. A struggle between unchanging tradition and a rapidly changing modern China emerges from the circular sense of time. This appears through phrases such as 'nuestros bellos cielos siempre iguales' or Lu's solemn attitude when feeding his cats, described as a 'ceremonia'.[87] In this way, Lu seems to embody an 'eternal' China. Even though he experiences strong changes

82 Amanda Holmes, 'China in Argentine Exotismo: Contemporary Inventions of the Orient', *Bulletin of Spanish Studies*, 85.1 (2008), pp. 71–83 (p. 76).

83 Travel to the PRC during the Cold War can be considered as part of the country's cultural diplomacy, expansion of its revolutionary project, and a search for legitimacy in an international context. See, among others, Rosario Hubert, 'Intellectual Cartographies of the Cold War: Argentinean Visitors to the People's Republic of China 1952-1958', in *Handbook of Literature and Space*, ed. by Robert Tally (London: Routledge, 2016), pp. 337–48; Jorge J. Locane and Maria Montt Strabucchi, 'Cultura china y Capricornio. Dos proyectos pioneros para el comercio simbólico (y material) entre América Latina y China', *Revista Izquierdas*, 49 (2020), pp. 2521–44; Jorge J. Locane and María Montt Strabucchi, 'El Viaje América Latina-China. Una Interacción Sur-Sur Sui Generis', *TRANSMODERNITY: Journal of Peripheral Cultural Production of the Luso-Hispanic World*, 9.3 (2020); Patricia Palma and Maria Montt Strabucchi, 'Percepción de la República Popular China en Chile a partir de la prensa: El Tarapacá de Iquique y El Mercurio de Santiago 1949-1960' (presented at the I Congreso Latinoamericano de Estudios Chinos, Universidad Nacional de La Plata, 2011); Matthew Rothwell, *Transpacific Revolutionaries: The Chinese Revolution in Latin America* (New York: Routledge, 2013); Brenda Rupar, 'El rol de la Revolución Cultural china en el maoísmo argentino', *Leste Vermehlo: revista de estudos críticos asiáticos*, 3.1 (2017), pp. 355–75; José Miguel Vidal Kunstmann, 'Entre lo local y lo global: Pablo de Rokha y el proyecto maoísta', *TRANSMODERNITY: Journal of Peripheral Cultural Production of the Luso-Hispanic World*, 9.3 (2020), pp. 161–94.

84 'Megan M. Ferry, 'China as Utopia: Visions of the Chinese Cultural Revolution in Latin America', *Modern Chinese Literature and Culture*, 12.2 (2000), pp. 236–69 (p. 239); Holmes, p. 76.

85 Holmes, p. 76.

86 Ferry, p. 239; Holmes, p. 76.

87 *Una novela china*, pp. 6, 9.

throughout his life, he does not change intrinsically, something bound to his wearing of traditional clothes.

The imagery, therefore, contributes to creating a revolutionary yet timeless and orientalized 'Chinese' space, interrupted by unclear or possibly invented elements that underline the fictional nature of literary discourse. The fictionality of narration is also recalled by the narrator himself, who evaluates the work of others who have written about China: 'Se decía que provenían del tronco originario manchú, pero era un rumor difundido por los cronistas antiguos, viciados de imbecilidad.'[88] This fictionality refers us back to the pattern presented at the beginning of the text: an eternal 'China' interrupted by events and stories, which, ultimately, pass and move on. The narrator highlights the illusoriness of events, filtered through his worldview. This further distances the illusion of 'reality', pointing to a postmodern shifting of perspectives and questioning of any totalizing system.[89]

Holmes has underlined how *Una novela china* makes use of an exotic setting as a way of opening up a fictional space, and of shifting perspectives. With China being as exotic as any fictionalized setting, Holmes shows how Aira exploits the setting to propose that perspective causes an imbalance in the identification of what is real, thus questioning the significance of contemporary artistic expressions and emphasizing the importance of the viewer's gaze within a context of globalization.[90] For this, she builds on Contreras and Laddaga, who observe the presence of 'miniaturas' in Aira's work, seeing things through a 'telescopio invertido'.[91] Héctor Hoyos's analysis of *Una novela china* engages with Holmes's by suggesting that exoticism allows Aira to 'emphasize the concept of perspective, rather than the idea of a strange and marvellous place'.[92] This recalls the words of Aira himself, who has stated that he invents spaces,

> [...] donde pueda funcionar una pura ficción como la China y por eso escribí *Una novela china* y nunca estuve allí. Son espacios de pura ficción, de pura invención, donde puede pasar cualquier cosa.[93]

Holmes claims that Aira develops an image of China built on preconceived notions of the Asian country, which he then uses as a landscape open to fictional experimentation.[94] Nevertheless, this 'exotic' landscape is grounded in material conditions that are tied to a 'real' China, even while Aira presents

88 Aira, *Una novela china*, p. 16.

89 Hutcheon, p. 67.

90 Holmes, pp. 73, 83.

91 Reinaldo Laddaga, 'Una literatura de la clase media: Notas sobre César Aira', *Hispamérica: Revista de Literatura*, 30.88 (2001), pp. 37–48 (p. 41); Contreras, p. 67.

92 Holmes, p. 78.

93 Luis Dapelo and César Aira, 'César Aira', *Hispamérica*, 36.107 (2007), pp. 41–53 (p. 51).

94 Holmes, p. 71.

it as 'pure fiction'. The use of specific words, places, or people implies a detailed knowledge of China. While this knowledge does not require one to have *been* there, it does recall a China beyond 'pure fiction'.

While I agree with Holmes that Aira's setting is shaped by 'authorial authority' and that the use of China-as-setting emphasizes the locus of enunciation of the gaze, I contend that Aira uses China not only as a tool by which to explore the concept of exoticism, but that he also uses China to subvert previous 'exotic' narratives, as the novel also emphasizes the partiality of 'prior histories' regarding China. He thus exposes the imagery and stereotypes themselves. In this sense, I agree with Ofelia Ros, who analyses how, for Aira, writing offers the 'possibility for reproducing structures of domination and repetition, or the contrary, for interrupting them with a symptomatic laughter'.[95] By plausibly presenting events, yet interrupting them via intermissions in register and theme, Aira seems to 'unfix' China while retaining elements which lead the reader to think of 'China'. The novel inscribes and only then subverts its mimetic engagement with the world. Interruption, furthermore, is stressed at the end of the novel, which ends with a significant change of register. As Contreras notes, while the narrator maintains the courtesy sustained through the text, the end is presented in an abrupt and unexpected way.[96] In this regard, the novel 'plays' with Latin American preconceptions of China, which may ultimately not be a mechanism that defies Orientalism.

In relation to this, Hoyos argues that '[...] para Aira el Oriente es una invención de la clase media argentina' or of 'cierta clase media criolla latinoamericana'.[97] Hoyos suggests that in *Una novela china*, as in Santiago Gamboa's *Los Impostores* and Ariel Magnus's *Un chino en bicicleta*, 'el orientalismo sur-sur incluye la fantasía imperialista sin reproducir su ideología de superioridad cultural'.[98] Nevertheless, it is possible to suggest that Aira's construction of China as the 'stranger' goes beyond Argentina and the Latin American *criollo* middle class, recalling the Western world. As Masiello shows, by testing and challenging boundaries of the 'Orient', the North/South, East/West or familiar/distant axes are removed.[99] Reading texts as a form of 'strange encounter' reveals how such encounters are always mediated and partial.[100]

95 Ofelia Ros, 'Restos de la ideología: la "idea siniestra" en la literatura de César Aira', *Revista de Crítica Literaria Latinoamericana*, 37.74 (2011), pp. 149–69 (pp. 149, 162).

96 Contreras, p. 120.

97 Héctor Hoyos, 'Orientalismo, globalización e imaginarios transpacíficos en la novela latinoamericana actual', *Cuadernos de Literatura*, 17.34 (2013), pp. 82–105 (pp. 89–99).

98 Hoyos, p. 100.

99 Masiello, p. 217.

100 Ahmed, p. 15.

This can be observed through the fact that Lu learns about the world by reading *Le Monde* and *Reader's Digest*.[101] This suggests that not only the novel but also its protagonist, is postmodern, which in the words of Jameson can be defined as someone '[...] fascinated precisely by [...] materials they no longer simply "quote" [...], but incorporate into their very substance'.[102] In this way, the novel makes explicit some of the 'prior histories' which inform Lu's encounter with the 'West', problematizing the histories of his determination.[103] The novel evades 'stranger fetishism' by exposing 'China' as fetish, exposed as a composite symbolic figure.[104] The 'encounter' goes beyond an imperialist fantasy or a removal of boundaries by being interrogative of holding 'others' in place.

The novel emphasizes the notion of perspective and otherness through the mention of mirrors and reflections, and the relation of the real and the oneiric. The different points of view are evoked when Lu himself reflects on perspective as he looks at his village from the mountains, in contrast to traditional Chinese paintings, which portray the mountains from below. This idea is further enhanced when Lu boards an aeroplane and looks at his village from a bird's-eye perspective.[105] The relevance of the point of view sheds light on how the novel is a reflection on Lu's life, exposing the mechanisms of representation. In this way, the novel problematizes representation even as it invokes it, something that becomes the text's defining characteristic. The 'stranger' is unfixed by opening up the text and focusing on the strangerness it evokes. While pointing to this 'reality' beyond discourse, its representations are shown to be discursive constructs, further problematizing narrative representation, exposing the crisis of grand narratives and acting as counter-discourse.[106]

Irene Depetris Chauvin has analysed how, from a Deleuzian conceptualization, Aira's novels expose the mechanisms which allow for the functioning of simulacra, while at the same time subverting them.[107] This comes close to my argument, as I agree that the China constructed by Aira 'already is' constructed as fetishized 'stranger', and this ontological being is challenged within the text itself. Aira reinvents 'China' as 'stranger', exposing the reader

101 Lisa Ubelaker Andrade, 'Connected in Print: Selecciones del Reader's Digest, U.S. Cultural Relations, and the Construction of a Global Middle Class', *Palabra Clave*, 22.4 (2019), pp. 1–32 <https://doi.org/10.5294/pacla.2019.22.4.7>.

102 Fredric Jameson, *Postmodernism, or, the Cultural Logic of Late Capitalism* (Durham: Duke University Press, 1991), p. 3.

103 Ahmed, p. 51.

104 Anne McClintock, *Imperial Leather: Race, Gender, and Sexuality in the Colonial Contest* (New York: Routledge, 1995), pp. 184–85.

105 Aira, *Una novela china*, p. 81.

106 Hutcheon, p. 40.

107 Irene Depetris Chauvin, 'La violencia gratuita y el poder de lo falso en César Aira', *Revista Chilena de Literatura*, 87 (2014), pp. 69–87 (p. 69).

to what 'we have already designated in the beyond' through our recognition of the one different from 'us'.[108] Yet at the same time, Aira challenges this ontology of the 'stranger' from within the text itself.

In *Una novela china* it is possible to observe predictable descriptions of the landscape, yet also words which are seemingly 'lies', through which contradictions are exposed. Hoyos argues that contemporary fiction about Sino-Latin American relations can be considered from a position somewhere between cultural comprehension and incomprehension; and that between these points there is a partial understanding, which Hoyos[109] refers to as 'opacity'. The evocation of Lu Xun through the character Lu Hsin, something that would only be noted by readers aware of the Chinese writer's existence, stands as an example of this 'opacity'.[110] This reference to Lu Xun can be seen as a provocation on the part of Aira, which contributes to an obliteration of boundaries between the local and the foreign, reflecting on the possibility of representing other cultures and the limitations embodied therein. It also reveals heteroglossia, with the relationship between Lu Xun/Lu Hsin standing as a way of relativizing borders created by history and society.

My analysis thus reveals that the notion of China as alien remains, encoding power relations, insofar as it is presented as a system in itself and hence recognizable as different. Aira's narrator fixes the place of enunciation, which reveals the narrator's capriciousness, questioning the authority of his knowledge and reminding us of the textual access to the past. In this way, the novel establishes a 'truth' only to subvert it from within.[111] China is presented and contested as the 'fetishised stranger', problematizing what is stated outright and emphasizing narrative *constructedness.*

Indeed, as noted by Hoyos, Lu Hsin becomes the epitome of multipolar interactions, challenging a division of the world between centre and periphery.[112] Yet I argue that the text not only challenges a centre–periphery approach, but portrays China as alien, insofar as it is presented as a hermetic world, real or invented. Chisu Teresa Ko argues, analysing *Una novela china*,

108 Ahmed, p. 3.

109 Hoyos.

110 Hoyos states that Lu Hsin is also a distorted image of the political role of Lu Xun. While Hoyos presents Lu Xun as '[...] el escritor oficial del régimen del presidente Mao', p. 101, it is arguable that this was the use that the Communist Party made of Lu Xun. While I agree that the use of Lu Hsin for the main character's name is something that should be further explored, and that Aira definitely presents a distorted figure of the original Lu, Hoyos's vision of Lu Xun as a Marxist-Leninist set against the Guomindang could be called into question. The real Lu Xun was not necessarily a blueprint of the Communist future, nor an obedient follower of Mao and of the Chinese Communist Party's line. Merle Goldman, 'The Political Use of Lu Xun', *The China Quarterly*, 91 (1982), pp. 446–61.

111 Hutcheon, p. xiii.

112 Hoyos, pp. 86–87.

El pequeño monje budista, and *El mármol* (see chapter 3), that Aira's novels search for a non-Orientalist representation of Asia, but in the process find themselves in a process of Orientalism and de-Orientalism. In this process, while the novels may allow some South–South connections, the 'East' remains in an Orientalized position.[113] Indeed, within this context, I suggest that *Una novela china* reaffirms a notion of cultural specificity by drawing on imagery which also stimulates the notion of 'China' as stranger. And yet, exposing 'China' as constructed—and therefore uncovering it as a created discourse—does not necessarily defy *constructedness* itself and may ultimately, as Ko shows, slip into '[...] a search for an essential Oriental subject, itself an act of Orientalism'[114] and a repetition of an 'Orient'.

And yet, the misleading aspects of the narration here suggest that more than one discourse on 'China' exists. This recalls the fragmentation of the 'master narratives' from Argentina by exploring different approaches to China, as the 'Shangai' group does with 'exotic' settings. By drawing attention to the authoritative, authorial techniques by which the 'stranger' emerges, the text makes available a worldview and a version of reality which cannot lay claim to an 'absolute truth'.[115] This challenges any specific ontology of China and the Chinese within the text. By displaying 'differentiation' (among 'strangers') as something that happens during the encounter, and not because the 'stranger' *is* inherently different, the text challenges cultural colonization[116] where the 'stranger' is still informed by the histories that have informed those encounters. The challenge China presents as an essential stranger and figure of otherness also appears in Laiseca's *La mujer en la Muralla*, as we shall now see.

A Traditional China: *La mujer en la Muralla*, by Alberto Laiseca

Alberto Laiseca (1941–2016) was considered a 'cult writer', partly because of his role reading horror stories on television, which raised his popularity in both the literary sphere and that of mass-media.[117] Even before he was published, he was well known by fellow Argentine authors who celebrated the quality and originality of his work. Aira praised him in 1989, calling him an 'artista maduro y consumado'.[118] Like Aira, Laiseca also plays with presentations of the 'East' in his literature, as in *La hija de Kheops* (1989) and

113 Ko, p. 153.

114 Ko, p. 164.

115 Bakhtin, p. 263.

116 Homi K. Bhabha, *The Location of Culture* (Oxon: Routledge, 1994).

117 Pedro Arturo Gómez and José Agustín Conde de Boeck, 'Canonización y actitud de culto. La presencia de Alberto Laiseca en El artista (2008) de Mariano Cohn y Gastón Duprat', *Imagofagia*, 7 (2013) <http://www.asaeca.org/imagofagia/index.php/imagofagia/article/view/345> [accessed 1 July 2017].

118 César Aira, 'Una máquina de guerra contra la pena', *Babel*, 2.12 (1989), p. 4.

La Puerta del Viento (2014). In addition, he often stated a specific interest in the Orient, China, and Chinese topics.[119] His work has become well-known and accessible in recent years, but there is as yet limited critical analysis of it. Most available works refer to his participation in 'Shangai' and the 'public figure of Laiseca', linked to his television and film appearances.

Ricardo Piglia observes that Laiseca was influenced by authors and trends from outside the Argentinean literary tradition, something with which Hernán Bergara concurs in his appraisal of Laiseca, as noted by Carlos Fernández González.[120] Bergara demonstrates this by listing how Laiseca's work has been described as strange or weird, disobedient to the canon, and Laiseca himself as erudite in strange things.[121] Regarding Laiseca's *La hija de Kheops*, Aira's *Una novela china*, and here I would also include *La mujer en la Muralla*, Montaldo suggests this is a literature that recognizes the existence of the foreign and speaks about it, thereby recovering the fictionality of literature. Fiction becomes a salient feature, as does the exercising of fiction beyond history.[122] And while Laiseca does indeed engage with literary traditions beyond Argentina, his novel *La mujer en la Muralla* can be described, on one level, as a rewriting of a story by Borges. Indeed, one could argue that his novel is an extended version of Borges' short story 'La muralla y los libros'[123] published in 1950, as a focus on the first emperor of China, the 'Great Wall', the Emperor's relationship with his mother, and books. However, this is something that has not been mentioned by Laiseca or has yet to be observed by the critics. While Borges hypothesizes how Shi Huang Ti's character was influenced by his sense of betrayal regarding his mother, Laiseca spends 312 pages exploring this possibility.

La mujer en la Muralla was published in Buenos Aires in 1990. A second edition of the novel, published in Spain in 2002, presented it as Laiseca's 'más fabuladora, más elaborada y más leída' novel.[124] Like *Una novela china*, the text discloses power imbalances through its construction of character, narrative structure, and imagery. It defies the authority of knowledge by

119 Federico Von Baumbach, 'Poemas Chinos de Laiseca', 2014 <http://www.dangdai.com.ar/joomla/index.php?option=com_content&view=article&id=3807:poemas-chinos-de-laiseca&catid=2:cultura&Itemid=9> [accessed 1 July 2021].

120 Carlos Fernández González, 'Alcances y dimensiones del plagio en la narrativa de Alberto Laiseca: alrededor de "Por favor ¡Plágienme!"', *Revista Chilena de Literatura*, 87 (2014), pp. 89–113 (p. 107).

121 Hernán Bergara, 'Plagios con un plagio de plagios', in *Por favor, ¡Plágienme!*, by Alberto Laiseca (Buenos Aires: Eudeba, 2013), p. 11.

122 Graciela Montaldo, 'Un argumento contraborgiano en la literatura argentina de los años 80 (sobre C. Aira, A. Laiseca y Copi)', *Hispamérica: Revista de Literatura*, 19.55 (1990), pp. 105–12 (p. 110).

123 Jorge Luis Borges, 'La muralla y los libros', in *Inquisiciones, Otras inquisiciones* (Barcelona: Debolsillo, 2011), pp. 151–54.

124 Tusquets, 'La mujer en la muralla' <http://www.tusquetseditores.com/titulos/andanzas-la-mujer-en-la-muralla> [accessed 1 July 2021].

contrasting subjectively constructed discourses narrated by different voices, stressing the subjective character of literary representation. In this sense, heteroglossia is present through the multiple narrators, allowing for specific worldviews to coexist, encounter each other, and conflict within the text.

Information as to the source of the knowledge presented in the novel is suggested via Laiseca's statements. He said that he drew his knowledge for the novel from Lin Yutang, who visited Argentina in 1959 and 1962,[125] even though, as Laiseca put it in 2005, he was 'un autor para señoras gordas',[126] suggesting Laiseca's reservations regarding Lin's academic significance. Laiseca claimed that he had considerable knowledge of Chinese culture, acquired after he read Lin's book *Sabiduría China*, which includes *The Tale of Meng Chiang*, the work that inspires Laiseca's title.[127] Laiseca also claimed 'mucha formación china' since his twenties, when Lin's visits to Argentina occurred.[128]

But throughout the book, that which is fiction and that which is based on 'real' history remain difficult to distinguish as original historiographic sources are not quoted. Hence, the text acts as a parody of genuine knowledge about China, casting doubt on the very possibility of 'any guarantee of meaning'.[129] As we shall see, historiographic sources come under scrutiny through the text's questioning of assumed correspondence between 'text' and 'reality'.[130] Bakhtin's concept of heteroglossia reveals language's connection to social

125 Lin Yutang (1895–1976) was one of the most influential writers from China of his generation. His prolific work was published in English and Chinese, and read in Latin America. Sergio Morero, 'Lin Yutang y la importancia de vivir', *Revista Vea y Lea*, 1962 <http://www.magicasruinas.com.ar/revistero/internacional/autores-lin-yutang.htm> [accessed 1 July 2021].

126 Facundo García, 'Los poemas sirven para no estar solo', *Página/12* (Argentina, 26 November 2005), section Cultura y Espectáculos <http://www.pagina12.com.ar/diario/suplementos/espectaculos/2-1125-2005-11-26.html> [accessed 1 July 2021].

127 Regarding *Sabiduría China*, Laiseca most probably means the Spanish edition of *The Wisdom of China and India* published in Buenos Aires in two separate volumes. The first part of the book would have been published in Spanish as Lin Yutang, *Sabiduría Hindú* (Buenos Aires: Editorial Biblioteca Nueva, 1959). *Sabiduría China* was translated by Alfredo A. Whitelow. Lin Yutang, *Sabiduría China*, trans. by Alfredo Whitelow, 3rd edition (Buenos Aires: Editorial Biblioteca Nueva, 1959). In English, it is only possible to find the text *The Wisdom of China and India*. *The Wisdom of China and India*, ed. by Lin Yutang (New York: Random House, 1942). See also Gabriel Palumbo and Diego Rossello, 'Laiseca', *Quilt*, 2010 <http://proyectoquilt.com.ar/page/10/> [accessed 1 August 2021]; Lin, *The Wisdom of China and India*, pp. 909–31.

128 Fernando Molle, 'Yo deliro pero con realismo', *Perfil*, 6 May 2011 <http://www.perfil.com/ediciones/cultura/Yo-delirio-pero-con-realismo-20116-578-0028.html> [accessed 1 July 2021].

129 Hutcheon, pp. 54–55.

130 Hutcheon, p. 56.

and historical spheres, exposing the fallacy of neutrality[131] and allowing us to detect the interplay of power positions within the novel. Simultaneously, this text draws attention to the forms of authorization concealed by stranger fetishism, which assumes the 'stranger' to be the one we do not know.[132]

The novel is set in historical China, and many characters are based on real historical figures, although only some are explicitly presented as such.[133] The text opens with a short story/chapter which narrates the events of the last day of King Nan, Emperor of the Chou dynasty (1046–256 BC). The main narrator's instructive tone establishes an underlying power imbalance between himself and the narratee, 'el lector'.[134] The rest of the novel tells the story of the Qin Emperor (Ch'in), describing how he gains power and how his Empire finally falls. The main text takes the reader back and forth, via jumps in time orchestrated through analepses, with stories told from a hypodiegetic level that emulates old Chinese novels, such as *Journey to the West*,[135] and with extracts from the diaries of characters, which partially complete the gaps in the main narrative. The gaps are formed by prolepsis, with the narrative taking an excursion into the future by introducing Lai Chú, a spiritualist who serves as advisor to the Ch'in Emperor and who, after being exiled by Ch'in, ends up serving as advisor to the Han dynasty. Lai Chú acts as a uniting thread throughout the book, where he is presented as reflective and ironic, caught between magical, economic, and ideological forces that he cannot control.

At the same time, the story is continuously commented upon by secondary narrators, introducing the notion of subjectivity. This 'Chinese box' narrative structure—in literary theory, a story within a story allowing for views from different perspectives, inspired by the idea of boxes of different sizes that fit insides larger ones—enacts the novel's main themes of control and power. The two-dimensional construction of the main narrator as both narrator (telling the story) and informant (providing historical detail) makes him an interpreter who positions himself as powerful. At the same time, the multiplicity of narratorial voices undermine his authority. The multivoicedness thus draws attention to the *constructedness* of the text, showing meaning to be discontinuous,[136] with no continuous narrative to be retrieved.

The narration begins with the presentation of King Nan, who is staged as representing an exception in Chinese history. His energetic attitude is

131 Bakhtin, pp. 300, 334.

132 Ahmed, p. 74.

133 Laiseca, *La mujer en la Muralla*; Nancy Fernández, 'Dos Viajes. Sobre Fogwill y Alberto Laiseca', *CELEHIS - Revista del Centro de Letras Hispanoamericanas*, 27.35 (2018), pp. 111–19.

134 Laiseca, *La mujer en la Muralla*, p. 9.

135 Cheng'en Wu, *The Journey to the West*, trans. by Anthony C. Yu, revised edition 2012 (London: University of Chicago Press, 1977).

136 Tambling, *Wong Kar-Wai's Happy Together*, pp. 14–15.

exposed by his lack of consideration for protocol, where 'sus faltas contra el ceremonial de la madrugada le trajeron no pocos problemas'.[137] Descriptions of empty places, such as the emptiness of his palace, which is described as being as empty as the Gobi desert, emphasize the King's solitude.[138] His active attitude towards work highlights the King's isolation, alienated from Chinese ceremonial structures, thus presenting him as an exception in relation to other Emperors because of his humane features within a context of authoritarianism. The humanity of King Nan, explicitly presented by the narrator, is contrasted with the horror perpetrated by his predecessors. This dissociation from other sovereigns evokes alienation, reinforced by the narrator's description of his custom of 'levantarse solo'.[139] Yet this exceptionality does not seem to undermine his power: he is constantly referred to as King and Emperor, reinforcing his centrality within the dynastic power system.

Other characters are also defined through their physical attributes and their particular expressions. For example, the narrator introduces Lü Pu Wei as severe, while a dialogue with his servant portrays him as violent. The insults and shy responses illustrate the specific social positions of both the servant and master, exposing their worldviews. These presentations establish the rank and status of characters in the story: Lü Pu Wei's attitude can be contrasted with that of the Emperor, while the servant represents those with no power. Seemingly powerless members of society are then silenced in different ways, underlining the weakness of the subject, who is distant from sources of power. Following Bakhtin, these descriptions, speeches, and actions expose the 'ideological positions' demarcated within the heteroglossia.[140] This relates to 'historiographic metafiction' and its signalling to the 'discursive nature of all references', which highlights the 'conditions of our mode of knowledge' of events.[141] Within this context, the imbalance of power relations is exposed through the panchronic main narrator, whose self-declared power is undermined within the text. His control over time and his assumed knowledge suggests his reliability and authority. Nevertheless, his unreliability is simultaneously disclosed through ellipses, gaps, notes, obvious omissions, dismissive opinions, and interpellations.

The main narrator explicitly filters or defers information that might 'horrify' the reader.[142] The leaps in time and stories told by fictional characters defer information of how events will develop, maintaining the tension throughout the narrative. The hypodiegetic level has both actional and explicative functions. For example, the story told by Lai Chú of how he became an astrologer explains the role he then plays as advisor to the Ch'in

137 Laiseca, *La mujer en la Muralla*, p. 10.
138 Laiseca, *La mujer en la Muralla*, pp. 9–11.
139 Laiseca, *La mujer en la Muralla*, p. 9.
140 Bakhtin, pp. 333–35.
141 Hutcheon, p. 119.
142 Laiseca, *La mujer en la Muralla*, p. 9.

Emperor. At the same time, other stories may also undermine the narrator's authority by indirectly questioning his knowledge.

Throughout the text, the narrator presents his personal knowledge, describing how eunuchs were castrated, commenting on the behaviour of prostitutes worldwide, or not explaining a joke that he judges to be untranslatable, but that does in fact work as a joke in Spanish: 'Ton Ton. Soy, en efecto, bastante tonto.'[143] His knowledge also appears in footnotes that have no referent but that are presented as if they were, in fact, there to explain the main text.[144] Furthermore, the text itself is stated to be a translation of another, unknown, text. Orthographic differences for the same words are included with no comment; in a note, he recalls his knowledge of sinology with no account of how he acquired it.[145] Through precise factual information, the narrator underlines his commitment to describing a 'reality' that is concrete and plausible.

In the novel, the main narrator's assumed scholarly authority is weakened by his pseudo-academic notes and non-academic register: he presents knowledge without quoting his sources and intervenes in the story with what are clearly his own opinions and reflections. His explanation of the 'rape of Nanjing', a real historical event, is described through his own evaluation with expressions such as 'tan horrible' and 'esto (sin nombre)'.[146] Colloquial and vernacular language also disrupt the narrative itself, with expressions such as 'súper', 'parranderos' or 'remolones'.[147] The narrator's dismissive and judgemental opinions of Chinese culture and historical characters undermine his academic knowledge, as indicated by his use of words such as 'tontos' or 'estupideces', by describing the practice of burying eunuchs with their organs as 'parodia estúpida', and by his presentation of the character Tchao Kao as 'este funesto personaje'.[148] The narrator also intrudes into the text by uttering his views in parenthesis, as in the following extract: '(si se me permite la malsonante y poco castiza expresión)', after using the slang term 'quilombo chino'.[149] This specific term, 'quilombo', relates the reader to Latin America.

The narrator's unreliability and obvious subjectivity also appear in swift changes of register. After a paragraph that refers to the horror executed by the troops of Ch'in, the narrator describes a street, 'una de las más hermosas y aristocráticas de Han Tan'.[150] The paragraph is constructed around an evocation of flowers and colours, in a sensuous, physical description of a Chinese street. Yet there is a shift midway through the paragraph, signifying

143 Laiseca, *La mujer en la Muralla*, pp. 46, 120, 98.
144 Laiseca, *La mujer en la Muralla*, p. 231.
145 Laiseca, *La mujer en la Muralla*, pp. 19, 21, 65, 99, 207.
146 Laiseca, *La mujer en la Muralla*, p. 21.
147 Laiseca, *La mujer en la Muralla*, pp. 19, 47.
148 Laiseca, *La mujer en la Muralla*, pp. 10, 46.
149 Laiseca, *La mujer en la Muralla*, p. 61.
150 Laiseca, *La mujer en la Muralla*, p. 22.

a change of register from a narrator who seems present, to one who almost disappears, giving way to a descriptive list, playing with 'the links and interrelationships between utterances and languages',[151] changing from a historical to a more philosophical register. The covert narrator thus enhances the textuality of the narration, thus creating a tension, with the elements described acting as ornaments, separated from their original functions. Likewise, the beauty of the place is then explained as resulting from the use of human excrement as fertilizer. The oxymoron stresses contrast and underlines once again the narrator's unreliability and subjectivity.

Finally, the narrator's unreliability is also disclosed by his constant expression of opinions and his vagueness in the construction of phrases. An example appears in the following extract, where the narrator presents an opinion attributed to the novel's author. While the paragraph starts by mentioning Sima Qian (145–90 BC), the Chinese historian,[152] as the main source for this specific narration, the way the phrase is constructed makes it unclear whether the narrator is the author or not. In this sense, the narrator's unstable location in the text is disclosed through the indirect intervention of an implied author:

> Ahora bien, cuenta la historia (en realidad lo cuenta Ssu Ma Chién, el Heródoto de China) [...] Es por lo tanto una opinión histórica del autor de esta novela, en la cual difiere de otros estudiosos, que la pretendida suba de impuestos al hierro y la sal nunca tuvo lugar durante los Ch'in, y decir lo contrario, es una deliberada mentira de los Han, siempre interesados en desprestigiar a la dinastía que les antecedió.[153]

The presence of this 'historical opinion' acts as an ironic reworking of narratives on China, calling into question their veracity and their access to any 'real' history of China, thus effectively parodying academic discourse. As is evident here, the narrator dissociates himself from the implied author, which makes us question the narrator's authority, as he is presumably controlled by the implied author. While the main narrator quotes Sima Qian as the source for his knowledge, for which the exact source is never mentioned, the implied author summons the implied reader. The authority of the narrator here relies on the powerlessness of the narratee, who is removed from the story and therefore unable to discuss or question the information presented. At the same time, the implied author differentiates himself from the main narrator by stating his disagreement with Sima Qian and 'other experts', thus intervening in the text.

This exchange between the main narrator and the implied author makes us, in turn, aware of the presence of other voices in the text. The reader gets lost among the different commentators: a 'comentarista ignoto'; a

151 Bakhtin, p. 263.

152 Burton Watson, *Ssu Ma Chien: Grand Historian of China* (London: Columbia University Press, 1958), p. vii.

153 Laiseca, *La mujer en la Muralla*, pp. 65–66.

'comentarista anónimo de la dinastía Sung'; 'Lin Yutón, dinastía mongola', whose name obliquely reminds the reader of Lin Yutang; 'Yin Hsí, oficial cuidafronteras, 1924, República de China'; and 'Kuo Wei'.[154] These multiple voices enhance the reader's awareness of the absence of any final, unifying authoritative/authorial voice, eliminating the possibility of certainty. The multivoicedness problematizes the multivalence of points of view and is also available through the inclusion of poems without specified authors. For example, a poem appears in the narration without previous mention, and because of this, it is not clear who the author is nor who is reciting this poem. The presence and style of the poem break the linearity of the prose and recall 'traditional' Chinese poetry, such as that by Li Bai or Wang Wei.[155] Lin Yutang has referred to poetry as the result of a 'Chinese literary genius' that is 'especially suitable to the writing of poetry'.[156] With the poem erupting in the text, the 'ambiguity concerning the speaker dramatizes the problematic relationship between any utterance and its origin',[157] recalling the 'languages' of heteroglossia, offering in this way a 'discourse' and its corresponding 'version' of reality. The presence of poems and the undisclosed information regarding the identity of the poet can be a way by which the main narrator reveals information by alternative means, for example, symbolically invoking a menacing atmosphere by the mention of blackbirds and spears, while the concealed identity of the poet reminds the reader of the narrator's power.

The unreliability of the narrator, the fragmentation of the text, and the persistent deconstruction of authoritative knowledge and epistemology also emerge through the presentation of the novel's cultural and historical imagery. The novel repeatedly generates tension between what is 'actually' Chinese and what is the representation of a stereotype. The presence of 'real', historical Chinese people, and the fact that the story is set in 'real' China serve to enhance the notion of a certain specificity inherent to Chinese culture. While this imagery may at times convey contradictory visions, as a whole the images chosen offer a cultural and historical context that is broadly recognizable to the reader as 'China'. The imagery thus assumes the existence of a definable 'traditional' Chinese culture, through representations of protocol, food, and names for people, actions, and places, positioned in a specific historical time, as the novel seems to invest 'China' with a 'life of its own'.[158] Yet, as shall be seen specifically in relation to Latin America, the novel challenges this ontology from within the text itself. In this way, the tension that emerges

154 Laiseca, *La mujer en la Muralla*, pp. 103, 157, 180, 188, 312.

155 *Three Chinese Poets: Translations of Poems by Wang Wei, Li Bai and Du Fu*, trans. by Vikram Seth (London: Phoenix, 1997), p. xvi.

156 Lin Yutang, *My Country and My People* (London: William Heinemann Ltd., 1936), p. 230.

157 Shlomith Rimmon-Kenan, *Narrative Fiction: Contemporary Poetics*, second edition (London: Routledge, 2002), p. 115.

158 Ahmed, pp. 5–6.

between a 'timeless' China and a specific historical time, or between China and Latin America, relates to power asymmetry in broader political and historical contexts, displaying the *constructedness* of grand narratives.

One way by which the *constructedness* of discourses is brought to the fore in the novel is through its continuous mention of protocol. The narrator is dismissive of protocol procedures while also presenting them as constitutive of Chinese culture, evoking yet challenging a notion of culture as static. Material descriptions also work to construct a textual imaginary of China as timeless, reinforced by the use of Chinese-style names for people, acts, and places. While men and empowered women are called by personal names, women subjected to men are called by euphemistic names such as 'Ojo del Cielo' or 'Espesura de Jade'.[159] These names are not necessarily rooted in actual Chinese naming practices and are likely the invention of the author, indicating the implied author's untrustworthy knowledge regarding China. Anne Anlin Cheng explores in this regard the figure of the 'yellow woman', the name she gives the process of racialization through which the real Asian or Asian American woman becomes a style, an aesthetic presence, or an ornament in Euro-American culture.

> She goes by many names: Celestial Lady, Lotus Blossom, Dragon Lady, Yellow Fever, Slave Girl, Geisha, Concubine, Butterfly, China Doll, Prostitute. She is carnal and delicate, hot and cold, corporeal and abstract, a full and empty signifier.[160]

The patriarchal representation of most women, via their euphemistic names, accounts for their lack of agency.

Textual imagery relating to specific acts and places emerge, in which punishments are figuratively referred to as 'Arena del Viento de Mongolia' or 'Cofre del Príncipe Yen'.[161] During a sexual encounter, body parts are called 'flauta de jade' or 'gruta de plata'.[162] Places are called 'calle del Tigre que Salta' or 'puente del Faisán Dorado'.[163] The use of symbolic terms for sex, places and women mocks *chinoiserie* by exaggerating and performatively overstating a certain aesthetic representation of a perceived 'China'. These textual expressions can be seen to act as 'ornamentations', revealing the authority and freedom the author has to name. This notion of an aestheticized China is enhanced by the inclusion of lists of food, where listings of delicacies remit the reader once again to a 'China' that appears timeless. The text's solemn representation of food functions as a textual cross-reference to traditional Chinese novels, in the sense emphasized here by Lin Yutang:

159 Laiseca, *La mujer en la Muralla*, pp. 11, 23, 95.

160 Anne A. Cheng, *Ornamentalism* (Oxford: Oxford University Press, 2019), p. 4.

161 Laiseca, *La mujer en la Muralla*, p. 106.

162 Laiseca, *La mujer en la Muralla*, p. 143.

163 Laiseca, *La mujer en la Muralla*, pp. 19, 114.

> The seriousness with which we [the Chinese] regard eating can be shown in many ways. Anyone who opens the pages of [...] any Chinese novel will be struck by the detailed and constant descriptions of the entire *menu* [...].[164]

The culinary as a literary device acts as an ambiguous and shifting marker for distance. While the food is determined culturally, as evidenced by the reference to the 'Thousand-Year Egg', the inclusion of universally recognized food—for example, fruit such as grapes and melon—[165] simultaneously makes the distance unstable. Thus, recalling Ahmed's reflections on 'strangerness', where the 'other' becomes 'familiar' or 'strange' as a 'mechanism for establishing the permeability of [...] boundary lines',[166] the novel highlights notions of distance from and closeness to the place and time in which the narrated events occur. The novel thus allows for the encountering of 'China' as 'stranger', through the disclosure of its fetishistic aspects.

At the same time, the romantic descriptions of 'China' are interrupted by references to Latin America in the use of words such as 'gliptodonte', a prehistoric South American mammal, the use of the slang word 'quilombo', or the mention of 'Victorias Regias' a plant originally from Latin America.[167] The narrator also explicitly directs the reader to a Latin American context when he speaks of the inflation of gold after the arrival of Europeans in Latin America.[168] By recalling the colonial history of Latin America in a Chinese setting, Laiseca ironizes and subverts a Eurocentric perspective. This irony signals the text's discontinuity, which suggests 'the impossibility of reading a text for a single isolatable truth'[169] but that, at the same time, still refers to a reality outside itself. Following Ahmed, this shows how 'communities cannot be understood as simply on one side of identity or the other'.[170] Even the mention of cheese, such as 'patos hervidos en queso',[171] can be seen as cutting across the description of Chinese food, since dairy products are generally not perceived as typical Chinese cuisine, acting as an ironic inversion of traditional Chinese foodstuffs.[172] The novel thus points towards the internal conflicts which result from the unequal flows and exchanges between different locations.[173] The use of disjunctive and incongruent terms in the

164 Lin, *My Country and My People*, p. 320.

165 Laiseca, *La mujer en la Muralla*, p. 296.

166 Ahmed, p. 119.

167 Laiseca, *La mujer en la Muralla*, pp. 10, 61, 22.

168 Laiseca, *La mujer en la Muralla*, p. 83.

169 Tambling, *Allegory*, p. 159.

170 Ahmed, p. 94.

171 Laiseca, *La mujer en la Muralla*, p. 132.

172 Hengyun Ma and Allan N. Rae, 'Projections of Dairy Product Consumption and Trade Opportunities in China', *Australasian Agribusiness Review*, 12 (2004), p. 1 <http://econpapers.repec.org/article/agsauagre/132084.htm> [accessed 1 July 2021].

173 Doreen Massey, *Space, Place and Gender* (Cambridge: Polity Press, 1994), pp. 1–9.

listing of food, or in the narrative itself, through the use of a non-academic register, reveals an ironic discontinuity at the heart of continuity.[174]

In this sense, the novel is highly parodic in its intertextual relationship to the generic conventions of the Chinese novel, while stressing the context in which this fiction is being produced. Although the narrator orientates the reader within 'Chinese' culture and history, in relation to a timeless Orient, it disorientates and re-orientates him/her by using words that refer the reader to Latin America with no previous warning. In this sense, it conspicuously does not hold a fetishized 'China' in place, and it draws attention to this fact through its various modes of narrative (de)construction. This suggests the novel's elasticity, giving up totalizing notions about what determines the encounter. By recalling cultural specificity and later disorienting the reader, it establishes and then undermines boundaries.

From this perspective, the 'stranger' can be seen to appear within the blurred borders, playing with what is, or is not, perceived as 'stranger'. For example, the narrator presents the 'West' and 'non-West' as a set of oppositions held in place, as seen in the description of events that happen 'no solamente en Occidente'.[175] However, the use of multiple narrators further underlines the destabilization of narrative authority, resisting the privilege of certain narratives, such as those which define East/West divisions.

The appearance of specific traits and stereotypes via cultural and historical imagery can be interpreted as an ironic subversion of established discourses of historiography and textbooks on China available in Latin America. As noted by David Martínez-Robles,[176] while Western historiography on China has set out to overcome the prejudices of the past, it has been unable to distance itself completely from the resources and stereotypes that the Western world had come to accept about China: as a country of 'miracles' and 'marvels' in medieval times, as a refined and erudite culture in early modern Europe, to a nation where history and progress ceased since the Enlightenment. Recalling Ahmed's 'stranger fetishism', 'China' here appears to embody a specific 'nature'. Martínez-Robles[177] argues that a historiography that criticizes such discourses on China has only emerged in recent decades, although it still fails to address them fully. The stereotyping effects of this history are exploited by Laiseca, who uses them to portray a particular 'China', while also undercutting them, and pointing the reader to Latin America. Disavowing any underlying, coherent meaning, the text is suggestive of the power imbalance that the ability to 'construct' embodies, making claims about China's 'nature'

174 Hutcheon, p. 26.

175 Laiseca, *La mujer en la Muralla*, p. 123.

176 David Martínez-Robles, 'The Western Representation of Modern China: Orientalism, Culturalism and Historiographical Criticism', in *Orientalism [online dossier]*, ed. by Carles Prado-Fonts, Digithum, 10, 2008, UOC <http://www.uoc.edu/digithum/10/dt/eng/martinez.pdf> [accessed 1 August 2021].

177 Martínez-Robles, UOC.

and, at the same time, subverting it. Resistance to categorized knowledge, and hence to 'stranger fetishism', becomes available from within the text itself.

Therefore, specific cultural and historical imagery is used to (de)construct a stereotyped, traditional and essential China, presented as prudent, individualist and respectful of the soul, and patriarchal, with most women subjected to men and named in artistic, symbolic terms. Yet the assumed authority of the narrator's knowledge helps (de)construct this China through (ironic) comments that act as anthropological generalizations. His authority is performed (ironically) in a condescending manner, to the extent that he presents Confucianism and Realism as sects, and even claims to 'know' what the Chinese 'think' at the moment of their death.[178]

The narrative construction, which purports to provide specific representations of China, presents an ironic, entertaining, and at times violent and shocking reworking of Chinese culture and society. The presence of ostensibly historical characters establishes a claim to represent real people and events. Still, veiled information about who is a historical character and who is not effectively maintains a constant tension between 'history' and 'fiction'. The perceived hermetic nature of China and the limited Latin American historiography on China permit this authorial liberty. So, one is hardly surprised that one of the main characters in the text shares with Laiseca the first syllable of his name, Lai. At the same time, Laiseca was sometimes called 'Lai', even figuring as 'Alberto LAI Laiseca' on his (apparently official) Twitter account.[179]

While the text seems to present a 'traditional China', indicators point to Latin America as Laiseca's real focal point. The novel releases itself from local historical reality yet retains and denies the 'pastness' of the 'histories' of colonialism and imperialism that determine, albeit not fully,[180] the encounter between China and Latin America. In doing this, it echoes concerns regarding the narratives of dictatorships, such as the Argentinean *Junta*, which appropriate or discredit past narratives to justify their predominant role. Broader relationships hence inform the 'encounter' of power and antagonism.[181] Unequal distribution of power is thus explored through the construction of narratives that question the validity of the information given, reflecting on the differing discourses at play in a post-dictatorship scenario.

The disputed power of the main narrator reveals his claim to authority as weak. The constant displacement of the narration draws attention to its constructed nature and a broad allegorical reading suggestive of power

178 Laiseca, *La mujer en la Muralla*, p. 89.

179 Alberto Laiseca, '@LAILaiseca' <https://twitter.com/lailaiseca> [accessed 1 August 2021]; Leonardo Oyola, 'Kryptonita (Fragmentos)', *Gramma*, 23.49 (2012), pp. 285–89.

180 Ahmed, p. 6.

181 Ahmed, p. 8.

imbalance.[182] The novel's unsystematic discourses allow the 'encounter' with the 'stranger' to challenge textbooks, which assume consensus regarding knowledge on China, and define a distinctive version of Chinese 'nature'.[183] In this sense, the novel critiques academic representations, mocking academic knowledge, undermining characterizations of what is typically 'Chinese' and exposing its contradictory possibilities. In so doing, the novel allows the reader to become aware of the differences involving power and antagonism present in the 'encounter'. As we shall now see in *La escuela dolor humano de Sechuán*, the contradictory possibilities of 'China' can be further problematized. While Aira's and Laiseca's texts interrupt discourses on 'China', the author Mario Bellatin takes this further in his novel by emphasizing the fetishist nature of 'China' in Latin America.

China at All? *La escuela del dolor humano de Sechuán* by Mario Bellatin

Bellatin's novel *La escuela del dolor humano de Sechuán* was published around ten years after the publication of *La mujer en la Muralla*, in 2001, just one year after a watershed moment in Mexican political history. The PRI, which had held power between 1929 and 2000, ended its seventy-one-year rule when the opposition candidate, Vicente Fox Quesada, was elected President. Viewed within this hugely complex socio-historical scenario, the Mexican narrative tradition does not seem readily reducible to any distinct or definitive trend or style. The novel in Mexico has been described by Raymond L. Williams as heterogeneous, influenced by the region's multiple indigenous groups, the *mestizo* culture, and subject to the literary influences of Europe and the United States.[184]

Postmodern literary texts began to appear in Mexico in the late 1960s, influenced by the workers' and students' movements of 1968, reinventing an indigenous and revolutionary literary style. Salvador Elizondo's *Farabeuf* (1965) stands out as an example, playing extensively as it does with language, characters, events, and aspects of 'Chineseness'. The publication of Carlos Fuentes's *Cambio de piel* (1967) also broke with established modernity by formulating questions, flaunting unresolved contradictions, and revelling in the different versions and alternative truths in which characters had no fixed identities.[185]

A second movement involved authors born since 1955, focusing on popular unrest within migratory and border contexts, and exploring the interplay

182 Tambling, *Allegory*, p. 165.

183 Lin, *My Country and My People*, p. 53.

184 Raymond L. Williams, *The Columbia Guide to the Latin American Novel since 1945* (New York: Columbia University Press, 2007), pp. 27–28.

185 Williams, *The Columbia Guide to the Latin American Novel since 1945*, p. 134; 'Fuentes the Modern; Fuentes the Postmodern', *Hispania*, 85.2 (2002), pp. 209–18 (p. 214).

between fiction and real life.[186] These themes include historiographical origins and games with language, while escaping formal rules and the judgmental evaluation of categorization. The texts position themselves, literarily and physically, in a transnational context. In many of these cases, national borders are also significantly blurred, and this phenomenon can be observed concerning Bellatin, who is usually referred to as 'Peruvian-Mexican'.

Born in 1960 in Mexico to Peruvian parents, Bellatin moved to Peru when he was four. After periods in Peru and Cuba, he later returned to Mexico in 1995. Like Aira, Bellatin is an author who is difficult to label and has also been loosely referred to as postmodern, and paradigmatic of new artistic and social forms.[187] Certainly his work exemplifies the continuous reworking of fiction through fragmentation.[188] Jorge Panesi suggests that Bellatin's aesthetic creed is to bring together parallel worlds whose relation to the everyday world is simultaneously evident, impossible and tangential.[189] Bellatin's work has been interestingly defined as 'literatura postautónoma', a term coined by Josefina Ludmer, which rejects literary borders, allowing for the narration of subject's daily lives positioned in territories produced and constituted by the media, new technologies, science, and modern politics.[190] The decoding of the novels therefore depends on their relationship to other works, including autobiographical insertions and their participation in other artistic activities. This also includes the relationship with author's essays, written as manifestos, that establish a relationship between literature and *performance*.[191]

The significance of a narrative based on fragments reveals itself, among other features, through intertextuality. Catalina Quesada Gómez, in her

186 Williams, *The Columbia Guide to the Latin American Novel since 1945*, pp. 28–32.

187 Diana Palaversich, 'Apuntes para una lectura de Mario Bellatin', *Chasqui*, 32.1 (2003), pp. 25–38 (p. 26); Samuel Steinberg, 'To Begin Writing: Bellatin, Reunited', *Journal of Latin American Cultural Studies*, 20.2 (2011), pp. 105–20 (p. 105).

188 Laddaga, *Espectáculos de realidad. Ensayo sobre la narrativa latinoamericana de las últimas dos décadas*, p. 163; Isabel A. Quintana, 'Escenografía del horror: cuerpo, violencia y política en la obra de Mario Bellatin', *Revista Iberoamericana*, 75.227 (2009), pp. 487–504 (p. 497).

189 Jorge Panesi, '"La escuela del dolor humano de Sechuán" de Mario Bellatin', 2005 <https://filologiaunlp.files.wordpress.com/2012/01/perros-heroes-por-panesi.pdf> [accessed 1 July 2021].

190 Silvia Roig, '¿Qué significa vivir en un Estado de derecho?: Vida, contaminación y muerte en "Salón de belleza" de Mario Bellatin', *Lucero*, 22.1 (2012), p. 39; Josefina Ludmer, 'Literaturas Postautónomas' <http://www.lehman.cuny.edu/ciberletras/v17/ludmer.htm> [accessed 1 July 2021].

191 Ángeles Mateo del Pino, 'Travistiendo la verdad en busca de la mentira. La escritura de Mario Bellatin', in *Identidad y simulación. Ficciones, performances, estrategias culturales*, ed. by José Ismael Gutiérrez Gutiérrez (Valencia: Aduana Vieja, 2009), pp. 119–62 (p. 119); Pablo Vergara, 'El vacío como gesto: Representación y crisis del sentido en la obra de Mario Bellatin', *Revista Laboratorio*, (2010) <http://revistalaboratorio.udp.cl/num2_2010_art6_vergara/> [accessed 1 July 2021]; Albornoz, p. 37.

study of Bellatin's association with Severo Sarduy's metafictional inclinations, notes how his works have been linked to Reinaldo Arenas, David Lynch, David Cronenberg, and Asian narrators, such as Kenzaburō Ōe or Yukio Mishima.[192] However, Palaversich notes that in his works, Bellatin never mentions the names of Borges, Julio Cortázar or Elizondo, with whom he nonetheless maintains a close intertextual dialogue.

What is 'true' and what is 'false' remains in constant tension in Bellatin's literature precisely because of the play of intertextuality.[193] This tension also emerges through the use of language itself, in a process where notions of identity and self are disarticulated, as observed by Megumi Andrade Kobayashi.[194] Palaversich observes how incorporating alternative narrative lines disavows the stabilization of the texts and disconcerts the reader.[195] Fragmentation thus appears to negate literary and cultural traditions, as López-Calvo notes.[196] Bellatin's work comes across as fictional, but it also performs a kind of testimonial function.[197] In this sense, as Laura Conde's analysis of Bellatin's work shows, the superposition of fragments from a 'poética de lo mutilado' finds a certain resonance in the mutilations committed by *Sendero Luminoso* and which, in the text, erupt as a mutilated archive.[198]

The way in which Bellatin plays with fragmentation through concealment and by leaving gaps is especially thought-provoking in his 'Oriental' works. The presence of 'Oriental' spaces in his literature has been stated by Bellatin himself to represent an arbitrary choice that does not disclose any special interest.[199] In his words, these worlds are 'un universo cargadamente inverosímil'.[200] Regarding his 'Japanese' texts, he says

192 Álvaro Martín Navarro also recalls intertextuality in Bellatin's 'Japanese' works, and how they present similarities with Japanese texts and authors directly (via quotes) and indirectly (via themes); see Catalina Quesada Gómez, 'Mutatis Mutandis: De Severo Sarduy a Mario Bellatin', *Boletín Hispánico Helvético*, 17.18 (2011), pp. 297–320 (p. 298).

193 Julia Azaretto, Entrevista a Mario Bellatin, 2009 <http://cle.ens-lyon.fr/espagnol/entrevista-a-mario-bellatin-68252.kjsp?STNAV=&RUBNAV=> [accessed 1 July 2021].

194 Megumi Andrade Kobayashi, 'Los héroes disecados de Mario Bellatin', *Estudios Avanzados*, 21 (2014), pp. 69–90 (pp. 69–70).

195 Palaversich, 'Apuntes para una lectura de Mario Bellatin', p. 32.

196 Ignacio López-Calvo, 'The Death of the Author through False Translation in Mario Bellatin's Orientalised Japan', *Bulletin of Latin American Research*, 32.3 (2013), pp. 339–53 (p. 340).

197 Facundo Ruiz, 'Vitrinas narrativas. Mario Bellatin y el relato fotográfico', *Revista de Crítica Literaria Latinoamericana*, 34.68 (2008), pp. 201–10 (p. 201).

198 'Mario Bellatin: Una Escritura Tridimensional' (presented at the VI Jornadas Internacionales de Filología y Lingüística, Universidad Nacional de La Plata, La Plata, 2003).

199 Emily Hind, 'Entrevista con Mario Bellatin', *Confluencia*, 2004, pp. 197–204 (p. 198).

200 Hind, p. 201.

> Sencillamente en estos hay una falsa retórica japonesa que hace que el lector inmediatamente deposite una serie de elementos que no están en el libro, sino que yo sé cómo va a reaccionar el lector. [...] [M]e interesa que crean que es Japón. Sí, que crean y después se den cuenta que no es porque el mismo texto tiene los elementos que decodifican esto [...].[201]

Emily Hind, however, suggests that Bellatin's choice of Japan and China, as in *La escuela*, is also used to contrast with the 'West', and therefore is not completely arbitrary. This contrast would reveal a struggle between 'lo moderno y lo tradicional' in Latin American literature, conducted in abstract terms. Bellatin argues that writing 'Japanese' texts as a way to go beyond 'tradition' and the canon is his way of responding to this struggle. Moreover, at the same time, he reveals his settings as conscious choices that gesture towards the global: 'no es gratuito que de pronto sea Japón, mañana China. Es crear toda esta cosa, pero para decir cosas que nos atañen a todos.'[202]

Isabel Quintana suggests that literature, as a reservoir of aesthetic material and symbolic forces, is relocated by Bellatin in different settings, with Mexican literature vanishing as an explicit referent.[203] His works would thus configure a poetics of desolation, where disrupted bodies are contained under the control of the state and its guardians—the very citizens that have internalized this discipline. The suffocating universes that shape Bellatin's narratives open up an interrogation regarding the possibility of justice in societies that have been and continue to be immersed in violence. In this sense, disrupted bodies, as in *La escuela*, create fantasies and modes of resistance and are also a means to represent pain as a kind of memory, denaturalizing violence. Quintana suggests that Bellatin takes on these interrogations by reimagining them as displaced from their political dimension. He does not escape from politics and history but stages them at their most monstrous extremes.[204] The choice of a foreign setting allows him to engage with politics and history, while playing with the abject and its/his/her displacement. In light of the above, *La escuela* deconstructs any fetishized understanding of 'China', not holding the other in place, and casting doubt on any guarantee of meaning.

La escuela was first published in Mexico in 2001. Other editions have been published in Buenos Aires in 2005 (Interzona), Mexico in 2005 (Alfaguara), San José in 2014 (Germinal), and Córdoba in 2016 (Borde Perdido Editora). There are major differences between the 2001 edition and the others regarding, for example, characters and narration. While the 2001 edition includes Chinese names and the word China, the editions published since

201 Hind, p. 198.
202 Hind, p. 199.
203 Quintana, pp. 487–89.
204 Quintana, p. 503.

2005 do not, yet the text still allows the reader to assume it is 'China' from the title and cultural references. I use the Interzona edition.

Through chapters/fragments presented with titles and explanatory notes, the reader is exposed to a multivoiced text with a non-linear timeframe. The story is presented through a heterodiegetic narrator and judgemental characters, told via internal viewpoints that alternate in focus throughout the text. The main characters are apparently a boy-man who grows up with his parents and must use a harness and an orthopaedic arm, who might be the founder of the 'School of Human Pain' and might have been castrated as a boy; a foreign woman whose husband has been buried in the village where events take place; and a woman in charge of drowning the third child of families, enforcing the law of the 'authorities'. The novel is arguably set during the Chinese Communist Party's rule, indicated through the mention of an uncapitalized '*república popular*',[205] grassroots elections and social planning. While it also refers on occasion to the Imperial past, these references are ambiguous. Through a game of angles and perspectives, as 'historiographic metafiction', the novel obscures the storyline, thus avoiding any commitment to a specific 'truth'.

By the novel's end, the text remains open, stressing the textual access to 'histories' while allowing for the (re)locating of the novel within alternative socio-historical contexts. Notions of asymmetrical power are thus revealed through this unstable narratorial construction. In line with Tambling's notion of the postmodern allegory, the novel presents a complex engagement with the representation of 'reality', stressing the notion of subjectivity through fragmentation, with the trappings of power appearing in bodies, places, and situations. The novel refuses to endorse any single point of view and does not hold the 'other' in place. In this sense, I argue that the allegory evokes asymmetrical power distribution as discontinuous, drawing attention to its constructed nature and allowing it to be displaced and re-situated.

The constructed nature of authority can be seen through Bellatin's use of 'Oriental' features, which appear regularly in his narrative. Palaversich suggests that

> El hecho de que algunos personajes sean japoneses y otros chinos o árabes es, otra vez, una trampa textual que tiene el efecto de *estrangement* en el lector: aquel puede llegar a pensar que no entiende el personaje a causa de su "extranjería." Sin embargo, estos personajes "exóticos" no poseen características adicionales que los distingan de otros del texto.[206]

López-Calvo agrees with Palaversich in so far as he believes that Bellatin's deliberate use of Japanese characters as a device for distancing himself from his text may also imply that he sees Japanese culture as the one farthest

205 Bellatin, *La escuela*, p. 56.
206 Palaversich, 'Apuntes para una lectura de Mario Bellatin', p. 33.

from his own, as he suggests 'in a way, perhaps these characters embody the author's 'Other'.[207] He further suggests that Bellatin's exploration of the 'potential relationship between writing, translation and physical deformity leads, perhaps unconsciously, to the continuation of exoticising stereotypes about "Oriental" cultures'.[208] But I argue that the construction of narrative and character of *La escuela* suggests otherwise.

While, as López-Calvo observed in the case of Japan, an *orientalized* image of China likewise emerges, its disavowal of difference and its overlap with Latin America function here as a critique of ontological difference. Furthermore, the text appears as a critique to any 'master narrative', something which would extend to China and Latin America, thus revealing what we have in common with the so-called 'stranger', destabilizing boundaries and creating new spaces through which this 'stranger' can be encountered.[209] In this sense, it is possible to discern an engagement with politics and history that may be considered in terms of allegory, something also suggested by Quintana,[210] Samuel Steinberg,[211] and Palaversich.[212]

According to Steinberg, Bellatin's writing '[...] toys with but cannot ultimately be made legible through the modes of national-political allegory that so often determine readings of Latin American texts'.[213] He suggests that Bellatin's groundlessness exposes history's virtual 'failure' to appear clearly, which in turn suggests a new way of understanding allegory during what he calls 'interregnal times'. Steinberg reads Bellatin from within an indeterminate historical periodization: he presents the waning of the PRI (Partido Revolucionario Institucional) as a nearly imperceptible process, as the vacuum of 'institutional power-in-legitimacy expresses precisely the continuity of the Mexican present with nearly 70 years of PRIist impunity and, in a sense, with the reigning impunities of the years before that as well'.[214] I build on this perspective, as I interpret the novel as one in which 'China' is summoned in order to problematize the grand narratives of history.

The novel opens with a recommendation that refers to 'reglas de juego para una posible puesta en escena', as a theatre play, and advises the reader how we should express the 'formas de representación'.[215] The narrator explains

207 'The Death of the Author through False Translation in Mario Bellatin's Orientalised Japan', p. 339.
208 López-Calvo, 'The Death of the Author through False Translation in Mario Bellatin's Orientalised Japan', p. 339.
209 Ahmed, pp. 8, 15.
210 Quintana.
211 Steinberg.
212 Diana Palaversich, 'Prólogo', in *Obra Reunida*, by Mario Bellatin (Mexico City: Alfaguara, 2015).
213 Steinberg, pp. 105–6.
214 Steinberg, p. 106. The PRI held power in Mexico for 71 years, from 1929 up to 2000.
215 Bellatin, *La escuela*, p. 9.

that these kinds of 'theatrical representations' were first encountered by anthropologists. He alerts the 'reader' to the fact that a sense of totality will emerge only at the end of the story.[216] Furthermore, the narrator warns us that, because at the end of this kind of theatre, spectators might enter into a state of catharsis 'bastante particular', its content is on occasions controlled by the 'authorities'. In this sense, the novel introduces a story about 'others' as 'strangers'; in this case, those studied by anthropologists. The narrator's warning, his withholding of information, and his explanations appear to confirm that the narrator holds authorial authority. Yet the different voices refuse to obey a hierarchy; the text's ambivalence denies us access to a 'truth'.

Dissimilar perspectives are revealed in the chapters/sections which have been described as 'miniatures'. As Facundo Ruiz shows, the term 'miniatures' suggests that the stories are exposed in the showcase of narration, presented as an imaginary diary or as a catalogue of scenes.[217] In the same section, sentences present different, contradictory 'miniatures', further emphasized by the fact that there is no direct speech. Contradictions emerge within the first-person narratives, revealing a tension between characters' psychological perspectives and their actual physical experiences.[218] In this way, the characters' monologues convey a denial of the self through contradictory statements about themselves.

Francisco Carrillo Martin has also noted how rupture is presented through the medium of theatre, with theatre acting as a space where the actors explain. At the same time, the author disappears, thus allowing for the catharsis of the audience, generating autonomous codes, which appear during the theatrical representation and disappear when it ends.[219] In this sense, the novel recalls Said's theatrical metaphor for Orientalism, as Orientalism tries 'at one and the same time to characterise the Orient as alien and to incorporate it schematically on a theatrical stage whose audience, manager, and actors are *for* Europe, and only for Europe'.[220] Yet the interference of the implied author in the text, together with the fragmented narration, renders any single characterization of it impossible. In this sense, the possibility of a single 'meaning' is disavowed.

The story is thus presented in a variety of inconsistent ways. While events seem to happen in Communist China, many elements refer back to Imperial China. This can be observed, for example, through the boy who listens to a distant television through a window, who might also be the founder of the 'Escuela del dolor humano' in Imperial China.[221] The novel is ambiguous

216 Bellatin, *La escuela*, p. 9.

217 Ruiz, p. 209.

218 *La escuela*, p. 75.

219 Francisco Carrillo Martin, 'La literatura como performance: Mario Bellatin y Severo Sarduy', *Hispamérica*, 39.115 (2010), pp. 37–47 (p. 40).

220 Edward Said, *Orientalism* (London: Penguin, 2003), pp. 71–72.

221 Bellatin, *La escuela*, p. 19.

throughout about the historical period. For example, there is no explicit information as to whether the founder of the 'Escuela' in imperial times is the same boy who is speaking from the 'present'. The titles and explanations appear as analepses, while the narration is in the present tense. The novel plays with linearity: events are in the past, yet the text itself holds the promise of repetition, presented both as a play and as fragments.

Inconsistency also characterizes the novel in several ways. For example, the following extract talks about the death of the 'pedagogo', founder of 'la escuela',

> El pedagogo murió decapitado y en la horca. Aquel fue el final de la historia del fundador de la *Escuela del dolor humano.* Cada quien lo vio en su muerte de distinta manera. Sin zapatos, con garras de pájaro, con el cuerpo cubierto de plumas, con los testículos colgándole como si de un camello viejo se tratara, con una erección presente como cuando introducía las uñas destruidas en el cuerpo de sus amantes, con los pies embalsamados como les corresponde a todos los padres del planeta e incluso con un pájaro mudo acurrucado en su cabeza.[222]

The paragraph evokes different points of view, suggesting that different people see/experience the same events in diverse ways. Contradiction also appears in the matter of temporality, as some of the individuals might belong to Imperial China and others to the 'república popular'. Simultaneously, it suggests that different characters might in fact be one, something enhanced by the fragmented narrative of the novel, which never introduces the characters as such. As Albornoz observes, the novel is presented as a mosaic of fragments which can never be evoked in their totality,[223] recognizing the text's foregrounding of the fictitious nature of 'master narratives'.[224]

This mosaic formation includes evidence which allows the reader to learn that the story is set in a recognizable 'China'. Yet, as we will see, this formation also directs the reader towards Latin America. As a result, the novel generates tension between what is implied to be 'Chinese', what is recognized as 'Chinese' by the reader, and what could be Latin American. An example of this is the depiction of rituals. In his interpretation of the novel, Alan Pauls recalls Bellatin's notion of regularity through the presence of ritual in *La escuela* and across Bellatin's works.[225] As noted by Panesi, Bellatin invents rituals in *La escuela*, such as the unearthing of the dead.[226] The ritual acts as a process by which 'China' can be retrieved and the 'foreign' can be

222 Bellatin, *La escuela*, p. 53.

223 Albornoz.

224 Hutcheon, p. 191.

225 Alan Pauls, 'El problema Bellatin', *El Interpretador. Literatura, Arte y Pensamiento*, (2005) <http://salonkritik.net/10-11/2011/05/el_problema_bellatin_alan_paul_1.php> [accessed 1 July 2021].

226 Panesi.

exposed. Yet the 'foreignness' is called into doubt by the explanatory note to a chapter that states '*es curioso constatar que las fiestas folklóricas son similares en todo el mundo*'.[227] The novel generates tension between what it shows that is implied to be Chinese, and what is recognized as 'Chinese' by the reader.

Furthermore, as noted by Albornoz, the traditions presented in the novel have a 'sabor andino', and the novel's exploration of pain can be related to Dr Farabeuf's obsessive need to understand what happens at the moment of death in Elizondo's *Farabeuf*.[228] In this sense, aspects of the text clearly signal their Latin American heritage, such as the presence of men with 'plumas de pájaro en el cuerpo', who recall the *voladores de Papantla*. These 'unfixed' references act as markers of ambiguity, recalling McClintock's notion of the fetish as involving a potential multitude of contradictions, housing the social contradictions that are experienced at a personal level.[229]

Indeed, Bellatin himself further plays with the book's contradictions and ambiguity. In August 2001, he published a piece featuring paragraphs and sentences that were later included in the published novel (released in September 2001). The 2001 edition includes an appendix which, as Palaversich notes, mocks the Aristotelian notion of catharsis, and includes a commentary which, it might be suggested, signals the arbitrary nature of the narrative montage.[230] In the Interzona edition, the mocking of catharsis fades as an implied author demands to be shown whether the spectators have uncovered the links between the fragments. This information allows for the appearance of 'some level of catharsis'.[231] The arbitrariness of the montage is thus less explicit, giving the text a broader uncertainty. While in the August 2001 text China is mentioned (for example, 'muchas veces, observadores internacionales se han cuestionado la cantidad tan alta de ejecutados que existe actualmente en China')[232] the 2001 and 2005 editions replace 'China' with 'region', and eliminate any temporal positioning.[233] While the 2001 online text can be seen as determined to show a specific Chinese context and uses capitals when referring to the 'Cultural Revolution' and 'People's Republic', in the 2005 edition China seems to fade into the background. However, the context remains 'Chinese'. This refers us back to Hutcheon, who shows how 'the refusal to integrate fragments [...] is a refusal of the closure and telos which narrative usually demands [...]'.[234]

227 Bellatin, *La escuela*, p. 40.

228 Albornoz, p. 5.

229 McClintock, p. 202.

230 Palaversich, 'Apuntes para una lectura de Mario Bellatin', p. 31.

231 Bellatin, *La escuela*, p. 81.

232 Mario Bellatin, 'Snapshots', 2001 <http://www.letraslibres.com/revista/portafolios/snapshots> [accessed 1 July 2021].

233 Mario Bellatin, *La escuela del dolor humano de Sechuán* (Córdoba: Borde Perdido Editora, 2016), p. 51; *La escuela*, p. 71.

234 Hutcheon, p. 121.

The author also plays with this 'openness' beyond the novel itself. For example, in 2008, in a piece written in the first person, he recalls a character from *La escuela*, but locates her in Latin America:

> El martes llega uno de mis personajes principales: la mujer de seattle [sic] que se dedica todos los años a desenterrar con sus propias manos a su marido en la cúspide de la montaña de un pueblo andino. El personaje aparece en mi libro *La escuela* del dolor humano de sechuánM.u< [sic]. Quiere visitar, después de treinta años, el primer pueblo en latinoamérica [sic] en el que se instaló. No creo estar en condiciones de realizar el viaje con ella.[235]

As is evident here, the author explicitly shifts towards a Latin American location. A comparison reveals the contradictions since in *La escuela* there is no information that would suggest the character is from Seattle or that the story is set in an Andean town. The novel continues to raise issues of power while simultaneously demonstrating that China's role as a referent for authoritarianism also applies to Latin America, thus extending the novel transnationally.

As Bellatin has mentioned elsewhere, he makes the reader imagine places through a rhetoric that intends to evoke specific locations.[236] In this sense, he reopens 'prior histories of encounter' between Latin America and China: even the somewhat eclipsed China of the 2005 edition can still be recognized through specific social references. In this sense, what is most relevant for my argument is to see how Bellatin plays with his audience's assumptions by evoking China without explicitly mentioning it. While the location can, in certain instances, be viewed as an Andean village, specific details refer to a 'real' China, such as 'república popular' or '*revolución cultural*',[237] leading the reader to consider the meaning of 'China'. The text thus creates a 'postmodern allegory' through its openness and the 'fragments [which] suggest the impossibility of reading a text for a single isolatable truth'.[238]

The nature of the novel allows the reader to doubt the veracity of quotes and information presented in the text. While in the 2001 edition the book further clarifies elements of the text as it includes a 'Señal para el lector' at the end, this is not present in the 2005 edition. This mischievous use of true and false quotes shows the way in which 'reality' and 'truth' may co-exist on the same ontological level, problematizing any correspondence between text and reality. Recalling McClintock's theory of the fetish, 'China' in the novel

235 Mario Bellatin, 'Pequeña muestra del vicio en el que caigo todos los días', *Literal*, 14 (2012) <http://literalmagazine.com/pequena-muestra-del-vicio-en-el-que-caigo-todos-los-dias/> [accessed 1 July 2021].

236 Bellatin, 'Pequeña muestra del vicio en el que caigo todos los días'.

237 Bellatin, *La escuela*, p. 65.

238 Tambling, *Allegory*, p. 159.

is shown to embody an impossible irresolution,[239] containing the negotiations and configurations of 'strangerness'. In the recognition of 'China' made available in the novel, the fragments that comprise this 'China' ultimately disclose it as a fetish of otherness.

Compositeness is also presented through the fragmentation of the body in *La escuela*, an element that Palaversich and other critics have noted as a distinct feature of Bellatin's work.[240] In this sense, we find traces of asymmetrically distributed power in and through traumatized bodies in *La escuela*, and the state and society significantly exercise this power. As Quintana shows, the novel reveals the exercise of power from within the 'gran relato del Estado' more precisely, in its double logic of power: the control over individual bodies and the regulation of the masses.[241] This can be seen in the 'democrats', a volleyball team who have no fingers on their right hand because the state had them cut off after they exercised their right to vote, or in the woman who drowns children that escape birth-control policies. The presence of the state is ubiquitous, and the 'Escuela' acts as a mechanism for resistance to this ubiquity. From this perspective, 'China' here can be seen, on one level, to embody an ultimate, tyrannical power.

Through detailed description, body parts are also presented as grotesque, thus exposing the subjection of bodies to socio-political control. The hedonistic relationship a man has with his nails and testicles can be read as a marker of a kind of madness. At the same time, it acts as a mechanism to protect him from external threats, such as the state, embodied by the woman who asks about him. She represents the state, as her responsibility is to drown

239 McClintock, p. 184.

240 In Bellatin's works, bodies are seen to destabilize the concept of the unity of the character and of the narrative construction. Palaversich links this to the fact that Bellatin was born without his right arm, in the sense that these bodies open up narratives which have not yet been explored. The presence of the body is something also noted by Javier Guerrero, Kathryn Méndez and Ángeles Donoso: Bellatin is constantly blurring lines between autobiography, perceived reality and fiction; Javier Guerrero, 'El experimento "Mario Bellatin". Cuerpo enfermo y anómalo en el tránsito material del seco', *Estudios. Revista de Investigaciones Literarias y Culturales*, 17.33 (2009), pp. 63–96 (pp. 63–64); Ángeles Donoso, '"Yo soy Mario Bellatin y soy de ficción" o el paradójico borde de lo autobiográfico en El Gran Vidrio', *Chasqui*, 40 (2011), pp. 96–110 (pp. 96–97); Katherine Méndez, 'Mario Bellatin: Ghosts, the Human Body and the Spaces Where They Meet', in *Orientalisms of the Hispanic and Luso-Brazilian World*, ed. by Araceli Tinajero (New York: Escribana Books, 2014), pp. 99–117 (pp. 99–117). His constructions, such as of the 'real' or the body, are fragmented, mutilated, and withhold complete information; Palaversich, 'Apuntes para una lectura de Mario Bellatin', pp. 36–37; Palaversich, 'Prólogo', pp. 12, 16; Alicia Vaggione, 'Literatura/enfermedad: el cuerpo como desecho. Una lectura de "Salón de belleza" de Mario Bellatin', *Revista Iberoamericana*, 75.227 (2009), pp. 475–86 (p. 475).

241 Quintana, pp. 495–96.

the third child of each family, exercising the state's policy on population control. The story's ambiguity allows us to think that the woman might be his castrated self, so that he knows about her because, in a sense, he could be her. Her practice of the 'mechanism of pain' can be seen as an example of how she embodies the lessons of the school he/she might have founded. At the same time, she is suggested to be the worst practitioner of the 'escuela'[242] thus effectively 'unfixing' the narration by rejecting any reliable meaning.

Carlos Cherri shows how violence finds its justification in the logic of its means, not its end, and, linking this to *La escuela*, he explores how, through performance, literature builds for itself a means with no end.[243] He concurs with Panesi's views on fragmentation and ellipsis,[244] and Florencia Garramuño's comments on the recreation of violence.[245] The capturing of the act of violence, Cherri shows, is presented paradoxically through its absence in the chapter entitled 'Los democráticos'. The withholding of information in this section, where there is no explanation about the lack of fingers, is then explained in 'Cerro de dedos': it is the ink on the fingers that will lead to their amputation. Only when the lack of fingers is clarified can the characters regain a discernible 'normality'.

Nevertheless, their bodies remind them of their past oppression. As Ángeles Donoso has observed, in Bellatin's writing malformations, anomalies, diseases, and eccentricities are always considered in relation to the parameters of normality imposed by others, such as parents, doctors or friends.[246] Palaversich suggests that the novel normalizes the singular and the anomalous, reminding the reader of Thomas Kuhn's notion that suggests that 'anomaly appears only against the background provided by paradigm'.[247] In this sense, the multiple readings that the novel opens up both present and interrogate the parameters of normality imposed by others, with characters contradicting themselves and removing any trace of regularity or normality.

The novel thus exposes the control of the state over its citizens, and the family's control, which duplicates this external coercion. As Quintana shows, the mother who disciplines and forces her child to use an orthopaedic harness

242 Bellatin, *La escuela*, p. 56.

243 Carlos Leonel Cherri, 'Políticas de sentimiento y políticas de muerte en un corpus latinoamericano: Estéticas de la violencia y del guerrero' (presented at the VIII Congreso Internacional de Teoría y Crítica Literaria Orbis Tertius, Universidad Nacional de La Plata, 2012), pp. 1–9 (p. 3).

244 Panesi.

245 Florencia Garramuño, 'Los restos de lo real', *Revista Z Cultural*, (2011) <http://revistazcultural.pacc.ufrj.br/los-restos-de-lo-real-de-florencia-garramuno-2/> [accessed 1 July 2021].

246 Donoso, pp. 96–110.

247 Thomas S. Kuhn, *The Structure of Scientific Revolutions*, 50th anniversary edn (Chicago: The University of Chicago Press, 2012), p. 65.

is moulding his body to 'fit in' to society.[248] The boy suffers under multiple forms of power imposed upon him: that of the parents, social stigma, and the intervention of the state. Yet the boy can also be viewed as the one exerting power over others if he is actually 'el pedagogo', the founder of 'La Escuela'. This representation of power is then fragmented through the multivoiced construction of the novel. For example, if we follow the chapter title, the boy without an arm can be read as the intrusion of the implied author, referencing the fact that Bellatin does not have his right arm. Heteroglossia also emerges within passages that suggest multivoicedness within the chapters/sections, such as when the boy talks about his dead brother, and his utterance is interrupted by the following phrase, 'a mi garfio hubo que colocarle un recubrimiento de espuma para evitar que dañara a mis compañeros de clase',[249] in this way toying with different versions of reality.

In the 2001 edition, the presence of the state and its exercise of power are explicit and personified, and experiences of pain are presented as something that can be 'captured' by the character Lin Pao. He is presented as the inventor of a game of mirrors through which pain can be fixed like a photograph. This capture of pain appears, Quintana suggests, as a way of capturing the memory of the people who suffered under state oppression. The staging of pain goes beyond death, with Lin Pao's school of images considered dangerous to the nation by the state, and Lin Pao himself being 'decapitated and hanged'.[250] In this sense, the 'Escuela' contains a disciplinary dimension with pedagogy as a mode of resistance: the 'Escuela' becomes a positive 'self-disciplinary' technique which empowers. This is the reason why it has the potential to be a threat to the authoritarian structure. Yet in the 2005 edition the location of resistance is less explicit, situated in different, unreachable spaces due to the new edition's narratorial ambiguity. In this edition, for example, Lin Pao is never named. The narrator's ambiguity is displayed through the characters' equivocal thoughts and the omission of key words, such as proper names.

As we have seen, these multiple readings do not allow for any closed interpretations. The characters' monstrosity is revealed throughout the story in terms of the traces of previous histories that inform their grotesque bodies: such as the woman who self-harms or the man with horrific nails. In this sense, monstrosity reveals its previous histories, while the absence of any judgment reveals the text to be a 'site of encounter'. While in both *Una novela china* and *La mujer en la Muralla*, a power imbalance is installed through powerful and unreliable narrators, and China is used as a way of exposing the fictitious nature of 'master narratives', in *La escuela* extreme fragmentation reveals the impossibility of any totalizing narrative at all. The discursive ambiguity and unpredictable utterances lead the reader to continuously

248 Quintana, p. 502.
249 Bellatin, *La escuela*, p. 50.
250 Quintana, p. 502.

doubt, revealing meaning to be precarious, allowing for an 'encounter' with China as 'stranger', even as it disavows any ontology of the stranger, hence rejecting 'stranger fetishism'. The 'stranger' here is arguably undefinable.

The characters in Bellatin's text can be considered as fetishized 'strangers', embodying otherness through their mutilated figures and experiences of violence. Any cultural antagonism that might raise the spectre of 'stranger fetishism' is negated by the presence of fragmented discourses. The fragmented construction opens up spaces where we, as readers, can, to some extent, 'identify' with these characters. Both apathy and empathy towards the same characters are experienced from one fragment to the other: while a child's concern about his testicles is worrying as an indicator of abuse, his description of his 'testículos palpables, sebosos, cargados de una pátina de grasa'[251] evokes power over his own touchable body, while simultaneously conveying the grotesque. In this way, 'China' in the novel embodies the abject through the estranged bodies of the practitioners of 'La escuela del dolor', such as the children drowned because of state policies. As Ahmed writes, encounters such as these 'surprise the subject' while they 'reopen the prior histories of encounter that violate and fix others in regimes of difference',[252] recalling histories of violence in both China and Mexico. The lack of things—such as fingers, clothes, a husband, a child, life, or death—opens up spaces to be filled by the reader. The 'stranger' is lacking things which can be given to them by the reader by 'remaking *what it is that we may yet have in common*',[253] opening up spaces of encounter and encouraging dialogue.

In this sense, reading *La escuela* as 'historiographical metafiction' opens it up to analysis as a broad allegory of power, questioning overarching discourses through a fragmented narrative. Throughout the different levels of the novel, such as the titles, explanatory notes, and main texts, and through the ubiquitous presence of the state, power imbalances emerge. This is also recalled through the parent-son, individual-community, state-subject or author-reader relationships. While the characters may engage voluntarily in these relationships, their conflicted internal monologues reveal difficulties embedded in these power dynamics. The state's ultimate power is developed and maintained through mechanisms of vigilance that permeate society and these internal relations. Ultimately, the novel questions the figure of the fetishized 'stranger' as the characters engage with the 'stranger' within themselves. That is, the 'stranger' is narratively displayed from within, allowing the reading of displaced internal narratives and exposing conflict.

Steinberg suggests that Bellatin's books are works that announce 'untimeliness', hoping to endure a Mexican interregnum. Regarding *La escuela*, Steinberg suggests that 'in a perhaps unintended irony, the text itself seems

251 Bellatin, *La escuela*, p. 42.
252 Ahmed, p. 8.
253 Ahmed, p. 181.

to thematise the critique of totalitarian political order [...]',[254] while allegory, as the political-historical functioning of the literary, has been the object of disavowal by Bellatin. Yet irony can also be considered here to be deliberate. Bellatin's explicit disavowal of allegory can be seen as a grand joke played on his readers, just as he plays with the format, inserting dramatized versions of himself. It is here that a key difference between Jameson's and Tambling's notions of 'allegory' comes into play. While Bellatin might be, through rhetorical operation, 'saving' art from the demands of a national-allegorical interpretation, it does not mean that the novel itself cannot be read in allegorical terms. *La escuela*, beyond the local Mexican context, can be read in terms of the 'postmodern allegorical', rejecting a single isolatable truth and revealing the *constructedness* of the narration. As such, allegory attaches itself to an asymmetrical distribution of power, which permeates different members of society within authoritarian or hegemonic rule, embodied and subverted in this novel through the figure of 'China' and its unfixed strangerness.

Although in Aira and Laiseca's works 'China' is deployed to embody master narratives of despotic power that are deconstructed in a variety of ways, as we have seen, in Bellatin's writing, the use of 'China' seems more gratuitous. In Aira's and Laiseca's texts, 'China' acts as marker of temporal-spatial distance, allowing for it to embody the fetishized 'stranger' in time and space, while simultaneously exposing the stranger as such. For Bellatin, 'China' embodies the openness of transnational links that evoke and subvert discourses about 'strangers'. The chronological distance between *Una novela china* and *La mujer en la Muralla* in relation to *La escuela del dolor humano de Sechuán*, which reveals a further removal of 'China' from the texts, seems to acknowledge the more ubiquitous presence of China in Latin America, influenced by China's patterns of growth and consumption since the late 1980s.[255] In this way, China as 'stranger' allows for diverse and contradictory narratives which, in a way, are responding to Ahmed's call for a 'politics of encounter', and rejecting any ontology of the 'stranger',[256] thus allowing for a space of 'encounter' and 'dialogue'. The novels disclose how the 'multiplicity, antagonisms and contrasting temporalities are the stuff of all places'.[257]

Conclusion: A Recognizable China

In his analysis of Borges's poem 'El Forastero', Robin Fiddian states that the poem adopts the perspective 'of an ancient and venerable Eastern civilization, in order to openly critique historic assumptions about Christian Europe and

254 Steinberg, p. 110.

255 *The Political Economy of China–Latin American Relations in the New Millennium: Brave New World*, ed. by Margaret Myers and Carol Wise (New York: Routledge, 2017).

256 Ahmed, p. 181.

257 Massey, *For Space*, p. 139.

the political and spiritual hegemony of the West'.[258] And while this seems to be what Aira, Laiseca, and Bellatin do in these novels, and one could say that this is precisely where the main difference with Borges can be found, they also emphasize the textual approach to 'China' and the constructedness of 'China' in Latin America. By doing this, they deconstruct a dualistic East/West vision which remains present in Borges's work. This is especially interesting in the case of Laiseca, where his text *La mujer en la Muralla* can be read as a (very long) rewriting of Borges's text 'La muralla y los libros'.[259] As Torres Estrada states regarding the short story, Borges here seems to configure reality through an aesthetic exercise.[260] Furthermore, the multiple narrators available in Laiseca's text enhance the effect of Borges's sole narrator, as the former text emphasizes the multiple perspectives and ultimate disavowal of any isolatable truth. Laiseca extends Borges's exercise and, like him, presents the suspension of truth and the coexistence of conjectures.

With the first two novels published in 1987 and 1991 respectively, they highlight the transition from imaginaries of China which seem to point out to the reader how 'China' has been imagined at a moment in which the influence of the People's Republic of China (PRC) and Taiwan, in both economic and discursive terms, was still perceived to be limited; and how this imaginary is based on a preconception of 'China' as other, which continues even with the exponential growth in presence of the PRC and Taiwan in Latin America. While *Una novela china* and *La mujer en la Muralla* interrupt discourses of an exotic and constructed 'China', in *La escuela del dolor humano de Sechuán*, 'China' is deconstructed to reveal 'China' as a fetish for Latin America. And yet, as can be seen through the Argentine Eduardo Berti's (1964–) *El país imaginado*[261] (Berti having won the Premio Emecé in 2011 and the Premio Las Américas de Novela in 2012), fetishized depictions of China are still reverted to when 'China' wants to be represented: 'China' remains a fetish.

In *El país imaginado*, set in China during the early twentieth century, as we learn by the car and references to the Shanghai cinema and Japanese invasion, two women develop a friendship. The events are narrated by Ling, a first-person narrator, and interrupted by sections in italics with dialogues Ling holds with the grandmother's ghost. Through Ling, the reader learns about the development of the relationship of the two girls and how Ling grows up. The novel can be described as a *Bildungsroman*, the unfolding of Ling's life until her marriage and first pregnancy—worlds which are also inhabited by ghosts. Chinese culture is at the centre of the narrative: it is seen

258 Robin Fiddian, 'Post-Colonial Borges', in *The Cambridge Companion to Jorge Luis Borges*, ed. by Edwin Williamson (Cambridge: Cambridge University Press, 2013), pp. 96–109 (p. 105).

259 Borges, 'La muralla y los libros'.

260 Andrés Camilo Torres Estrada, 'A pesar de la muralla y los libros', *Hallazgos*, 12.24 (2015), pp. 125–37 (p. 137).

261 Berti, *El país imaginado*.

in the arranged marriage, in foot-binding, and in the knowledge of *nu-shu*, a secret language of women in China. Within this context the reader learns of the relationship between Ling and Xiaomei. The nuances keep the girl's relationship a mystery; the reader is unable to define if it's friendship or a romantic relationship. This ambiguity is possible because of the narrator's exquisite description and fascination with Xiaomei, the daughter of a blind man, Liu Feihong.

If Bellatin removes all specificity in *La escuela*, Berti shows specific ways of recognizing China and Chineseness through Chinese names and traditions. What was removed in the second edition in *La escuela*, is brought to the forefront in *El país imaginado*. The novel starts with a section called Xiaomei, indicator of a Chinese name, and the first paragraphs describe traditional Chinese customs and the relevance given to traditional rites. And yet, while traditional aspects of Chinese culture are continuously recalled, Ling, as well as the other women in the story, are described as having more agency than what the rites described suggest (such as funerary traditions, marriages, or foot binding). In the novel, women play a central role: the grandmother, mother, daughter, and Xiaomei.

Berti builds on a Chinese and 'Oriental' imaginary, in dialogue with previous traditions and literature, as Adrián Ferrero also notes.[262] The 'imagined' place recalls the 'China' of *Una novela china*, where estrangement results from difference and where difference seems to remain at the level of culture. When centred around the relationship between Xiaomei and Ling, the novel becomes more about people and their feelings, detached from the Saidian orientalism in which the novel is immersed. In the prologue to the book, Alberto Manguel warns the reader that Berti's China is 'imagined' and not 'imaginary', and warns that the distinction is crucial.[263] Manguel explains that China is '[...] en la imaginación occidental, el otro lado del Espejo',[264] recalling an alterity central to the idea of China. Because of this, it seems unproblematic that the story appropriates an imagined 'China' to tell a story. This imagined China is recognized as such precisely because of its specificity. 'El país imaginado', the reader learns towards the novel's end, is how the grandmother referred to death. 'El último de una serie de países imaginados; el país que nunca dejamos de imaginar porque no tenemos de él ninguna imagen real.'[265] And yet, the 'imagined' China of Berti's novel is very much engrained in traditional culture, although change and modernity (through which the reader learns because of hair or clothes style, or what seems like an honest relationship with her husband) are embraced rather than challenged.

262 Ferrero.

263 Alberto Manguel, 'Introducción. Cuento de la Enamorada', in Eduardo Berti, *El país imaginado* (Madrid: Impedimenta, 2012), pp. 7–11 (p. 8).

264 Manguel, p. 9.

265 Eduardo Berti, *El país imaginado* (Madrid: Impedimenta, 2012), p. 189.

The narrator, whose real name we never get to know—while the reader does know that Ling is a name that she makes up when she introduces herself to Xiaomei—is unreliable, and she lets the reader know of her relationship with ghosts. But while in *La escuela* the narrator's unreliability recalls transnationalism, in *El país imaginado* the continuous recalling of specific aspects of Chinese culture reminds us, as readers of a Latin American writer, of the ways in which Chineseness is constructed. In this sense, that the story is set in China only provides an atmosphere; because the centre is on the girl, and Ling is the narrator, the whole world of China depicted in the novel could be an invention of Ling herself. Although it constructs an essentialist and stereotypical Chinese atmosphere and performance of Chineseness, the novel seems to be centred as a *Bildungsroman* where the girl exercises agency: at the story's centre is a girl's experience of love and growing up.

In this sense, and to borrow from Bakhtin, I suggest that a 'chronotope of encounter' emerges in the novels discussed here. Bakhtin's notion of the chronotope (time-space) asserts the intrinsic connectedness of temporal and spatial relationships artistically expressed in literature: the representation of China as setting and cultural context interacts with the plot, history and characters, emerging through unreliable and unstable narrative constructions. For Bakhtin, time and space are inseparable, a combination of setting and plot, with their intersections creating an integral whole. Following Bakhtin, analysing a chronotope entails attention to the narrative structure and the external social and political contexts. This 'China' chronotope embodies the existence of multiple conflicting discourses, revealed through utterances, evoking power imbalances by embodying the abject, and disturbing all notions of conventional identities and cultures. In this way, China emerges as a kind of 'uncanny', foreign yet familiar, the known and unknown 'stranger', exposing spatialized social practices, and articulating subjective transnational experiences.

The 'chronotope of encounter' provides the novels' grounding for the 'representability of events', allowing for the 'strange encounter'.[266] By depicting a static China, an ontological perspective on 'China' is made available and then disrupted through irony and parody. To this end, the stagnant nature of 'historiographic' accounts, which attribute certain traits to China as 'ontological other', are constantly displaced. In this sense, these novels address China's 'strangerness' by 'unfixing' certain boundaries concerning access to history, power and knowledge.

Narrative estrangement disturbs naturalized assumptions about where we are and how we position ourselves with relation to the world, while simultaneously playing out within borders. This in turn makes possible a geographical reversal: the imbalance of power and its physical embodiment and practice relate not only to China, but also to Latin America. In this way, the novels

266 Bakhtin, p. 250.

unsettle the distance between 'strangers', while still acknowledging them to be 'strangers' in unfixed and open ways. In this sense, the presence of China here performs a political function. The authors expose the idiosyncrasies and contradictions of discourses that present a somewhat invisible China in Latin America, simultaneously challenging binary understandings between notions of 'East' and 'West'.

The choice of 'China' as a motif for the narrative thread thus serves to (de) legitimize discourses on the 'other', while revealing 'China' to be an ultimately distant, relatively invisible, exoticized and unknown place in Latin American literary discourses. The chronotope of China as encounter mobilizes existing socio-political relations at the same time as renegotiating them, destabilizing existing hierarchies of power in Latin American contexts through a partly allegorical China. The authors seem to resort to China specifically because of China's historically hermetic image in the Latin American imagination. 'China' as a setting allows for a performance of Chineseness. This performance positions 'China' as an 'ultimate other', precisely the 'fetishised stranger' in Ahmed's terms, a notion which is simultaneously disavowed through the novels' narrative strategies and (de)constructions. The defiance of the authority of knowledge disclosed in the novels reminds the reader of the fictionality of literature as demonstrative of the fictionality of all discursive constructs, including that which 'China' invents for itself. By exposing contradictions, these texts reveal and denounce the processes through which some others are rendered 'stranger than other others'.[267]

In this way, it is tacitly implied that China as 'stranger' is admitted as possibly knowing differently from what it represents. The displacement of 'China' here leaves its 'strangerness' hidden and designates it unmistakably.[268] 'China' is thus chosen to reveal the fragmentation and blurring of the known and unknown. The novels reveal their 'openness' to the 'stranger', acting as a 'space of encounter', allowing dialogue and finding through these discursively reinvented and destabilized 'Chinas', different ways to talk about contemporary power relations and forms of strangerness.

References

Ahmed, Sara, *Strange Encounters: Embodied Others in Post-Coloniality* (London: Routledge, 2000)

Aira, César, *El mármol*, Kindle 2012 (Buenos Aires: La Bestia Equilátera, 2011)

———, *El pequeño monje budista* (Buenos Aires: Mansalva, 2005)

———, *El volante* (Rosario: Beatriz Viterbo Editora, 1992)

———, 'Una máquina de guerra contra la pena', *Babel*, 2.12 (1989)

———, *Una novela china* (Buenos Aires: Javier Vergara, 1987)

267 Ahmed, p. 25.

268 Jacques Derrida, *Of Grammatology* (Baltimore: Johns Hopkins University Press, 2016), p. 182.

———, *Una novela china* (Buenos Aires: Debolsillo, 2005)
Albornoz, Carla Victoria, 'La pedagogía del dolor en la escritura fragmentaria de Mario Bellatin', *Hipertexto*, 13 (2011), pp. 3–23
Alfieri, Carlos, 'César Aira: El mejor Cortázar es un mal Borges', *Revista de Cultura Ñ, Clarín*, (2014) <http://www.elortiba.org/aira.html> [accessed 1 July 2021]
Andrade Kobayashi, Megumi, 'Los héroes disecados de Mario Bellatin', *Estudios Avanzados*, 21 (2014), pp. 69–90
de Arriba, María Laura, 'Raras ficciones nuevas', *Revista del CELEHIS*, 5.6–7–8 (1996), pp. 213–53
Azaretto, Julia, Entrevista a Mario Bellatin, 2009 <http://cle.ens-lyon.fr/espagnol/entrevista-a-mario-bellatin-68252.kjsp?STNAV=&RUBNAV=> [accessed 1 July 2021]
Bakhtin, Mikhail, *The Dialogic Imagination: Four Essays*, ed. by Michael Holquist (Austin: University of Texas Press, 1981)
Bellatin, Mario, *La escuela del dolor humano de Sechuán* (Mexico City: Tusquets Editores, 2001)
———, *La escuela del dolor humano de Sechuán* (Buenos Aires: Interzona, 2005)
———, *La escuela del dolor humano de Sechuán* (Córdoba: Borde Perdido Editora, 2016)
———, 'Pequeña muestra del vicio en el que caigo todos los días', *Literal*, 14 (2012) <http://literalmagazine.com/pequena-muestra-del-vicio-en-el-que-caigo-todos-los-dias/> [accessed 1 July 2021]
———, 'Snapshots', 2001 <http://www.letraslibres.com/revista/portafolios/snapshots> [accessed 1 July 2021]
Bergara, Hernán, 'Plagios con un plagio de plagios', in *Por favor, ¡Plágienme!*, by Alberto Laiseca (Buenos Aires: Eudeba, 2013)
Berti, Eduardo, *El país imaginado* (Buenos Aires: Planeta, 2011)
———, *El país imaginado* (Madrid: Impedimenta, 2012)
Bhabha, Homi K., *The Location of Culture* (Oxon: Routledge, 1994)
Borges, Jorge Luis, 'El escritor argentino y la tradición', in *Discusión*, essay originally published 1953 (Madrid: Alianza, 1976), pp. 128–37
———, 'La muralla y los libros', in *Inquisiciones, Otras inquisiciones* (Barcelona: Debolsillo, 2011), pp. 151–54
Caparrós, Martín, 'Nuevos avances y retrocesos de la nueva novela argentina en lo que va del mes de abril', *Babel*, 2.10 (1989), pp. 43–45
Carrillo Martin, Francisco, 'La literatura como performance: Mario Bellatin y Severo Sarduy', *Hispamérica*, 39.115 (2010), pp. 37–47
Chen, Xiaolan, 'Primitive and Modern: Two Faces of Shanghai in Chinese and Western Literature', *Frontiers of Literary Studies in China*, 1.4 (2007), pp. 543–54
Cheng, Anne A., *Ornamentalism* (Oxford: Oxford University Press, 2019)
Cherri, Carlos Leonel, 'Políticas de sentimiento y políticas de muerte en un corpus latinoamericano: Estéticas de la violencia y del guerrero' (presented at the VIII Congreso Internacional de Teoría y Crítica Literaria Orbis Tertius, Universidad Nacional de La Plata, 2012), pp. 1–9

Conde, Laura, 'Mario Bellatin: Una Escritura Tridimensional' (presented at the VI Jornadas Internacionales de Filología y Lingüística, Universidad Nacional de La Plata, La Plata, 2003)

Contreras, Sandra, *Las vueltas de César Aira* (Rosario: Beatriz Viterbo Editora, 2002)

Dapelo, Luis, and César Aira, 'César Aira', *Hispamérica*, 36.107 (2007), pp. 41–53

Depetris Chauvin, Irene, 'La violencia gratuita y el poder de lo falso en César Aira', *Revista Chilena de Literatura*, 87 (2014), pp. 69–87

Derrida, Jacques, *Of Grammatology* (Baltimore: The Johns Hopkins University Press, 2016)

Donoso, Ángeles, '"Yo soy Mario Bellatin y soy de ficción" o el paradójico borde de lo autobiográfico en El Gran Vidrio', *Chasqui*, 40 (2011), pp. 96–110

Escobar Ulloa, Ernesto, 'Entrevista a César Aira', *The Barcelona Review*, 2004 <http://www.barcelonareview.com/44/s_ca.htm> [accessed 1 July 2021]

Fernández González, Carlos, 'Alcances y dimensiones del plagio en la narrativa de Alberto Laiseca: alrededor de "Por favor ¡Plágienme!"', *Revista Chilena de Literatura*, 87 (2014), pp. 89–113

Fernández, Nancy, 'Dos Viajes. Sobre Fogwill y Alberto Laiseca', *CELEHIS - Revista del Centro de Letras Hispanoamericanas*, 27.35 (2018), pp. 111–19

Ferrero, Adrián, 'Reviewed Work: *El país imaginado* by Eduardo Berti', *Chasqui*, 41.2 (2012), pp. 221–24

Ferry, Megan M., 'China as Utopia: Visions of the Chinese Cultural Revolution in Latin America', *Modern Chinese Literature and Culture*, 12.2 (2000), pp. 236–69

Fiddian, Robin, 'Post-Colonial Borges', in *The Cambridge Companion to Jorge Luis Borges*, ed. by Edwin Williamson (Cambridge: Cambridge University Press, 2013), pp. 96–109

García, Facundo, 'Los poemas sirven para no estar solo', *Página/12* (Argentina, 26 November 2005), section Cultura y Espectáculos <http://www.pagina12.com.ar/diario/suplementos/espectaculos/2-1125-2005-11-26.html> [accessed 1 July 2021]

García Márquez, Gabriel, *Cien años de soledad* (Madrid: Espasa-Calpe, 1983)

Garramuño, Florencia, 'Los restos de lo real', *Revista Z Cultural*, (2011) <http://revistazcultural.pacc.ufrj.br/los-restos-de-lo-real-de-florencia-garramuno-2/> [accessed 1 July 2021]

Ginzburg, Carlo, *Threads and Traces: True False Fictive*, trans. by Anne C. Tedeschi and John Tedeschi (Berkeley: University of California Press, 2012)

Goldman, Merle, 'The Political Use of Lu Xun', *The China Quarterly*, 91 (1982), pp. 446–61

Gómez, Pedro Arturo, and José Agustín Conde de Boeck, 'Canonización y actitud de culto. La presencia de Alberto Laiseca en El artista (2008) de Mariano Cohn y Gastón Duprat', *Imagofagia*, 7, 2013 <http://www.asaeca.org/imagofagia/index.php/imagofagia/article/view/345> [accessed 1 July 2017]

Guerrero, Javier, 'El experimento "Mario Bellatin". Cuerpo enfermo y anómalo en el tránsito material del seco', *Estudios. Revista de Investigaciones Literarias y Culturales*, 17.33 (2009), pp. 63–96

Hind, Emily, 'Entrevista con Mario Bellatin', *Confluencia* (2004), pp. 197–204

Holmes, Amanda, 'China in Argentine Exotismo: Contemporary Inventions of the Orient', *Bulletin of Spanish Studies*, 85.1 (2008), pp. 71–83

Hoyos, Héctor, 'Orientalismo, globalización e imaginarios transpacíficos en la novela latinoamericana actual', *Cuadernos de Literatura*, 17.34 (2013), pp. 82–105

Hubert, Rosario, 'Intellectual Cartographies of the Cold War: Argentinean Visitors to the People's Republic of China 1952–1958', in *Handbook of Literature and Space*, ed. by Robert Tally (London: Routledge, 2016), pp. 337–48

Hutcheon, Linda, *A Poetics of Postmodernism: History, Theory, Fiction* (New York: Routledge, 1988)

Jameson, Fredric, *Postmodernism, or, the Cultural Logic of Late Capitalism* (Durham: Duke University Press, 1991)

Ko, Chisu Teresa, 'Orientalism and De-Orientalism in Contemporary Latin America: Reading César Aira', *TRANSMODERNITY: Journal of Peripheral Cultural Production of the Luso-Hispanic World*, 8.3 (2018), pp. 149–67

Kuhn, Thomas S., *The Structure of Scientific Revolutions*, 50th anniversary edn (Chicago: The University of Chicago Press, 2012)

Kurlat Ares, Silvia G., 'Post-Utopian Imaginaries: Narrating Uncertainty', in *A Companion to Latin American Literature and Culture*, ed. by Sara Castro-Klaren (Chichester: Wiley-Blackwell, 2013), pp. 620–35

Laddaga, Reinaldo, *Espectáculos de realidad. Ensayo sobre la narrativa latinoamericana de las últimas dos décadas* (Buenos Aires: Beatriz Viterbo Editora, 2007)

———, 'Espectáculos de realidad. Ensayo sobre la narrativa latinoamericana de las últimas dos décadas', *Comunicação & Política*, 24.3 (2006), pp. 159–78

———, 'Una literatura de la clase media: Notas sobre César Aira', *Hispamérica: Revista de Literatura*, 30.88 (2001), pp. 37–48

Laiseca, Alberto, *La mujer en la Muralla* (Buenos Aires: Planeta, 1990)

———, '@LAILaiseca' <https://twitter.com/lailaiseca> [accessed 1 August 2021]

Lin Yutang, *My Country and My People* (London: William Heinemann Ltd., 1936)

———, *Sabiduría China*, trans. by Alfredo Whitelow, 3rd edn (Buenos Aires: Editorial Biblioteca Nueva, 1959)

———, *Sabiduría Hindú* (Buenos Aires: Editorial Biblioteca Nueva, 1959)

———, ed., *The Wisdom of China and India* (New York: Random House, 1942)

Locane, Jorge J., and Maria Montt Strabucchi, 'Cultura china y Capricornio. Dos proyectos pioneros para el comercio simbólico (y material) entre América Latina y China', *Revista Izquierdas*, 49 (2020), pp. 2521–44

Locane, Jorge J., and María Montt Strabucchi, 'El Viaje América Latina-China. Una Interacción Sur-Sur Sui Generis', *TRANSMODERNITY: Journal of Peripheral Cultural Production of the Luso-Hispanic World*, 9.3 (2020), pp. 1–5

López-Calvo, Ignacio, *Dragons in the Land of the Condor: Writing Tusán in Peru* (Tucson: The University of Arizona Press, 2014)

———, 'The Death of the Author through False Translation in Mario Bellatin's Orientalised Japan', *Bulletin of Latin American Research*, 32.3 (2013), pp. 339–53

Ludmer, Josefina, 'Literaturas Postautónomas' <http://www.lehman.cuny.edu/ciberletras/v17/ludmer.htm> [accessed 1 July 2021]

Ma, Hengyun, and Allan N. Rae, 'Projections of Dairy Product Consumption and Trade Opportunities in China', *Australasian Agribusiness Review*, 12 (2004) <http://econpapers.repec.org/article/agsauagre/132084.htm> [accessed 1 July 2021]

Manguel, Alberto, 'Introducción. Cuento de la Enamorada', in *El país imaginado*, by Eduardo Berti (Madrid: Impedimenta, 2012), pp. 7–11

Martínez-Robles, David, 'The Western Representation of Modern China: Orientalism, Culturalism and Historiographical Criticism', in *Orientalism [online dossier]*, ed. by Carles Prado-Fonts, Digithum, 10, 2008, UOC <http://www.uoc.edu/digithum/10/dt/eng/martinez.pdf> [accessed 1 August 2021]

Masiello, Francine, 'Bodies in Transit: Travel, Translation and Gender', in *Voice-Overs, Translation and Latin American Studies*, ed. by Daniel Balderston and Schwartz (New York: State University of New York Press, 2002), pp. 213–23

Massey, Doreen, *For Space* (London: SAGE, 2005)

———, *Space, Place and Gender* (Cambridge: Polity Press, 1994)

Mateo del Pino, Ángeles, 'Travistiendo la verdad en busca de la mentira. La escritura de Mario Bellatin', in *Identidad y simulación. Ficciones, performances, estrategias culturales*, ed. by José Ismael Gutiérrez Gutiérrez (Valencia: Aduana Vieja, 2009), pp. 119–62

McClintock, Anne, *Imperial Leather: Race, Gender, and Sexuality in the Colonial Contest* (New York: Routledge, 1995)

Méndez, Katherine, 'Mario Bellatin: Ghosts, the Human Body and the Spaces Where They Meet', in *Orientalisms of the Hispanic and Luso-Brazilian World*, ed. by Araceli Tinajero (New York: Escribana Books, 2014), pp. 99–117

Molle, Fernando, 'Yo deliro pero con realismo', *Perfil*, 6 May 2011 <http://www.perfil.com/ediciones/cultura/Yo-delirio-pero-con-realismo-20116-578-0028.html> [accessed 1 July 2021]

Montaldo, Graciela, 'Aira, un arte basado en la incorrección. El cuestionamiento de las instituciones en una vanguardia finisecular', in *De Alfonsín al Menemato (1983-2001)*, ed. by Rocco Carbone and Ana Ojeda, Literatura Argentina siglo XX (Buenos Aires: Fundación Crónica General, 2010), VII, pp. 94–106

———, 'Un argumento contraborgiano en la literatura argentina de los años 80 (sobre C. Aira, A. Laiseca y Copi)', *Hispamérica: Revista de Literatura*, 19.55 (1990), pp. 105–12

———, 'Una literatura que lo puede todo', in *Literatura Latino-Americana do século XXI*, ed. by Beatriz Resende (Rio de Janeiro: Aeroplano, 2005), pp. 127–39

Montoya Juárez, Jesús, 'Aira y los aireanos. Literatura argentina y cultura masiva desde los noventa', in *Entre lo global y lo local: La narrativa latinoamericana en el cambio de siglo (1990–2006)*, ed. by Jesús Montoya Juárez and Esteban Ángel (Madrid: Vervuert, Iberoamericana, 2008), pp. 51–76

———, 'Dos sentidos del humor de fin de Siglo: César Aira y Leo Maslíah', in *Encuentro de Latinoamericanistas Españoles: Viejas y nuevas alianzas entre América Latina y España* (Santander: CEEIB, 2006), pp. 1668–84

Montt Strabucchi, Maria, Carol Chan, and María Elvira Ríos, *Chineseness in Chile: Shifting Representations during the Twenty-First Century*, Studies of the Americas (Cham: Palgrave Macmillan, 2022) <https://doi.org/10.1007/978-3-030-83966-6>

Moore, Marianne, 'Silence' <http://www.poets.org/poetsorg/poem/silence-2> [accessed 19 February 2021]

Morero, Sergio, 'Lin Yutang y la importancia de vivir', *Revista Vea y Lea*, (1962) <http://www.magicasruinas.com.ar/revistero/internacional/autores-lin-yutang.htm> [accessed 1 July 2021]

Myers, Margaret, and Carol Wise, eds, *The Political Economy of China–Latin American Relations in the New Millennium: Brave New World* (New York: Routledge, 2017)

Nagy-Zekmi, Silvia, 'Relocation of Knowledge: The Postcolonial Debate in Latin America', *Phoebe: Gender and Cultural Critique*, 16.1 (2004), pp. 1–9

Oyarzún, Pablo, *La desazón de lo moderno. Problemas de la modernidad* (Santiago: Cuarto Propio / Arcis, 2001)

Oyola, Leonardo, 'Kryptonita (Fragmentos)', *Gramma*, 23.49 (2012), pp. 285–89

Palaversich, Diana, 'Apuntes para una lectura de Mario Bellatin', *Chasqui*, 32.1 (2003), pp. 25–38

———, *De Macondo a McOndo. Senderos de la postmodernidad latinoamericana* (Barcelona: Plaza y Valdés, 2005)

———, 'Prólogo', in *Obra Reunida*, by Mario Bellatin (Mexico City: Alfaguara, 2015)

Palma, Patricia, and Maria Montt Strabucchi, 'Percepción de la República Popular China en Chile a partir de la prensa: El Tarapacá de Iquique y El Mercurio de Santiago 1949–1960' (presented at the I Congreso Latinoamericano de Estudios Chinos, Universidad Nacional de La Plata, 2011)

Palumbo, Gabriel, and Diego Rossello, 'Laiseca', *Quilt*, (2010) <http://proyecto-quilt.com.ar/page/10/> [accessed 1 August 2021]

Panesi, Jorge, '"La escuela del dolor humano de Sechuán" de Mario Bellatin', 2005 <https://filologiaunlp.files.wordpress.com/2012/01/perros-heroes-por-panesi.pdf> [accessed 1 July 2021]

Patiño, Roxana, 'Revistas literarias y culturales argentina de los 80', *Ínsula*, 715–716 (2006), pp. 2–5

Pauls, Alan, 'El problema Bellatin', *El Interpretador. Literatura, Arte y Pensamiento*, (2005) <http://salonkritik.net/10-11/2011/06/el_problema_bellatin_alan_paul_1.php> [accessed 1 July 2021]

Porrúa, Ana, 'César Aira: Implosión y juventud', *Punto de Vista*, 81 (2005), pp. 24–29

Quesada Gómez, Catalina, 'Mutatis Mutandis: De Severo Sarduy a Mario Bellatin', *Boletín Hispánico Helvético*, 17.18 (2011), pp. 297–320

Quintana, Isabel A., 'Escenografía del horror: cuerpo, violencia y política en la obra de Mario Bellatin', *Revista Iberoamericana*, 75.227 (2009), pp. 487–504

Reber, Dierdra, 'Cure for the Capitalist Headache: Affect and Fantastic Consumption in César Aira's Argentine "Baghdad"', *MLN*, 122.2 (2007), pp. 371–99

Remón-Raillard, Margarita, 'La narrativa de César Aira: Una sorpresa continua e ininterrumpida', *Foro Hispánico*, 24.1 (2003), pp. 53–64

Richard, Nelly, 'Latinoamérica y la posmodernidad', *Escritos. Revistas de Ciencias del Lenguaje* (1996), pp. 271–80

Rimmon-Kenan, Shlomith, *Narrative Fiction: Contemporary Poetics*, 2nd edn (London: Routledge, 2002)

Ríos, María Elvira, María Montt, and Carol Chan, 'El imaginario de lo chino en las revistas magazinescas chilenas de principios del siglo XX', *Revista Rumbos TS. Un espacio crítico para la reflexión en Ciencias Sociales*, 24 (2021), pp. 129–50 <https://doi.org/10.51188/rrts.num24.434>

Roig, Silvia, '¿Qué significa vivir en un Estado de derecho?: Vida, contaminación y muerte en "Salón de belleza" de Mario Bellatin', *Lucero*, 22.1 (2012)

Ros, Ofelia, 'Restos de la ideología: la "idea siniestra" en la literatura de César Aira', *Revista de Crítica Literaria Latinoamericana*, 37.74 (2011), pp. 149–69

Rose, Arthur, *Literary Cynics: Borges, Beckett, Coetzee* (London: Bloomsbury, 2017)

Rothwell, Matthew, *Transpacific Revolutionaries: The Chinese Revolution in Latin America* (New York: Routledge, 2013)

Ruiz, Facundo, 'Vitrinas narrativas. Mario Bellatin y el relato fotográfico', *Revista de Crítica Literaria Latinoamericana*, 34.68 (2008), pp. 201–10

Rupar, Brenda, 'El rol de la Revolución Cultural china en el maoísmo argentino', *Leste Vermehlo: revista de estudos críticos asiáticos*, 3.1 (2017), pp. 355–75

Said, Edward, *Orientalism* (London: Penguin, 2003)

Saítta, Sylvia, 'En torno al 2001 en la narrativa argentina', *Literatura y Lingüística*, 29 (2013), pp. 131–48

Seth, Vikram, trans., *Three Chinese Poets: Translations of Poems by Wang Wei, Li Bai and Du Fu* (London: Phoenix, 1997)

Sommer, Doris, *Foundational Fictions: The National Romances of Latin America* (Berkeley: University of California Press, 1991)

Speranza, Graciela, *Fuera de campo: Literatura y arte argentinos después de Duchamp* (Barcelona: Anagrama, 2006)

Steinberg, Samuel, 'To Begin Writing: Bellatin, Reunited', *Journal of Latin American Cultural Studies*, 20.2 (2011), pp. 105–20

Tambling, Jeremy, *Allegory* (London: Routledge, 2010)

———, *Wong Kar-Wai's Happy Together* (London: Hong Kong University Press, 2003)

Torres Estrada, Andrés Camilo, 'A pesar de la muralla y los libros', *Hallazgos*, 12.24 (2015), pp. 125–37

Tusquets, 'La mujer en la muralla' <http://www.tusquetseditores.com/titulos/andanzas-la-mujer-en-la-muralla> [accessed 1 July 2021]

Ubelaker Andrade, Lisa, 'Connected in Print: Selecciones Del Reader's Digest, U.S. Cultural Relations, and the Construction of a Global Middle Class', *Palabra Clave*, 22.4 (2019), pp. 1–32 <https://doi.org/10.5294/pacla.2019.22.4.7>

Vaggione, Alicia, 'Literatura/enfermedad: el cuerpo como desecho. Una lectura de "Salón de belleza" de Mario Bellatin', *Revista Iberoamericana*, 75.227 (2009), pp. 475–86

Vergara, Pablo, 'El vacío como gesto: Representación y crisis del sentido en la obra de Mario Bellatin', *Revista Laboratorio*, (2010) <http://revistalaboratorio.udp.cl/num2_2010_art6_vergara/> [accessed 1 July 2021]

Vidal Kunstmann, José Miguel, 'Entre lo local y lo global: Pablo de Rokha y el proyecto maoísta', *TRANSMODERNITY: Journal of Peripheral Cultural Production of the Luso-Hispanic World*, 9.3 (2020), pp. 161–94

Villanueva, Graciela, 'El "enfrente del enfrente": Circuitos urbanos en las novelas de César Aira', in *Ciudades y el fin de siglo XX en América Latina: literaturas, culturas, representaciones*, ed. by Teresa Orecchia Havas (Bern: Peter Lang, 2007), pp. 369–81

Vitale, Ida, 'Un vestido rosa y después: César Aira', *Vuelta*, 165 (1990), pp. 42–45

Von Baumbach, Federico, 'Poemas Chinos de Laiseca', 2014 <http://www.dangdai.com.ar/joomla/index.php?option=com_content&view=article&id=3807:poemas-chinos-de-laiseca&catid=2:cultura&Itemid=9> [accessed 1 July 2021]

Watson, Burton, *Ssu Ma Chien: Grand Historian of China* (London: Columbia University Press, 1958)

Williams, Raymond L., 'Fuentes the Modern; Fuentes the Postmodern', *Hispania*, 85.2 (2002), pp. 209–18

———, *The Columbia Guide to the Latin American Novel since 1945* (New York: Columbia University Press, 2007)

Wu, Cheng'en, *The Journey to the West*, trans. by Anthony C. Yu, revised edition 2012 (London: University of Chicago Press, 1977)

CHAPTER TWO

China Here

Remapping China in Latin America

Novels where Chinese topics or Chinese protagonists are set in Latin America have grown continuously since the Mexican Juan José Rodríguez published *Asesinato en una lavandería china*[1] in 1996, a novel set in contemporary Mexico in which the protagonist is exposed to a Mexican-Chinese vampire drug cartel, and which—by inserting a flashback to 1917—recalls the violence to which the Chinese were subject in the early twentieth century.[2] Then Ariel Magnus published *Un chino en bicicleta* in 2007 and, in addition to the publication of *Verde Shanghai* and *El mármol* in 2011, and *La casa del dolor ajeno* in 2016, we can find other novels published in Mexico, Peru, and Argentina. In 2009, the Mexican Bernardo Fernández, or BEF (1972–) published *Ojos de lagarto*. In it, the reader is exposed, through the different chapters with different narrators, to multiple stories set in different times and places, all linked through fascinating fantastic creatures. Fernández is an iconic figure in Mexican contemporary science fiction, while Sánchez Prado describes *Ojos de lagarto* not as science fiction but rather as a multiperspective historical novel.[3] Set in the 1920s, the novel spans Africa, China, Mexico, and the United States, following scientific interest in exotic animals, dragons, and the greed of men. Ultimately, the story centres around an underground city run by the Chinese in Mexicali, a mysterious city hidden in plain sight,

1 Juan José Rodríguez, *Asesinato en una lavandería china* (Mexico D.F: Consejo Nacional para la Cultura y las Artes, 1996).

2 For a detailed analysis of *Asesinato en una lavendería china* and the way in which the Chinese are depicted in Mexico see the work of Svetlana V. Tyutina, 'The Peripheral and the Ephemeral: Power Struggle, Violence and Fear in the Depiction of Chinos in Mexican Literature and Visual Arts', *TRANSMODERNITY: Journal of Peripheral Cultural Production of the Luso-Hispanic World*, 8.3 (2018), pp. 64–85.

3 Ignacio M. Sánchez Prado, 'Ending the World with Words: Bernardo Fernández (BEF) and the Institutionalization of Science Fiction in Mexico', in *Latin American Science Fiction: Theory and Practice*, ed. by M. Elizabeth Ginway and J. Andrew Brown (New York: Palgrave Macmillan US, 2012), pp. 111–32 <https://doi.org/10.1057/9781137312778_7>.

which serves as a comment on the historical presence of the Chinese there. Mystery linked to the Chinese communities, as well as a commentary on the historical presence of the Chinese in Latin America, is also available in *El misterio del barrio chino* by the Peruvian author José Güich Rodríguez.[4] In the novel, also set in the early twentieth century, a young journalist-detective helps solve mysteries in Lima's *barrio chino* (Chinatown), responding to a request by his friend Antonio Loo, a member of the Chinese community. The novel is informed by Lima's history and the Chinese community,[5] and includes real historical people as characters in the plot. In both *Ojos de lagarto* and *El misterio del barrio chino*, the fictional narration comments on the local perspective, where the plots combine places and events that put in dialogue the historical with the imaginary, as Svetlana V. Tyutina[6] explores in her analysis of *Asesinato en una lavandería china*.[7] All these novels explore in different nuanced ways how the Chinese have been 'othered' in both symbolic and real ways in their local contexts.

The novels analysed in this chapter are linked to the presence of Chinese communities and *barrios chinos* (Chinatowns) in Latin America. The novel *Un chino en bicicleta* (2007, henceforth, *Un chino*) by the Argentine author Ariel Magnus is set in the *barrio chino* of Buenos Aires, while the story of *El mármol*[8] by César Aira occurs around two 'supermercados chinos', as supermarkets owned or administered by Chinese people in Buenos Aires are known.[9] In the novel *Verde Shanghai*[10] by Mexican author Cristina Rivera Garza, the protagonist goes to a non-specified *barrio chino*, presumably that of Mexico City.[11] I contend here that by focusing on Chinatowns and the Chinese, these novels offer an evaluation of the discourses that support a racially homogeneous Latin America by emphasizing its heterogeneity

4 José Güich Rodríguez, *El misterio del barrio chino* (Lima: Ediciones SM, 2013).

5 Fernando de Trazegnies Granda, *En el país de las colinas de arena: Reflexiones sobre la inmigración china en el Perú del S. XIX desde la perspectiva del derecho* (Lima: Pontificia Universidad Católica del Perú, 1994); Patricia Palma and José Ragas, 'Enclaves sanitarios: higiene, epidemias y salud en el barrio chino de Lima, 1880–1910', *Anuario Colombiano de Historia Social y de la Cultura*, 45.1 (2018), pp. 159–90 <https://doi.org/10.15446/achsc.v45n1.67555>.

6 Tyutina.

7 Rodríguez.

8 César Aira, *El mármol*, Kindle 2012 (Buenos Aires: La Bestia Equilátera, 2011).

9 Sections of my analysis of *Un chino en bicicleta* and *El mármol* have been published in *Documentos de trabajo REDCAEM*, see Maria Montt Strabucchi, 'Encuentros con la comunidad china en Buenos Aires: Un análisis de dos novelas', *Working Paper Series (WPS) de REDCAEM*, 4 (2018), pp. 1–26.

10 Cristina Rivera Garza, *Verde Shanghai*, Kindle (Mexico City: Tusquets, 2011).

11 A similar version of my analysis of *Verde Shanghai* here is published as 'Mexico City's "Chinos" and "Barrio Chino": Strangerness and Community in Cristina Rivera Garza's "Verde Shanghai" (2011)', *Verge: Studies in Global Asias*, 3.2 (2017), pp. 144–68.

and hybridity beyond 'local' black and indigenous cultures. Read through Jean-Luc Nancy's idea of 'being singular plural',[12] the postcolonial scholar Graham Huggan's 'postcolonial exotic',[13] and further engaging with Sara Ahmed's theorizations on the 'stranger',[14] these novels can be shown to converse with contemporary questions regarding multiculturalism,[15] to unfix binaries,[16] and to challenge the idea of a post-racial Latin America.[17]

These novels reflect upon, and challenge fixed conceptions of race, gender, and national identity, hinting towards alternative views on alterity, the state of being different or other, and community. Through Chinatowns and Chinese people, the novels both disclose and condemn racism in Latin America. On another level, these novels also shed light on China's economic and political role in Latin America today, reflecting on the structures which have intensified the economic, political, and, to a lesser extent, cultural exchange between the regions. The novels thus depict the changing demographic landscapes of Latin American cities, influenced by Chinese engagement in the region and informed by racism. Thus, the novels are shown to expose and critique binary constructions in the definitions of identity and community in Latin American cities. *Un chino* explores the role and impact of the different communities that coexist in Buenos Aires, whilst *El mármol* questions the notion of community through its depiction of a biased discourse of self-identity. Finally, *Verde Shanghai* challenges any notion of difference between self and other. I argue that the three novels disclose the nuances of the word 'chino', linked to the marketization of the Chinatowns in Buenos Aires and Mexico and the ubiquity of Chinese supermarkets in Buenos Aires 'at a moment when

12 Jean-Luc Nancy, *Being Singular Plural* (Stanford: Stanford University Press, 2000).

13 Graham Huggan, *The Postcolonial Exotic: Marketing the Margins* (London: Routledge, 2001).

14 Sara Ahmed, *Strange Encounters: Embodied Others in Post-Coloniality* (London: Routledge, 2000).

15 Ignacio Aguiló, 'Tropical Buenos Aires: Representations of Race in Argentine Literature during the 2001 Crisis and Its Aftermath', in *Argentina since the 2001 Crisis: Recovering the Past, Reclaiming the Future*, ed. by Cara Levey, Daniel Ozarow, and Christopher Wylde (New York: Palgrave Macmillan, 2014), pp. 177–94; Chisu Teresa Ko, 'From Whiteness to Diversity: Crossing the Racial Threshold in Bicentennial Argentina', *Ethnic and Racial Studies*, 37.14 (2014), pp. 2529–46; Chisu Teresa Ko, '"Argentina te incluye": Asians in Argentina's Multicultural Novels', *Symposium: A Quarterly Journal in Modern Literatures*, 69 1 (2015), pp. 1–13.

16 Anne-Marie Lee-Loy, *Searching for Mr. Chin: Constructions of Nation and the Chinese in West Indian Literature* (Philadelphia: Temple University Press, 2010), p. 24.

17 Mónica G. Moreno Figueroa and Emiko Saldívar Tanaka, '"We Are Not Racists, We Are Mexicans": Privilege, Nationalism and Post-Race Ideology in Mexico', *Critical Sociology*, 42.4–5 (2016), pp. 515–233; Alexandre Emboaba Da Costa, 'Thinking "Post-Racial" Ideology Transnationally: The Contemporary Politics of Race and Indigeneity in the Americas', *Critical Sociology*, 42.4–5 (2016), pp. 475–90.

cultural difference has become a valuable consumer item'.[18] In this sense, the novels display the idea of China as fetishized 'stranger' in Latin America, simultaneously disavowing the racism that informs the literary and cultural discourses of Latin American identity in the region.

In relation to this, Huggan's 'postcolonial exotic', described as 'the oppositional system of postcolonial resistance and the profit-driven system of the transnational culture industries and global trade',[19] further reveals how the idea of 'strangerness' is deployed in these novels to challenge constructions of alterity. Acknowledging Huggan's limitations,[20] these three novels can all be seen in different ways to act through what he terms 'strategic exoticism', 'working from within exoticist codes of representation, either manag[ing] to subvert those codes [...], or succeed[ing] in redeploying them for the purpose of uncovering differential relations of power'.[21]

Indeed, as Selma Siew Li Bidlingmaier observes, Chinatowns are 'often imagined to be spaces where time is suspended, conserving cultural authenticity, traditions, and all cultural artifacts'.[22] This conceptualization allows for a loose deployment of the term, where Chinatowns can be defined around a geographical and economic area and according to a certain imaginary about China.[23] Particularly in the Chinatowns of Latin America, it is possible to find people from Taiwan, the People's Republic of China (PRC), and people from different generations of migrants.[24] Furthermore, it is also possible

18 Huggan, p. 243.

19 Huggan, p. 263.

20 Huggan's anglophone bias, as well as his lack of attention to gender and sexual difference, has been noted by Ana Margarida Martins in *Magic Stones and Flying Snakes: Gender and the 'Postcolonial Exotic' in the Work of Paulina Chiziane and Lídia Jorge* (Oxford: Peter Lang, 2012), pp. 1–62. Furthermore, Huggan's postcolonial exotic is limited with regards to Latin America, as he signals that the 'development of a global alterity industry in which the commodified signs of cultural otherness become a currency to be negotiated and traded by *metropolitan interest groups*', Huggan, p. 259, my italics.

21 Huggan, p. 32.

22 Selma Siew Li Bidlingmaier, 'Spaces of Alterity and Temporal Permanence: The Case of San Francisco's and New York's Chinatowns', in *Selling Ethnicity: Urban Cultural Politics in the Americas*, ed. by Olaf Kaltmeier (Surrey: Ashgate, 2011), pp. 275–86 (p. 275).

23 Wai-ki Luk, *Chinatown in Britain: Diffusions and Concentrations of the British New Wave Chinese Immigration* (Youngstown: Cambria Press, 2008), pp. 8, 80–81.

24 Ien Ang, 'Chinatowns and the Rise of China', *Modern Asian Studies*, 54.4 (2020), pp. 1367–93 <https://doi.org/10.1017/S0026749X19000179>; Luciana Denardi, 'Ser chino en Buenos Aires: Historia, moralidades y cambios en la diáspora china en Argentina', *Horizontes Antropológicos*, 21.43 (2015), pp. 79–103; Luciana Denardi, 'Casetes, redes y banquetes. Prácticas comerciales de chinos, taiwaneses y argentinos en Buenos Aires', *Etnografías Contemporáneas*, 2.2 (2016), pp. 134–60; Luciana Denardi and Alejandra Conconi, 'Reflexiones Metodológicas sobre Investigaciones

to find 'Chinese' products from other Asian countries that are taken to be 'Chinese', such as the maneki-neko figurine, which is originally Japanese. Overall, there is an assumption that things are 'Chinese' in Chinatown. This notion allows us to see how Chinatowns can be perceived, in the words of Ruth Mayer, as 'sites of mystery and sites of fascination',[25] their histories intrinsically linked to Chinese communities and their impact.[26]

By suggesting the *constructedness* of 'China' and the Chinatown as 'exotic', the novels here engage with what Huggan terms the 'postcolonial imperative to demystify "foreign" cultures and, ultimately, to show the constructed nature of discourses about culture itself',[27] thus decentring assumptions regarding a metropolitan centre. While in *Verde Shanghai* this is revealed by the fact that it is impossible for the main character to identify with any race, gender, or culture, in *Un chino* and *El mármol*, it is made available through the text's double-voicedness. As developed by Bakhtin, and as seen

Etnográficas con "Chinos" y "Taiwaneses" en Argentina', *Asian Journal of Latin American Studies*, 31.2 (2018), pp. 41–61; Alejandro Grimson, Gustavo Ng, and Luciana Denardi, 'Las organizaciones de inmigrantes chinos en Argentina', *Migración y Desarrollo*, 14.26 (2016) <http://www.redalyc.org/resumen.oa?id=66046498002> [accessed 1 August 2021]; Lucía Rud, 'Representaciones de las migraciones y diásporas de Asia del Este en el audiovisual argentino', *Nuevo Mundo Mundos Nuevos*, (2020) <https://doi.org/10.4000/nuevomundo.80888>; Luciana Denardi, 'Chinese Migrations to Argentina: Diasporic Bureaucracy, Identifications and Rituals', in *Chinese Immigration in Latin America: Some Cultural Contributions*, ed. by Pablo Baisotti (Newcastle upon Tyne: Cambridge Scholars Publishing, 2020), pp. 69–88; Palma and Ragas; Evelyn Hu-DeHart, 'Chinatowns and Borderlands: Inter-Asian Encounters in the Diaspora', *Modern Asian Studies; Cambridge*, 46.2 (2012), pp. 425–51 <http://dx.doi.org/10.1017/S0026749X11000965>; Rayén Amancay Torres, 'Los barrios chinos en Buenos Aires: entre diversidades, tensiones e interculturalidad', *Diversidad*, 11.7 (2015), pp. 1–24; Luciana Denardi and Chenxi Luo, 'El estudio era el único camino para cambiar mi destino: Posicionamientos de mujeres migrantes chinas en Buenos Aires respecto a su rol en la familia', *Revista del Museo de Antropología*, 15.1 (2022) <https://doi.org/10.31048/1852.4826.v15.n1.35367>.

25 Ruth Mayer, 'Introduction', in *Chinatowns in a Transnational World: Myths and Realities of an Urban Phenomenon*, ed. by Vanessa Künnemann and Ruth Mayer (New York: Routledge, 2011), pp. 1–25 (p. 1); Ruth Mayer, '"The Greatest Novelty of the Age": Fu-Manchu, Chinatown, and the Global City', in *Chinatowns in a Transnational World: Myths and Realities of an Urban Phenomenon*, ed. by Vanessa Künnemann and Ruth Mayer (New York: Routledge, 2011), pp. 116–34 (p. 118).

26 Nicolás Borcoski, 'El nuevo plan del alcalde de Santiago: Un "Barrio chino" en la Estación Central', *La Nación*, 25 May 2018 <http://lanacion.cl/2018/05/25/el-nuevo-plan-del-alcalde-de-santiago-un-barrio-chino-en-la-estacion-central/> [accessed 25 January 2023]. Because of their histories, Chinatowns are different throughout Latin American cities, and countries: in some cases they are linked to older generations of migrants, like in Lima or La Habana, in other cases they are yet unfulfilled projects like a Chinatown in Santiago, Chile.

27 Huggan, p. 19.

in the previous chapter, double-voicedness in the novel reveals the utterance to be 'contradiction-ridden, [a] tension-filled unity of two embattled tendencies in the life of language',[28] a result of the fact that every utterance serves as a point where centrifugal and centripetal forces are brought to bear. Double-voicedness means that two voices are dialogically interrelated in each utterance, allowing for heteroglossia, which serves 'to express authorial intentions but in a refracted way'.[29] Dialogism denies the availability of transcendental unity in the novel, challenging official closure, and opening up meaning and signification.

From this Bahktininian perspective, I argue that Ahmed's 'fetishised others' and Huggan's 'postcolonial exotic' enter a productive dialogue in this chapter. While these theories have not yet been combined in a Latin American context and do not account for the specific implications of race in Latin America,[30] they reveal how the 'China' available in Chinatown is simultaneously constructed and dismissed as 'exotic'. In the novels, the exotic nature of 'China' is deconstructed, challenging ideas of 'difference' and 'distance' associated with China in Latin America, destabilizing the notions of North/South, of an East and West opposition, or a West/non-West binary, through explorations of an 'exotic East' in a 'Western' Latin America. The novels can be seen to simultaneously redeploy their versions of exoticism to critique discourses of national homogeneity and to question structures of domination.

In this sense, the novels also respond to Brett Levinson's and Chisu Teresa Ko's critiques of the perpetuation of binaries, as embodied by orientalism and de-orientalism, which ontologize alterity and cultural difference in Latin America[31] by exposing how 'difference is a *praxis*, an engagement with

28 Mikhail Bakhtin, *The Dialogic Imagination: Four Essays*, ed. by Michael Holquist (Austin: University of Texas Press, 1981), p. 272.

29 Bakhtin, p. 324.

30 Peter Wade, *Race and Ethnicity in Latin America* (London: Pluto Press, 1997), pp. 1–162; Peter Wade, 'Racism and Liberalism: The Dynamics of Inclusion and Exclusion', *Ethnic and Racial Studies*, 38.8 (2015), pp. 1292–97 (pp. 1292–97); Edward Telles and Liza Steele, 'Pigmentocracia en las Américas: ¿cómo se relaciona el logro educativo con el color de piel?', *Proyecto Afrolatin@*, 2012.73 (2012) <http://afrolatinoproject.org/2012/06/28/pigmentocracia-en-las-americas-como-se-relaciona-el-logro-educativo-con-el-color-de-piel/> [accessed 5 January 2021]; Edward Eric Telles and PERLA, *Pigmentocracies: Ethnicity, Race, and Color in Latin America* (Chapel Hill: University of North Carolina Press, 2014).

31 Chisu Teresa Ko, 'Orientalism and De-Orientalism in Contemporary Latin America: Reading César Aira', *TRANSMODERNITY: Journal of Peripheral Cultural Production of the Luso-Hispanic World*, 8.3 (2018), pp. 149–67; Brett Levinson, 'The Death of the Critique of Eurocentrism: Latinamericanism as a Global Praxis/Poiesis', in *Orientalism and Identity in Latin America: Fashioning Self and Other from the (Post) Colonial Margin*, ed. by Erik Camayd-Freixas (Tucson: University of Arizona Press, 2013), pp. 19–34.

alterity, that is also a *poiesis*, a making'.[32] As Gayatri Spivak states in 'Can the Subaltern Speak?', what is 'useful is the sustained and developing work in the *mechanics* of the constitution of the Other'.[33] It is useful because it allows us to expose the arbitrariness that those mechanics may contain. In this way, the novels studied here challenge essentialism and deconstruct fixed notions of the 'other' by exposing the mechanisms at play in the practice and (re) making of difference. In other words, the novels deconstruct how 'China' is made to embody a fetishized other.

By reading these novels through Nancy's ideas on ontology, and in their exposure and decentring of the subject and community, i.e., the way they reveal the mechanisms at play in the practice and (re)making of difference, they can be considered as moving away from the terminology of the 'other' and thinking instead of being-with as 'contiguity, contact, and touch'.[34] In this way, these novels can propose new understandings of the subject, race, and notions of community. In light of this and starting with my analyses of *Un chino* and *El mármol*, this chapter explores how the practice and (re)making of these discourses on nation and race are both exposed and disavowed in these novels.

As Ko and Ignacio Aguiló note, debates about nationhood and race in Argentina need to consider the impact of the 2001 crisis as a key event that led to the interrogation of dominant discourses on 'Argentineness and whiteness'.[35] Indeed, Aguiló, Peter Wade, and others have shown how narratives of whiteness have been central to the production of dominant discourses on the Argentine nation, rooted in the large-scale immigration from Europe and the extinction of indigenous and Afro-Argentine populations in the late nineteenth and early twentieth centuries.[36] Aguiló argues that the crisis led to heightened racism, not only through anti-immigration rhetoric, 'as the racialisation of immigrants allowed the identification of an internal threat – which is also external – on which to blame social malaise',[37] but also through the idea of migrant communities as figures of non-Western exoticism, leading to a growth in interest in ethnic, cultural products and images of diversity.

Since the crisis, institutional and non-institutional efforts have also contributed to the notion of diversity and a multicultural state. Ko states

32 Levinson, p. 33.

33 Gayatri Chakravorty Spivak, 'Can the Subaltern Speak?', in *Marxism and the Interpretation of Culture*, ed. by Cary Nelson and Lawrence Grossberg (Urbana: University of Illinois Press, 1988), pp. 271–313 (p. 294).

34 Marie-Eve Morin, *Jean-Luc Nancy* (Cambridge: Polity, 2012), p. 20.

35 Aguiló, p. 191; Ko, '"Argentina te incluye"'.

36 Aguiló, p. 178; Peter Wade, 'Race in Latin America', in *A Companion to Latin American Anthropology*, ed. by Deborah Poole (Oxford: Blackwell, 2008), pp. 177–92 (p. 182); *Rethinking Race in Modern Argentina: The Shades of the Nation*, ed. by Paulina L. Alberto and Eduardo Elena (New York: Cambridge University Press, 2016).

37 Aguiló, p. 180.

that the economic crisis of 2001 profoundly affected how the Argentines see themselves, while the governments of Néstor Kirchner and Cristina Fernández replaced an 'Argentine exceptionalism' with a 'Latin Americanist' position, and the global pursuit of diversity created a new space for formerly marginalized peoples.[38] Also following Ahmed, she argues that the challenge to Argentina's myth of whiteness embodies what she describes as a shift from the notion of 'stranger danger' to 'welcoming the stranger' typical in contemporary multiculturalism.[39] That is, the dominant subject retains its normativity and requires the stranger to inhabit degrees of subalternity. Ko also observes how the multicultural project in Argentina has mostly excluded the Chinese.[40] Not only were they excluded from the 2010 Bicentennial National Census, but there is a circular omission and minimization of the Asian population that rests on the presumption of their insignificance to the country's demographic.[41] As Ko explains, the estimates of the Asian population in Argentina are usually outdated and limited in scope as they can, for example, overlook those who do not participate actively in ethnic associations, or they ignore people of mixed descent and Argentine nationals.[42] Within this context, Ko sees multicultural novels in Argentina as addressing the question of whom the Argentine nation includes. They also uncover the violent process of Argentina's whitening, something also recognized by Aguiló.[43] Indeed, as we shall now see, both *Un chino* and *El mármol* engage in this debate.

Mapping Diversity in Chinatown: *Un chino en bicicleta*, by Ariel Magnus

Un chino was written by the writer, academic, translator, and journalist Ariel Magnus (1975–) and won the prize *La Otra Orilla* upon its release in 2007.[44] Building on Chisu Teresa Ko's and Héctor Hoyos's analyses, the novel can be linked to the dynamics of globalization,[45] and read as part of Argentina's post-2001 'multicultural turn', that increased the visibility of and granted

38 Ko, 'From Whiteness to Diversity', p. 2530.

39 Ko, '"Argentina te incluye"', p. 3.

40 Chisu Teresa Ko, 'Between Foreigners and Heroes: Asian-Argentines in a Multicultural Nation', in *Rethinking Race in Modern Argentina*, ed. by Eduardo Elena and Paulina L. Alberto (New York: Cambridge University Press, 2016), pp. 268–88 (p. 277).

41 Mara Loveman, *National Colors: Racial Classification and the State in Latin America* (Oxford: Oxford University Press, 2014), p. 200; Ko, 'Between Foreigners and Heroes: Asian-Argentines in a Multicultural Nation', p. 277.

42 Ko, 'Between Foreigners and Heroes: Asian-Argentines in a Multicultural Nation', p. 272.

43 Aguiló, p. 185; Ko, '"Argentina te incluye"', p. 3; See also Erika Denise Edwards, 'The Making of a White Nation: The Disappearance of the Black Population in Argentina', *History Compass*, 16.7 (2018), e12456 <https://doi.org/10.1111/hic3.12456>.

44 Héctor Hoyos, 'Orientalismo, globalización e imaginarios transpacíficos en la novela latinoamericana actual', *Cuadernos de literatura*, 17.34 (2013), pp. 82–105 (p. 94).

45 Hoyos, p. 84.

unprecedented protagonism to racial others in Argentine culture and public life, particularly those who were previously marginalized by discourses of the nation's whiteness.[46] Drawing on the ostensibly essentialist representations of the Chinese available in the novel, the text exposes the conflicting nature of such representations based on 'the lay belief that social categories possess underlying attributes that are immutable and are indicative of the characteristic of group members'.[47] Through diverse epigraphs, the novel reveals the ideology of an implied author who is aware and critical of the essentialist discourses on China that the main male narrator espouses. In other words, the text challenges the existence of any 'underlying attribute' in its understandings of alterity, community, and the subject.

Un chino en bicicleta opens with the main protagonist and narrator, Ramiro Valestra, being kidnapped from the Courts of Justice in Buenos Aires, establishing a corrupt and frail justice system not only through the failure of the security system itself but also by Valestra's reflections. Through his use of slang and expressions that reveal his disillusionment with life in general, the reader learns that Valestra is a disheartened young man who had been called to trial as a witness and seemed paradoxically quite relaxed about being kidnapped. Mainly through Valestra's first person testimony, the reader learns about the way in which he is taken to the *barrio chino* in the Belgrano neighbourhood by Li, nicknamed 'Fosforito', his abductor, who stands accused of igniting a series of fires in the city. Although Li has brought Valestra there by force, he asks Valestra to help him find the real culprit of the fires. The reader later learns that Valestra has been laid off from his job, his father has been diagnosed with cancer, and his girlfriend has left him for his best friend. Valestra decides to stay in the *barrio chino*, where he makes friends, falls in love, and ultimately remains.

In the *barrio chino*, Valestra is shown around traditional 'oriental' places such as Chinese restaurants,[48] a practitioner of Chinese medicine, and a temple, revealing an 'unknown' world right on his doorstep. Even though he experiences and becomes part of this 'other world', symbolized by his falling

46 Ko, '"Argentina te incluye"', pp. 1–3; Chisu Teresa Ko, 'Toward Asian Argentine Studies', *Latin American Research Review*, 51.4 (2016), pp. 271–89 (p. 201); Maria Montt Strabucchi and Carol Chan, 'Questioning the Conditional Visibility of the Chinese: (Non)Normative Representations of China and Chineseness in Chilean Cultural Productions', *Journal of Chinese Overseas*, 16.1 (2020), pp. 90–116 <https://doi.org/10.1163/17932548-12341414>.

47 Melody M. Chao and Franki Y. H. Kung, 'An Essentialism Perspective on Intercultural Processes', *Asian Journal of Social Psychology*, 18.2 (2015), pp. 91–100 (p. 91).

48 See, among others, Carol Chan and Maria Montt Strabucchi, 'Creating and Negotiating "Chineseness" through Chinese Restaurants in Santiago, Chile', in *American Chinese Restaurants: Society, Culture and Consumption*, ed. by Jenny Banh and Haiming Liu (New York: Routledge, 2020), pp. 3–25.

in love with a 'local', he continues to think of himself as part of a 'Western' Argentine community. Even when Valestra suggests that his perception of the Chinese is changing, through expressions such as 'la decoración, un bochinche de rojo y dorado, me pareció de lo más sobria',[49] he continues to define himself in contrast to the Chinese. For example, he contrasts his reaction, that of a 'clásico argentino histérico',[50] with a stereotypical Chinese one, 'que prefieren pensar que llueve para no ver que lo están meando, ellos lo llaman budismo zen',[51] a play on a well-known graffiti popularized by Uruguayan writer Eduardo Galeano, which states 'nos mean y la prensa dice que llueve'. Continuously using inappropriate expressions that he seems to find amusing and perhaps ironic, including the latter, he remains resolutely within the dichotomies of same/other and East/West while also confusing Chinese and Japanese traditions.

Valestra works through the familiarity of the 'stranger', ignoring the histories that inform the relationship that led him to perceive them as 'strangers' in the first place. However, a critique of this 'ontology of strangers' is simultaneously disclosed through epigraphs that reveal an implied author's ideology. The epigraphs are selected from diverse sources, including theorists, philosophers, writers, films, and popular culture. He curates them, choosing European, Chinese, Latin American, Argentine, and indigenous sources, such as Mozi, Mao Zedong, Marco Polo, the Mesoamerican Popol Vuh, the popular musical humour band Les Luthiers and Jorge Luis Borges. The novel uses them to critique Valestra's dismissal of the histories of racism and power imbalance and the essentialism that informs the construction of the discourses embodied by the protagonist.

In this sense, the novel engages with Huggan's 'postcolonial exotic', as Valestra's presentation of the cultural other is 'effectively *repoliticised*'[52] by Magnus in order to critique discourses on strangers that have been informed by differential power relations within contexts of globalization and multiculturality. Valestra suggests a worldview that commits itself to giving a voice to minorities and the injustice of their living conditions. However, through highly humorous discourses, the novel simultaneously reveals him to be ignorant of those people's 'real' conditions and forms of sociality.[53] As Ko shows, although Valestra 'believes that he understands the "authentic" Chinatown and is eager to share his insight with other Argentines, whom he now considers ignorant and culturally insensitive',[54] he 'continue[s] to

49 Ariel Magnus, *Un chino en bicicleta* (Bogota: Grupo Editorial Norma, 2007), p. 46.

50 Magnus, p. 185.

51 Magnus, p. 185.

52 Huggan, pp. ix–x.

53 Soledad Pereyra, 'Terrorismos postautónomos en la literatura argentina actual, en torno a Washington Cucurto, escritor' (unpublished doctoral dissertation, Albert Ludwigs Universität Freiburg i. Br., 2010), p. 183.

54 Ko, '"Argentina te incluye"', p. 8.

construct the *chinos* at [...] [his] own whim'[55] with his narration 'persistently reducing the other to an essentialised and orientalised figure'.[56]

Ko questions the 'deeply flawed places' where Valestra finds 'the truth',[57] describing Chinatown as the emblematic site of an exoticized other. There, Valestra learns that all Chinese are not the same and that the first 'Chinese' actor in Argentina, Lito Ming, is actually of Japanese descent.[58] From this perspective, 'China' emerges as a metonym of the exotic 'other'. Indeed, Lito Ming also enhances the idea of the *barrio chino* as a site of exoticism, as his current job is eating by the window of a Chinese restaurant to confer authenticity on the place, as noted by Ko.[59] The novel again evokes Huggan's 'postcolonial exotic', where 'minorities are encouraged, in some cases obliged [for economic reasons], to stage their racial/ethnic identities in keeping with white stereotypical perceptions of an exotic cultural other'.[60] Furthermore, the abbreviation 'Lito' can be a Latin American Spanish nickname, although it also encompasses the possibility of being a Chinese name. In this sense, Lito Ming embodies the description that Mónica Lacarrieu and Andrea Pappier give of the Chinatown: a place for intercultural consumption and the staging of difference.[61]

Chinese immigration and the *barrio chino* are relatively recent phenomena in Argentina. An initial migration current occurred towards the end of the nineteenth and at the beginning of the twentieth centuries due to struggles in China. At the same time, the presence of Chinese in the Belgrano neighbourhood and the establishment of the *barrio chino* began in the 1980s with (Taiwanese) Chinese immigrants.[62] As Luciana Denardi argues, to be 'Chinese' in Buenos Aires has various meanings: a strict meaning regarding

55 Ko, '"Argentina te incluye"', p. 11.
56 Ko, '"Argentina te incluye"', p. 5.
57 Ko, '"Argentina te incluye"', p. 7.
58 Magnus, p. 53.
59 Ko, '"Argentina te incluye"', p. 7.
60 Huggan, p. 95.
61 Mónica Lacarrieu, '"... De todos lados y de ningún lado...": Visibles/visibilizados e invisibles/invisibilizados en busca de un lugar en la Buenos Aires del siglo XXI', *Kairos*, 11 (2002) <http://www.revistakairos.org/k11-07.htm> [accessed 1 August 2021]; Andrea Pappier, 'Inmigración china en Argentina: el barrio chino de Bs As como caso de estudio intercultural' (presented at the Asociación Latinoamericana de Estudios de Asia y África, XIII Congreso Internacional de ALADAA, Bogota, 2011).
62 Laura Bogado Bordazar, 'Migraciones internacionales: Influencia de la migración china en el Río de la Plata' (unpublished master's dissertation, Universidad Nacional de La Plata, 2002); Susana Sassone and Carolina Mera, 'Barrios de migrantes en Buenos Aires: Identidad, cultura y cohesión socioterritorial', *Réseau Amérique Latine*, (2006), pp. 1–14 (p. 6); Bernardo Trejos and Lan-Hung Nora Chiang, 'Young Taiwanese Immigration to Argentina: The Challenges of Adaptation, Self Identity and Returning', *International Journal of Asia-Pacific Studies*, 8.2 (2012), pp. 113–43 (pp. 117, 118); Amancay Torres; Denardi and Conconi.

people from the PRC and a broader meaning, which includes Taiwanese communities.[63] The existing differences between the Chinese groups are, however, invisible in the *barrio chino* and cultural events across the city.

The *barrio chino* of Buenos Aires contains temples, restaurants, and shops that sell articles from China, as well as from other Asian and Latin American countries. It was founded as a *barrio chino* in 2005 for 'touristic and promotional purposes',[64] and it appears regularly in the press and tourist guides to Buenos Aires.[65] It is described as one of the city's attractions and is also promoted by its local government.[66] The website's description of 'typical restaurants' and 'typical products' evokes an essentialist 'orient'. It has also been described as a place to find 'exotic' products and 'extremely rare treats'.[67] These websites and texts contribute to the city's imaginary of the Chinatown, providing a different level of discourse regarding the understanding of 'chino' available in Buenos Aires.

In her study on multiculturalism in Buenos Aires, in which she examines the celebration of the Chinese New Year in the *barrio chino* and its sponsorship by the city, Lacarrieu terms this 'light multiculturalism', according to which the minority group conforms to a schematic image of their country of origin which coincides with one promoted for tourism.[68] The Chinatown is thus precisely what Huggan describes as a staging through which the arguably 'white stereotypical perception of an exotic cultural other'[69] can be maintained and consumed. Indeed, the visibility of race increased after the economic crisis. One of its effects was the growing interest of certain sectors of Buenos Aires's middle class in 'ethnic cultural products and images of diversity'.[70] In this context, the shifting uses of the word 'chino' in Latin America and Chinatown worldwide require further clarification to stabilize

63 Denardi, 'Ser chino en Buenos Aires: Historia, moralidades y cambios en la diáspora china en Argentina', p. 89.

64 'Barrio Chino Belgrano Buenos Aires Argentina', *Barrio Chino* <http://www.barriochino.net/index.php/10-tapa/30-barriochinonet-barrio-chino-belgrano-buenos-aires-argentina> [accessed 1 July 2021]; 'Barrio Chino en Belgrano', *Mi Belgrano* <http://www.mibelgrano.com.ar/barriochinovie.htm> [accessed 1 July 2021].

65 María del Carmen González Viaña, 'Cambios en la vocación del territorio. Estudio de tres enclaves porteños: Avenida de Mayo, La Boca y Barrio Chino' (unpublished doctoral dissertation, Universidad Complutense de Madrid, 2014), p. 403.

66 González Viaña, pp. 17, 518. A new *barrio chino* was inaugurated in 2015 in Tigre (Greater Buenos Aires); Amancay Torres, pp. 19–21.

67 Verónica Ocvirk, 'Guía para conocer lo mejor del Chinatown porteño', *Revista OhLaLá!* <http://www.revistaohlala.com/1348595-guia-para-conocer-lo-mejor-del-chinatown-porteno> [accessed 1 May 2021].

68 Lacarrieu.

69 Huggan, p. 95.

70 Aguiló, p. 184.

their tendency to shift meaning between academic studies and, indeed, across branches of literary studies.

In Latin America, the words 'oriental' and 'chino' are often wandering signifiers that mean 'Far East Asian'. Specifically, for the case of Argentina, Ko argues that Argentines consider Asians' differences to be both 'insurmountable and incomprehensible', evidenced through the use of 'oriental' in everyday language and the interchangeability of 'chino', 'japonés' and 'coreano'.[71] The word 'chino' is effectively used in this way and, as Ko argues, sometimes followed by the insult 'de mierda'. Ko states that in Argentina, the word 'chino' is a permeable, derogatory term for Asians and that the category 'chino' creates a pejorative meaning, which can then produce a semantically charged socio-racial boundary, structuring hierarchies of difference in Argentina.[72] According to Ko, the permeability of the term 'chino', ascribed by the dominant subject, would always be on the threshold of divergent meanings informed by a notion of the Chinese immigrant as 'entirely undesirable', revealing the complex mechanisms of multiculturality.[73] From this perspective, then, 'chino' might *not* signify something entirely undesirable. In other words, the undesirability of the Chinese and the marketization of cultural differences embody the paradox of the postcolonial exotic. This, in turn, informs the imaginaries and physical aspects of the Chinatown as represented in *Un chino.*

Hoyos argues that the novel's 'imprecise' recreation of the 'Orient' is linked to the image of China held by a 'certain Latin American middle class'.[74] He argues that the novel offers an inflection point in China's recognition process: instead of 'luxurious and depersonalised *chinoiserie*', it makes available a China that manifests itself through cheap products. This goes hand in hand with the depiction of Valestra's growing familiarity with the *barrio chino*,[75] an image informed by the increased economic and cultural engagement between the PRC in Latin America.[76] As the novel shows, the recognition of China in this context continues to be, at least in Argentina, informed by xenophobic discourses. Valestra embodies traditional depictions of the 'Argentine' attitude towards the Chinese in Buenos Aires, as described by Florencia Alam, where the ignorance of Spanish is perceived to be representative of the Chinese refusal to integrate, hence becoming linked to a 'justified' exclusion, to conspiracy, threat, and fears of invasion.[77]

71 Ko, '"Argentina te incluye"', p. 2.
72 Ko, 'From Whiteness to Diversity', pp. 2533, 2538.
73 Ko, 'From Whiteness to Diversity', p. 2543.
74 Hoyos, p. 99.
75 Hoyos, p. 99.
76 Robert Evan Ellis, *China on the Ground in Latin America: Challenges for the Chinese and Impacts on the Region* (New York: Palgrave Macmillan, 2014), pp. 3–12.
77 Florencia Alam, 'Representaciones sociolingüísticas en la comunidad inmigrante chino-taiwanesa: Posibles abordajes para la enseñanza' (presented at the IV Coloquio

For example, when visiting his former house (after some time in the *barrio chino*, he gains sufficient independence to move around freely), Valestra is not recognized by his alcoholic mother, who says to him '[...] pasa que los chinos de al lado no me dejan vivir, los chinos se llevaron a mi hijo, los vechinos [sic] de mierda, ellos tienen la culpa de todo...'[78] After this scene, which displays the racism experienced by the Chinese community, he leaves his house and feels closer to the Chinese family who have just moved to his neighbourhood and whom he greets with a 'hello' in Chinese.[79] This also recalls the fact that not all the Chinese are concentrated spatially within the *barrio chino*, hence suggesting a new spatial configuration of immigrants in Buenos Aires. Valestra and his mother are presented in contrast: her intoxicated rant embodies white Argentina's racism and xenophobia towards the Chinese, and she no longer recognizes Valestra, who greets their Chinese neighbours in a friendly manner. On one level, Valestra represents the multicultural 'new Argentina' in contrast to his mother, who embodies a normative subject who is nationalistic and racist. However, he continues to construct the Chinese in essentialist terms. The novel thus shows how, despite the difference of opinions between Valestra and his mother, he continues to essentialize in less obvious ways. From this perspective, the novel reveals the essentialism within and beyond the ideas of *mestizaje*. While Valestra can be considered *mestizo*, his biased views reveal how the notion of mixture can continue to essentialize difference.

Unable to succeed in neoliberal Buenos Aires, Valestra feels ironically 'at home' in a place he arguably misinterprets. 'Aware' of the Chinese presence in Buenos Aires, in the *barrio chino* and beyond, he speculates about Chinese domination of the world, only to conclude that things would not change much; 'menos hamburguesa y más chao fan, menos MTV y más karaoke',[80] the latter a Japanese word. Valestra seemingly celebrates a multicultural Buenos Aires contrary to the 'ethnic and racial fears of the stereotypically white Porteño discourse'.[81] In his attempt to clarify the misconstructions around the Chinese in Argentina, Valestra equates Latin American and Asian cultures[82] and thus essentializes both. In this way, while he seems to undermine a Eurocentric structure of power, he does not stop thinking of himself as Argentine and continues to construct the Chinese as what Ahmed would term 'fetishised strangers'. By referring to China through 'chao fan', a common fried rice dish in Chinese American and Latin American Chinese cuisine, and 'karaoke', which is also very popular in Japanese and Korean

CELU: La interculturalidad y la internacionalización en las prácticas evaluativas, Universidad Nacional del Litoral, Santa Fe, 2008).

78 Magnus, p. 193.

79 Magnus, p. 194.

80 Magnus, p. 95.

81 Aguiló, p. 183.

82 Magnus, p. 146.

communities, he seemingly ignores the histories through which China has come to be associated with those terms. He thus exposes the complex and fragmented identity of an Argentine middle-class man whose own experiences are inflected by ignorance and cultural incompetence.

Through the *barrio chino*, Valestra displays how racial meanings are produced, reiterated and normalized. The novel highlights the ways in which Argentine official discourses and media help to perpetuate racial hierarchies and essentialist understandings of culture and race. This emerges through Valestra's comments about the news coverage of *Crónica TV*, or his ironic remark on medical doctors who declare Li insane: 'no todo está perdido para el mundo occidental mientras dos personas se puedan poner de acuerdo para declarar insana a una tercera.'[83] And within this context, he is economically displaced: unable to find a job and economic success, he is happy to abandon his previous life and stay in the *barrio chino*. In other words, although Valestra is critical of the injustices of the neoliberal dynamics of Argentina, he continues to describe the Chinese in asymmetric and discriminatory terms. This emerges, for example, when he refers to Chinese women with euphemistic invented names as 'Flor de Loto' and 'Jazmín de Jade',[84] a mocking form of mimicry that we have also seen in *La mujer en la Muralla*, that embodies discourses of essentialist otherness.

Ko argues that Valestra 'certainly want[s] to include Asians in Argentina, but by confirming [...] [its] version of hyperorientalized Asians, the *novel* [...] fail[s] to realize [...] [its] best intentions'.[85] However, it is arguably Valestra who 'fails', while an implied narrator critiques his ideology through the epigraphs included in most of the chapters, a distinctive feature of the novel. Valestra's limited views are pointed out to the reader by an implied author who is revealed through the epigraphs. I argue that a new notion of alterity and community emerges precisely through the inclusion of epigraphs.

Hoyos describes the epigraphs as one of the most original characteristics of the novel, as they invite speculative considerations, as well as a less abstract approximation of the story, due to the reader's identification with the protagonist, a middle-class Latin American.[86] He claims that they allow the readers to situate themselves in Valestra's shoes while at the same time positioning that experience in the broader context of relations between East and West. For Hoyos, the epigraphs try to reconfigure the relationship between readers and that which is Chinese by showing truth in foolishness, prejudice in children's songs, or a long tradition of thoughtless assumptions about the East.

These epigraphs create a second narrative beyond the main story, making the ideology of the otherwise silent implied author available. Furthermore, these epigraphs establish a narrative distance between the implied author and

83 Magnus, p. 22.
84 Magnus, p. 37.
85 Ko, '"Argentina te incluye"', p. 12, my italics.
86 Hoyos, p. 96.

the narrator, providing a context through which different ideologies can be regarded as conflicting. In this way, a Bakhtinian double-voicedness emerges through the epigraphs, which reframe Valestra and his utterances alongside longer and broader histories and essentialist discourses of asymmetry and discrimination. By this exposure, the implied author can be regarded as opposing Valestra's worldview while simultaneously taking an ironic stance towards the common usage of Chinese proverbs as stereotypical 'Chinese wisdom'.

The epigraphs thus reveal new dimensions to the content of each chapter they introduce, as the following examples show. The novel's first epigraph is a quote by Victor Segalen, read in relation to Segalen's 'Essay on the Exoticism', where he proposes that exoticism is 'nothing other than the notion of difference, the perception of diversity, the knowledge that something is other than one's self; and Exoticism's power is nothing other than the ability to conceive otherwise'.[87] The novel emphasizes the 'ability to conceive otherwise' which, for Valestra, seems to be impossible. On one level, the implied author can hint at Valestra's trip to an 'exotic China' situated in the *barrio chino* while simultaneously revealing this 'China' to be a constructed other. Valestra's unreliable narration contrasts with the recognition of what is 'real', emphasizing the constructedness of discourses.

Another example is given in the chapter that marks the beginning of Valestra's relationship with Yintai, his Sino-Cuban girlfriend, and which is preceded by an epigraph quoting from a song popular through, among others, the television show *Topo Gigio*:

> En un bosque de la China
> La chinita se perdió
> Y como yo andaba perdido
> Nos encontramos los dos.

Popular in Latin America since the 1960s, many generations have sung this song about a meeting between a lost Chinese woman who encounters a lost (most probably) man in the woods. However, the song's racialized and gendered naming of the Chinese woman, since the diminutive 'chinita' implies a degree of subordination which is not usually accredited as racist and sexist, has not been commented upon. In this context, the implied author draws on the ongoing history of the normalization of racial constructions in Latin America, which does not consider the term 'chinita' or 'chinito' as a racist way of referring to Chinese people. Even if Valestra does not use the term to refer to Yintai, or Chinese people, he continues to think of her as a 'fetishized other'. The 'oriental' woman is sexualized, in line with stereotypical gendered representations of Asian women (associated with the idea of the

87 Victor Segalen, *Essay on Exoticism: An Aesthetics of Diversity*, trans. by Yaël Rachel Schlick (Durham: Duke University Press, 2002), p. 19.

'geisha' or hentai manga). The epigraphs concerning the following text can be seen to demand an awareness of essentialism, histories of power imbalance and racialized constructions, which in turn can reveal the construction of fetishized strangers.

Through the epigraphs and double-voicedness, the novel includes reflections on other migrant communities in Buenos Aires and the conflicts between them. For example, not only is Valestra's ex-girlfriend Jewish but the arsonists behind the fires are revealed to be from the Jewish community, according to what Li tells Valestra. They allegedly intended to punish the Chinese for taking over certain areas of the city they had previously dominated. Other examples appear through the mention of Brazilians, Galicians, and Bolivians in the city. Valestra's biased and inappropriate appraisals of other cultures contrast markedly with the actual conflicts between migrant communities revealed in the novel:

> Mi pálpito es que los porteños en general no solemos hacer muchas diferencias entre las nacionalidades, bien lejos están los chinos y un poco más acá los turcos, después vienen en el sur los tanos y en el norte los piratas, de los Pirineos para acá sólo hay Gallegos y del Amazonas para abajo son todos brazucas o bolitas, más de uno ni se debe haber dado cuenta de que en el Once los coreanos ya casi desplazaron a los judíos, [...].[88]

In the above quotation, Valestra explicitly outlines the city's landscape through a self-other dichotomy. In his desire to make all migrant communities equal, he not only presents them in racist and derogatory terms, but he also presents them in contrast to his being 'porteño' (from the City of Buenos Aires), which, furthermore, elevates the 'porteños' in contrast to the rest of Argentina. This recalls what Tanja Bastia observes about Buenos Aires, where the city and the nation are often in conflict.[89] As she demonstrates, 'ethnicity continues to be used to demarcate "others," particularly migrants, with the purpose to delegitimise their claims to space'.[90] As Bastia shows, while the state has, at least in principle, improved the conditions of migrants, this contrasts with how the city's representatives blame migration from neighbouring countries (which is the focus of her study) for the growth of informal settlements.

In this sense, Valestra's narration brings new dimensions into discussion, as it exposes conflicts that go beyond the state and the city, and migration from neighbouring countries, in its disclosure of struggles at a very local level. The novel thus emphasizes the heterogeneity of Buenos Aires and how these conflicts are informed by imaginaries and stereotypes linked to those communities. This, for example, emerges again in the following extract, a

88 Magnus, p. 148.

89 Tanja Bastia, 'Transnational Migration and Urban Informality: Ethnicity in Buenos Aires' Informal Settlements', *Urban Studies*, (2014), pp. 1–16 (p. 2).

90 Bastia, p. 7.

speech made by an Argentine woman regarding the fires supposedly lit by Li, as she explains why there were no witnesses at Li's trial,

> Por miedo a la mafia. Son gente peligrosa. Hoy te incendian el negocio, mañana te incendian a vos. Eso está en el carácter de los chinos. Yo estuve investigando en Internet y es así, el fuego para ellos es como un juego, está en su cultura, es algo que traen de nacimiento. Es como los judíos, que tienen problemas de estómago y se mueren de cáncer. Bueno, a ellos les gusta el fuego y muchos terminan pirómanos.[91]

This evokes common myths about the Chinese in Argentina, as exposed by Julia Reagan in her documentary *Argenchino*,[92] such as that Chinese supermarkets sell stolen goods or that they are a mafia.

Moreover, state campaigns risk essentializing race as visible and biological, and the multicultural discourse of the nation continues to preserve the 'we' by requiring 'strangers' to fit in modes of difference, as Ko notes.[93] Yet *Un chino* goes beyond this discourse and explores the coexistence of communities in the city and the relationships within those communities. For example, when Li explains to Valestra that the Jewish communities are responsible for the fires, Li refers not only to the conflicts between those communities but also to how the Jewish community is not aware of the differences between Chinese and Korean communities, and to how the Chinese are not aware of the differences among Ashkenazi and Sephardic Jews.[94] In this way, the novel reflects on the constructedness of 'communities', which makes the conflicts within them invisible. As Silvia Rivera Cusicanqui argues in the case of Bolivia, multiculturalism has been the concealing mechanism par excellence of new forms of colonization.[95] The novel thus discloses how discourses of multiculturalism may indeed be hegemonic and dismissive of internal differences and distinct identities.

In this way, through indirect dialogue between the narrator and the implied author and the narrator's and character's own voices, the novel opens the discussion regarding the construction and repetition of the stereotype itself. For Homi Bhabha, the stereotype is an ideological operation that constructs people or groups as 'the other'. Building on Sigmund Freud and Jacques Lacan's psychoanalysis and semiotics, as well as the ambivalent fetish figure, Bhabha shows how the stereotype proclaims fixity while the repetition of the stereotype questions that same fixity.[96] However he fails to

91 Magnus, pp. 188–89.

92 *Argenchino*, dir. by Julia Reagan, 2009.

93 Ko, '"Argentina te incluye"', p. 3.

94 Magnus, p. 205.

95 Silvia Rivera Cusicanqui, 'Ch'ixinakax Utxiwa: A Reflection on the Practices and Discourses of Decolonization', *South Atlantic Quarterly*, 111.1 (2012), pp. 95–109 (p. 99).

96 Homi K. Bhabha, *The Location of Culture* (Oxon: Routledge, 1994), p. 66.

recognize the 'specific role played by gendered power relations in historically male-protagonized negotiations of cultural and political authority'.[97] In this sense, similar to what Bhabha maintains regarding the stereotype, the novel both recognizes and disavows racial and cultural differences. Thus, it can be regarded as an ironic and paradoxical rewriting of discourses of otherness. In this sense, the absence of Asians that Ko objects to might be exactly what the implied author denounces. Magnus works throughout this paradox, engaging not only with racial and cultural differences but also with the literary market.

Magnus wrote this novel after relinquishing his intention to write a realist account of the Chinese community in Buenos Aires; an idea his publishers rejected.[98] Magnus thus seems to strategically exoticize 'Chinatown' as a way of mocking the lack of interest from Buenos Aires publishing houses. Regarding his choice, Magnus states that he decided to write on the subject because:

> [...] me atrevería a decir que es el país más importante del mundo. Más que un chino o la China, el protagonista es nuestra (mi) visión de los chinos y la China. Desde ahí está narrada la novela, que además ocurre en el barrio chino de Buenos Aires, que me atrevería a decir que es el menos importante del mundo.[99]

Magnus thus exposes the relative unimportance of the *barrio chino* within a global imaginary while at the same time suggesting that he frames the novel this way for his own reasons. Through Valestra's narration, China is shown to be perceived as the unknown, a notion reinforced by this book, which exposes how 'different' China is perceived to be even while experienced as spatially close. In his appraisal of the novel, for example, Michel Emiliano Nieva states that the protagonist does not have to travel far to find the unknown. By doing so, he explicitly associates Chinatown with the unknown, yet one that is only blocks away from 'home'.[100] While Magnus explains the relative importance of China and the Buenos Aires *barrio chino*, he also seems to maintain notions of centre and periphery. Moreover, the above quotation presents a new, if personal, 'authorial voice' on the Chinese and China in Buenos Aires.

However, the fact that Magnus explains that he wrote the novel only after he had tried to write a realist account casts a different light on his statement. Just as Huggan argues for Arundhati Roy's *The God of Small Things*, Valestra

97 Hilary Owen, *Mother Africa, Father Marx: Women's Writing of Mozambique, 1948–2002* (Lewisburg: Bucknell University Press, 2007), p. 29.

98 Olman Castro, 'Un chino en bicicleta da fama a un argentino', *Revista Perfil*, 2008 <http://wvw.revistaperfil.com/node/4617> [accessed 1 August 2021].

99 'Premian la novela de un argentino', *La Nación*, 21 July 2007, section Cultura <http://www.lanacion.com.ar/945949-premian-la-novela-de-un-argentino> [accessed 1 May 2021].

100 Michel Emiliano Nieva, 'Ariel Magnus: Un chino en bicicleta', *Soles Digitial*, (2009) <http://www.solesdigital.com.ar/libros/magnus.html> [accessed 1 May 2021].

can be seen to employ 'strategic exoticism', 'designed to trap the unwary reader into complicity with Orientalisms of which the novel so hauntingly relates'.[101] While Roy is an Indian author and Valestra is a 'white' narrator, the novel reveals how 'myths' are constructed through and beyond white and non-white exoticisms. The novel builds on the 'myth', only to ultimately subvert it. Magnus hence deposits his complete potential imaginary about 'China' into the novel, playing with what is 'expected' of the Chinese, feeding into an imaginary of 'China' in Argentina.

This exposure of imaginaries is emphasized through an unexpected intertextual reference. Valestra is introduced to a Chinese professor, who tells him he is studying the 'Grupo Buenos Aires de Shangai', offering an ironic reworking of the 'Shangai group' to which, as seen in the previous chapter, Aira and Alberto Laiseca were both linked. The novel turns the global map upside down, something that Francine Maisello has explored in Argentine literature, displacing location and knowledge, questioning not only the paradigms and preconceptions of China available in Argentina but also those of Argentina available to the Chinese.[102] The character then explains the work of this literary group and amusingly offers altered descriptions of *Una novela china* and *La mujer en la Muralla*. This quote exemplifies the humour that is present throughout the novel, while the implied author plays with and ironically mocks the Argentine tradition of *gaucho* literature,

> [...] después estaba *Una novela argentina* de Po-Fu-Chan, que es la historia de un gaucho gay que cría a un indiecito para hacerlo su esclavo sexual pero cuando el chico tiene edad de servirlo Pu-Toh (así se llama el gaucho) se da cuenta de que lo que en realidad le gustan son las vacas; y por último estaba *La mujer en la toldería* de Lai Ts Chiá, una historia de Argentina en clave gauchesco-pornográfica con muchos pasajes de mal gusto (por ejemplo aquel en que el autor cita uno de sus libros anteriores) pero con una frase memorable: "Cuan grande es el parecido entre un Maestro de verdad y un loco. La única diferencia consiste en que uno es un loco y el otro un Maestro."[103]

As we see here, the narrator makes up names, toying with the masculinity of the *gaucho*, as the name 'Pu-toh' brings to mind a male prostitute and can also be used to refer to a gay man. The novel thus takes *Una novela china* and subverts the story on every level by changing genders, events, and its title. Regarding *La mujer en la Muralla*, it also brings the text to Latin America through the figure of the *toldería* (camp of indigenous awnings or huts), with the 'Chinese' name of the author recalling 'Laiseca'.

101 Huggan, p. 77.

102 Francine Masiello, *The Art of Transition: Latin American Culture and Neoliberal Crisis* (London: Duke University Press, 2001), p. 7.

103 Magnus, pp. 174–75.

The 'Shangai' group, as seen in the previous chapter, has been regarded as a response to Borges's essay 'El escritor argentino y la tradición',[104] first presented at a conference in 1951 and then published in 1953, which argued for freedom for the Argentinean author from using 'local colour' in literary expression. If in the previous chapter the resort to the 'Orient' was seen to parody the choice of what could still be termed 'foreign local colour', here Magnus subverts the very concept of 'local colour' as a whole by satirically ironizing the Argentine literary tradition and recalling the misunderstandings of cultural translation. Through the figure of the 'gaucho' and its connotations of 'Argentineness', the novel calls into question who is actually Argentine, what 'Argentineness' is and what 'local colour' or 'local essence' are, i.e., nationalist stereotypes.

And the novel finds yet another way of altering the map: the epigraph of that chapter is a quote from the poem 'El Go' by Jorge Luis Borges himself.[105] Here, the implied author chooses a poem whose title is the Japanese name of a game of Chinese origin: Weíqí. The implied author not only refers to the Japanese name through which the Chinese game is known in Latin America, but the poem itself speaks of a labyrinth whose path will never be taken, a glimpse of a reality that will never be understood. The epigraph thus interrogates both the 'Shangai group of Buenos Aires' and the counterfactual, invented possibility of a 'Buenos Aires group of Shanghai' and the partiality and limitations that inform each group's knowledge.

By swapping names, locations, and topics, the professor echoes the cultural misappropriations and misunderstandings that Valestra himself displays. The novel thus allows the reader to view the *barrio chino* as displacing notions of cultural specificity without converting the 'we' into a significant and exclusive identity, but rather opening up the meanings and understandings of community. Following Nancy, the novel can be seen to expose how, within the community as a whole, difference, as diversity, 'is nothing *itself*'.[106] As Nancy explains, cultures do not mix, but rather 'encounter each other, mingle, modify each other, reconfigure each other'.[107] Nancy describes this as *mêlée*, as 'an action rather than a substance';[108] rather than emphasizing an idea of mixture, he favours *mêlée* as a non-definable unity in which each singularity is a *mêlée* of traits.[109] From this perspective, there is no essential community and no essentialism available in the Nancean notion of community. In being-with, what is held in common simultaneously differentiates and distinguishes

104 Jorge Luis Borges, 'El escritor argentino y la tradición', in *Discusión*, essay originally published 1953 (Madrid: Alianza, 1976), pp. 128–37.

105 Originally published in his book *La cifra* (Madrid: Alianza, 1981).

106 Nancy, *Being Singular Plural*, p. 151.

107 Nancy, *Being Singular Plural*, p. 151.

108 Nancy, *Being Singular Plural*, p. 150.

109 Morin, p. 37.

between us.[110] Valestra embodies the discourse of a community that believes in a shared essence. At the same time, the novel exposes how there is no shared essence, emphasizing the conflict that encounters contain and the relational aspect of Valestra's being-there.

In this way, Nancy's notion of the 'inoperative community' as a shared experience of finitude, based on 'being-with',[111] sheds light on the ways through which community operates in *Un chino*. As Ana Luszczynska argues, attempting to locate moments when community flourishes 'allows a glimpse into the possibilities and the power of being, which subverts an often dominating and always totalizing will to essentialize'.[112] Although community resists institution, it still allows us to recognize the moments when the being-with emerges. As Hoyos argues, Valestra's old 'self' disappears through his life in the *barrio chino*, immersed in a Chinese life symbolized by the novel's conclusion, which is presented in untranslated, simplified Chinese characters.[113] From this perspective, all that is left of Valestra is a hybrid future, symbolized by the baby expected by his Sino-Cuban girlfriend. And like Bill Ashcroft, Gareth Griffiths and Helen Tiffin explain, untranslated words have an important function in inscribing difference, as 'the absence of explanation is, therefore, first a sign of distinctiveness, though it merely makes explicit the alterity which is implicit in the gloss'.[114] Even if Valestra continues to essentialize his girlfriend, the pregnancy itself embodies the possibility of openness, made available through love. This recalls Nancy's discussion of love, as it 'renders the inoperative community more accessible to us', as articulated by Joseph Twist.[115]

However, the last chapter's epigraph, a quote from a song from 1967 popularized by a group of Spanish clowns, which ends with the phrase 'chinito tú, chinita yo; y nuestro amol así selá; siemple siemple igual',[116] recalls us to the sense that although Valestra thinks he has understood the other culture, he continues to differentiate based on a racial interpretation and to rely on a self-other dichotomy. This is epitomized in the racist use of 'l' rather than 'r', mocking 'Chinese' pronunciation. Although it suggests a happy ending to the story, an ironic reading of the epigraph shows that

110 Nancy, *Being Singular Plural*, p. 155.

111 Jean-Luc Nancy, *The Inoperative Community* (Minneapolis: University of Minnesota Press, 1991), p. 2.

112 Ana Luszczynska, 'The Opposite of the Concentration Camp: Nancy's Vision of Community', *The New Centennial Review*, 5.3 (2005), pp. 167–205 (pp. 167, 204).

113 Hoyos, p. 97.

114 Bill Ashcroft, Gareth Griffiths, and Helen Tiffin, *The Empire Writes Back: Theory and Practice in Post-Colonial Literatures* (London: Routledge, 2005), p. 64.

115 Joseph Twist, '"The Crossing of Love": The Inoperative Community and Romantic Love in Feridun Zaimoglu's "Fünf klopfende Herzen, wenn die Liebe springt" and Hinterland', *German Life and Letters*, 67.3 (2014), pp. 399–417 (p. 399).

116 Magnus, p. 221.

Valestra is still unable to grasp plurality The estranged gaze of the implied author, available through the epigraph, condemns Valestra as the colonizing white man, as he continues to think of Yintai as a 'fetishised stranger'. Magnus thus makes the reader aware of the asymmetrical, gendered power implications contained in 'strange encounters'.

The novel thus suggests the failure of Valestra's quest to engage with the 'Chinese'. Valestra subordinates his relationships with the Chinese as the stranger to a self/other dichotomy and continues to ontologize the other.[117] Valestra is even disappointed when he becomes aware of the unexotic nature of the Chinese people he encounters.[118] In dialogue with Hoyos, the novel can be seen to shed light on the less celebrated aspects of globalization through its depiction of a biased and prejudiced main character who is never able to totally abandon binarial othering. While exposing the vestiges of a colonial white/Latin American binary, the novel simultaneously points to the incorporation of a new 'other', which still allows for building new discourses of subordination and conflicts between communities. Thus, the novel sheds light on the failure of a multicultural society that continues to ontologize self and 'stranger'.

In his analysis of the novel, Hoyos argues that the text presents an original viewpoint on the relations between East and West.[119] Hoyos stresses how this novel, as well as *Una novela china* by Aira and *Los impostores* by Santiago Gamboa, engages with the anxieties of globalization. He sees these novels' use of humour as a mechanism that reveals social anxiety—the result of losing the economic game of globalization and several other factors. These might include a shift in cultural values or the unpredictable structural changes that globalization might bring, such as China challenging a representative, multiparty democracy like Argentina's as the natural state of things.[120] Hoyos shows the ways in which China passes from mystification to banalization, at once acknowledging that Latin American fiction is aware that these oriental stereotypes are not the 'Orient' but that it has not yet constructed any imaginary with which to replace it.[121]

Ko similarly notes how 'the ubiquity of Asians in contemporary Argentina has permeated the popular imaginary, without inspiring reformulations of nationhood that would include them'.[122] Ko includes *Un chino* within a group of novels in which the 'hyperbolic orientalism' and 'deliberate fictionality' act as a critique of a multiculturalism that continues to grant unequal power to the dominant culture.[123] She argues that the novel reveals 'some uncertainties

117 Ahmed, *Strange Encounters*, p. 6.
118 Magnus, pp. 143, 146.
119 Hoyos, p. 94.
120 Hoyos, pp. 102–3.
121 Hoyos, pp. 100, 103.
122 Ko, '"Argentina te incluye"', p. 11.
123 Ko, '"Argentina te incluye"', pp. 1, 3.

as to Asians' place in the current national narrative that, regardless of its appreciation of diversity, does not grant racial or cultural citizenship to Asian-Argentines'.[124]

However, the novel arguably engages with the prospect of a new imaginary, only to suggest the impossibility of any stable imaginary of 'China'. *Un chino* can be seen to reveal the failure of a multicultural and post-racial community, which is shown to continue to define a national identity through essentialist notions of otherness. From this perspective, the novel can be regarded as critiquing this understanding of community, suggesting a new cosmopolitan identity instead, as developed by Berthold Schoene,[125] in line with Nancy's notion of Being, where the I is necessarily constituted in relation to a plurality.[126] As we shall now see, a critique of a post-racial, multicultural Argentina is also identifiable in César Aira's *El mármol*. However, in *Un chino*, the emphasis is on the community, while in *El mármol*, the focus is on the subject.

Aliens in the City: *El mármol*, by César Aira

El mármol, signed off in 2009, belongs to what has been described by Sandra Contreras as the second period of Aira's writing, characterized by periodical publications, a continuing writing process that does not stop to make corrections until the text is complete; and surprising and unexpected endings.[127] By focusing on the dialogical aspects of the novel, as studied by Mikhail Bakhtin, where double-voicedness 'serves two speakers at the same time and expresses simultaneously two different intentions',[128] an implied author de-authorizes the narrator, exposing him as a stereotype of middle-class Argentina. The novel thus effectively ironizes anti-Chinese racism while engaging with broader critiques of a multicultural Argentina.

In *El mármol*, a middle-aged man from Buenos Aires tells a story in the first person. He states that he is sitting on a piece of marble, relieved to be looking at his legs, genitals, and thighs.[129] The linear narrative, interspersed with pauses indicated by the narrator, begins with the narrator trying to recall what has led him to his current situation. He declares that because he is not able to remember why and how he got there, he will write in order to remember.

The narrator's incredible and confusing recollections then become chronological. Whilst paying for goods in a Chinese supermarket, he is made to select additional, cheap objects to make up for a lack of change. After taking

124 Ko, '"Argentina te incluye"', p. 3.
125 Berthold Schoene, *The Cosmopolitan Novel* (Edinburgh: Edinburgh University Press, 2011).
126 Nancy, *Being Singular Plural*, pp. 1–99.
127 Sandra Contreras, *Las vueltas de César Aira* (Rosario: Beatriz Viterbo Editora, 2002).
128 Bakhtin, p. 324.
129 Aira, loc. 10.

what he describes as an excessively long time to select the objects, the last thing he chooses is a set of 'glóbulos de mármol'.[130] As noted by Rafael Arce, the 'baratijas' chosen go on to dictate the course of the adventure.[131] When leaving the supermarket, the narrator is intercepted by a young Chinese man called Jonathan. Unpredictably, the reader is then informed that the narrator will later be found riding a moped with Jonathan while holding a stone toad with a beating heart under his arm. The narration then returns to the original time of the events and, after going to the narrator's house, Jonathan and the narrator decipher a series of clues for which the objects he has chosen at the supermarket become functional, such as finding a code by zapping through television channels and discovering a stone toad which 'pulsates'. Together, they go on Jonathan's moped to a second Chinese supermarket, where the selected articles' tasks and roles continue.

The second supermarket, owned by Chinese people who are present there, is supposedly the prize to be won by anyone who solves a vague, undefined competition made up of specific tasks. This is revealed to be what Jonathan is trying to win. In the narrator's recollection, the Chinese end up being extra-terrestrials from outer space who have started to feel nostalgic for their world, a world exactly the same as Earth. The extra-terrestrials have set up a competition in which participants can collect the elements which would bring the marble globules together, as this would allow the Chinese/aliens to return home. After a box containing a collection of images is opened, which the narrator states were fuel for the spaceship, the supermarket explodes, perhaps allowing the 'aliens' to return to their 'world'. Because of the explosion, the narrator and Jonathan are ejected from the store and then travel in the form of images. While placing a ring on his finger, another of the 'baratijas' he bought, the narrator lands next to the supermarket. After helping Jonathan, who has been hurt during the fall, he sits on a piece of marble. The novel ends with him relieved to see that although they have travelled as images, everything is in the 'right place'.[132]

The novel plays with a posited author who is the narrator in the text, incorporated as the carrier of a 'particular verbal-ideological linguistic belief system'[133] that distances him from the implied author. Read through Bakhtin's notion of double-voicedness, the novel reveals the existence of this implied author. They de-authorize the narrator, exposing him as the stereotype of a racist, middle-class Argentinean embedded in discourses of multiculturalism. Stories told about his life, at a hypodiegetic level, have an explanatory function which underlines the character's social identity as a stereotypically middle-class Argentine who has taken early retirement:

130 Aira, loc. 162.

131 Rafael Arce, 'César Aira: "Entre los indios"; "Festival"; "El náufrago"; "El mármol"', *Cuadernos de Literatura*, 17.34 (2013), pp. 341–47 (p. 343).

132 Aira, loc. 1200.

133 Bakhtin, p. 312.

married to a psychoanalyst who supports him financially, he sits around in parks, waiting for time to pass. While the novel's entire text is presented in the voice of this main narrator, his actions, as he recounts, contradict his words and thoughts, leading the reader to question the narrator's morality and ethical values. This, in turn, allows for emphasis to be placed on a particular belief system that belongs to someone other than the implied author, as this belief system 'is able [...] to show the object of representation in a new light [...] and [...] illuminate [...] the horizon against which the particularities of the teller's tale are perceivable'.[134]

The reader learns about the male Argentine narrator, whom we can assume thinks of himself as white, and whose name is never disclosed. The nondisclosure of his name points to a certain indistinctiveness—a stereotype. He is the kind of person whose personality and attitudes can be taken for granted, who is kept by his wife because of his early retirement due to health issues. Like Aira, he lives in the Flores neighbourhood of Buenos Aires. His prejudices are on display throughout the novel.

When confronted with a Chinese person who addresses him in perfect Spanish, his surprise suggests that the knowledge of language can be a way of disavowing exclusive notions of racial difference, revealing the constructedness of race. Furthermore, he never cares to specify whether Jonathan speaks Mandarin, Cantonese, or another 'Chinese' language. In contrast to 'other' well-dressed, Spanish-speaking Chinese people, the narrator's portrayal of Jonathan suggests, as discussed by Álvaro Fernández Bravo,[135] a variation and displacement of the stereotype, simultaneously revealing its contingency. The condescending, racist narrator operates alongside the fantasy of the stereotype of the 'Chinese'.

The novel's double-voicedness exposes the conflicts which inhabit the same utterance. For example, the narrator states that he would never go on an adventure, but then he expresses a desire for alterations to his routine. Furthermore, the narrator's ideology seems to clash with his experience: his reticence to engage with the Chinese cashier and his racist comments about him are explicitly confronted by his closeness to Jonathan. The disclosure of the contradictions between the narrator's actions and his statements reveal how he remains locked in his worldview. In this way, the morally questionable views of the narrator on the Chinese are presented in contrast to the views of the implied author, who engages with the visibility of Chinese migrants.

Aira himself has already been described as engaging with the 'growing visibility and racialization of the migrant'[136] in his novel *La Villa*. Yet when

134 Bakhtin, pp. 312–13.

135 Álvaro Fernández Bravo, 'Apropiaciones de la cultura china en la literatura sudamericana contemporánea: Contribución para un mapa tentativo a partir de obras de César Aira, Bernardo Carvalho y Siu Kam Wen', *452oF Revista de Teoría de la literatura y Literatura Comparada*, 13 (2015), pp. 50–70 (pp. 62–66).

136 Aguiló, p. 191.

asked about his de-stigmatization of Chinese communities in *El mármol*, he responded: 'no se me ocurrió ni remotamente que los chinos puedan estar discriminados o estigmatizados, y si se me hubiera ocurrido, habría buscado otro tema.'[137] However, the continuous reflection on distance and alienation available in the novel, linked to the explicit racism and xenophobic attitudes of the narrator, sheds new light on Aira's statement. The novel can be seen to engage critically, as Aguiló notes for other works of the period, 'with historical representations of race and the way in which these were affected by the crisis'.[138] Aira produces a critique of historical and contemporary racism in Buenos Aires by focusing on the Chinese as an ethnic group that escapes Argentina's narratives of whiteness, racial homogeneity, and multiculturalism.

As argued above, the rise of multiculturalism and the crisis of 2001 contributed to the emergence of discourses that challenged Argentina's narrative of whiteness and racial homogeneity. In this sense, the novel points to contemporary forms of exclusion in Latin America,[139] in which the Chinese are excluded from the discourses embodied by those of the narrator. It is the narrator's insight into the Chinese as 'human' that 'awakens' him to his own racism:

> Tuve un pensamiento en cierto modo premonitorio: ellos también eran seres humanos. Mi distracción anterior podía provenir, culpable, de haber estado pensando en todos ellos solo como chinos. Es asombroso cómo aun en alguien más o menos culto, de izquierda [...] puede caer en las trampas del racismo, que muchas veces, si no siempre, es cuestión de palabras.[140]

As we see in this extract, his amazement at the fact that 'cultivated', 'leftist' people such as himself can still be racist may be read as an ironizing double voice. At the same time as the narrator criticizes racism, an implied author sheds light on how the same narrator continues to perpetuate racialized views. Whilst the narrator realizes that the Chinese are 'human beings', the implied author exposes the ignorance of a certain erudite left in Argentina regarding racism, communism, China and immigration as a whole. The narrator himself states that the 'traps of racism' are linked to the use of words, yet he continues to use 'racist' expressions throughout the text. By showing how unaware the protagonist is of his racism, even though he does (partly) recognize it, the text brings racial constructions in Argentina to the fore. The double-voicedness discloses a conflict between two different worldviews, which is unresolved, pointing out the continuity of racism within what is expected to be a multicultural context.

137 '"El mármol", una aventura literaria de la mano de César Aira', *El Sol*, 2011 <http://www.elsol.com.ar/nota/92392> [accessed 1 May 2021].

138 Aguiló, p. 177.

139 Peter Wade, 'Mestizaje, Multiculturalism, Liberalism, and Violence', *Latin American and Caribbean Ethnic Studies*, 11.3 (2016), pp. 323–43.

140 Aira, loc. 718.

This is further enhanced by the fact that throughout the novel, there are suggestions that the main narrator might change, yet he never does. When they go on the moped, the narrator expresses that he feels a kind of awakening, an experience evoked through bodily awareness. He feels his body against Jonathan's body. He states he starts to see things differently, but he is unsure if he has changed or if things have changed. His body is moved 'towards' excitement and adventure, as well as difference, embodied in the figure of Jonathan. The physical contact with Jonathan is described as 'sin resquicios, pegado, animal'.[141] This elusive desire for Jonathan recalls the historical marginalization of homosexuals and exposes the narrator's alienation from an Argentine 'macho' stereotype. Sexual otherness seems to signal towards subjectivity and change. However, even while the protagonist tries to make sense of events, which may be linked to the notion of 'awakening', underlined by his statement: 'El barrio gris y humilde se transformaba, ¿o era yo?'[142] his expressions continue to fix him within discourses of otherness and alienation. The novel thus exposes the different discourses at play here.

From this perspective, the protagonist can be read as trying to make sense of his encounter with the Chinese immigrant community in Buenos Aires but, unable to engage with them, or in other words, to complete any real process of 'awakening', he reads them as aliens. The interpretation of the Chinese as aliens suggests the expression of authorial intentions in a refracted sense. Aira's declaration ironically exposes the failed incorporation of immigrants, especially the Chinese, within the Argentine nation. Aira's stated blindness to the discrimination against and stigmatization of Chinese in Argentina, included in his statement above, thus appears to be a disingenuous answer to the question posed.[143] In this, there is a denunciation by the implied author of an Argentine society which continues to construct essentialist stereotypes of immigrants. The novel parodies racist constructions, which are taken to an extreme by the use of aliens.

On one level, *El mármol* evidently caricatures views of Argentines who read themselves as non-racist, whilst the Chinese community is presented as an arrival to Argentina from outside and are ultimately perceived as different. The process of awakening, which is never completed, also evokes an incomplete awakening of Argentina to the question of its whiteness, both during and after the 2001 crisis. As Ko shows, discourses of multiculturality in Argentina continue to have embedded racist constructions. The narrator's essentialism can be summarized through his statement, 'después de todo, estos chinos eran chinos';[144] only, in the end, that means that they are extra-terrestrials, or 'aliens'.[145]

141 Aira, loc. 462.

142 Aira, loc. 402.

143 '"El mármol", una aventura literaria de la mano de César Aira'.

144 Aira, p. loc. 720.

145 The Real Academia Española does not recognize the word 'alien' in the Spanish language; it does include 'alienígena'; 'alien', *Diccionario de la Lengua Española* (Real Academia Española, 2017) <http://dle.rae.es/> [accessed 1 May 2021].

The figure of the alien is worth exploring further. As Ahmed explains in her introduction to *Strange Encounters*, the 'alien, on one hand, is so over-represented in popular culture that it has become quite recognisable'. Yet, on the other hand, 'there is always the possibility that we might not recognise the alien if we see one'.[146] The double-bind of the alien figure is exploited in the novel, exposing the discursive mechanisms through which the alien is recognized and considered different from a discursive 'us' and also exposing how the 'other' is designated 'beyond' the nation. The 'alien' here becomes a fetish in psychoanalytical terms, recovering all that is beyond the human into the singularity of a given form.

Through his narration, the protagonist discloses the mechanisms available for differentiating between humans. At the same time, the physical closeness of the 'alien' finally reveals that they, as Chinese, are actually contained within the nation. In other words, while the migrant may be a legal resident, the condition of being alien and foreign remains. This is something on which the narrator himself reflects in the novel. Not only does he comment on the presence of Chinese youth in Buenos Aires as becoming 'almost typical', he also comments on the growing presence of Chinese supermarkets in Buenos Aires, noting changes within the city itself.

The Argentine press has widely registered the increase in Chinese supermarkets and the changes to the Buenos Aires commercial landscape.[147] Ko states that in Argentina, 'the word *chino* has become synonymous with "grocer"'.[148] She even argues that the word 'supermarket' has been actually largely replaced by 'chino' due to the concentration of Chinese immigrants in the grocery business.[149] Although it can be argued that the word 'chino' replaces the 'Chinese supermarket' instead of the 'supermarket' as a whole, this differentiation is still a stereotype, as this kind of business is associated with the Chinese owners or administrators, although the products sold are largely the same as the ones sold in any supermarket. Highlighting the stereotypical association of the Chinese with 'supermercados chinos', Valestra recalls in *Un chino*: 'al último chino que había intentado abrir una tintorería en Buenos Aires le había ido como al primer japonés que intentó abrir un minimercado.'[150]

146 Ahmed, *Strange Encounters*, p. 1.

147 Verónica Jordana, 'Mi gran casamiento chino | Conexión Brando' <http://www.conexionbrando.com/1092794-mi-gran-casamiento-chino> [accessed 1 May 2021]; Franco Varise, 'Los chinos en la Argentina, más allá del supermercado', *La Nación*, (2011) <http://www.lanacion.com.ar/1413378-los-chinos-en-la-argentina-mas-alla-del-supermercado> [accessed 1 May 2021]; Silvia Rodiño, 'El secreto de los negocios chinos', *Clarín*, 6 March 2006 <http://edant.clarin.com/suplementos/pymes/2006/03/06/y-01150880.htm> [accessed 1 May 2021].

148 Ko, '"Argentina te incluye"', p. 2.

149 Ko, 'From Whiteness to Diversity', p. 2533.

150 Magnus, p. 54.

Denardi states that in Buenos Aires there is a Chinese supermarket every two or three blocks.[151] The growth of Chinese supermarkets even led the French-origin multinational chain of supermarkets Carrefour in 2006 to air a TV commercial that openly criticized Chinese supermarkets.[152] The association of supermarkets owned by Chinese residents legally forced Carrefour to edit the commercial and remove the images of Chinese people and supermarkets in it.[153] In the novel, the narrator expresses the idea that Chinese supermarkets are ubiquitous in the city, stating that 'estos establecimientos proliferan hasta el exceso'.[154] The novel thus parodies the discourses that refer to the proliferation of Chinese supermarkets, by producing yet another text referring to this phenomenon. The novel portrays the Argentinean discourse on those supermarkets through a narrator who ultimately repeats the racist stereotypes associated with them.

As Ko expresses it: 'Asians in Argentina were considered "eternally foreign" [...] because of their distinctive condition as "physiognomic outsiders" [...] in essence, considered absolutely foreign and unable to assimilate';[155] according to her, this novel is at once Orientalist, de-Orientalist, and critical of de-Orientalism. Ko actualizes this to state that the newly multicultural Argentine nation continues to essentialize race. However, the Chinatown, and the Chinese supermarket, may subvert its own notion of undesirability by embodying the racialized subjects in order to position themselves in the market. Furthermore, and paraphrasing Huggan, in the simulation of conditions in which dominant cultures perceive 'minorities', marginalized groups may reveal the underlying structures of their oppression.[156] The text hence simultaneously reveals the complexities which the staging of 'Chineseness' and 'China' contains.

Today, Fernández Bravo argues, after Bhabha, it is Chinese economic productivity which confirms and alters the nature of the Chinese stereotype, as he describes the objects selected at the supermarket as representative of properties associated with the Chinese imaginary:

> Dimensiones pequeñas que pueden subdividirse hasta el infinito, calidad dudosa, producción industrial que por su cantidad desafía la misma noción de valor económico, reduciéndolo (y por eso mismo multiplicándolo) hasta casi hacerlo desaparecer.[157]

151 Denardi, 'Ser chino en Buenos Aires: Historia, moralidades y cambios en la diáspora china en Argentina', p. 86.

152 *Argenchino*.

153 Claudio Zlotnik, 'Guerra sino-francesa por los precios', *Página|12*, (2006) <http://www.pagina12.com.ar/diario/elpais/1-63669-2006-02-28.html> [accessed 1 May 2021].

154 Aira, loc. 182.

155 Ko, 'From Whiteness to Diversity', p. 2533.

156 Huggan, p. 88.

157 Fernández Bravo, p. 66.

The cheap objects selected at the supermarket operate as fetishized objects, associated with contemporary, industrial China. Fernández Bravo sees China in *El mármol* as evoking notions of disproportionate quantity and dimension for the narrator, and thereby summoning terrifying (Latin American) fantasies associated with the Chinese population.[158] The stereotype is simultaneously disrupted and confirmed, whilst also revealing new meanings, which Fernández Bravo reads as a Chinese present-future, into which the world has entered, and of which the supermarket is a projection.[159] As we have seen before, Bhabha explicitly builds on Lacan, to argue that identity is paradoxical, contradictory, and constantly shifting, locating the stereotype as a fetishist mode of representation.[160] In the protagonist's recognition of the coherence of the stereotype as an imaginary, the difference is disavowed symbolically through the figure of the 'alien'.

In this sense, the complexity of the multiculturalism exposed in the novel can be approached through Nancy's notion of existence, where existence can only 'be grasped in the paradoxical simultaneity of togetherness [...] and disseminated singularity'.[161] Emerging in the novel through the narration and the narrator himself, that which is Chinese is, as a fetish, never totally undesirable, enhancing an idea of coexistence. Simultaneously, the novel exposes and interrupts discourses of multiculturalism and the way in which it continues to operate through an aestheticizing, exoticist discourse, which is far from being resolved.[162] From this perspective, 'China' as 'alien' is revealed as a fetish, accommodating the social contradictions which the narrator experiences at a personal level. Allegedly secondary to a Latin American *mestizo* identity, a 'Chinese' identity is revealed to have been excluded from Argentine identity discourses.

Through this disclosure, the novel's deployment of double-voicedness toys with notions of distance, boundaries, and difference. The specific figure of a toad which blends in with the garden[163] evokes the notion of a 'discovery' amidst a landscape that has been naturalized. It is echoed by the narrator's surprise at being addressed in perfect Spanish by a young Chinese man, an experience that clashes with the narrator's expectations of understanding the Chinese. His growing understanding of somebody he had initially perceived as different transforms his arrival at the second supermarket into an undoing of notions of difference. This is further enhanced by his becoming 'dis-oriented' inside the neat, clean supermarket, which contrasts with government denunciations of Chinese supermarkets as unhygienic and failing to fulfil minimum health and safety procedures, a widely disseminated

158 Fernández Bravo, p. 65.
159 Fernández Bravo, p. 66.
160 Bhabha, pp. 5, 57–93.
161 Nancy, *Being Singular Plural*, p. 7.
162 Huggan, p. 126.
163 Aira, loc. 401.

discourse on popular online social networks.[164] The narrator's worldview collapses when confronted with the unexpected, while the implied author discloses his critique of stereotypical images of Chinese supermarkets.

This use of a narrator who exposes his biased and stereotyped views and who is disorientated when challenged by a 'real' situation that runs contrary to his expectations leads to a collapsing of the assumptions that had informed notions of difference. Or, in other words, the 'stranger', whom he has perceived as 'stranger', cannot be defined or read through his own traditional paradigms. The singular is only expressed in relation to others. When the narrator is unable to accept this, he discovers, or convinces himself, that the Chinese are 'aliens'. His narration allows us to hypothesize that this results from his inability to incorporate the Chinese into his discourse on the Argentine nation which, read through Ko, arises from the fact that Argentines consider Asian difference both insurmountable and incomprehensible.[165]

Ko ultimately argues that these 'Asian' novels do not grant racial or cultural citizenship to Asian-Argentines.[166] However, while it can be argued that the narrator does not grant citizenship to the Chinese and 'reads' them as aliens, the novel's emphasis on the constructedness of the character's account exposes his bias. This subjectivity, in turn, leads the reader to question the narrator's moral authority and, in its double-voicedness, it arguably does effectively grant citizenship to the Chinese in Argentina. This, in turn, reveals the narrator as further alienated.

Although the narrator refers to a relatively comfortable middle-class life at the beginning of the text, the narration simultaneously includes darker aspects of his life. His reflections present him as unhappy due to his miserable pension, while he describes being dependent on his wife as 'una sorda tortura permanente'.[167] His confessed ignorance about national news underlines his isolation.[168] His description of the places he inhabits shows him as disillusioned and hopeless. He is socially 'alienated' and emasculated, which further suggests his projection of the 'alien' status of the Chinese. The narrator's identification with a white, patriarchal Argentine nation contrasts with his life, in which his wife economically supports him and is, therefore, a failure in the eyes of a white, patriarchal, neoliberal society.

The narrator's 'failure' recalls the period before the crisis of 2001 in which, as Aguiló shows, 'social malaise and impoverishment become more

164 'Clausuran 4 supermercados chinos', *Buenos Aires Ciudad—Gobierno de la Ciudad Autónoma de Buenos Aires*, (2015) <http://www.buenosaires.gob.ar/noticias/clausuran-4-supermercados-chinos> [accessed 1 May 2021]; 'Supermercados chinos - Taringa!' <http://www.taringa.net/posts/info/9483558/Supermercados-chinos.html> [accessed 1 May 2021].

165 Ko, '"Argentina te incluye"', p. 2.

166 Ko, '"Argentina te incluye"', p. 3.

167 Aira, loc. 298.

168 Aira, loc. 189.

acute as a result of neoliberal policy'.[169] Indeed, the narrator's racism recalls the post-crisis heightening of racism and interest in images of ethnic cultural products and diversity.[170] This context suggests that Aira's depiction of the Chinese is not haphazard. As Ko shows, discourses on the 'chino' present them as the most 'alien' to Argentina.[171] And yet the Chinatown is simultaneously marketed as part of a 'multicultural' Buenos Aires, and Chinese supermarkets are described as part of the city's landscape. The novel exposes the 'alien' condition of the Chinese while simultaneously revealing and questioning the discourses that construct and maintain that 'foreignness'.

In the novel, the description of the Chinese as aliens from outer space exposes the notions of otherness linked to the Chinese community in Buenos Aires. It accentuates the primacy of images of modernity and whiteness in that construction of a white Argentina, which the novel interrupts. Unlike the Chinese, who own supermarkets in Buenos Aires, the narrator owns nothing—something he acknowledges is his own responsibility due to his 'moral weakness'.[172] The better-dressed and apparently more educated Chinese man they encounter at the second supermarket contrasts with Jonathan's poor Spanish and modest clothes. While Jonathan's clothes enhance the idea that the crisis has affected the whole of society, including the migrant communities not traditionally included in the discourses of 'the nation', the difference between both Chinese men and between the Chinese and Argentine men, points to forms of exclusion and the economic asymmetry of neoliberalism.

As *El mármol* shows, re-orientation may reduce notions of strangerness. By offering us the possibility of challenging the figure of the stranger as such, the novel is able to critique 'stranger fetishism'. Nevertheless, this re-orientation, which allows the character to enter a place he has not had access to in the past, is shown to occur only when a major event happens (being dragged into an adventure, for instance). Although the narrator acts as the empowered white man, his existence is simultaneously miserable and devoid of all agency. At a certain point, he even states his surprise at the fact that the Chinese man is asking *him* questions, further enhancing his lack of authority as the reader is aware that it is actually the Chinese character who has been making the decisions ever since they met. This enhances the notion of a community that is neither homogeneous nor an accumulation of differences. Rather, the plural is the collection of singularities, and the novel reminds us that power imbalances still inform it. In the novel, the agency and authority reside with the Chinese, ultimately disrupting any set idea of who is the 'stranger' in Argentina.

169 Aguiló, p. 179.
170 Aguiló, p. 184; Lacarrieu.
171 Ko, 'From Whiteness to Diversity', p. 2533.
172 Aira, loc. 1114.

Through the narration, two different world-views are brought into contact: that of the implied author, which reveals a failed multicultural Argentina and acknowledges the racism that still permeates the nation's discourse, and that of the narrator, revealing an old-fashioned nation, which continues to 'whiten' its national discourse. In *El mármol*, the protagonist identifies himself as 'Western' and Argentine and is shown to be displaced from his own 'imagined community', to use Benedict Anderson's term,[173] because of his failure within neoliberal structures and his inability to 'understand' the changing immigrant landscape of the city. As a result, the novel questions what informs the 'imagined community' that the character seems to identify with. The jobless, broke narrator is displaced from society. This sense of displacement informs his encounter with the 'stranger', only to ultimately reveal his racist ideology. If in Aira, we find a disruption of the constructions of 'fetishized strangers' through the novel's deconstruction of racist multiculturalism, in *Verde Shanghai*, by Rivera Garza, the possibility of any notion of 'otherness' is challenged, as well as any naturalization of gendered, racial, and cultural differences.

Strangers in the City: *Verde Shanghai*, by Cristina Rivera Garza

The last novel studied is *Verde Shanghai*, by Cristina Rivera Garza (1964–). Through its main character, *Verde Shanghai* is seen as evading boundaries, emphasizing ambiguity instead and operating in a pluralistic mode.[174] Through the female protagonist(s), the novel rejects the Chinatown as a place of the 'exotic'. Instead, it regards it as a space that allows for exposing the performativity of gendered and racialized bodies. Bringing together Nancy's 'being singular plural' with Gloria Anzaldúa's notion of 'borderlands',[175] the novel can be read as a critique of constructions of gender and race in Mexico. Although she was raised on the border between Mexico and the United States of America (U.S.), which has caused her to be linked to Mexican 'narrators of the North', the position of Rivera Garza within any particular literary group is contested.[176] 'De-territorialisation'[177] appears as

173 Benedict Anderson, *Imagined Communities: Reflections on the Origin and Spread of Nationalism*, 3rd edn (London: Verso, 2006), pp. 6–7.

174 Gloria Anzaldúa, *Borderlands/La Frontera: The New Mestiza* (San Francisco: Aunt Lute Books, 2007), p. 101.

175 Anzaldúa, pp. 19–20.

176 Jungwon Park, 'Manicomio y locura: Revolución dentro de la revolución mexicana en "Nadie me verá llorar" de Cristina Rivera Garza', *Anclajes*, 17.1 (2013), pp. 55–72 (pp. 57–58); Tomás Regalado López, 'The Crack and Contemporary Latin American Narrative: An Introductory Study', in *New Trends in Contemporary Latin American Narrative, Post-National Literature and the Canon*, ed. by Timothy R. Robbins and José Eduardo González (New York: Palgrave Macmillan, 2014), pp. 55–83 (pp. 55–73).

177 Diana Palaversich, 'The New Narrative of the North: Moving Frontiers of Mexican Literature', *Symposium*, 61.1 (2007), pp. 9–26 (p. 24).

a central characteristic of her work. Rivera Garza has lived in recent years between Mexico and the U.S. She has taught history and creative writing in both countries and writes in both English and Spanish.[178] Enjoying an intense social media presence,[179] her life across borders can be said to underpin her understanding of immigrant experience, gender, and citizenship. Her work explores mental territories or stories that resist explanation and covers topics such as madness, love, and silence, consistently rejecting notions of essential, stable identities.

Various critics and academics have described her work in terms of exploring limits, major and unresolved gaps, impenetrable passages, the challenging of genre and gender conventions, and as an enclave of transgression in contemporary Mexican literature. She has received many Mexican and international prizes. Her novel *Nadie me verá llorar*[180] was praised by Carlos Fuentes as 'una de las obras de ficción más notables de la literatura [...] en castellano, de esta vuelta de siglo'.[181] The madness of the protagonist of *Nadie me verá llorar* illustrates Rivera Garza's preference for what Diana Palaversich calls 'sujetos des-centrados'. That is, characters who unfold continuously, which can be many or one, gradually disclosing gender and exposing the interplay of different discourses.[182] The disclosure of 'sujetos des-centrados' and narratological fragmentation is also present in the novel *Verde Shanghai*. Aniela Rodríguez Zapata has argued that the feminist alterity available in the novel acts as a symbol for feminist, poststructural perspectives.[183] Eduardo Sabugal has described it as a Chinese box and as using language to conceal and reveal simultaneously.[184]

178 Cheyla Rose Samuelson, 'Writing at Escape Velocity: An Interview with Cristina Rivera Garza', *Confluencia*, 23.1 (2007), pp. 135–45 (p. 135); Cristina Rivera Garza, 'Cristina Rivera Garza: Matamoros, México, 1964', *Nuevo Texto Crítico*, 21.2 (2008), pp. 21–32 (pp. 21–32).

179 Edmundo Paz Soldán, '"Cristina Rivera Garza's Tweets"', ed. by Christine Hensler and Deborah Castillo, *Hispanic Issues Online*, 9 (2012), pp. 38–39 (pp. 38–39); Niamh Thornton, 'Fairies at the Bottom of the Garden: Writers Crossing Digital Borders', *Forum for Inter-American Research*, 5.1 (2012); Betina Keizman, 'El blog de Cristina Rivera Garza: experiencia literaria y terreno de contienda', *Chasqui*, 42.1 (2013), pp. 3–15 (pp. 3–4).

180 Cristina Rivera Garza, *Nadie me verá llorar* (Mexico City: Tusquets, Conaculta, 1999).

181 Carlos Fuentes, 'Cristina Rivera Garza' (El Norte, 2002).

182 Palaversich, p. 15.

183 Aniela Rodríguez Zapata, 'La otredad en la literatura femenina: un acercamiento posestructural a "Verde Shanghai" de Cristina Rivera Garza', in *La Palabra. Lenguaje, Medios y Sociedades Digitales*, ed. by Ysela Y. de Pablo Porras et al. (Chihuahua: Universidad Autónoma de Chihuahua, 2013), pp. 141–48 (p. 141).

184 Eduardo Sabugal, 'La caja verde de Cristina', *Crítica*, 145 (2011) <http://revistacritica.com/contenidos-impresos/vigilia/verde-shanghai-de-cristina-rivera-garza> [accessed 1 May 2021].

Although not stated explicitly, the story is seemingly set in Mexico City, constructed through a main narrative interrupted by different narrators and literary styles, such as prose, poetry, short stories, extracts from other books, and press notes. The text is fragmented: different sections use different typefaces and are interrupted by quotes from unknown authors whose references are only given at the end of the novel; this is impossible to trace back in a Kindle edition, enhancing the perplexing aspects of the novel. Events are presented in ways that lead the reader to question whether they have actually 'happened' or if they are just dreams or thoughts. The settings are also ambiguous. The blurriness reinforces ambiguity regarding the duration of events and the people involved in them, while details of time and place abound in conflicting ways. As Jennifer Prince notes, names are changed, confused, and non-existent in the novel, and identities are ambiguous, transient, and temporary.[185] The reader is ultimately not allowed to make sense of the text, which questions all information provided. In this sense, the novel not only questions the ways in which reality is made coherent but shows that reality itself is not coherent.

Verde Shanghai tells the story of Marina Espinoza, a woman married to the medical doctor Horacio Oligoechea. The story opens with a car accident in which Marina breaks her arm, prompting time in the hospital. After the accident, Marina becomes haunted by the image of another woman named Xian, and although their thoughts seem to intertwine, her identity remains a mystery. Feeling the urge to understand her thoughts, Marina searches for Xian in Chinatown, moved by a desire which she describes in a letter to Xian as 'el animal salvaje'.[186] The idea that Marina could also be Xian is suggested through phrases such as 'alguien dentro de ella había tomado la decisión sin consultarla',[187] while Prince has suggested that Xian is an 'oriental "Other"' due to her Chinese name, her location in Chinatown, and the fact that Marina finds similarities between Xian and Chiang Wei, who is of Chinese descent and the fiancée of Marina/Xian in an arranged marriage.[188] There is nothing in the novel that directly suggests this. Instead, through writing and her encounters with other characters, including Chiang Wei, a self who was silenced in Marina's life with Horacio gradually emerges. From this perspective, and resonant with the fact that the character slides from one to another, the figure of Marina/Xian allows for a re-reading of the figure 'La Malinche', not only because she moves along borders, as Malinche does between Aztec and Spanish, but also because Malinche's Christian name was, indeed, Marina.

185 Jennifer Prince, 'Ella, Yo y El Yotro: Orientalisms and Identities in Cristina Rivera Garza's "Verde Shanghai"', in *Orientalism of the Hispanic and Luso-Brazilian World*, ed. by Araceli Tinajero (New York: Escribana Books, 2014), pp. 118–36 (p. 120).

186 Rivera Garza, *Verde Shanghai*, loc. 1445.

187 Rivera Garza, *Verde Shanghai*, loc. 476.

188 Prince, p. 127.

Alberto Cabezas has described *Verde Shanghai* as a game with time through which the novel gets close to 'our most extreme other': the Chinese community in Mexico.[189] Rivera Garza herself describes the novel as a way of showing how a city has changed in multiple ways: 'inicialmente con el fenómeno de la inmigración, después con las críticas radicales al sistema en el México de finales del siglo XX.'[190] In this sense, the novel engages with the way in which the Chinatown is 'marketed', not caring to distinguish between different generations of immigrants. As Bhabha shows regarding colonial discourse in relation to the production of the colonized as a social reality, the Chinatown allows for a reality which is at once 'other' and entirely knowable.[191] From this perspective, a critique of fixed otherness emerges throughout the novel as, through Marina, it displays and challenges Chinatown in Mexico City as a space of otherness, exposing and questioning the power asymmetry of encounters.

The first Chinese immigrants arrived in Mexico during Spanish colonial rule, linked to the Manila Galleon's trade route between America and Asia.[192] A stronger current of migration developed in the nineteenth century, linked to the Mexican interest in attracting labour for farming and mining, and as consequence of the Chinese Exclusion Act in the U.S. in 1882.[193] Many of them worked as local businessmen, seizing commercial opportunities resulting from the growth in mining and railroad activities.[194] When the U.S. passed its exclusion law, authorities from both China and Mexico encouraged Chinese migration to Mexico.[195] The Chinese believed Latin America

189 Alberto Cabezas, 'Cristina Rivera Garza: "La mirada de los migrantes no descansa nunca"', *Revista Arcadia*, (2011) <http://www.revistaarcadia.com/libros/articulo/cristina-rivera-garza-la-mirada-migrantes-no-descansa-nunca/25644> [accessed 1 May 2021].

190 Fabiola Palapa Quijas, 'Cristina Rivera Garza explora formas de la memoria para escapar al olvido', *La Jornada*, (2011), section Cultura <http://www.jornada.unam.mx/2011/07/06/cultura/a06n1cul> [accessed 1 May 2021].

191 Bhabha, p. 101.

192 Homer H. Dubs and Robert S. Smith, 'Chinese in Mexico City in 1635', *The Far Eastern Quarterly*, 1.4 (1942), pp. 387–89 (pp. 387–89).

193 Erika Lee, 'The "Yellow Peril" and Asian Exclusion in the Americas', *Pacific Historical Review*, 76.4 (2007), pp. 537–62 (pp. 541–42); Grace Peña Delgado, *Making the Chinese Mexican: Global Migration, Localism, and Exclusion in the U.S.-Mexico Borderlands* (Stanford: Stanford University Press, 2012), pp. 13–40; Evelyn Hu-DeHart, 'Inclusion and Exclusion. The Chinese in Multiracial Latin America and the Caribbean', in *Routledge Handbook of the Chinese Diaspora*, ed. by Tan Chee-Beng (London: Routledge, 2013), pp. 89–107 (p. 100); Tatiana Seijas, 'Asian Migrations to Latin America in the Pacific World, 16th–19th Centuries', *History Compass*, 14.12 (2016), pp. 573–81.

194 Evelyn Hu-DeHart, 'Coolies, Shopkeepers, Pioneers: The Chinese of Mexico and Peru (1849-1930)', *Amerasia*, 15.2 (1989), pp. 91–116 (pp. 91, 96).

195 Robert Chao Romero, *The Chinese in Mexico, 1882–1940* (Tucson: University of

to be a convenient alternative to the racial hostility and discriminatory laws found in the U.S.; for example, during the Porfiriato (1876–1910), foreign immigration was regarded as an essential ingredient for the development of the country.[196] Lee explains that although Mexican officials found Chinese immigrants '"undesirable," they also admitted that Chinese labour was beneficial and necessary'.[197]

The post-Revolutionary state aimed to build an identity that claimed, simultaneously and without hierarchies, peasants, workers, and indigenous groups to be at the heart of 'mexicanidad'. Nevertheless, xenophobia in general and Sinophobia in particular, were strong,[198] reaching a climax during the 1930s. Indeed, even by 1925, the Chinese population had declined sharply,[199] and in the 1930s almost 10,000 Chinese persons were expelled from Mexico.[200] In 2012, Adrian Hearn suggested that Chinese communities in contemporary Mexico were still being made to feel that they posed a threat to national interests, a narrative that resurfaces during times of economic hardship, as also noted by Aguiló and Ko in Argentina,[201] and fuelled by China's growing global influence and the role that overseas Chinese are thought to play in it.[202]

Within the Mexican nation, Mexico City's Chinatown defines itself through a discourse based on otherness, as can be seen, for example, on their official website[203] and in other writing aimed at tourists.[204] The website states

Arizona Press, 2010); Erika Lee, 'Enforcing the Borders: Chinese Exclusion along the U.S. Borders with Canada and Mexico, 1882–1924', *The Journal of American History*, 89.1 (2002), pp. 54–86; Elliott Young, *Alien Nation: Chinese Migration in the Americas from the Coolie Era Through World War II* (University of North Carolina Press, 2014).

196 Jürgen Buchenau, 'The Limits of the Cosmic Race: Immigrant and Nation in Mexico, 1850-1950', in *Immigration and National Identities in Latin America*, ed. by Nicola Foote and Michael Goebel (Gainsville: University Press of Florida, 2014), pp. 66–90 (pp. 72, 73).

197 Lee, 'Enforcing the Borders', p. 59.

198 Evelyn Hu-DeHart, 'Indispensable Enemy or Convenient Scapegoat? A Critical Examination of Sinophobia in Latin America and the Caribbean, 1870s to 1930s', in *The Chinese in Latin America and the Caribbean*, ed. by Walton Look Lai and Chee-Beng Tan (Leiden: Brill, 2010), pp. 65–102.

199 Hu-DeHart, 'Coolies, Shopkeepers, Pioneers'; Hu-DeHart, 'Indispensable Enemy or Convenient Scapegoat?'

200 Flora Botton Beja, 'La persecución de los chinos en México', *Estudios de Asia y África*, 43.2.136 (2008), pp. 477–86 (pp. 483–84); Adrian Hearn, 'Harnessing the Dragon: Overseas Chinese Entrepreneurs in Mexico and Cuba', *The China Quarterly*, 209 (2012), pp. 111–33 (p. 112).

201 Aguiló; Ko, 'From Whiteness to Diversity'; Ko, '"Argentina te incluye"'.

202 Hearn, pp. 112–13.

203 'Historia del Barrio Chino CDMX' <http://barriochinomexico.com/historia/> [accessed 1 May 2021].

204 J.C. Cavallero, 'Barrio Chino y Calle de Dolores, D.F. (Visita y Semblanza)',

that in the 1940s, the restaurant Shan Ghai was settled in the 'callejón de las damas' off Dolores Street, establishing the *barrio chino*. The description on the website evokes a mysterious 'Orient', stating it to be a place where people can go and 'deleitarse con las costumbres orientales que en él se realizan'.[205] The idea of 'oriental customs' continues racist constructions by relying on a euphemistic cultural specificity. The Chinatown of Mexico City is expected both to 'contain' difference and to provide a space of encounter with the 'other culture'. The website thus disregards the persecutions that led the Chinese to eventually settle in Mexico City while remaining within discourses of fixed otherness.

One of the other ways in which *Verde Shanghai* challenges fixed notions of otherness is through Marina's acceptance of ambiguity. For example, the impossibility of Marina identifying herself, or Chiang Wei, through race, contrasts with quotes within the text that tell the reader about explicit historical discrimination towards the Chinese in Mexico.[206] These extracts, which include a quote from an academic journal,[207] echo Ariel C. Armony and Nicolás Velásquez's conclusion regarding the ways in which the symbolic construction of China as the 'favourite villain' has served an array of actors behind the notion of China as an 'evil other' in Mexico today.[208] In other words, how an 'other' is constructed through race is something the novel exposes and critiques through Marina, as her racial fluidity contrasts with a quoted historical source referring to a stereotyped idea of 'Chinese race'.[209] Although the reader is never told Marina's 'race', her body is read racially when doña Aída, owner of Verde Shanghai, the restaurant that Marina goes to in Chinatown, recognizes her as a member of the 'Chou' family.[210] Another example appears when Chiang Wei talks about his grandfather, who was told to go to a place where 'todos son como tú [...] mientras se estiraban los ojos con ambas manos',[211] a physically expressed racist insult.

On her arrival in Chinatown, Marina subverts the distance informed by class and racial discourses. As shown by Ahmed, 'proximity' and 'distance' come to be lived by being associated with specific bodies and places.[212] From

Bici-tando la Ciudad de México, (2013) <https://bicitando.wordpress.com/2013/08/27/barrio-chino-y-calle-de-dolores-d-f-visita-y-semblanza/> [accessed 1 May 2021].

205 'Historia del Barrio Chino CDMX'.

206 Rivera Garza, *Verde Shanghai*, loc. 2026–2210.

207 Rivera Garza, *Verde Shanghai*, loc. 2179.

208 Ariel C. Armony and Nicolás Velásquez, 'Anti-Chinese Sentiment in Latin America: An Analysis of Online Discourse', *Journal of Chinese Political Science*, 20.3 (2015), pp. 319–46 (p. 320).

209 Rivera Garza, *Verde Shanghai*, loc. 2143.

210 Rivera Garza, *Verde Shanghai*, loc. 1131.

211 Rivera Garza, *Verde Shanghai*, loc. 2132.

212 Sara Ahmed, *Queer Phenomenology: Orientations, Objects, Others* (Durham: Duke University Press, 2006), p. 112.

this perspective, Marina subverts the limited contact between the multiple layers of Mexico City. After the accident, her unexplained orientation towards Chinatown reveals the spatial arrangement of the Chinese in the city, disclosing class divisions, as she needs to leave her upper/middle-class house in order to move towards the *barrio chino*. Marina's house is described as illuminated and spacious, with 'sábanas blancas [que] olían a limpio, un leve aroma a limón',[213] while Chinatown is described as an 'acumulación de coches, cuerpos, ruidos'.[214]

Marina's undermining of gender performativity also enhances this slippage between racialized worlds. From this perspective, Marina/Xian can be read in relation to the work of queer theorist Judith Butler, who suggests that the gendered body 'has no ontological status apart from the various acts which constitute its reality'.[215] Rivera Garza herself has stated, acknowledging Butler's influence on her, that 'el género es sobre todo un *performance* que varía y se *enacta* de acuerdo a negociaciones específicas en contextos específicos'.[216] The exposure of the performativity that Chinatown offers Marina rejects clear-cut binaries of gender and race, playing along the Marina/Xian identity axes. Marina challenges any essentialist understanding of identity, pointing towards the significance of context and subjective experience.

Indeed, Marina can be seen to challenge normative codes by not being restricted to any stable form of gender performativity. In the novel, although presented as a female subject, Marina performs masculinity, as seen through her relationship with Chiang Wei. She also performs femininity, as seen in relation to Xian; heterosexuality, as seen in her relationship with Horacio; and homosexuality, as seen through her desire for Julia, a woman whose identity is never clear.[217] However, she displays no consistent sexual preference, something also present in other works by Rivera Garza.[218] Marina reveals how normative codes of masculinity, femininity and heterosexuality may be contingent, opening up the possibility that the authority of these normative codes is being undermined. This suggests that bodies could be more adequately understood as a continuum rather than as clear-cut binaries

213 Rivera Garza, *Verde Shanghai*, loc. 1242.

214 Rivera Garza, *Verde Shanghai*, loc. 1061.

215 Judith Butler, *Gender Trouble: Feminism and the Subversion of Identity* (London: Routledge, 1990), p. 136. For Butler, both gender and sexuality are 'performances' enacted by continuous repetition.

216 Emily Hind, *Entrevistas con quince autoras mexicanas* (Madrid: Iberoamericana, 2003), p. 189.

217 Rivera Garza, *Verde Shanghai*, loc. 3232.

218 Maricruz Castro Ricalde, 'Diversidad sexual y liminalidad en "Nadie me verá llorar" de Cristina Rivera Garza', in *Reflexiones en torno a la escritura femenina*, ed. by Adriana Sáenz Valadez and Cándida Elizabeth Vivero Marín (Mexico City: Universidad de Guadalajara y Universidad Michoacana de San Nicolás de Hidalgo, 2011), pp. 241–69 (pp. 244, 250).

between female and male bodies, thus disavowing fixed notions of gendered identity.

Within this context, Horacio's scientific and rational perspective, characterized by his being a medical doctor, posits him as the male gazer, a role performed through his photography of the ill Marina.[219] Prince's analysis of this novel suggests that the 'orientalization' of Marina through her experience in the *barrio chino* exposes her as the 'other' of the rational and scientific male, Horacio, whilst Chiang Wei is also shown to be her 'other'. As Prince shows, Horacio's control over and desire for Marina allow the reader to think of him as the epitome of the white, male, orientalist gaze.[220] In her class-determined existence, Marina is 'esposa de médico'[221] as she articulates it, invoking belonging and control. And yet Marina escapes the power that Horacio intends to have over her. Her dismissal of Horacio's hegemony, slipping away psychologically from him while in his house after being dragged there, acts as a critique of and a challenge to male domination over the female subject.

The contrast between Marina's aesthetic appreciation of shades and tones and Horacio's fascination with the static photograph stresses their differences. Marina's references to green in different sections of the novel, such as in including a quote from Rivera Garza's own poem 'Conjurar', which discusses recommendations of colours for different tones of green,[222] suggests the relevance that shades, and not fixity, have for Marina. The disavowal of a fixed subject position in favour of one that slides and refuses any definition acknowledges the centrality of the subject position without fixing the subject. In this sense, it opens up the title *Verde Shanghai*, allowing its meaning to slide and evade definition. Furthermore, self and other similarly avoid definition in the novel.

The most extreme problematization of self and other in the novel is the relationship between Marina and Xian. The possibility that Marina and Xian are the same person is, Prince suggests, one of the book's most intriguing questions. While ambiguous sentences or the confusion of names supports the idea of a split identity, it is not actually clear who is 'self' and who is 'other'.[223] This is explored by the text through a dialogue in which Marina and Chiang Wei decide that the word 'Yotro' best describes the concept. This term can be seen to suggest that people exist in common, disavowing a self-other dichotomy. In so doing, it recalls Nancy's idea that 'togetherness *is* otherness'.[224] Although Prince emphasizes the convergences and blurri-

219 Rivera Garza, *Verde Shanghai*, loc. 1254.

220 Prince, pp. 121–24.

221 Rivera Garza, *Verde Shanghai*, loc. 378.

222 Rivera Garza, *Verde Shanghai*, loc. 1062; the poem was published in Rivera Garza Cristina Rivera Garza, *El disco de Newton, Diez ensayos sobre el color* (Mexico City: Bonobos, Universidad Nacional Autónoma de México, 2011).

223 Prince, p. 127.

224 Christopher Watkin, 'A Different Alterity: Jean-Luc Nancy's "Singular Plural"', *Paragraph*, 30.2 (2007), pp. 50–64 (p. 61).

ness of subject and other, and Orient and Occident, her analysis seems to rely on either the distinctness or indistinctiveness of subjects and others, as she focuses on blurriness that does not necessarily challenge the realities of 'East' or 'West'. An alternative reading of the novel suggests that through Chinatown, Marina and Xian ultimately let go of any notion of self and other, characterizing existence as a kind of being-with. One of the final sentences of the novel serves to illustrate this: 'Y se hundió en el otro rostro'.[225] The unclear notion of who the 'otro rostro' belongs to unfixes identity and allows Marina to pass between borders while her body is under Horacio's control, in his house. Marina's singularity is exposed in this way as she interrupts Horacio's hegemonic power over her, escaping his control, even if only through her imagination.

From this perspective, Marina can be viewed as an example of what Alicia Gaspar de Alba has termed 'bad women': she is a woman who refuses to comply with the social discourses by which 'good girls' and 'good women' are constructed.[226] Horacio's attempt to control Marina is invested in discourses which position her as a 'bad woman'. Still, Marina escapes any framing by which bodies are described within 'a particular discourse and patriarchal imperatives, which are capitalist, racist, and imperialist imperatives'.[227] Marina ultimately escapes these discourses or frames by passing through her other selves, which have been present throughout the text and are made available to her via Chinatown. In Nancean fashion, Marina embodies the mingling, modification, and reconfiguration that occurs when different systems of differentiation encounter each other.

This blurriness is reinforced by the description of places that seem to have inexact borders or that exhibit transparency. Within these border uncertainties, Marina/Xian's body acts as a reminder of existence. Marina is aware through her bodily existence that she is Marina, as when a doctor touches her to confirm that no bones have been broken in the accident.[228] The novel's suggestion of the body as a site informed by histories and integral to the construction of meaning, as noted by Cheyla Samuelson in relation to Rivera Garza's writings,[229] can be seen in the following quote: 'Justo en medio de la historia, albergando entre las células la significación violenta de la historia, el

225 Rivera Garza, *Verde Shanghai*, loc. 4114.

226 Alicia Gaspar de Alba, *[Un]Framing the 'Bad Woman': Sor Juana, Malinche, Coyolxauhqi and Other Rebels with a Cause* (Austin: University of Texas Press, 2014), p. 7.

227 Gaspar de Alba, p. 18.

228 Rivera Garza, *Verde Shanghai*, loc. 158.

229 Cheyla Rose Samuelson, '"Algo destrozado sobre la calle": La guerra no importa como obra precursora en la narrativa de Cristina Rivera Garza', in *Cristina Rivera Garza. Ningún crítico cuenta esto...*, ed. by Oswaldo Estrada, Kindle (Mexico City: Ediciones Eón, 2010), loc. 725.

cuerpo es uno, sólo uno, no puede ser más.'[230] But Marina asks, 'Quien te dijo que la carne es real?'[231] questioning the notion of existence beyond the body while also questioning the body and essentialist and racialized understandings of it. Marina's inability to identify fully as either Chinese or Mexican, or otherwise, challenges any element that might foster the sustenance of any borders between class, race, or gender. Not only does Marina's existence have traces of both male and female identities, but she embodies different races and cultures. The text suggests a breaking of dichotomies, which places Marina as a site of Anzaldúa's 'borderland', a 'vague and undetermined place created by the emotional residue of an unnatural boundary'.[232]

Anzaldúa's *Borderlands/La Frontera: The New Mestiza* describes the constant collision between two cultures. Identity in the borderland is shifting, unresolvable, fluid, and in a constant state of transition. Although Anzaldúa's notion of the borderland is specific to a Chicana/o identity in relation to the U.S., Marina can also be seen to stand for notions of borders and unfixedness. Marina embodies the impossibility of 'hold[ing] concepts or ideas in rigid boundaries' while showing 'a tolerance for contradictions, a tolerance for ambiguity'.[233] However, if Chicana/o theory presupposes the hegemonic gaze of a White Anglo U.S., *Verde Shanghai* seems to go beyond this theory challenging the validity of any hegemony. In this sense, Marina/Xian sheds light on the parameters of Mexico's sociocultural identity. Marina can be interpreted as what Nancy terms the 'interruption of myth that reveals the disjunctive or hidden nature of community'.[234] By displacing borders, the novel suggests a redefinition from an indigenous/European mestizo identity to a transnational, transcultural, beyond hybrid, 'borderland' identity. Although the characters write and speak in Spanish, the conquerors' language, Marina pronounces Chinese correctly, in contrast to Horacio's incorrect transcription of it.[235]

Concerning racial or gendered positions, Marina exists as shifting and blending points on a continuum. In passing between races and genders, she is shown to be aware of the histories that inform her body. The novel reveals the racism and violence to which the Chinese in Mexico have been subjected, as we saw earlier in this chapter. From this perspective, Marina uses the Chinatown to open up the possibilities granted by less rigid distinctions of gender and race. Ambiguity allows Marina to be represented not as an assemblage or addition of identities, but as the coexistence of identities, the

230 Rivera Garza, *Verde Shanghai*, loc. 2634.
231 Rivera Garza, *Verde Shanghai*, loc. 3613.
232 Anzaldúa, p. 25.
233 Anzaldúa, p. 101. This certainly describes Rivera Garza herself, who not only grew up on the Mexican–U.S. border, but continues to travel between the U.S. and Mexico. *Verde Shanghai* itself is signed off 'Mexico, 1987 – San Diego, 2001 – Tijuana, 2010'.
234 Nancy, *The Inoperative Community*, p. 58.
235 Rivera Garza, *Verde Shanghai*, loc. 1306–07.

'"with" at the heart of the Being'.[236] In the encounters informed by histories and affectivity that are simultaneously positional and impossible to grasp in the present,[237] it is the relation itself which is given primacy. Indeed, Marina reminds the reader that 'strangerness' is not intrinsic to the subject but results from encounters between people.

The fact that the novel takes its title from the restaurant 'Verde Shanghai' (mentioned in the novel), which can be interpreted as a reference to 'Shan Ghai', the first restaurant in Mexico's *barrio chino*, suggests a return to the foundational moment of a space, which recalls the encounter between cultures and the histories of racism that inform these cultures. The Chinatown stands for a difference that is shown to have no 'essential' foundation. By challenging hegemonic constructions around gender, class and race, *Verde Shanghai* critiques essentialism, interrogating the paradigms around which cultural definitions have been structured. By using the Chinatown as a resource, this novel exposes the fictionality of the borders between cultures, race, and gender, and the narratives those discourses contain. In doing this, it exposes precisely the economic and racial realities that the novel aims to challenge.

Although access to 'truth' is denied, the novel nevertheless reveals how history may be 'real' in that it affects not only discourse but people themselves. The novel does not expose history as another discourse but rather explores the effects that specific historical discourse can have on people's lives. Rivera Garza has stated that immigrants, other than the Spanish Civil War exiles, are poorly regarded in Mexico.[238] However, the novel goes beyond the traditional idea of the migrant and emphasizes the notion of displacement within the self and at home; the novel reveals the various discourses at play through which Marina/Xian can define herself. In this sense, the text exceeds Anzaldúa's concept of the border in its discussion of internal otherness in Mexico, with the Chinatown as a space of disidentification. As originally defined by queer theorist José Esteban Muñoz, building on previous writings, disidentification 'both exposes the encoded message's universalizing and exclusionary machinations and recircuits its workings to account for, include, and empower minority identities and identifications'.[239] The novel thus exposes the racial discrimination towards the Chinese and the dominant culture's need for subaltern others. At the same time, it reveals the means through which those subject positions can be evaded and subverted. In so doing, *Verde Shanghai* both uses and displaces the *barrio chino*, challenging an idea of 'China' as different or distant.

Indeed, *Verde Shanghai* challenges any carefully orchestrated setting of the Chinatown and recalls instead a history linked to migration and racism.

236 Nancy, *Being Singular Plural*, p. 30.

237 Ahmed, *Strange Encounters*, p. 9.

238 Cabezas.

239 José Esteban Muñoz, *Disidentifications: Queers of Color and the Performance of Politics* (London: University of Minnesota Press, 1999), p. 31.

Chinatown, therefore, is where Marina's multiple identities are uncovered without erasing or ignoring the histories of her past. The denial of a stable identity is reiterated by the way she is named, or recognized, differently by different characters: as Xian, Marina, and Mar. Chinatown becomes the place where she is able to slip between worlds, being able to '[...] mirar como ellos, como hombre y como mujer'.[240]

From this perspective, as Debra Castillo notes, Marina comes closer to Norma Alarcón's explicit critique of Nancy's 'imprecise and universalising gesture'[241] of the *mestizo* as someone on the border of meaning, where ('his somewhat loose use of the term')[242] *mestizaje* is not the basis for identity because, he argues, everyone is a *mestizo*.[243] While reminding us that 'anti-essentialist theories of race [are] dominated by men who do not bother to remark [upon] gender',[244] Alarcón puts forward a middle ground between a traditional notion of ethnic identity and unbound heteroglossia. She thus suggests the presence of a continuous recreating of subjective identities through 'differences' and not through correspondence to an 'authentic core'.[245] Furthermore, the novel precisely embodies a challenge to a contemporary problem in Mexico, denounced by Mónica G. Moreno Figueroa and Emiko Saldívar Tanaka: that a 'raceless' ideology of *mestizaje* can become a concrete strategy of power, overlapping with current post-racial politics, and thus concealing the workings of racism.[246] Marina's dismissal of any notion of fixity through racial slippage disavows race as a category of identity whilst acknowledging the histories of racial discrimination and violence that the Chinese have suffered.

Rivera Garza offers a rewriting of the history of the *barrio chino*, where the descriptions available in the novel are far from the idealized and essentialized descriptions of the Chinatown's own website and other tourist sources, and closer to what Héctor de Mauleón describes as 'relato horrible de xenophobia'.[247] Focusing on the Chinatown and addressing a historical target of Mexico's racism,[248] the novel brings to the fore notions of inclusion

240 Rivera Garza, *Verde Shanghai*, loc. 2487.

241 Debra Castillo, '"An Other Tongue: Nation and Ethnicity in the Linguistic Borderlands" by Alfred Arteaga, Ed. (Book Review)', *Discourse*, 18.1 (1995), pp. 190–93 (p. 192).

242 Castillo, p. 192.

243 Jean-Luc Nancy, 'Cut Throat Sun', in *An Other Tongue*, ed. by Alfred Arteaga (Durham: Duke University Press, 1994), pp. 113–24 (pp. 113–23).

244 Norma Alarcón, 'Conjugating Subjects: The Heteroglossia of Essence and Resistance', in *An Other Tongue*, ed. by Alfred Arteaga (Durham: Duke University Press, 1994), pp. 125–38 (p. 131).

245 Alarcón, pp. 125–38.

246 Moreno Figueroa and Saldívar Tanaka, pp. 516–17, 527–28.

247 Héctor de Mauleón, 'Barrio Chino', *Nexos*, (2013) <http://www.nexos.com.mx/?p=15232> [accessed 1 May 2021].

248 Jason Oliver Chang, 'Racial Alterity in the Mestizo Nation', *Journal of Asian American Studies*, 14.3 (2011), pp. 331–59 (p. 332); Moreno Figueroa and Saldívar Tanaka, p. 14.

and exclusion and racial politics in Mexico. Read in dialogue, Nancy and Anzaldúa's conceptualizations illuminate Marina's radical unfixedness, reformatting ideas of community and 'in-betweeness'. While Aira and Magnus point to the fictitiousness of stable and essentialist identities by depicting Marina's embracing of ambiguity and the borderland, *Verde Shanghai* reveals a preference for being-with and coexistence as constitutive of the subject and the community.

As Elena Barabantseva argues, Chinatowns can create a restrictive delineation of space associated with a narrowly conceived cultural tradition, evoking limited images of Chineseness.[249] In her study on Chinatowns as heterotopic spaces in the U.S., Li Bidlingmaier argues that the myths associated with them as separate places within the city continue to render them as 'exotic, dangerous, uncanny, and perpetually other'.[250] Building on Butler, she argues that Chinatowns are performative spaces, affirming and perpetuating spatial otherness, as well as commodified ethnic spaces creating consistent products for consumption.[251] In her exploration of how the image and myth of Chinatowns have evolved into a transnational fantasy based on 'invented traditions', Mayer shows how literary and filmic narratives act as particularly compelling means of mediation across cultures and continents.[252] Within this context, literature acts as a platform for subverting and demystifying these same images and myths. If the Chinatown is now changing in light of the growing influence of the PRC, at the expense of dissidents, undocumented migrants and asylum seekers, the Chinatown fantasy and historical reality are very much alive.[253]

Conclusion: China in Latin America

'La historia perdida de los 303 chinos masacrados en Torreón durante la Revolución. Julián Herbert narra con gran maestría este hecho olvidado' states the publicity paper that comes with the edition by Random House Mondadori of the Mexican author Julián Herbert's (1971–) *La casa del dolor ajeno*.[254] Like the books analysed in the first chapter, this novel can also be defined, on one level, as historiographic metafiction:[255] while a work of fiction, it recourses to historiography and chronicle to explore the racism and

249 Elena Barabantseva, 'Seeing beyond an "Ethnic Enclave": The Time/Space of Manchester Chinatown', *Identities*, 23.1 (2016), pp. 99–115 (p. 2).

250 Li Bidlingmaier, p. 280.

251 Li Bidlingmaier, p. 281.

252 Mayer, 'Introduction', pp. 1–2.

253 Mayer, 'Introduction', p. 20.

254 Julián Herbert, *La casa del dolor ajeno* (México, D.F: Literatura Random House, 2015).

255 Linda Hutcheon, *A Poetics of Postmodernism: History, Theory, Fiction* (New York: Routledge, 1988).

violence to which the Chinese in Mexico have been subject to. Furthermore, the books explore how the violence of Mexican history is embedded in the history of the Chinese community in the country, as the narrator/investigator/author explores the 'lost story' of the 303 Chinese massacred in Torreón in 1911. While historically it had been blamed on the Mexican revolutionary context, Herbert explores the responsibility of ordinary people (rather than organized troops led by Pancho Villa). Indeed, the novel plays 'upon the truth and lies of the historical record', reminding us that we name and constitute events as historical facts by selection and narrative positioning, admitting 'the paradox of the *reality* of the past but its *textualized accessibility* to us today';[256] the subtitle of the novel is *Crónica de un pequeño genocidio en La Laguna*. It is a moving text, which, with a first-person narrator, retells the story of the genocide through a discussion with historical sources, and oral interviews (such as talking to taxi drivers), while simultaneously commenting on the structural violence at both the global and local (Mexican) level. The latter is in part achieved by also commenting on the forced disappearance of 43 students in Ayotzinapa in September 2014 and impunity in Mexico.[257]

Both Ignacio Sánchez-Prado and Jorge Locane argue that the text can be considered as non-fiction, and rather like a way of thinking about history from a different perspective, from the archive and building on the discursive elements of the past, like oral history, they see it as a way to explore hegemonic historical narratives.[258] Julio Enrique Ornelas[259] states Herbert rewrites Mexican history by including the event in his own version of the history of the period through a chronicle. According to Rebecca Janzen, who describes the text as 'an imaginative reconstruction of history',[260] the massacre was a 'consequence of systems that implicitly foster and condone violence'[261] rather than an example of lawlessness. The novel challenges traditional histories, which silence the crime and assassination of 303 Chinese persons by

256 Hutcheon, pp. 97, 114.

257 Ignacio López-Calvo, 'Entrevista a Julián Herbert sobre su obra La casa del dolor ajeno', *A Contracorriente: Revista de Historia Social y Literatura en América Latina*, 16.3 (2019), pp. 254–60.

258 Jorge Locane, 'China en América Latina o los límites del cosmopolitismo (liberal): A propósito de La casa del dolor ajeno (2015)', *A Contracorriente: una revista de estudios latinoamericanos*, 16.3 (2019), pp. 302–16 (p. 303); Ignacio M. Sánchez Prado, 'Más allá del mercado. Los usos de la literatura latinoamericana en la era neoliberal', in *Libro mercado: literatura y neoliberalismo*, ed. by José Ramón Ruisánchez (México: Universidad Iberoamericana, 2015), pp. 15–40 (p. 16).

259 Julio Enríquez Ornelas, 'Sinofobia a la vuelta de siglo: la matanza de chinos en Torreón, México', *Textos Híbridos*, 6.1 (2018) <https://doi.org/10.15691/textoshibridos.v6i1.76>.

260 Rebecca Janzen, 'Mexican Lawlessness: Genocide and Massacre in Julián Herbert's La Casa Del Dolor Ajeno', *TRANSMODERNITY: Journal of Peripheral Cultural Production of the Luso-Hispanic World*, 8.3 (2018), p. 88.

261 Janzen, p. 87.

showing that it was not an irrational or exceptional event but that it was part of a structural violence based around capitalism and ruthless competition, where in this specific event, it was directed towards the Chinese community, perceived as a threat. This, as we saw, was also available in *Verde Shanghai* by Cristina Rivera Garza. While the book is usually referred to as a novel, it does not adhere to the conventional aspects of the genre and has also been referred to as a chronicle,[262] as a historiographical chronicle, and a hybrid artifact.[263] Jorge Quintana Navarrete proposes that, in the book, Herbert plays with the methods of historians and the concepts of historicity in ways that question the political implications of historical memory.[264] Meanwhile, Juan Leal Ugalde describes the text as a 'historic-literary work'[265] as he discusses how the photographs in the book interrupt historicist narratives on the event while simultaneously allowing for a critical reflection on both the past and the present.

Sánchez Prado has also referred to the text as a 'hybrid';[266] and as 'una apuesta más amplia por la materialidad del archivo como estrategia de socavación del consenso hegemónico y el sujeto soberano constituidos de manera intermitente en los momentos traumáticos de la historia'.[267] And yet, while *La casa del dolor ajeno* does explore the limits of the historical record and the archive, and Herbert states in an interview that 'la obra no tiene nada de ficción',[268] in the text fiction becomes a discourse through which versions of reality are constructed. Indeed, the text itself calls attention to the versions of reality themselves, and how fiction is offered as another of the discourses by which we construct our versions of reality, played out in terms of parody and metafiction.[269] In the text the narrator states (more than once) 'Las cosas

262 Miguel Ángel Hernández Acosta, 'La recepción crítica de la narrativa de Herbert', in *La memoria cercena lo que une: Lecturas críticas a la obra de Julián Herbert*, ed. by Velázquez Soto and Armando Octavio (Universidad Nacional Autónoma de México. Facultad de Filosofía y Letras., 2019), pp. 41–60.

263 Nieves Marín Cobos, 'La autoficción como contrapunto a la "novela histórica" de los vencedores: hibridismo y metaficción en La casa del dolor ajeno (2015), de Julián Herbert', *Impossibilia. Revista Internacional de Estudios Literarios*, 14 (2017), pp. 74–92.

264 'El puente del horror: imagen dialéctica y soberanía en La casa del dolor ajeno de Julián Herbert', *A Contracorriente: una revista de estudios latinoamericanos*, 16.3 (2019), pp. 317–31 (p. 317).

265 Juan Leal Ugalde, 'Fotografía, literatura y muerte en La casa del dolor ajeno: el horror de la revolución mexicana en el norte de México', *A Contracorriente: una revista de estudios latinoamericanos*, 16.3 (2019), pp. 332–58 (p. 332).

266 Ignacio M. Sánchez Prado, 'La casa del dolor ajeno de Julián Herbert. No-ficción, memoria e historicidad en el México contemporáneo', *MLN*, 132.2 (2017), pp. 426–40 (p. 427) <https://doi.org/10.1353/mln.2017.0025>.

267 Sánchez Prado, 'La casa del dolor ajeno de Julián Herbert. No-ficción, memoria e historicidad en el México contemporáneo', p. 433.

268 López-Calvo, p. 258.

269 Hutcheon, pp. 40, 45.

le pertenecen al lenguaje'.[270] Herbert's novel explores the historical presence of Chinese persons in Mexico, shedding light on the way in which they are perceived in Latin America.

In *Chinardos*, by Fernando del Río, *Chineseness* and *Orientalness* are deployed and intersect in the text, exposing how 'strangerness' is enacted while simultaneously commenting on the spatial and migrant landscapes in Argentina, as events occur beyond the capital city of Buenos Aires, in Mar del Plata.[271] Like *Un chino en bicicleta* and *El mármol*, it also interrupts discourses of national homogeneity. *Tacos altos*,[272] by the Argentine Federico Jeanmaire, is a coming-of-age novel that recounts a 15-year-old girl's first-hand account of her daily life. The beginning of the book finds her in China, later travelling to Argentina; the text also includes intermissions in which she recalls her previous life in the Latin American country. Although her family is originally from China, the protagonist had spent ten years living in Argentina, where she arrived when she was five years old. Her return to China, the reader later learns, is the result of the death of her father, who was attacked by a local mob that burnt his shop with him in it. Her reflections on her identity permeate the book, as she continuously asks herself (always in Spanish): '¿soy realmente china?' On one level, this is a tale of a girl who embarks upon an emotional and physical journey prompted by a crisis of identity.[273] On another level, the novel engages with transnationalism, migration, and racism, as well as with the growing engagement between China and Latin America. Through both dimensions, the novel sheds light on the complexity of the experiences of the Chinese in Latin America and the connections between both regions.[274]

In Latin America, Mexico City's and Buenos Aires's *barrios chinos* can be seen to invoke the cultural imaginary around 'China' and the Chinese in a manner that resonates with Chinatowns worldwide. Kathleen López argues that Chinese immigration played a central role in the construction of the nation in Latin America in the late nineteenth and early twentieth centuries, and specifically in Mexico, Peru and Cuba, where they were at once 'promoted as efficient workers for progress and prosperity and criticized

270 Herbert, loc. 899.

271 For a more detailed analysis, see Montt Strabucchi '"Muertos somos todos iguales": Una lectura de Chinardos de Fernando del Río', in *Narrativas de lo chino en las Américas y la Península Ibérica*, ed. by Maria Montt Strabucchi and Amelia Sáiz López (Barcelona: Edicions Bellaterra, 2020), pp. 135–52.

272 Federico Jeanmaire, *Tacos altos* (Barcelona: Editorial Anagrama, 2016).

273 Jennifer Ann Ho, *Consumption and Identity in Asian American Coming-of-Age Novels*, ed. by Franklin Ng (New York & London: Routledge, 2005), p. 9.

274 For a detailed analysis, see Maria Montt Strabucchi, '(Trans)National Narratives of Identity in Federico Jeanmarie's Tacos Altos (2016)', in *Cultural and Literary Dialogues Between Asia and Latin America*, ed. by Axel Gasquet and Gorica Majstorovic (New York: Palgrave Macmillan, 2021), pp. 19–35.

as harmful to the physical and moral well-being of the nation'.[275] Although Chinese communities have had a relatively limited role in the recent economic engagement of China with Latin America, this presence has deeply impacted their social and political position in the countries in which they are located.[276] Ellis states that distinctions between 'new' Chinese, linked to the import-export business of China in Latin America, and the 'old' Chinese in Latin America, are 'fuzzy', tainted by a combination of respect for the perceived work of Chinese people, but mixed with prejudice over their 'perceived otherness'.[277] Indeed, many of these discourses echo the anti-Chinese voices of the twentieth century.[278]

From this perspective, through their portrayal of the Chinatown and Chinese, the novels analysed in this chapter demand the acknowledgement of race as central to the power dynamics in Latin America today. In this sense, the use of China can be linked to the real presence of China both in Mexico and Argentina. It can be argued that China, as a mirror, can also trigger questions concerning issues of identity, regarding both subject and community.[279] In line with Jacques Derrida's discussion of the supplement, 'China' here shows how 'what is no longer deferred is also absolutely deferred'.[280] As the Chinese stand out from other immigrant communities because of their 'perceived otherness' and construction as a 'fetishized stranger', the novels expose the impossibility of locating them within stable, known cartographies such as East/West, North/South or West/non-West. In their choice of Chinese communities and Chinatowns, and precisely because the implied authors do not see the 'Chinese' as 'fitting' these cartographies, the novels expose and critique how Latin America continues to rely on fixed

275 Kathleen López, 'In Search of Legitimacy: Chinese Immigrants and Latin American Nation Building', in *Immigration and National Identities in Latin America*, ed. by Nicola Foote and Michael Goebel (Gainsville: University Press of Florida, 2014), pp. 182–204 (pp. 182–83).

276 Carol Chan, 'Imagining and Linking Latin America: Chinese Regional Mobilities and Social Networks in Chile', *Journal of Latin American Geography*, 17.2 (2018), pp. 23–45; Ellis, pp. 179–81; Montt Strabucchi and Chan; Jorge Moraga Reyes, 'Reparto comunitario y gasto agonístico: diferenciaciones y hegemonías entre antiguos y nuevos migrantes chinos en Chile', *Rumbos TS*, 17 (2018), pp. 133–52; *China's Foreign Direct Investment in Latin America and the Caribbean: Conditions and Challenges*, ed. by Enrique Dussel Peters (México, D.F: Universidad Nacional Autónoma de México, 2019).

277 Ellis, pp. 181–82.

278 López, p. 201.

279 Armony and Velásquez; Carol Chan and Maria Montt Strabucchi, 'Many-Faced Orientalism: Racism and Xenophobia in a Time of the Novel Coronavirus in Chile', *Asian Ethnicity*, 22.2 (2021), pp. 374–94 <https://doi.org/10.1080/14631369.2020.1795618>.

280 Jacques Derrida, *Of Grammatology* (Baltimore: The Johns Hopkins University Press, 2016), p. 167.

discourses of self and other, however nuanced they may be, such as those contained in the discourses of *mestizaje*. In this exposure and critique, they hint towards a community close to that described by Nancy, disavowing race and exposing and challenging the mechanisms for the construction of 'strangerness'.

In the novels studied here, the image of 'China' as different or distant is challenged through characters who disturb those discourses and engage with the Chinese at home, challenging the myths of a 'white' Argentina and opening up the meaning of a 'mestizo' Mexico. As Jane Hiddlestone argues, 'with its capacity for experimentation and singular invention [literature can constitute a discourse that may] remove any ground, or any essential content, from terms such as "the subject" and "the community"'.[281] The novels can thus be read as engaging with Nancy precisely because 'it is the interruption of myth that reveals the disjunctive or hidden nature of community'.[282] In this sense, as Masiello explores in *The Art of Transition*, these novels' imaginings of China 'alter the paths of citation that depend on a northern center';[283] although she refers to Argentina specifically, her analysis can be extended to other Latin American cultural expressions. By incorporating the Chinese into national discourses, the novels subvert and alter a North/South binary, interrogate fixed relationships between stable categories, and reconstruct those categories removed from a North/South lens.[284] In this context, the novels may be said to 'test the boundaries of home and foreign and chart courses for racialized bodies',[285] borrowing Masiello's word. While *Un chino en bicicleta* and *El mármol* mostly disclose and dismiss fixed discourses, *Verde Shanghai* seems to explicitly embrace unfixedness. The novels thus produce city landscapes in which the *barrio chino* and the Chinese supermarkets are intrinsically constitutive and transformative, revealing the changing cultural, economic, and political landscapes of Buenos Aires and Ciudad de Mexico, and beyond that, unveiling varying notions of alterity and community in Latin America.

References

Aguiló, Ignacio, 'Tropical Buenos Aires: Representations of Race in Argentine Literature during the 2001 Crisis and Its Aftermath', in *Argentina since the 2001 Crisis: Recovering the Past, Reclaiming the Future*, ed. by Cara Levey, Daniel Ozarow, and Christopher Wylde (New York: Palgrave Macmillan, 2014), pp. 177–94

281 Jane Hiddlestone, 'The Politics of Literary Criticism: Nancy and Rushdie', *Oxford Literary Review*, 27 (2005), pp. 119–38 (pp. 119, 121).

282 Nancy, *The Inoperative Community*, p. 58.

283 Masiello, p. 17.

284 Masiello, pp. 7, 146.

285 Masiello, p. 156.

Ahmed, Sara, *Queer Phenomenology: Orientations, Objects, Others* (Durham: Duke University Press, 2006)

———, *Strange Encounters: Embodied Others in Post-Coloniality* (London: Routledge, 2000)

Aira, César, *El mármol*, Kindle 2012 (Buenos Aires: La Bestia Equilátera, 2011)

Alam, Florencia, 'Representaciones sociolingüísticas en la comunidad inmigrante chino-taiwanesa: Posibles abordajes para la enseñanza' (presented at the IV Coloquio CELU: La interculturalidad y la internacionalización en las prácticas evaluativas, Universidad Nacional del Litoral, Santa Fe, 2008)

Alarcón, Norma, 'Conjugating Subjects: The Heteroglossia of Essence and Resistance', in *An Other Tongue*, ed. by Alfred Arteaga (Durham: Duke University Press, 1994), pp. 125–38

Alberto, Paulina L., and Eduardo Elena, eds, *Rethinking Race in Modern Argentina: The Shades of the Nation* (New York: Cambridge University Press, 2016)

Amancay Torres, Rayén, 'Los Barrios Chinos en Buenos Aires: entre diversidades, tensiones e interculturalidad', *Diversidad*, 11.7 (2015), pp. 1–24

Anderson, Benedict, *Imagined Communities: Reflections on the Origin and Spread of Nationalism*, 3rd edn (London: Verso, 2006)

Ang, Ien, 'Chinatowns and the Rise of China', *Modern Asian Studies*, 54.4 (2020), pp. 1367–93 <https://doi.org/10.1017/S0026749X19000179>

Anzaldúa, Gloria, *Borderlands/La Frontera: The New Mestiza* (San Francisco: Aunt Lute Books, 2007)

Arce, Rafael, 'César Aira: "Entre los indios"; "Festival"; "El náufrago"; "El mármol"', *Cuadernos de Literatura*, 17.34 (2013), pp. 341–47

Argenchino, dir. by Julia Reagan, 2009

Armony, Ariel C., and Nicolás Velásquez, 'Anti-Chinese Sentiment in Latin America: An Analysis of Online Discourse', *Journal of Chinese Political Science*, 20.3 (2015), pp. 319–46

Ashcroft, Bill, Gareth Griffiths, and Helen Tiffin, *The Empire Writes Back: Theory and Practice in Post-Colonial Literatures* (London: Routledge, 2005)

Bakhtin, Mikhail, *The Dialogic Imagination: Four Essays*, ed. by Michael Holquist (Austin: University of Texas Press, 1981)

Barabantseva, Elena, 'Seeing beyond an "Ethnic Enclave": The Time/Space of Manchester Chinatown', *Identities*, 23.1 (2016), pp. 99–115

'Barrio Chino Belgrano Buenos Aires Argentina', *Barrio Chino* <http://www.barriochino.net/index.php/10-tapa/30-barriochinonet-barrio-chino-belgrano-buenos-aires-argentina> [accessed 1 July 2021]

'Barrio Chino en Belgrano', *Mi Belgrano* <http://www.mibelgrano.com.ar/barriochinovie.htm> [accessed 1 July 2021]

Bastia, Tanja, 'Transnational Migration and Urban Informality: Ethnicity in Buenos Aires' Informal Settlements', *Urban Studies*, 52.10 (2014), pp. 1–16

Bhabha, Homi K., *The Location of Culture* (Oxon: Routledge, 1994)

Bogado Bordazar, Laura, 'Migraciones internacionales: Influencia de la migración china en el Río de la Plata' (unpublished master's dissertation, Universidad Nacional de La Plata, 2002)

Borcoski, Nicolás, 'El nuevo plan del alcalde de Santiago: Un "Barrio chino" en la Estación Central', *La Nación*, 25 May 2018 <http://lanacion.cl/2018/05/25/el-nuevo-plan-del-alcalde-de-santiago-un-barrio-chino-en-la-estacion-central/> [accessed 25 January 2023]

Borges, Jorge Luis, 'El escritor argentino y la tradición', in *Discusión*, essay originally published 1953 (Madrid: Alianza, 1976), pp. 128–37

———, *La cifra* (Madrid: Alianza, 1981)

Botton Beja, Flora, 'La persecución de los chinos en México', *Estudios de Asia y África*, 43.2.136 (2008), pp. 477–86

Buchenau, Jürgen, 'The Limits of the Cosmic Race: Immigrant and Nation in Mexico, 1850-1950', in *Immigration and National Identities in Latin America*, ed. by Nicola Foote and Michael Goebel (Gainsville: University Press of Florida, 2014), pp. 66–90

Butler, Judith, *Gender Trouble: Feminism and the Subversion of Identity* (London: Routledge, 1990)

Cabezas, Alberto, 'Cristina Rivera Garza: "La mirada de los migrantes no descansa nunca"', *Revista Arcadia*, (2011) <http://www.revistaarcadia.com/libros/articulo/cristina-rivera-garza-la-mirada-migrantes-no-descansa-nunca/25644> [accessed 1 May 2021]

Castillo, Debra, '"An Other Tongue: Nation and Ethnicity in the Linguistic Borderlands" by Alfred Arteaga, Ed. (Book Review)', *Discourse*, 18.1 (1995), pp. 190–93

Castro, Olman, 'Un chino en bicicleta da fama a un argentino', *Revista Perfil*, (2008) <http://wvw.revistaperfil.com/node/4617> [accessed 1 August 2021]

Castro Ricalde, Maricruz, 'Diversidad sexual y liminalidad en "Nadie me verá llorar" de Cristina Rivera Garza', in *Reflexiones en torno a la escritura femenina*, ed. by Adriana Sáenz Valadez and Cándida Elizabeth Vivero Marín (Mexico City: Universidad de Guadalajara y Universidad Michoacana de San Nicolás de Hidalgo, 2011), pp. 241–69

Cavallero, J.C., 'Barrio Chino y Calle de Dolores, D.F. (Visita y Semblanza)', *Bici-tando la Ciudad de México*, (2013) <https://bicitando.wordpress.com/2013/08/27/barrio-chino-y-calle-de-dolores-d-f-visita-y-semblanza/> [accessed 1 May 2021]

Chan, Carol, 'Imagining and Linking Latin America: Chinese Regional Mobilities and Social Networks in Chile', *Journal of Latin American Geography*, 17.2 (2018), pp. 23–45

Chan, Carol, and Maria Montt Strabucchi, 'Creating and Negotiating "Chineseness" through Chinese Restaurants in Santiago, Chile', in *American Chinese Restaurants: Society, Culture and Consumption*, ed. by Jenny Banh and Haiming Liu (New York: Routledge, 2020), pp. 3–25

———, 'Many-Faced Orientalism: Racism and Xenophobia in a Time of the Novel Coronavirus in Chile', *Asian Ethnicity*, 22.2 (2021), pp. 374–94 <https://doi.org/10.1080/14631369.2020.1795618>

Chang, Jason Oliver, 'Racial Alterity in the Mestizo Nation', *Journal of Asian American Studies*, 14.3 (2011), pp. 331–59

Chao, Melody M., and Franki Y. H. Kung, 'An Essentialism Perspective on Intercultural Processes', *Asian Journal of Social Psychology*, 18.2 (2015), pp. 91–100

Chao Romero, Robert, *The Chinese in Mexico, 1882–1940* (Tucson: University of Arizona Press, 2010)

'Clausuran 4 supermercados chinos', *Buenos Aires Ciudad—Gobierno de la Ciudad Autónoma de Buenos Aires*, (2015) <http://www.buenosaires.gob.ar/noticias/clausuran-4-supermercados-chinos> [accessed 1 May 2021]

Contreras, Sandra, *Las vueltas de César Aira* (Rosario: Beatriz Viterbo Editora, 2002)

Da Costa, Alexandre Emboaba, 'Thinking "Post-Racial" Ideology Transnationally: The Contemporary Politics of Race and Indigeneity in the Americas', *Critical Sociology*, 42.4–5 (2016), pp. 475–90

Denardi, Luciana, 'Casetes, redes y banquetes. Prácticas comerciales de chinos, taiwaneses y argentinos en Buenos Aires', *Etnografías Contemporáneas*, 2.2 (2016), pp. 134–60

———, 'Chinese Migrations to Argentina: Diasporic Bureaucracy, Identifications and Rituals', in *Chinese Immigration in Latin America: Some Cultural Contributions*, ed. by Pablo Baisotti (Newcastle upon Tyne: Cambridge Scholars Publishing, 2020), pp. 69–88

———, 'Ser chino en Buenos Aires: Historia, moralidades y cambios en la diáspora china en Argentina', *Horizontes Antropológicos*, 21.43 (2015), pp. 79–103

Denardi, Luciana, and Alejandra Conconi, 'Reflexiones Metodológicas sobre Investigaciones Etnográficas con "Chinos" y "Taiwaneses" en Argentina', *Asian Journal of Latin American Studies*, 31.2 (2018), pp. 41–61

Denardi, Luciana, and Chenxi Luo, 'El estudio era el único camino para cambiar mi destino: Posicionamiento de mujeres migrantes chinas en Buenos Aires respecto a su rol en la familia', *Revista del Museo de Antropología*, 15.1 (2022), <https://doi.org/10.31048/1852.4826.v15.n1.35367>

Derrida, Jacques, *Of Grammatology* (Baltimore: The Johns Hopkins University Press, 2016)

Dubs, Homer H., and Robert S. Smith, 'Chinese in Mexico City in 1635', *The Far Eastern Quarterly*, 1.4 (1942), pp. 387–89

Dussel Peters, Enrique, ed., *China's Foreign Direct Investment in Latin America and the Caribbean: Conditions and Challenges* (México, D.F: Universidad Nacional Autónoma de México, 2019)

Edwards, Erika Denise, 'The Making of a White Nation: The Disappearance of the Black Population in Argentina', *History Compass*, 16.7 (2018), e12456 <https://doi.org/10.1111/hic3.12456>

'"El mármol", una aventura literaria de la mano de César Aira', *El Sol*, (2011) <http://www.elsol.com.ar/nota/92392> [accessed 1 May 2021]

Ellis, Robert Evan, *China on the Ground in Latin America: Challenges for the Chinese and Impacts on the Region* (New York: Palgrave Macmillan, 2014)

Fernández Bravo, Álvaro, 'Apropiaciones de la cultura china en la literatura sudamericana contemporánea: Contribución para un mapa tentativo a partir de obras de César Aira, Bernardo Carvalho y Siu Kam Wen', *452°F Revista de teoría de la literatura y literatura comparada*, 13 (2015), pp. 50–70

Fuentes, Carlos, 'Cristina Rivera Garza' (El Norte, 2002)

Gaspar de Alba, Alicia, *[Un]Framing the 'Bad Woman': Sor Juana, Malinche, Coyolxauhqi and Other Rebels with a Cause* (Austin: University of Texas Press, 2014)

González Viaña, María del Carmen, 'Cambios en la vocación del territorio. Estudio de tres enclaves porteños: Avenida de Mayo, La Boca y Barrio Chino' (unpublished doctoral dissertation, Universidad Complutense de Madrid, 2014)

Grimson, Alejandro, Gustavo Ng, and Luciana Denardi, 'Las organizaciones de inmigrantes chinos en Argentina', *Migración y desarrollo*, 14.26 (2016) <http://www.redalyc.org/resumen.oa?id=66046498002> [accessed 1 August 2021]

Güich Rodríguez, José, *El misterio del barrio chino* (Lima: Ediciones SM, 2013)

Hearn, Adrian, 'Harnessing the Dragon: Overseas Chinese Entrepreneurs in Mexico and Cuba', *The China Quarterly*, 209 (2012), pp. 111–33

Herbert, Julián, *La casa del dolor ajeno* (México, D.F: Literatura Random House, 2015)

Hernández Acosta, Miguel Ángel, 'La recepción crítica de la narrativa de Herbert', in *La memoria cercena lo que une: Lecturas críticas a la obra de Julián Herbert*, ed. by Velázquez Soto and Armando Octavio (Mexico: Universidad Nacional Autónoma de México, Facultad de Filosofía y Letras, 2019), pp. 41–60

Hiddlestone, Jane, 'The Politics of Literary Criticism: Nancy and Rushdie', *Oxford Literary Review*, 27 (2005), pp. 119–38

Hind, Emily, *Entrevistas con quince autoras mexicanas* (Madrid: Iberoamericana, 2003)

'Historia del Barrio Chino CDMX' <http://barriochinomexico.com/historia/> [accessed 1 May 2021]

Ho, Jennifer Ann, *Consumption and Identity in Asian American Coming-of-Age Novels*, ed. by Franklin Ng (New York & London: Routledge, 2005)

Hoyos, Héctor, 'Orientalismo, globalización e imaginarios transpacíficos en la novela latinoamericana actual', *Cuadernos de literatura*, 17.34 (2013), pp. 82–105

Hu-DeHart, Evelyn, 'Chinatowns and Borderlands: Inter-Asian Encounters in the Diaspora', *Modern Asian Studies; Cambridge*, 46.2 (2012), pp. 425–51 <http://dx.doi.org/10.1017/S0026749X11000965>

———, 'Coolies, Shopkeepers, Pioneers: The Chinese of Mexico and Peru (1849–1930)', *Amerasia*, 15.2 (1989), pp. 91–116

———, 'Inclusion and Exclusion. The Chinese in Multiracial Latin America and the Caribbean', in *Routledge Handbook of the Chinese Diaspora*, ed. by Tan Chee-Beng (London: Routledge, 2013), pp. 89–107

———, 'Indispensable Enemy or Convenient Scapegoat? A Critical Examination of Sinophobia in Latin America and the Caribbean, 1870s to 1930s', in *The Chinese in Latin America and the Caribbean*, ed. by Walton Look Lai and Chee-Beng Tan (Leiden: Brill, 2010), pp. 65–102

Huggan, Graham, *The Postcolonial Exotic: Marketing the Margins* (London: Routledge, 2001)

Hutcheon, Linda, *A Poetics of Postmodernism: History, Theory, Fiction* (New York: Routledge, 1988)

Janzen, Rebecca, 'Mexican Lawlessness: Genocide and Massacre in Julián Herbert's La Casa Del Dolor Ajeno', *TRANSMODERNITY: Journal of Peripheral Cultural Production of the Luso-Hispanic World*, 8.3 (2018)

Jeanmaire, Federico, *Tacos altos* (Barcelona: Editorial Anagrama, 2016)

Jordana, Verónica, 'Mi gran casamiento chino | Conexión Brando' <http://www.conexionbrando.com/1092794-mi-gran-casamiento-chino> [accessed 1 May 2021]

Keizman, Betina, 'El blog de Cristina Rivera Garza: experiencia literaria y terreno de contienda', *Chasqui*, 42.1 (2013), pp. 3–15

Ko, Chisu Teresa, '"Argentina te incluye": Asians in Argentina's Multicultural Novels', *Symposium: A Quarterly Journal in Modern Literatures*, 69.1 (2015), pp. 1–13

———, 'Between Foreigners and Heroes: Asian-Argentines in a Multicultural Nation', in *Rethinking Race in Modern Argentina*, ed. by Eduardo Elena and Paulina L. Alberto (New York: Cambridge University Press, 2016), pp. 268–88

———, 'From Whiteness to Diversity: Crossing the Racial Threshold in Bicentennial Argentina', *Ethnic and Racial Studies*, 37.14 (2014), pp. 2529–46

———, 'Orientalism and De-Orientalism in Contemporary Latin America: Reading César Aira', *TRANSMODERNITY: Journal of Peripheral Cultural Production of the Luso-Hispanic World*, 8.3 (2018), pp. 149–67

———, 'Toward Asian Argentine Studies', *Latin American Research Review*, 51.4 (2016), pp. 271–89

Lacarrieu, Mónica, '"... De todos lados y de ningún lado...": Visibles/visibilizados e invisibles/invisibilizados en busca de un lugar en la Buenos Aires del siglo XXI', *Kairos*, 11 (2002) <http://www.revistakairos.org/k11-07.htm> [accessed 1 August 2021]

Leal Ugalde, Juan, 'Fotografía, literatura y muerte en La casa del dolor ajeno: el horror de la revolución mexicana en el norte de México', *A Contracorriente: una revista de estudios latinoamericanos*, 16.3 (2019), pp. 332–58

Lee, Erika, 'Enforcing the Borders: Chinese Exclusion along the U.S. Borders with Canada and Mexico, 1882–1924', *The Journal of American History*, 89.1 (2002), pp. 54–86

———, 'The "Yellow Peril" and Asian Exclusion in the Americas', *Pacific Historical Review*, 76.4 (2007), pp. 537–62

Lee-Loy, Anne-Marie, *Searching for Mr. Chin: Constructions of Nation and the Chinese in West Indian Literature* (Philadelphia: Temple University Press, 2010)

Levinson, Brett, 'The Death of the Critique of Eurocentrism: Latinamericanism as a Global Praxis/Poiesis', in *Orientalism and Identity in Latin America: Fashioning Self and Other from the (Post)Colonial Margin*, ed. by Erik Camayd-Freixas (Tucson: University of Arizona Press, 2013), pp. 19–34

Li Bidlingmaier, Selma Siew, 'Spaces of Alterity and Temporal Permanence: The Case of San Francisco's and New York's Chinatowns', in *Selling Ethnicity: Urban Cultural Politics in the Americas*, ed. by Olaf Kaltmeier (Surrey: Ashgate, 2011), pp. 275–86

Locane, Jorge, 'China en América Latina o los límites del cosmopolitismo (liberal): A propósito de La casa del dolor ajeno (2015)', *A Contracorriente: una revista de estudios latinoamericanos*, 16.3 (2019), pp. 302–16

López, Kathleen, 'In Search of Legitimacy: Chinese Immigrants and Latin American Nation Building', in *Immigration and National Identities in Latin America*, ed. by Nicola Foote and Michael Goebel (Gainsville: University Press of Florida, 2014), pp. 182–204

López-Calvo, Ignacio, 'Entrevista a Julián Herbert sobre su obra La casa del dolor ajeno', *A Contracorriente: Revista de Historia Social y Literatura en América Latina*, 16.3 (2019), pp. 254–60

Loveman, Mara, *National Colors: Racial Classification and the State in Latin America* (Oxford: Oxford University Press, 2014)

Luk, Wai-ki, *Chinatown in Britain: Diffusions and Concentrations of the British New Wave Chinese Immigration* (Youngstown: Cambria Press, 2008)

Luszczynska, Ana, 'The Opposite of the Concentration Camp: Nancy's Vision of Community', *The New Centennial Review*, 5.3 (2005), pp. 167–205

Magnus, Ariel, *Un chino en bicicleta* (Bogota: Grupo Editorial Norma, 2007)

Marín Cobos, Nieves, 'La autoficción como contrapunto a la "novela histórica" de los vencedores: hibridismo y metaficción en La casa del dolor ajeno (2015), de Julián Herbert', *Impossibilia. Revista Internacional de Estudios Literarios*, 14 (2017), pp. 74–92

Martins, Ana Margarida, *Magic Stones and Flying Snakes: Gender and the 'Postcolonial Exotic' in the Work of Paulina Chiziane and Lídia Jorge* (Oxford: Peter Lang, 2012)

Masiello, Francine, *The Art of Transition: Latin American Culture and Neoliberal Crisis* (London: Duke University Press, 2001)

de Mauleón, Héctor, 'Barrio Chino', *Nexos*, (2013) <http://www.nexos.com.mx/?p=15232> [accessed 1 May 2021]

Mayer, Ruth, 'Introduction', in *Chinatowns in a Transnational World: Myths and Realities of an Urban Phenomenon*, ed. by Vanessa Künnemann and Ruth Mayer (New York: Routledge, 2011), pp. 1–25

———, '"The Greatest Novelty of the Age": Fu-Manchu, Chinatown, and the Global City', in *Chinatowns in a Transnational World: Myths and Realities of an Urban Phenomenon*, ed. by Vanessa Künnemann and Ruth Mayer (New York: Routledge, 2011), pp. 116–34

Montt Strabucchi, Maria, 'Encuentros con la comunidad china en Buenos Aires: un análisis de dos novelas', *Working Paper Series (WPS) de REDCAEM*, 4 (2018), pp. 1–26

———, 'Mexico City's "Chinos" and "Barrio Chino": Strangerness and Community in Cristina Rivera Garza's "Verde Shanghai" (2011)', *Verge: Studies in Global Asias*, 3.2 (2017), pp. 144–68

———, '"Muertos somos todos iguales": Una lectura de Chinardos de Fernando del Río', in *Narrativas de lo chino en las Américas y la Península Ibérica*, ed. by Maria Montt Strabucchi and Amelia Sáiz López (Barcelona: Edicions Bellaterra, 2020), pp. 135–52

———, '(Trans)National Narratives of Identity in Federico Jeanmarie's Tacos Altos (2016)', in *Cultural and Literary Dialogues Between Asia and Latin America*, ed. by Axel Gasquet and Gorica Majstorovic (New York: Palgrave Macmillan, 2021), pp. 19–35

Montt Strabucchi, Maria, and Carol Chan, 'Questioning the Conditional Visibility of the Chinese: (Non)Normative Representations of China and Chineseness in Chilean Cultural Productions', *Journal of Chinese Overseas*, 16.1 (2020), pp. 90–116 <https://doi.org/10.1163/17932548-12341414>

Moraga Reyes, Jorge, 'Reparto comunitario y gasto agonístico: diferenciaciones y hegemonías entre antiguos y nuevos migrantes chinos en Chile', *Rumbos TS*, 17 (2018), pp. 133–52

Moreno Figueroa, Mónica G., and Emiko Saldívar Tanaka, '"We Are Not Racists, We Are Mexicans": Privilege, Nationalism and Post-Race Ideology in Mexico', *Critical Sociology*, 42.4–5 (2016), pp. 515–33

Morin, Marie-Eve, *Jean-Luc Nancy* (Cambridge: Polity, 2012)

Muñoz, José Esteban, *Disidentifications: Queers of Color and the Performance of Politics* (London: University of Minnesota Press, 1999)

Nancy, Jean-Luc, *Being Singular Plural* (Stanford: Stanford University Press, 2000)

———, 'Cut Throat Sun', in *An Other Tongue*, ed. by Alfred Arteaga (Durham: Duke University Press, 1994), pp. 113–24

———, *The Inoperative Community* (Minneapolis: University of Minnesota Press, 1991)

Nieva, Michel Emiliano, 'Ariel Magnus: Un chino en bicicleta', *Soles Digitial*, (2009) <http://www.solesdigital.com.ar/libros/magnus.html> [accessed 1 May 2021]

Ocvirk, Verónica, 'Guía para conocer lo mejor del Chinatown porteño', *Revista OhLaLá!* <http://www.revistaohlala.com/1348595-guia-para-conocer-lo-mejor-del-chinatown-porteno> [accessed 1 May 2021]

Ornelas, Julio Enríquez, 'Sinofobia a la vuelta de siglo: la matanza de chinos en Torreón, México', *Textos Híbridos*, 6.1 (2018) <https://doi.org/10.15691/textoshibridos.v6i1.76>

Owen, Hilary, *Mother Africa, Father Marx: Women's Writing of Mozambique, 1948–2002* (Lewisburg: Bucknell University Press, 2007)

Palapa Quijas, Fabiola, 'Cristina Rivera Garza explora formas de la memoria para escapar al olvido', *La Jornada*, 2011, section Cultura <http://www.jornada.unam.mx/2011/07/06/cultura/a06n1cul> [accessed 1 May 2021]

Palaversich, Diana, 'The New Narrative of the North: Moving Frontiers of Mexican Literature', *Symposium*, 61.1 (2007), pp. 9–26

Palma, Patricia, and José Ragas, 'Enclaves Sanitarios: Higiene, Epidemias y Salud En El Barrio Chino de Lima, 1880-1910', *Anuario Colombiano de Historia Social y de la Cultura*, 45.1 (2018), pp. 159–90 <https://doi.org/10.15446/achsc.v45n1.67555>

Pappier, Andrea, 'Inmigración china en Argentina: el barrio chino de Bs As como caso de estudio intercultural' (presented at the Asociación Latinoamericana de Estudios de Asia y África, XIII Congreso Internacional de ALADAA, Bogota, 2011)

Park, Jungwon, 'Manicomio y locura: Revolución dentro de la revolución mexicana en "Nadie me verá llorar" de Cristina Rivera Garza', *Anclajes*, 17.1 (2013), pp. 55–72

Paz Soldán, Edmundo, '"Cristina Rivera Garza's Tweets"', ed. by Christine Hensler and Deborah Castillo, *Hispanic Issues Online*, 9 (2012), pp. 38–39

Peña Delgado, Grace, *Making the Chinese Mexican: Global Migration, Localism, and Exclusion in the U.S.-Mexico Borderlands* (Stanford: Stanford University Press, 2012)

Pereyra, Soledad, 'Terrorismos postautónomos en la literatura argentina actual, en torno a Washington Cucurto, escritor' (unpublished doctoral dissertation, Albert Ludwigs Universität Freiburg i. Br., 2010)

'Premian la novela de un argentino', *La Nación*, 21 July 2007, section Cultura <http://www.lanacion.com.ar/945949-premian-la-novela-de-un-argentino> [accessed 1 May 2021]

Prince, Jennifer, 'Ella, Yo y El Yotro: Orientalisms and Identities in Cristina Rivera Garza's "Verde Shanghai"', in *Orientalism of the Hispanic and Luso-Brazilian World*, ed. by Araceli Tinajero (New York: Escribana Books, 2014), pp. 118–36

Quintana Navarrete, Jorge, 'El puente del horror: imagen dialéctica y soberanía en La casa del dolor ajeno de Julián Herbert', *A Contracorriente: una revista de estudios latinoamericanos*, 16.3 (2019), pp. 317–31

Real Academia Española, 'alien', *Diccionario de la Lengua Española* (Real Academia Española, 2017) <http://dle.rae.es/> [accessed 1 May 2021]

Regalado López, Tomás, 'The Crack and Contemporary Latin American Narrative: An Introductory Study', in *New Trends in Contemporary Latin American Narrative, Post-National Literature and the Canon*, ed. by Timothy R. Robbins and José Eduardo González (New York: Palgrave Macmillan, 2014), pp. 55–83

Rivera Cusicanqui, Silvia, 'Ch'ixinakax Utxiwa: A Reflection on the Practices and Discourses of Decolonization', *South Atlantic Quarterly*, 111.1 (2012), pp. 95–109

Rivera Garza, Cristina, 'Cristina Rivera Garza: Matamoros, México, 1964', *Nuevo Texto Crítico*, 21.2 (2008), pp. 21–32

———, *El disco de Newton, Diez ensayos sobre el color* (Mexico City: Bonobos, Universidad Nacional Autónoma de México, 2011)

———, *Nadie me verá llorar* (Mexico City: Tusquets, Conaculta, 1999)

———, *Verde Shanghai*, Kindle (Mexico City: Tusquets, 2011)

Rodiño, Silvia, 'El secreto de los negocios chinos', *Clarín*, 6 March 2006 <http://edant.clarin.com/suplementos/pymes/2006/03/06/y-01150880.htm> [accessed 1 May 2021]

Rodríguez, Juan José, *Asesinato en una lavandería china* (Mexico D.F: Consejo Nacional para la Cultura y las Artes, 1996)

Rodríguez Zapata, Aniela, 'La otredad en la literatura femenina: un acercamiento posestructural a "Verde Shanghai" de Cristina Rivera Garza', in *La Palabra. Lenguaje, Medios y Sociedades Digitales*, ed. by Ysela Y. de Pablo Porras, Brenda Sánchez Aguirre, Emma Escobedo Chávez, Angélica Sandoval Pineda, Eduardo Fernandez Armendáriz, and Humberto Payán Fierro (Chihuahua: Universidad Autónoma de Chihuahua, 2013), pp. 141–48

Rud, Lucía, 'Representaciones de las migraciones y diásporas de Asia del Este en el audiovisual argentino', *Nuevo Mundo Mundos Nuevos*, (2020) <https://doi.org/10.4000/nuevomundo.80888>

Sabugal, Eduardo, 'La caja verde de Cristina', *Crítica*, 146 (2011) <http://revistacritica.com/contenidos-impresos/vigilia/verde-shanghai-de-cristina-rivera-garza> [accessed 1 May 2021]

Samuelson, Cheyla Rose, '"Algo destrozado sobre la calle": La guerra no importa como obra precursora en la narrativa de Cristina Rivera Garza', in *Cristina Rivera Garza. Ningún crítico cuenta esto...*, ed. by Oswaldo Estrada, Kindle (Mexico City: Ediciones Eón, 2010)

———, 'Writing at Escape Velocity: An Interview with Cristina Rivera Garza', *Confluencia*, 23.1 (2007), pp. 135–45

Sánchez Prado, Ignacio M., 'Ending the World with Words: Bernardo Fernández (BEF) and the Institutionalization of Science Fiction in Mexico', in *Latin American Science Fiction: Theory and Practice*, ed. by M. Elizabeth Ginway and J. Andrew Brown (New York: Palgrave Macmillan US, 2012), pp. 111–32 <https://doi.org/10.1057/9781137312778_7>

———, 'La casa del dolor ajeno de Julián Herbert. No-ficción, memoria e historicidad en el México contemporáneo', *MLN*, 132.2 (2017), pp. 426–40 <https://doi.org/10.1353/mln.2017.0025>

———, 'Más allá del mercado. Los usos de la literatura latinoamericana en la era neoliberal', in *Libro mercado: literatura y neoliberalismo*, ed. by José Ramón Ruisánchez (México: Universidad Iberoamericana, 2015), pp. 15–40

Sassone, Susana, and Carolina Mera, 'Barrios de migrantes en Buenos Aires: Identidad, cultura y cohesión socioterritorial', *Réseau Amérique Latine*, (2006), pp. 1–14

Schoene, Berthold, *The Cosmopolitan Novel* (Edinburgh: Edinburgh University Press, 2011)

Segalen, Victor, *Essay on Exoticism: An Aesthetics of Diversity*, trans. by Yaël Rachel Schlick (Durham: Duke University Press, 2002)

Seijas, Tatiana, 'Asian Migrations to Latin America in the Pacific World, 16th–19th Centuries', *History Compass*, 14.12 (2016), pp. 573–81

Spivak, Gayatri Chakravorty, 'Can the Subaltern Speak?', in *Marxism and the Interpretation of Culture*, ed. by Cary Nelson and Lawrence Grossberg (Urbana: University of Illinois Press, 1988), pp. 271–313

'Supermercados chinos - Taringa!' <http://www.taringa.net/posts/info/9483558/Supermercados-chinos.html> [accessed 1 May 2021]

Telles, Edward Eric and PERLA, *Pigmentocracies: Ethnicity, Race, and Color in Latin America* (Chapel Hill: University of North Carolina Press, 2014)

Telles, Edward, and Liza Steele, 'Pigmentocracia en las Américas: ¿cómo se relaciona el logro educativo con el color de piel?', *Proyecto Afrolatin@*, 2012.73 (2012) <http://afrolatinoproject.org/2012/06/28/pigmentocracia-en-las-americas-como-se-relaciona-el-logro-educativo-con-el-color-de-piel/> [accessed 5 January 2021]

Thornton, Niamh, 'Fairies at the Bottom of the Garden: Writers Crossing Digital Borders', *Forum for Inter-American Research*, 5.1 (2012)

de Trazegnies Granda, Fernando, *En el país de las colinas de arena: Reflexiones sobre la inmigración china en el Perú del S. XIX desde la perspectiva del derecho* (Lima: Pontificia Universidad Católica del Perú, 1994)

Trejos, Bernardo, and Lan-Hung Nora Chiang, 'Young Taiwanese Immigration to Argentina: The Challenges of Adaptation, Self Identity and Returning', *International Journal of Asia-Pacific Studies*, 8.2 (2012), pp. 113–43

Twist, Joseph, '"The Crossing of Love": The Inoperative Community and Romantic Love in Feridun Zaimoglu's "Fünf klopfende Herzen, wenn die Liebe springt" and "Hinterland', *German Life and Letters*, 67.3 (2014), pp. 399–417

Tyutina, Svetlana V., 'The Peripheral and the Ephemeral: Power Struggle, Violence and Fear in the Depiction of Chinos in Mexican Literature and Visual Arts', *TRANSMODERNITY: Journal of Peripheral Cultural Production of the Luso-Hispanic World*, 8.3 (2018), pp. 64–85

Varise, Franco, 'Los chinos en la Argentina, más allá del supermercado', *La Nación*, (2011) <http://www.lanacion.com.ar/1413378-los-chinos-en-la-argentina-mas-alla-del-supermercado> [accessed 1 May 2021]

Wade, Peter, 'Mestizaje, Multiculturalism, Liberalism, and Violence', *Latin American and Caribbean Ethnic Studies*, 11.3 (2016), pp. 323–43

———, *Race and Ethnicity in Latin America* (London: Pluto Press, 1997)

———, 'Race in Latin America', in *A Companion to Latin American Anthropology*, ed. by Deborah Poole (Oxford: Blackwell, 2008), pp. 177–92

———, 'Racism and Liberalism: The Dynamics of Inclusion and Exclusion', *Ethnic and Racial Studies*, 38.8 (2015), pp. 1292–97

Watkin, Christopher, 'A Different Alterity: Jean-Luc Nancy's "Singular Plural"', *Paragraph*, 30.2 (2007), pp. 1292–97

Young, Elliott, *Alien Nation: Chinese Migration in the Americas from the Coolie Era Through World War II* (University of North Carolina Press, 2014)

Zlotnik, Claudio, 'Guerra sino-francesa por los precios', *Página|12*, (2006) <http://www.pagina12.com.ar/diario/elpais/1-63669-2006-02-28.html> [accessed 1 May 2021]

CHAPTER THREE

Next Stop

'China'

Like the novels studied in the second chapter, those studied here also disclose forms of contemporary othering. However, here the emphasis results in the equivalence of different locations in the world, challenging hegemonic Eurocentric structures and 'national' epistemologies. While the novels critique essentialist views on culture, they also negotiate subjectivities beyond fixed global cartographies.[1] These novels can be seen to emphasize subjectivities while simultaneously campaigning for a sense of fluidity and open-endedness. From this perspective, the novels reveal the limitations of essentialist bounded identities while calling for a reconsideration of community and potentially a 'new cosmopolitanism'[2] as an existing practical stance that is provisional and can lead to strategic alliances and networks across borders.[3]

Caren Kaplan notes, in *Questions of Travel: Postmodern Discourses of Displacement*, since the twentieth century, 'increasing numbers of people have become disengaged or dislocated from national, regional, and ethnic locations and identities'[4] and 'in the midst of these displacements, new concerns over borders, boundaries, identities, and locations arise'.[5] Kaplan warns that to conflate migratory experiences may lead to 'mythologized narrativizations of displacement [that do not question] [...] the cultural, political, and economic grounds of [...] different professions, privileges, means and limitations'.[6]

1 *Scattered Hegemonies: Postmodernity and Transnational Feminist Practices*, ed. by Inderpal Grewal and Caren Kaplan (London: University of Minnesota Press, 1994), pp. 1–33.

2 Pnina Werbner, *Anthropology and the New Cosmopolitanism: Rooted, Feminist and Vernacular Perspectives* (Oxford: Berg, 2008), p. 2.

3 Pheng Cheah, 'The Cosmopolitical', in *The Ashgate Research Companion to Cosmopolitanism*, ed. by Maria Rovisco and Magdalena Nowicka (Farnham: Ashgate, 2011), pp. 211–24 (p. 218).

4 Caren Kaplan, *Questions of Travel: Postmodern Discourses of Displacement* (London: Duke University Press, 1996), pp. 101–2.

5 Kaplan, pp. 101–2.

6 Kaplan, p. 2.

In other words, the conflation of different displacements can veil power imbalance.

Indeed, Kaplan demonstrates how approaches to travel offer a range of accounts that go from the overemphasizing of difference to the overemphasizing of similarities, both of which risk losing sight of a world where 'new subjectivities' produce 'new relationships to space as well as time'.[7] It is these new subjectivities that this chapter aims to explore. Along these lines, my analysis focuses on Latin American novels whose main theme is travel to contemporary China. The storylines of *Los impostores*[8] and *Hotel Pekín*,[9] both by the Colombian Santiago Gamboa, recount tales of male travellers to contemporary China, while Mexican author Ximena Sánchez Echenique's *El ombligo del dragón*[10] narrates the story of a woman who travels to rural China and Hong Kong. The last work to be analysed is part of the *Shanghai* collection (2013–2014) by the Uruguayan author Gabriel Peveroni, where events occur in different places globally but are centred around Shanghai.

Travel to China, as depicted in these novels, leads the characters to reflect on their idea of 'home' and belonging, as well as culture, community, and cosmopolitanism. As Sara Ahmed shows, it is precisely the opposition between 'home' and 'away' that must be questioned, and which can only 'be addressed by considering the question of affect: being-at-home is a matter of *how one feels or how one might fail to feel*'.[11] While Ahmed's text informs this book as a whole, this chapter focuses specifically on her examination of migration and estrangement narratives. Ahmed's position, which attends to the effects of globalization, migration, and multiculturalism in the relationship between communities and strangers,[12] is particularly useful to my analysis because it pays attention to the intersection of multiple factors in the articulation of strangerness. Furthermore, approached through the theme of travel, these novels reveal that while 'the experience of cultural difference is now internal to a culture [...] it *is* implacably also a question of different others in distant lands'.[13]

According to Debbie Lisle, in her study of contemporary travel writing, the spatial coding of home/away appears as a means of entrenching complex and multilayered views regarding cosmopolitanism.[14] Following Mary Louise Pratt's argument that Enlightenment travel writing reinforced a 'planetary

7 Kaplan, p. 142.
8 Santiago Gamboa, *Los impostores* (Barcelona: Seix Barral, 2002).
9 Santiago Gamboa, *Hotel Pekín* (Bogota: Editorial Planeta Colombiana, 2008).
10 Ximena Sánchez Echenique, *El ombligo del dragón* (Mexico City: Tusquets, 2007).
11 Sara Ahmed, *Strange Encounters: Embodied Others in Post-Coloniality* (London: Routledge, 2000), p. 89.
12 Ahmed, *Strange Encounters*, p. 13.
13 Doreen Massey, *For Space* (London: SAGE, 2005), p. 194.
14 Debbie Lisle, *The Global Politics of Contemporary Travel Writing* (Cambridge: Cambridge University Press, 2011), p. 42.

consciousness',[15] which silenced or justified the less palatable effects of colonial rule, Lisle argues that when travel writing 'reproduces spatial divisions between here and there *as if* these cartographies were unproblematic or somehow neutral, it willingly reproduces the prevailing discourse of modern cartography'.[16]

From this perspective, the novels' explorations of the relationship to the 'other' become a means through which they challenge the binary and fixed notions of centre and periphery. By viewing literature as a discursive strategy from which to discuss Latin America's and China's position in the world, the novels disclose an engagement with cosmopolitanism. To refer to these novels as 'cosmopolitan', my analysis focuses on the ways they depict a global community. However, as I argue, by following the work of Jean-Luc Nancy and Berthold Schoene, this notion of a global community is not informed by embracing a utopic united community. On the contrary, the analysis of these novels will show not a future ideal but rather a diagnosis and an understanding of contemporary forms of alterity in Latin America and beyond.

Nancy's formulations of being-in-common and community as inoperative shed light on a literature that suggests a global community beyond an essential notion of the subject or the community, i.e., nation or region, and beyond fixed frames of reference. He presents this non-identitarian and non-foundational notion of community in opposition to a fusion of individuals with an allegedly common identity. And while Nancy dismisses the term 'cosmopolitan', his theoretical reconceptualization allows for a new, non-identitarian understanding of cosmopolitanism. From this perspective and following Schoene's ideas developed in his book *The Cosmopolitan Novel*,[17] I suggest that a new cosmopolitanism is available in these novels. One that is in opposition to a traditional notion of cosmopolitanism, which overlooks power imbalance by conflating cosmopolitanism with privileged circumstances of travel. In sum, these novels do not suggest the excision of local affiliations, but rather that they are receptive to Schoene's Nancean understanding of cosmopolitanism, a 'radical unlearning of all definitive modes of identification',[18] which can accommodate the whole world.

The theme of travel thus appears to interrupt narratives on China by revealing that the 'East' is a signifier that can be displaced while at once emphasizing Latin America as being shaped by its interactions with the rest of the world. The novels thus explore what Doreen Massey refers to as 'the challenge of our constitutive interrelatedness [...] the radical contemporaneity

15 Mary Louise Pratt, *Imperial Eyes: Travel Writing and Transculturation* (London: Routledge, 1992), pp. 4–5.

16 Lisle, p. 138.

17 Berthold Schoene, *The Cosmopolitan Novel* (Edinburgh: Edinburgh University Press, 2011).

18 Schoene, p. 21.

of an ongoing multiplicity of others [...]; and the ongoing and ever-specific project of the practices through which that sociability is to be configured',[19] suggesting new understandings of cosmopolitanism concerning the Latin American subject. It is precisely this idea of community which seems to be displayed in Gamboa's *Los impostores*.

The Subjectivity of a Global Community: *Los impostores*, by Santiago Gamboa

Indeed, by exploiting the descriptions of a Colombian journalist, a Peruvian academic, and a German sinologist and their travel experience in China, Gamboa destabilizes and complicates national and regional subjectivities. By emphasizing that all fixed points of reference have to be acknowledged as fiction, questioning the position of Latin America and highlighting the hegemonic power dynamics which have established paradigmatic antinomies such as North and South, or East and West, *Los impostores* sheds light on the imaginary which, as Jan Campbell argues, 'is always embodied within culture'.[20] By showing how North/South, East/West or self/other are hegemonic constructions, the novel questions the position of Latin America in a worldwide context regarding fixed cartographies of reference, altering paradigms of identity and literature. Building on Ahmed's formulations of 'home', the characters in Gamboa's novel expose how a concept of global citizenship obscures power imbalances. Thus, on one level, the novel indicates power imbalance in a global context. On another level, it highlights a community which, from a global outlook, thinks of community as finite, with subjects in relation to each other, and without a fixed teleology.[21]

By exposing the fictitiousness of the stereotype as a way of making sense of 'other' subjectivities, the novel critiques discourses of cosmopolitanism which build on essentialism. Instead, it suggests forms of new cosmopolitanism closer to that developed by Schoene, in which cosmopolitans 'must stay alert to their own positionality as well as the complex enmeshment of other people's historical legacy, economic capital, and ensuing degree of cosmopolitan competence and ambition'.[22] This form of cosmopolitanism, rather than claiming a homogeneous arena, calls for the recognition of the unevenness of such an arena.

As Ahmed explains, transnational journeys and detachment from a particular home grant the nomadic subject an ability to see the world that becomes the basis for a new global identity and community. However, identity may develop as a fetish in such narratives since, as Ahmed states, it becomes

19 Massey, p. 195.

20 Jan Campbell, *Arguing with the Phallus. Feminist, Queer, and Postcolonial Theory: A Psychoanalytic Contribution* (London: Zed Books, 2000), p. 218.

21 Schoene, p. 179.

22 Schoene, p. 5.

'detached from the particularity of places which allow for its formation as such'.[23] There is thus no inevitable link between forms of travel and, Ahmed continues, the 'transgression and destabilisation of identity [due to] migration [that] can allow identity to become a fetish under the sign of globality'.[24] To explore *Los impostores*' critique of power imbalance in textual detail, I build on the figure of the fetish as it informs my reading: through its structuring of the notions of stereotype and identity.

Indeed, for Homi Bhabha, stereotyping is an ideological operation that occurs through the construction of signs, oscillating between what is already known and what must be anxiously repeated.[25] As explained in the introduction, this paradox is what Bhabha calls 'productive ambivalence', as stereotyping involves both the recognition and disavowal of differences. A psychoanalytical dimension emerges as Bhabha sees the stereotype discourse as fetishistic, where the subject being stereotyped and those engaging in the stereotype are thought to be essentially coherent. Building on Jacques Lacan's Imaginary, Bhabha shows how this coherence, however, is recognized as a fantasy. In other words, difference is constituted through discourse, thus remaining unstable. Bhabha therefore identifies hybridity as a paradigm of colonial anxiety, where identities are constantly shifting. In this hybrid third space, hegemonic practices can be rearticulated, allowing for new identities to emerge. While Bhabha's reworking of the fetish is concerned with the male body, Anne McClintock shows how the ambivalence of the fetish can involve multiple contradictions.[26] From this perspective, the hybrid space allows for new identities beyond binary oppositions, male-centred understandings of fetishism, and essentialist understandings of identity.

Arguing that hybridity, as a noun, can essentialize the nature of Being, Wolff-Michael Roth suggests using Nancy's concept of the *mêlée*.[27] While arguing that Bhabha's notion of hybridity does not in any way essentialize the nature of Being and, on the contrary, allows the idea of an essential nature to be questioned, Nancy's conceptualization of the *mêlée* is indeed useful for my analysis. In reference to culture and language, among others, Nancy uses the *mêlée* to theorize the processes of mixture, as opposed to purity and essence, as mixture is action, not substance.[28] As Angharad Closs Stephens shows, the idea of the *mêlée* points towards imagining 'community

23 Ahmed, *Strange Encounters*, p. 86.

24 Ahmed, *Strange Encounters*, p. 86.

25 Homi K. Bhabha, *The Location of Culture* (Oxon: Routledge, 1994), pp. 94–95.

26 Anne McClintock, *Imperial Leather: Race, Gender, and Sexuality in the Colonial Contest* (New York: Routledge, 1995), p. 200.

27 Wolff-Michael Roth, 'In Praise of the Mêlée: Toward a New Conception of Scientific Identity and Literacy', 2007 <http://web.uvic.ca/~mroth/teaching/600-13Fall/1007/Melee.pdf> [accessed 1 March 2021].

28 Jean-Luc Nancy, *Being Singular Plural* (Stanford: Stanford University Press, 2000), pp. 145–58.

as encounters'.[29] From this perspective, subjects cannot be understood as 'on one side of identity or the other, or on one side of the community or the other'.[30] Drawing on Ahmed, for whom being at home involves the enveloping of subjects in a space which is not simply outside them but that overlap, enables my understanding of subjects as being-in-common and community as complex and diverse.

Born in Bogotá in 1965, Gamboa studied Literature in Colombia, later studying in Madrid and Paris. He published his first book in 1995, and since then, his work has been widely translated. Catalina García García-Herreros has described Gamboa's novels as 'novelas del movimiento', where characters physically move or travel.[31] He has published three texts related to China: in 2001, a travelogue entitled *Octubre en Pekín*; in 2002, the novel *Los impostores*; and in 2008 the novel *Hotel Pekín*.

Los impostores tells the story of a lost manuscript and the quest to find it undertaken by three foreigners in China: Suárez Salcedo (Suárez), a Colombian journalist, based in Paris and working for a French radio station; Gisbert Klauss, a German sinologist who has never been to China; and Nelson Chouchén Otárola (Chouchén), a Peruvian academic of Chinese ancestry based in Texas, who has been suspended from his university. In China, their paths cross due to a manuscript that belonged to the 'Yi Ho Tuan' movement, a real historical moment that gave rise to the Boxer Rebellion in 1899. The main storyline focuses on these characters' relation to the manuscript, which can best be described as a 'MacGuffin'. Alfred Hitchcock's cinematic term is useful to our understanding of the role of the manuscript in the plot, as a MacGuffin is a plot device which is under-explained within the narrative and largely irrelevant in and of itself, yet essential to the plot.[32] Although they are strangers at the novel's beginning, the three characters' stories intertwine in pursuit of the 'MacGuffin' manuscript.

The novel is divided into three main sections and an epilogue. The first section comprises ten chapters in which the narrators vary, and so does the focalization. The story is introduced by a certain Régis Cerard, who addresses an implied narratee and relates his guarding of a mysterious manuscript. The following chapters introduce the three main characters through a first-person narrator called Suárez and an undisclosed narrator who writes in the third person. This undisclosed narrator identifies with the 'Western' world and is gradually revealed to be Cerard, whom the reader learns is a French priest.

29 Angharad Closs Stephens, *The Persistence of Nationalism: From Imagined Communities to Urban Encounters* (Abingdon: Routledge, 2013), p. 120.

30 Ahmed, *Strange Encounters*, p. 94.

31 Catalina García García-Herreros, 'Personajes que viajan: Una tipología del desplazamiento global en la narrativa de Santiago Gamboa' (presented at the V Congreso Europea CEISAL de Latinoamericanistas, Bruselas, Bélgica, 2007).

32 Mike Digou, 'Hitchcock's MacGuffin in the Works of David Mamet', *Literature-Film Quarterly*, 31.4 (2003), pp. 270–75 (p. 270).

A complex narrator, Cerard unveils his omnipresence beyond time and space when the story ends. Inconsistencies throughout the narration emphasize the sense of imposture and deception, as an instance of pretending to be someone else to deceive others, recalling the novel's title.

In the first section, the reader learns that Suárez is travelling to Beijing at the orders of his superior, thinking that he has to write an article on Chinese Catholicism, but he is actually sent to get hold of the manuscript. Chouchén wants to explore his Chinese heritage and write a novel but is really escaping from the humiliation of the sanction imposed on him by his university. Finally, Klauss is travelling to experience what he has studied all his life. This first section ends with their simultaneous arrival at Beijing airport at 12:30 am, each unaware of the others' presence. Their arrival at this symbolic location of the contemporary world occurs in what the French anthropologist Marc Augé would call a 'non-place', a space where human beings remain anonymous and is not significant enough to be called a place.[33] With their arrival, a series of coincidental events is set in motion. The second section informs us about the characters once they have arrived in China; narrative voices are differentiated by leaving extra space between paragraphs. The text gives 'voice' to other narrators by including the transcriptions of Klauss's recorded diary or copies of Chouchén's grandfather's letters.

In the third section, the focus is on those characters still active in the plot. The text abandons Klauss as he has been kidnapped and disappears from view. When all the characters meet up at a warehouse, the different viewpoints become one. The novel cryptically ends with Cerard addressing the narratee from a different story, time, or dimension. The questioning of what is 'real' in the narration is reinforced by embedding fictional elements based on historical facts and 'real' events. This metafictional aspect is further emphasized by Gamboa's Suárez, the first-person narrator, a Colombian journalist who has lived in Paris.

The characters' engagement with the places they visit and their opinions of other travelogues reveal how their expectations of China are mediated by the travel writers they have read, evoked in the novel through Pierre Loti, André Malraux, Victor Segalen or Henri Michaux, among others. The novel thus summons the discourses of travel writing, in a way that reveals a double coding of their understanding of the present.[34] In this sense, it reveals the impossibility of detaching Latin American travel to China from the dominant European narrative of travel to the 'East', exemplified by mentioning specific real travel writers and their texts as guides to the characters' experience in China.[35] The novel reveals and critiques this travel writing by depicting

33 Marc Augé, *Non-Places: Introduction to an Anthropology of Supermodernity* (London: Verso, 2009).

34 Simon Dentith, *Parody* (London: Routledge, 2000), p. 183.

35 Héctor Hoyos, 'Orientalismo, globalización e imaginarios transpacíficos en la novela latinoamericana actual', *Cuadernos de literatura*, 17.34 (2013), pp. 82–105 (p. 94);

non-Westerners in the position of the 'traditional Western traveller' as 'imposters'. From this perspective, the novel intervenes in what James Clifford describes as the 'long history of travel': 'predominantly Western-dominated, strongly male, and upper-middle class'.[36]

Indeed, the writers that the characters read, as well as the characters themselves, in some way fit Clifford's description. Throughout this text and, as we shall see later, particularly in *Hotel Pekín*, we find a parody of the writings and experiences of previous European travel writers in China. For example, both Loti and Segalen were employed by the French government,[37] like Suárez. Likewise, Loti was in China precisely during the aftermath of the Boxer Rebellion, when the country lay open to Westerners, and would have known about the manuscript, as Klauss deduces from his reading of Loti's *The Last Days of Pekin*.[38] Indeed, Klauss can also be described in the terms Yvonne Ying Hsieh uses for Loti—to represent Eurocentric perceptions of China.[39] Furthermore, when Klauss reflects on publishing his thoughts on China, it brings to mind Michaux's *A Barbarian in Asia*,[40] which aims to explain to a European public the countries he visited, including China.[41] Michaux also travelled to Latin America and published a travelogue about his trip to Ecuador. This reveals how hegemonic European worldviews of both China and Latin America emerge through reference to these authors in the novels.

On another level, Chouchén's expressions, such as when he hopes to have a 'chinita bien rica de compañera'[42] on the airplane, coincide with Loti's 'excessive sentimentalism, his egoism, ethnocentrism, and sexism'.[43] However, Chouchén's utterance appears to the reader exaggerated and in a spirit of ridicule. The novel thus revises an 'imperialist nostalgia' which, according to Patrick Holland and Graham Huggan, manifests particularly clearly in

Rosario Hubert, 'Rewriting Travel Literature: A Cosmopolitan Critique of Exoticism in Contemporary Latin American Fiction', in *Peripheral Transmodernities: South-to-South Intercultural Dialogues between the Luso-Hispanic World and 'the Orient'*, ed. by Ignacio López-Calvo (Newcastle upon Tyne: Cambridge Scholars Publishing, 2012), pp. 42–61 (pp. 55–56).

36 James Clifford, *Routes: Travel and Translation in the Late Twentieth Century* (Cambridge: Harvard University Press, 1997), p. 66.

37 Yvonne Ying Hsieh, *From Occupation to Revolution: China Through the Eyes of Loti, Claudel, Segalen, and Malraux (1895–1933)* (Birmingham: Summa Publications, 1996), p. 3.

38 Pierre Loti, *The Last Days of Pekin*, trans. by Myrta L. Jones (Boston: Little, Brown and Company, 1902).

39 Hsieh, p. 6.

40 Henri Michaux, *A Barbarian in Asia* (New York: New Directions, 2016).

41 Hsieh, p. 6.

42 Gamboa, *Los impostores*, p. 100.

43 Hsieh, p. 2.

travel writing.[44] Through stereotyping and preconceived ideas about China, and through the disjuncture between the travel accounts they read and their real experience in China, the novel reveals the 'Orient' the characters expect to encounter to be entirely constructed. The novel thus parodies and questions any existence of the 'Orient' as such. Gamboa rejects generalizations regarding identity[45] and exposes their constructedness by marking the excess of stereotypes and deploying humour.

Héctor Hoyos and Rosario Hubert both note that stereotypes are applied to all nationalities using the style of text specific to each character, as related to their profession. The stereotypes emerge as preconceptions about places and people beyond China itself. For example, the text reveals Klauss's understanding of China when he thinks of the places and buildings having a 'sello de Oriente: en la forma de los techos, en los colores, en su estructura'.[46] An 'oriental' stereotype also emerges when Suárez states that he hears a voice 'con un lejano acento oriental'.[47] The notion of an 'oriental' aura or accent exposes the generalizations regarding 'Far Eastern cultures', showing how China is made to represent the 'orient'.

Asian stereotypes are also reiterated throughout the novel, such as when Suárez states: 'En esto de la comodidad y el lujo, la verdad es que los asiáticos son insuperables – recuérdese, si no, la expresión "lujo asiático"',[48] evoking the notion of Asian luxury, the sensual, and the decadent;[49] an 'Asian mystique'.[50] Another example is when the narrator describes Chouchén as being dressed with a 'bata de seda con brocados que le daba un vago aire de filósofo taoísta',[51] associating a certain kind of clothing with a philosophical tradition and recalling the kind of Imperial clothes that Loti describes.[52]

44 Patrick Holland and Graham Huggan, *Tourists with Typewriters: Critical Reflections on Contemporary Travel Writing* (Ann Arbor: University of Michigan Press, 1998), p. 29.

45 Hubert, p. 54.

46 Gamboa, *Los impostores*, p. 116.

47 Gamboa, *Los impostores*, p. 126.

48 Gamboa, *Los impostores*, p. 126.

49 This can also be found in different representations of China in Latin America, see Daisy Saravia, *Migración china y orientalismo modernista. Análisis en la revista Variedades (1909-1919)* (Lima: Ediciones MyL, 2020); Maria Montt Strabucchi, Carol Chan, and María Elvira Ríos, *Chineseness in Chile: Shifting Representations during the Twenty-First Century*, Studies of the Americas (Cham: Palgrave Macmillan, 2022) <https://doi.org/10.1007/978-3-030-83966-6>; María Elvira Ríos, María Montt, and Carol Chan, 'El imaginario de lo chino en las revistas magazinescas chilenas de principios del siglo XX', *Revista Rumbos TS. Un espacio crítico para la reflexión en Ciencias Sociales*, 24 (2021), pp. 129–50 <https://doi.org/10.51188/rrts.num24.434>.

50 Sheridan Prasso, *The Asian Mystique: Dragon Ladies, Geisha Girls, & Our Fantasies of the Exotic Orient* (London: PublicAffairs, 2006), p. xi.

51 Gamboa, *Los impostores*, p. 342.

52 Loti, p. 119.

Simultaneously, the layering of Asian and Chinese stereotypes discloses a certain vision of China and Asia in Latin America, which is conflated under the notion of a fetishistic and stereotyped 'Oriental'. Frequently occurring throughout the text, these stereotypes are exposed as parodic. Gamboa thus rejects generalizations of identity by exposing what Hubert calls a 'hilarious catalogue' of Latin American clichés, ridiculing all references to specific particularities of the 'Oriental'.[53]

Misunderstandings about the Orient are forced on the reader in comical ways, as also noted by Hoyos.[54] For example, the hilarious dialogue in a sex scene between Suárez and a stereotype of Cuba, the independent doctor, Omaira Tinajo:

> Entonces le dije [...] "Omaira, emperatriz de Oriente," y ella me respondió, [...] "¿Cómo supiste que soy de Gibara, [...]" y yo, [...] pregunté, "¿Qué es eso de Gibara?," a lo que ella, [...] respondió, "Gibara, provincia de Oriente, Cuba, [...]" [...] y murmuré, "Yo decía emperatriz de Oriente por Pekín, no por Cuba, pero es lo mismo, Señora de Gibara, Podestá del Oriente," y ella, [...] me dijo "Ah, ya entiendo, creí que lo decías por Cuba [...]."[55]

Suárez addresses an exotic Cuban woman as an 'Oriental' empress, revealing his preconceptions regarding a powerful, sexually attractive woman. Her response to this is banal, as she explains that 'Oriente' is the name of eastern Cuba. At a moment in which rational thought is replaced by desire and instinct, the novel displaces the location of the 'East' and places it in Latin America. It is provocative that in China, it is an 'Eastern' Latin American, not a Chinese woman, who catches Suárez's attention. To question Western mythologies, as Hoyos discusses,[56] Gamboa parodies the search for authenticity characteristic of Orientalist travel writing and empties the term 'Orient' of mythical connotation.

Stereotypes beyond China also arise when Suárez proposes a toast with other Latin Americans he has met at his hotel. He recites a long list of Latin American clichés, celebrating a 'Latin American unity'.[57] In his words, the stereotype, while reductive, is not necessarily portrayed as negative. From this perspective, a cosmopolitan desire for community close to what Jacques Derrida defines as unconditional hospitality emerges in their evocation of national stereotypes, 'offered *a priori* to every other [...] *whoever they may be*'.[58] However, their reliance on stereotypes reveals the nation-bound nature of

53 Hubert, p. 54.
54 Hoyos, p. 89.
55 Gamboa, *Los impostores*, p. 255.
56 Hoyos, p. 91.
57 Gamboa, *Los impostores*, pp. 194–95.
58 Jacques Derrida, *On Cosmopolitanism and Forgiveness* (London: Routledge, 2001), p. 22.

their cosmopolitanism, simultaneously parodying discourses of 'integración latinoamericana',[59] emphasized by the lengthy wording of the discourse. Indeed, the fact that the discourse is delivered under the influence of alcohol allows the reader to question the genuine feelings of solidarity. Following Derek Hook, the quote reveals a 'paradox of otherness' operating at the levels of discourse and identification alike.[60]

In this sense, as discourse and as a form of identification, the stereotype continues to reduce the other to an ontological essential other. As the toast's desire for unity relies on essentialist views of culture and self-exoticization as an alibi that does not recognize power imbalance, cosmopolitanism as a supposed shift of perspectives and a questioning of one's openness to the other is itself interrogated. However, the impossibility of ultimately fixing the subject discloses the layering of identities made available throughout the text.

More precisely, all of the characters are linked by displacement, their identities becoming disarticulated between countries, occupations, dreams, and aspirations. For example, Suárez's anxiety when arriving at the Chinese border reveals the persistence of a Colombian stereotype linked to drugs and violence.[61] The narrator links the feeling to a nationality rather than to a personal feeling. This linking of stereotypes with nationality also emerges through Suárez himself, as the first thing he does when he learns he will be going to Beijing is 'lo que haría cualquier francés, es decir, sacar de la biblioteca esa vieja edición en Gallimard que todos tenemos de *Un bárbaro en Asia*, de Henri Michaux [...].'[62] At once, this quote sheds light on the power imbalance contained in the process of stereotyping, since by taking it for granted that all French people would have an edition of the book, he overlooks differences in education levels and interests.

The displacement of fixed cartographies and hegemonic relationships between people and places, and the movement through those places, is also found in the novel's layering of literature, narrative voices and experiences, which never allows a single layer to predominate. This discloses new subject positions that emerge through the intertwining of beliefs and practices, which bear the traces of the feelings and practices that inform these subject positions.[63] For example, layering occurs through Chouchén's literary ambitions when he imagines a phrase and immediately thinks, 'se parecía un

59 Sergio González Miranda and Cristián Ovando Santana, 'Hacia un Nuevo Pensamiento Integracionista Latinoamericano: Aproximación a una lectura de segundo orden', *Polis*, 7.21 (2008), pp. 265–85 (pp. 266–79).

60 Derek Hook, 'The Racial Stereotype, Colonial Discourse, Fetishism, and Racism', *Psychoanalytic Review*, 92.5 (2005), pp. 701–34 (p. 701).

61 Gamboa, *Los impostores*, p. 110.

62 Gamboa, *Los impostores*, pp. 24–25.

63 Jonathan Rutherford, 'The Third Space: Interview with Homi Bhabha', in *Identity: Community, Culture, Difference* (London: Lawrence and Wishart, 1990), pp. 207–21 (p. 211).

poco a Rulfo, pero qué importa, se dijo, ¿Quién es dueño de las palabras?'[64] His consideration of plagiarism is enhanced by his question, which is in itself a cliché. In this respect, Hoyos views Chouchén's orientalist fantasies, delirious recreations, and daydreaming about authors from the Boom as a questioning of the Latin American Boom literary tradition.[65] He sees this as suggestive of an isomorphic relationship between a vision of the 'East' as a place of wonders and luxury and a view of the Boom as the epitome of sophistication. As Hoyos argues, through Chouchén's distorted vision of the Latin American Boom literary group as a jet set taking place in China, Gamboa provides a way of thinking of the prestige of Latin American writers beyond a Europe–Latin American axis. In other words, it demands a reflection on the effects of globalization.

According to Hubert Pöppel, globalization makes things verisimilar and generalizes stories that used to be considered exceptional.[66] Indeed, this context allows Gamboa to set his novel in Beijing, playing with what may be considered 'foreign'. In this respect, Hubert argues that the novel 'do[es] not exoticize the Oriental but instead use[s] the Oriental setting as a rhetorical device to discuss the notion of exoticism, that is, the treatment of *any* cultural particularity as distant and fixed'.[67] To write against Orientalism, she argues, is a way of criticizing the self-exoticization of Latin American magical realism, where the choice of an Oriental setting constitutes a critique of the legacy of the Boom and its excessive accentuation of Latin American specificity.

From this perspective, we can see how superimposed layers are displayed to explore how we make sense of places and people in the novel. For example, an exploration of Latin American identities is represented by Chouchén, whose combination of Hispanicized Chinese and Basque surnames mirror a Latin American *mestizaje* that goes beyond a Spanish–indigenous mix. This is flagged up by Chouchén himself, who considers himself discriminated against because of his looks, which he describes in the following words: 'Tal vez a la vista de su piel oscura y achinada – la sangre india confluyendo en el torrente sinológico –, creyó que era un filipino vietnamita, y se quizo burlar.'[68] A Latin American *mestizo* identity, which has traditionally excluded the Chinese,[69] is imagined as interpreted to be 'Filipino Vietnamese', thus adding to the superimposition of layers which inform identities.

64 Gamboa, *Los impostores*, p. 102.

65 Hoyos, p. 91.

66 Hubert Pöppel, 'Fuerzas centrífugas y centrípetas en Santiago Gamboa y Gonzalo España: La novela policíaca colombiana en el contexto de la glocalización', *Revista Iberoamericana*, 76.231 (2010), pp. 359–76 (p. 360).

67 Hubert, p. 48.

68 Gamboa, *Los impostores*, pp. 122–23.

69 Kathleen López, 'The Asian Presence in *Mestizo* Nations: A Response', in *Critical Terms in Caribbean and Latin American Thought*, ed. by Yolanda Martínez-San

Furthermore, this superimposition of layers also transpires through the novel's challenge to the traditional detective novel genre. As Clemencia Ardila shows, the novel surpasses the conventional detective genre, combining a detective-style novel with a metafictional reflection on literature itself, and constructing a fiction (the resurgence of a conflict centred around the manuscript) based on a historical event (the Boxer uprising). Ardila explores the former through her analysis of the novel's two epigraphs: a quote from Graham Greene, novelist, travel writer and spy,[70] and one from Witold Gombrowicz, a Polish writer who migrated to Argentina before the outbreak of the Second World War. The epigraphs, Ardila argues, warn the reader of the impostures or deceptions that the novel will disclose: such as the impostures of the characters, the imposture of the narrative voices, or the imposture entailed in the obtaining of the manuscript and how this is resolved.[71]

Greene's quote comes from an interview in which he claims he never wanted to belong to the secret service and did not want to be a spy. It was the result, he states, of 'las circunstancias, la guerra, un vago interés por las atmósferas oscuras, el hastío…'[72] Indeed, his words insist on the fact that circumstances are central to events, beyond desire, and that one sometimes ends up doing things one did not intend to do in the first place. Broadly reminding us of Greene, Suárez is a journalist-cum-spy in China. As such, Ardila notes, he challenges a stereotype of the literary spy, as he is not good-looking or elegant, he is not successful with women, does not know how to use a gun, and is easily frightened.[73]

Gombrowicz's quote is from his book *Ferdydurke*.[74] The extract discusses the role of the second-rate writer: repudiated by the common reader, repudiated by his own reality, which exposes him as the imitator of the great authors and repudiated by Art for being incompetent and deficient.[75] In this case, the quote explores the formation of identity, and the way in which time and

Miguel, Ben. Sifuentes-Jáuregui, and Marisa Belausteguigoitia (New York: Palgrave Macmillan, 2016), pp. 125–31 (p. 125).

70 Graham Dann, 'Writing out the Tourist in Space and Time', *Annals of Tourism Research*, 26.1 (1999), pp. 159–87 (pp. 159–60); Peter Hulme, *Cuba's Wild East: A Literary Geography of Oriente* (Liverpool: Liverpool University Press, 2011), pp. 361–62.

71 Clemencia Ardila and Grupo de Especialización en Hermenéutica Literaria Eafit, '"Los impostores" de Santiago Gamboa: El juego de la escritura', *Estudios de Literatura Colombiana*, 13 (2003), pp. 121–38 (pp. 122–24).

72 Gamboa, *Los impostores*, p. 8.

73 Clemencia Ardila, 'Cronistas, investigadores y reporteras -policíacos- en la narrativa colombiana contemporánea', *América: Cahiers du CRICCAL*, 43.1 (2013), pp. 69–78 (p. 77).

74 Witold Gombrowicz, *Ferdydurke*, trans. by Danuta Borchardt (New Haven: Yale University Press, 2000).

75 Gamboa, *Los impostores*, p. 8.

circumstance have real effects on people's lives. While its reference to the second-rate writer is echoed in the figure of Chouchén, the statement itself allows that reality may be more complex and points instead to its hegemonic stance, uttered by a narrator with the power to judge and decide. By revealing this powerful narrator, the novel opens by suggesting the existence of other possibilities for this secondary writer. Furthermore, Ricardo Piglia once stated that Gombrowicz was the greatest modern writer in Argentina. At the same time, Ernesto Sábato and Juan José Saer, among other Argentine authors, also discussed Gombrowicz in relation to the Argentine literary canon.[76] Indeed, Gombrowicz is also known for the following statement: 'cuando escribo, no soy ni chino ni polaco.'[77] The epigraph thus also questions what is 'Argentine' or 'Latin American', as well as authenticity and the writer's position in a global context, evoking Jorge Luis Borges's essay 'El escritor argentino y la tradición'.[78] Indeed, this is further emphasized by the fact that, in the end, the reader learns that two copies of the manuscript have been made, so each character can retrieve a version. The manuscript is thus never again a unique original document.

Resolving the conflict by producing copies, the novel references China's economic productivity[79] while also allowing a playful and open interpretation. In the style of postmodern narrative, these new manuscript copies involve the reader in a process of conjecture. In the postscript to his novel *The Name of the Rose*,[80] Umberto Eco argues that the appeal of detective fiction is conjecture, where a hypothesis is formed by speculation that also works through narrative. Eco explains the 'rhizomatic maze', building on Gilles Deleuze and Félix Guattari's metaphor of the rhizome. Deleuze and Guattari use the rhizome to picture the way things relate to other things, providing an alternative to linear models of interpretation and suggesting that language also works in this way.[81] While they argue that there are always numerous meanings suggested in language, Eco argues that 'the rhizome is so constructed that [it has] no centre, no periphery, no exit, because it is potentially infinite'.[82]

76 Ewa Kobylecka-Piwonska, 'Ricardo Piglia, Lector de Witold Gombrowicz', *Neophilologus*, 97.2 (2012), pp. 333–47 (pp. 333–35).

77 Fernando Aínsa, 'Nueva cartografía de la pertenencia. La pérdida del territorio en la narrativa latinoamericana', *Iberoamericana*, 14.54 (2014), pp. 111–26 (p. 113).

78 Jorge Luis Borges, 'El escritor argentino y la tradición', in *Discusión*, essay originally published 1953 (Madrid: Alianza, 1976), pp. 128–37.

79 Álvaro Fernández Bravo, 'Apropiaciones de la cultura china en la literatura sudamericana contemporánea: Contribución para un mapa tentativo a partir de obras de César Aira, Bernardo Carvalho y Siu Kam Wen', *452oF Revista de Teoría de la literatura y Literatura Comparada*, 13 (2015), pp. 50–70 (p. 65).

80 Umberto Eco, *The Name of the Rose* (London: Vintage, 2004).

81 Gilles Deleuze and Félix Guattari, *A Thousand Plateaus: Capitalism and Schizophrenia* (London: Athlone, 1987), p. 7.

82 Umberto Eco, 'Reflections on "The Name of The Rose"', *Encounter*, (1985), pp. 7–19 (p. 15).

From this perspective, the production of copies evokes Borges's parody of detective fiction; when the manuscript is found, copies are produced, offering closure to the detective story, but not in the way expected from the genre's classics.[83] Indeed, the novel offers a structure, but it simultaneously reveals that it is never definitively structured.[84]

Hoyos also notes how, throughout the novel, layers of identities and experiences come to be superimposed. He argues that Gamboa signals how, for Latin Americans, the encounter with China is never a 'direct relation', and thus is always mediated. The manuscript, according to Hoyos, is a metonym for the Orient itself, and does not resolve the enigma of otherness, but rather dissolves it;[85] he states that finding the other means getting over misunderstandings. However, otherness cannot be dissolved, as the novel does not permit China to be discovered by the characters. Instead, they become aware of the constructedness of the 'other'. Gamboa thus offers a critique of the negative connotations of imposture, positing it instead as part of a new kind of cosmopolitanism, one which takes into consideration power imbalance. From this perspective, layering is not rejected but rather embraced as part of identity. The novel thus defies exclusive identities, as in the following words uttered by Suárez: '[…] todos aquí son ex algo. Ex jesuitas, ex sacerdotes, ex alcohólicos. Al fin y al cabo todo el mundo fue antes otra cosa.'[86] In doing this, the novel intervenes in discourses of belonging and identity.

Precisely at the moment when the Latin Americans restore the peace, with each group possessing a copy of the manuscript, the novel dismisses any hierarchical differentiation through which Latin America could be posited as peripheral. Hoyos states that the fact that the Latin Americans restore peace can be read as a strengthening of Sino-Latin American relations or as recognition of how rare and almost impossible these relations now are. He also notes how Chouchén and Suárez go to China because of the positions they occupy in Texas and Paris, as if indicating that a South–South relation would need the mediation of the First World.[87] However, while the novel sheds light on the histories of engagement between China and Latin America, mentioning the Peruvian exploitation of Chinese workers, for example, it suggests an unmediated link between them. The fact that the manuscript belonged to the group that led the 'Boxer Rebellion', which was countered by a military campaign led by a multinational coalition involving eight countries,[88] seems ironic. It is

83 Bran Nicol, *The Cambridge Introduction to Postmodern Fiction* (Cambridge: Cambridge University Press, 2009), p. 175.

84 Eco, 'Reflections on "The Name of The Rose"', p. 15.

85 Hoyos, p. 94.

86 Gamboa, *Los impostores*, p. 182.

87 Hoyos, p. 93.

88 Eric Ouellet, 'Multinational Counterinsurgency: The Western Intervention in the Boxer Rebellion 1900–1901', *Small Wars & Insurgencies*, 20.3–4 (2009), pp. 507–27 (p. 507).

foreigners again who restore the peace, albeit this time by non-violent means and through people who are not nationals of major Western powers.

Hoyos goes on to argue that in the novel, a direct relationship between Asia and Latin America seems fragile, mediated by travel permits and language barriers, as material conditions affect the characters' freedom to roam around the world like early-modern European adventurers.[89] This, he argues, recalls the precariousness of Latin American cosmopolitanism in real life. However, I contend that instead of pointing to a fragility linking Asia and Latin America or to the precariousness of a Latin American cosmopolitanism, Gamboa emphasizes the power imbalance contained in the relationship by making the novel's characters aware of this. In other words, Gamboa shows how the Latin American characters are aware of the historical and material conditions that mediate their freedom to roam the world. By emphasizing subjectivities, he grants agency to the Latin American subject, making him (the male characters in his novel) aware of the surrounding power imbalance and thus establishing a cosmopolitanism that accounts for such difference. In this cosmopolitan context, the connection between Asia and Latin America is relational and contingent, as 'no one person or group of persons is ultimately in charge in the sense of plotting or controlling the general course of events'.[90]

The characters and the ways they relate to China are defined by their diasporic displacement and by being 'between cultures', as Hubert also notes.[91] This 'third space' reveals their cosmopolitan condition. For example, Chouchén is a Peruvian of Chinese origin who lives in Texas, and Suárez is a Colombian journalist settled in Paris. The novel thus displaces the notion of belonging, continuously deferred or made available, for example, by Chouchén and his fetishistic attachment to Peruvian themes. The superimposition of layers, as well as the hybrid or interstitial emergences of identity, might correspond to the notion of an 'imposter' divested of its negative connotation.

According to this reading, the notion of the 'imposture' emerges instead as a script of superimposed layers, accessible through the characters' identities and the narrative structure. By acknowledging the contradictions contained in the imposture, the novel uncovers the power imbalance inherent in any encounter. Thus, Gamboa questions binary alterities, removes a fetishistic notion of the other, and discloses the fetishistic impulse of the stereotype as developed by Bhabha. Simultaneously, he engages with Ahmed's critique of the fetishized stranger cut off from its histories of determination.[92] The 'imposter' and 'imposture', when separated from the intention to deceive, and combined with the embodiment of the multiple aspects that inform our

89 Hoyos, p. 93.

90 Schoene, p. 2.

91 Hubert, p. 55.

92 Ahmed, *Strange Encounters*, p. 6.

identities, might be seen in Gamboa's writing to characterize a different form of cosmopolitanism.

In this sense, Gamboa may be read as engaging with Charles Hatfield's critique of Latin American cultural and literary studies for their repudiation of universalism and their commitment to identity and difference, as presented in his book, *The Limits of Identity*.[93] While Hatfield's view of the cosmopolitan is restricted since he considers it reliant on the occupation of 'vast, cosmopolitan' subject positions,[94] his call for non-identitarian readings sheds significant light on my interpretation of the novel as a call for a new Latin American cosmopolitanism. Hatfield notices how solving issues of economic injustice entails erasing difference, while cultural injustice entails celebrating and indeed preserving difference; as he observes in Latin America, 'the politics of cultural dehierarchization has created a machine by which hierarchies are endlessly redescribed as difference, which in turn is celebrated as such'.[95] Hatfield explains that distinguishing between economic injustice and cultural difference remains difficult and proposes instead that we think of an alternative future for Latin America in terms that are no longer identitarian.[96] From my perspective, Hatfield's emphasis on the challenge that an understanding of a Latin American identity entails indicates a notion of community that is 'inoperative' in Nancy's terms: non-essentialist, complex, and diverse. Indeed, Hatfield's arguments coincide with Kaplan's awareness of how 'discourses of location can be used to naturalize boundaries and margins under the guise of celebration, nostalgia, or inappropriate assumptions of sameness'.[97] What Hatfield is calling for is an acknowledgement of Ahmed's notion of 'stranger fetishism', which is inscribed in difference; this is central to Gamboa's understanding of cosmopolitan identities.

From this perspective, I agree with Hubert, who argues that the choice of an Oriental setting in *Los impostores*, and the challenge to *Orientalism*, is a critique of the legacy of the Boom and its accentuation of Latin American specificity and the self-exoticizing operations of magical realism. She sees this as entailing an affirmation of 'the potential expression of literature, understood as a cosmopolitan sphere where national boundaries of enunciation are overcome and the discursive space is de-centered, [and] it is imagined universal'.[98] This affirmation, she argues, establishes a homogeneous arena allowing the Latin American writer to embark on a discussion of the 'European tradition of Romantic travel writing that forwarded the orientalist

93 Charles Hatfield, *The Limits of Identity: Politics and Poetics in Latin America* (Austin: University of Texas Press, 2015), pp. 1–10.

94 Hatfield, p. 6.

95 Hatfield, p. 108.

96 Hatfield, p. 109.

97 Kaplan, p. 187.

98 Hubert, p. 46.

imagination they deconstruct'.[99] However, Hubert seems to dismiss the power imbalance embedded in the cosmopolitan call that the novel shares with the reader. As emphasized by Kaplan, there is always something at stake when valorizing a generalized hybridity that is presumed to construct a cosmopolitan identity without considering the 'diverse and complex shifts in the organization of capital, geographies, and populations'.[100] The novel does not take a homogeneous arena for granted but rather emphasizes the power imbalance it contains. Instead of pointing to the precariousness of Latin American cosmopolitanism specifically[101] or claiming a homogeneous arena,[102] the novel informs us of the precariousness of cosmopolitanism per se when it masks the power imbalances that being a free traveller conceals, as Hoyos also notes when he discusses the freedom of characters to wander the world.[103]

Throughout the text, the reader learns about different kinds of travellers whose experience abroad discloses power imbalances. On the one hand, the main characters are shown to be privileged travellers who choose to go to China and mostly move through spaces which foreigners usually use. But simultaneously, the novel itself suggests differences between these same travellers. For example, there seem to be no material restrictions to Klauss' experiences in China, facilitated by his knowledge of Chinese, which allows him to navigate the city freely. However, a limitation to his movement is the French Embassy's requirement of a permit to access their archives. Yet this is easily resolved by his secretary in Germany, who arranges everything for him.

Chouchén also emerges as privileged, a Peruvian academic with a career in the U.S. at the prestigious 'Austin University'. While he self-exoticizes his Latin Americanness, such as by drinking Inca Kola and pisco sour, or the fact that his e-mail is elcondorpasa@yahoo.com, the reader is told he is an internationally recognized literary critic. When suspended from his academic post for his unscrupulous attitude, he still can fly to China, showing that the change in his career does not significantly affect his finances. However, the reader is told that his hotel in Beijing is not as impressive as Klauss's. While this could be due to their relative academic positions, the characterization highlights the construction of a stereotypical 'Western' academic in contrast to a 'not-so-Western' one, pointing to a power imbalance between East and West. In the case of Suárez, while he also emerges as a privileged traveller, his choices are limited. French officials remind him that his status in France depends on their authority, so he must travel to China at their request.

99 Hubert, p. 46.
100 Kaplan, p. 136.
101 Hoyos, p. 93.
102 Hubert, p. 46.
103 Hoyos, p. 93.

The characters' subject positions are thus disclosed as historically informed and dynamic, where just to 'articulate multiplicity is not enough'.[104] Indeed, the circumstances of the different characters emerge within different subject positions and are never narrowed down. Their subject positions are instead revealed as multiple, constructed out of the complex positioning of different kinds of 'nomads'. For example, while Tinajo can travel to China for an international conference, she discusses with Suárez the limitations preventing others from travelling internationally.

As Ahmed shows, the ease of movement or transgression of borders becomes a mechanism for the reproduction of social privilege, granting 'particular subjects with the ability to see and to move beyond the confined spaces of a given locality'.[105] While the privileged travellers in the novel have somewhat limited agency, they can still travel. Furthermore, they have access to spaces to which they can retreat. In *Los impostores*, the hotel acts as a 'neutral' space where there are apparently no language barriers or threats. While at first the hotel room also emerges as Augé's 'non-place', in the novel, it is closer to Peter Merriman's critique of Augé, which argues that Augé 'fails to acknowledge the heterogeneity and materiality of the social networks bound up with the production of such environments'.[106] The threats within the city that appear in the novel, such as the secret societies that want to get hold of the manuscript, intervene in this protected space, as rooms get broken into, and their privileged condition is interrupted. This is reflected in the unequal situations in which the travellers find themselves.

Chouchén is also presented as conscious of power imbalances beyond his frantic hyper-awareness of the racism he experiences. While he blames his nationality for his problems,[107] he admits that the country cannot be blamed, suggesting a non-essentialist view of community. This awareness of subjectivity is further emphasized by the novel's contrasts with other characters that are unaware of their privilege, such as when Klauss is described in a matter-of-fact way that seems to parodically highlight the power distribution contained in privilege. As a German 'ivory tower' academic, Klauss seems unaware of power inequality. Following Ahmed, who argues that communities become established '*as a way of moving through space*',[108] the novel reveals a cosmopolitan calling that emphasizes power imbalance and makes the reader aware of it. By suggesting this new cosmopolitanism, the novel emphasizes that there is no 'level playing field'[109] for either the Latin

104 Kaplan, p. 176.

105 Ahmed, *Strange Encounters*, p. 85.

106 Peter Merriman, 'Driving Places: Marc Augé, Non-Places, and the Geographies of England's M1 Motorway', *Theory, Culture & Society*, 21.4–5 (2004), pp. 145–67 (p. 147).

107 Gamboa, *Los impostores*, p. 20.

108 Ahmed, *Strange Encounters*, p. 34.

109 Sharae Deckard and others, *Combined and Uneven Development: Towards a New Theory of World-Literature* (Liverpool: Liverpool University Press, 2015), p. 22.

American subject or the Latin American writer. This, in turn, reveals an uneven cosmopolitanism which sheds light on how communities, specifically Latin American communities, are thought about.

Following Kaplan, the age of telecommunication and transnational cultural production requires the imagining of distance, and I would add, epistemological enunciation, in complicated ways. This situation, she explains, leads to 'new subjectivities that produce new relationships to space as well as time so that distance is [...] a terrain that houses new subjects of criticism'.[110] While stressing the unevenness of epistemological enunciation can also lead to the essentializing of difference, it is useful as it demands the acknowledgment of uneven power distribution.

In the novel, new subjectivities appear informed by the characters' awareness of the distribution of power implicit in the description of 'others', such as when Suárez reads Michaux's description of the Chinese and states:

> ¿En qué año escribió Michaux esta estupidez? Todo el mundo ha visto un chino. En todas las ciudades grandes de Europa y América hay chinos, y entonces, ¿qué sentido tiene describirlos? No lo entiendo. ¡Es un acto arrogante y burlón que no estoy dispuesto a tragar![111]

By telling the reader that the travellers are aware and are critical of canonical Western travelogues of China, the novel shows it is not China itself that the characters have previously engaged with but rather a mediated representation of it. As Lisle suggests, 'the travelogue is an excellent illustration of how discursive power is always characterised by an antagonism between the articulation of hegemony and the inclusion of difference'.[112] In their reading of travelogues, the characters are exposed to this antagonism of hegemony and difference. So, while Suárez stereotypes the Chinese, he simultaneously demands a revision of those precise representations. Gamboa thus appears wary of '"thin" cultural cosmopolitanism approaches that tend to conflate certain cultural phenomena that are typical of the current global condition [...] with mundane and everyday expressions of cosmopolitanism'.[113] Indeed, these 'thin' approaches to cultural cosmopolitanism can remain oblivious to the hierarchies of power and material conditions underpinning any encounter.[114]

The need to be aware of subjectivity also emerges in the words of a Chinese priest who tells his story to Suárez, 'Estuve en la policía secreta que luchó contra la revuelta de estudiantes, en Tiananmen, y le digo una

110 Kaplan, p. 142.

111 Gamboa, *Los impostores*, p. 25.

112 Lisle, p. 277.

113 Maria Rovisco and Magdalena Nowicka, 'Introduction', in *The Ashgate Research Companion to Cosmopolitanism*, ed. by Maria Rovisco and Magdalena Nowicka (Farnham: Ashgate, 2011), pp. 1–14 (p. 7).

114 Helen Gilbert and Jacqueline Lo, *Performance and Cosmopolitics: Cross-Cultural Transactions in Australasia* (Basingstoke: Palgrave Macmillan, 2007), pp. 8–9.

cosa: ustedes, en Occidente, no entendieron nada de lo que pasó aquí.'[115] Interrupting the narration with a serious, non-parodic moment, the novel does not go on to explain what actually happened. A key ellipsis, the utterance reveals the difference between something that has been perceived as a mere object of study and a defining image of Chinese Communism in the 'West' and an event that was experienced intimately by a real person. By not explaining what actually happened, the novel leaves the interpretation open, offering the possibility of new readings of past events, emphasizing subjectivity and concealing a defining moment from 'Western' consumption and global appropriation.

However, the novel does not endorse relativism. On the contrary, it emphasizes the importance of what Ahmed terms 'histories of determination',[116] which inform our experiences in the world, alerting us to the interpellation of the past in the present. Indeed, the novel seems to emphasize the different aspects of life and the impossibility of privileging one over the other. Suspension of judgement and the problems of generalization are recalled, for example, in a discussion between Tirajo and Suárez. When he questions her decisions, she replies, 'no es el momento de dar lecciones morales, *sweet heart*. Pronto ambos estaremos muertos y nuestros cuerpos serán devorados por hordas de gusanos cuyas larvas ya viven en nuestro intestino.'[117] Just as the novel exposes the illusion of an essential notion of community, with death as the reminder of this, the narrator of the final section interrupts the laws of physics, addressing the reader from an unknown dimension that he calls 'la nada'.[118] From this perspective, the novel embraces Nancy's notion of community, with death as the figure through which a non-essential condition of community can be apprehended. As Nancy explains, community is revealed in the death of others; as community presents its members with their mortal truth, death reveals the impossible, 'inoperative' community.[119]

In this sense, the novel discloses a Nancean-informed notion of cosmopolitanism, aware of power imbalances in which the Chinese setting extends and questions the geographical boundaries of Latin America. Linking it to Borges's call for no boundaries,[120] Hubert argues that Gamboa's choice of an Oriental setting 'responds to a relocation of the subject position of the Latin American writer from a point of *repression* (marginal) to one of *emancipation* (cosmopolitan)',[121] thus inverting the prescriptive formula of the peripheral writer who presents a vision of Latin America to the world and offering

115 Gamboa, *Los impostores*, p. 178.
116 Ahmed, *Strange Encounters*, p. 7.
117 Gamboa, *Los impostores*, p. 343.
118 Gamboa, *Los impostores*, p. 349.
119 Jean-Luc Nancy, *The Inoperative Community* (Minneapolis: University of Minnesota Press, 1991), p. 15.
120 Borges.
121 Hubert, p. 46.

instead a Latin American vision of 'the world'. This approach sheds significant light on the Latin American writer with regard to their position in the world. Still, it locates them according to contrasting terms—the marginal and the cosmopolitan—a difference that I do not consider to be fixed in the novel or in Borges's essay. Hubert sees the novel as rewriting travel literature into fictions of travel. She sees this as evidence of the cosmopolitan attitude of the Latin American writer, who intervenes from a peripheral point of enunciation.[122] However, I see the writer as challenging the bearing of *any* point of enunciation, developing a critique of the hegemonic ideas of centre and periphery, suggesting an idea of community that is no longer nationally or essentially bounded.

From this perspective, the novel opens up to Schoene's understanding of cosmopolitanism as he states that this 'new cosmopolitanism promotes an open and flexible practice of community that can accommodate the whole world'.[123] The novel insists on a de-centred space yet is still historically informed by power imbalance. From this perspective, Gamboa exposes power imbalance while evoking a specific cosmopolitanism that acknowledges imaginaries and myths working at both individual and social levels.

Dynamic Encounters in *Hotel Pekín*, by Santiago Gamboa

Like *Los impostores*, *Hotel Pekín* also plays with stereotypes and emphasizes the failures of an essentialist understanding of 'China' as a fixed community. Also, by Gamboa, *Hotel Pekín*[124] recounts the main character, Frank Michalski's professional trip to China. In his encounters with other characters, Michalski's stereotyped constructions fall apart, revealing his self-acknowledged 'cosmopolitanism' to be precarious while pointing to the power imbalance of these encounters. From this perspective, and through the idea of mixture and hybridity in Nancy's conceptualization of the *mêlée*,[125] the novel also seems to expose the failure of globalization as integration.

The story commences with Frank Michalski seated on a United Airlines flight taking off from New York on his way to Beijing. A heterodiegetic narrator tells the reader that Michalski is a middle-aged Colombian national who has settled in the U.S., and whose original name was Francisco Munévar. He is sent to China by his company *Enhancing the Future* to lead a course for Chinese businessmen. His mission is to enlighten them on the 'Western' ways of doing business, including how to serve wine or how to dress. On the flight, he meets Bordewich, a journalist of Brazilian origin who has also settled in the U.S. In China, Michalski is met by Ming Cheng, a woman

122 Hubert, p. 56.

123 Schoene, p. 21.

124 Gamboa, *Hotel Pekín*.

125 Jean-Luc Nancy, 'Eulogy for the Mêlée', in *The Inoperative Community* (Minneapolis: University of Minnesota Press, 1991), pp. 145–58.

who assists him during his time in Beijing. There he also meets Li Qiang, a wealthy Chinese man taking his course.

Michalski's identity is revealed to be torn three ways between the 'West', Latin America, and exoticized notions of the 'East'. His simplistic views on China, made available through his notes, reveal him to be naive regarding human nature. He believes, for example, that he can change how people think by following his company's manual.[125] The narrator knows all about the characters and is also judgemental, making jokes and showing off their knowledge of China. The novel also includes Bordewich's adventures in Beijing and tells us about Li's personal life. Michalski's interactions with these characters will lead him to question his life until that point, thus affording him a new perspective.

Throughout the novel, Michalski perceives China as different from a 'Western' existence. Because he ultimately changes due to his encounters with other people and not because of China itself, the novel reveals 'China' to be a fetish of difference and distance. In this sense, the text emerges as somewhat similar to existing texts and discourses on obtaining knowledge on China. It reveals itself as a parody, understood as a chain of utterances that destabilizes the essential knowledge[127] of these texts and discourses.

Focusing on the exchanges between Michalski and the other characters, and the metafictional aspect disclosed through the apparent conflation of Bordewich, the narrator, and Gamboa himself, the novel challenges essentialist positions on culture and identity, evoking what Kaplan terms 'new subjectivities'.[128] From this perspective, the novel seems to explore the potential of the transnational, suggesting a new understanding of the subject. To my mind, it is in the encounter that these new meanings are created.

Bordewich is Michalski's first interlocutor during his trip. On the aeroplane where they meet, Bordewich tells Michalski that he is a journalist writing for magazines, including *Selecciones* of the *Reader's Digest*, the same magazine that Lu Hsin, the protagonist of *Una novela china*[129] liked to read. In common with contemporary travel writers, as described by Lisle, Bordewich 'fashion[s] a self characterised by solitude, masculinity and irony'.[130] His personality emerges as a very good interlocutor for the philosophical views he discusses with Michalski. With different worldviews, they both think they know how to conquer or truly know the Chinese.[131] Both Michalski and Bordewich seem to build and rely on prejudice, thus setting the tone for the rest of the novel. For example, as they discuss globalization, Bordewich insists on the importance of local culture and the impossibility of a global culture. According to Camilo

126 Gamboa, *Hotel Pekín*, pp. 43–44.
127 Dentith.
128 Kaplan, p. 142.
129 César Aira, *Una novela china* (Buenos Aires: Javier Vergara, 1987), p. 73, see chapter 1.
130 Lisle, p. 77.
131 Gamboa, *Hotel Pekín*, p. 27.

Malagón, the narrative addresses the opposition between the global and the local.[132] In contrast, Michalski seems to embody a universal worldview in which 'cualquier individuo puede ser sensible a los dramas de Shakespeare, la música dodecafónica o el pecado original'.[133]

Most exchanges with Bordewich occur in the hotel bar, a place Bordewich 'adores'.[134] The hotel, as a temporary home, can be considered a paradigmatic chronotope (time and space image) of globalization. Augé has described the hotel run by international chains as one of the emblematic non-spaces of postmodernity, as a transit space without historicity or any specific original characteristics.[135] According to Augé, the hotel becomes a cosmopolitan space by containing different cultures in one space. Yet it concurrently undermines its cosmopolitanism by offering isolation from its surrounding culture. In this sense, it is especially interesting that the hotel in the novel is the famous Hotel Beijing on Chang'an Avenue, in the novel described as 'con una gran leyenda y mil anécdotas',[136] and where the footage of the famous Tank Man near Tian'anmen Square was filmed from. This underlining of the iconic historicity of the area challenges Augé's theory. Yet, simultaneously, it evokes a globally recognized image from history.

However, if we follow Augé, the 'Beijing Hotel' in the novel is certainly a suspended place; while being, on one level, a symbol in China, it is also a place where China is not present. For example, Michalski drinks Lagavulin and Talisker whisky there, and international music is played.[137] Furthermore, the characters seem unaware of the local labour force employed in the hotel. From this perspective, it also seems to evoke the consumer culture that has developed in China since Deng Xiaoping's reforms. In this capitalist China, the hotel evokes a 'neutral' and 'international' space without apparent language barriers. From the point of view of Michalski and the narrator, the hotel is a calm and protected space where illegal topics in China, such as Falun Gong, can be talked about freely. Beyond the hotel, Michalski is always aided by Ming Cheng, disclosing his need for a guide in China.

Michalski acts arrogantly in his attempts to seduce her. While he tells her that he has no stable partner and that this kind of relationship can happen between 'personas lo suficientemente cultas y cosmopolitas como para saber

132 Camilo A. Malagón, 'Dislocated Subjects in the Global City: Santiago Gamboa's Hotel Pekín', in *Urban Spaces in Contemporary Latin American Literature*, ed. by José Eduardo González and Timothy R. Robbins, Hispanic Urban Studies (Cham: Palgrave Macmillan, 2019), pp. 153–74 <https://doi.org/10.1007/978-3-319-92438-0_8>.

133 Gamboa, *Hotel Pekín*, p. 19.

134 Gamboa, *Hotel Pekín*, p. 29.

135 Augé, p. 79; Estefanía Bournot, 'Rutas y encrucijadas: Cronotopos de la narrativa contemporánea latinoamericana', *Anales de Literatura Hispanoamericana*, 44 (2015), pp. 139–48 (p. 142).

136 Gamboa, *Hotel Pekín*, p. 31.

137 Gamboa, *Hotel Pekín*, pp. 83, 109, 202.

que no sólo hay un modo de vivir la vida',[138] revealing a 'liberal' attitude towards relationships, he also states that a woman needs a man. He then pays the bill, a classic 'macho' trope. His lack of sensitivity is depicted through his relationship with Ming, as he uses expressions such as 'la economía global experimentará un gran salto adelante, como se dijo aquí hace cuatro décadas',[139] decisively ignoring the history of Mao Zedong's Great Leap Forward as he uses the term as shorthand for economic development in general.

While Ming initially rejects him, they later get closer, and she ends up acting as his confidant. Ming seems to be the only person with whom he is honest, while she criticizes him directly for his paternalistic, biased and stereotyped approach to China.[140] The narrator tells us how Michalski had an inaccurate idea of how Chinese women looked,[141] in his recognition of the 'other' as 'other' based on their appearance. The 'stranger', as Ahmed explains, is produced precisely as that which we already recognize as a 'stranger'.[142] Michalski conceptualizes 'strangers' as different from his own essentialized 'Western' persona, establishing a boundary between him and them. However, Michalski's Colombian origin, disclosed by the novel, allows the reader to question the character's own 'Westernness' in terms of Ahmed's critique of multiculturalism which, she warns, 'implies that differences *can be* reconciled through the [...] framework which has historically defined Western values as neutral and universal'.[143] The novel thus seems to signal the reigning Western epistemology that blinds Michalski's ability to consider himself non-Western.

Ming's words also seem to echo the way Li thinks of Michalski. Li is *nouveau riche*, and while wealthy and successful, he has continued to be traditional and relatively austere. While both have certain things in common, including their status as 'self-made men',[144] their worldviews clash throughout the novel. Li's aversion to change does not fit with Michalski's welcoming of change, progress, and universal values. Michalski is revealed as naïve in that he is unable to convince Li to endorse his project. Li explains to him instead, 'usted debe saber adaptar sus teorías a nuestra cultura, de lo contrario fracasará'.[145] In their relationship of opposites, Michalski defines Li as a 'reticent' actor, a term that he uses in his work for people who are difficult to convince. Indeed, this reveals his role as course leader as a theatrical one, a performance which assumes its audience will be convinced. Indeed,

138 Gamboa, *Hotel Pekín*, p. 144.
139 Gamboa, *Hotel Pekín*, p. 117.
140 Gamboa, *Hotel Pekín*, p. 184.
141 Gamboa, *Hotel Pekín*, p. 115.
142 Ahmed, *Strange Encounters*, p. 3.
143 Ahmed, *Strange Encounters*, p. 110.
144 Gamboa, *Hotel Pekín*, p. 11.
145 Gamboa, *Hotel Pekín*, p. 127.

Michalski seems to use very 'technical' and 'rational' language to approach his relationship with Li, who, in contrast, is presented as instinctive. This emerges as a mapping process regarding gender stereotypes onto national differences. This mapping of the relationship also appears when Li invites Michalski to his country house, where the 'Colombian-American' is surprised at the beauty of the place as he judges it with hegemonic authority, further revealing his self-sanctioned, prejudiced ideas of China.

Li continuously disagrees with Michalski, emphasizing China's differences, while Michalski believes in 'universal' methods, as he states, 'China no puede ser tan diferente del resto del mundo'.[146] Michalski's 'overemphasizing of similarities', while relying on differences, reminds us of Ahmed's warning in her explorations of multiculturalism: that the dominant subject retains its normativity and requires the stranger to inhabit degrees of subalternity. In Ahmed's words, 'the act of welcoming "the stranger" [...] produces the very figure of "the stranger"'.[147] This contradiction is highlighted by Ming, as she states, 'curioso que admires culturas diferentes cuando tu trabajo es hacer que todas se parezcan'.[148] As Ahmed warns, markers of difference can become barriers that 'restrict the movement and capacities of essentially disembodied individuals'.[149] Both Li's and Michalski's construction of the 'stranger' reveal how the 'mythologized narrativization of displacement' does not 'question[...] the cultural, political, and economic grounds of [...] privileges, means, and limitations'.[150]

For example, Li explains to Michalski how teaching the Chinese how to deal with the 'West' can be just as important as teaching the 'West' how to deal with China. Li emphasizes the differences between them, as he depicts a communal aspect of Chinese politics and society, which continues to reinforce binaries such as communist/non-communist.[151] Following Mariano Siskind's ideas, I see the novel as denouncing the nationalistic patterns of self-marginalization that reinforce hegemonic 'Western' centric structures.[152] In Michalski's change from an essentialist view on culture to a sensitive awareness of its nuances, he eventually seems aware of what Lisle describes as 'the distinctions between here and there with familiar binary oppositions between a safe, civilised home and a dangerous, uncivilised elsewhere'.[153] The novel thus challenges all the ways a 'Western' centre is maintained,

146 Gamboa, *Hotel Pekín*, p. 128.
147 Ahmed, *Strange Encounters*, p. 97.
148 Gamboa, *Hotel Pekín*, p. 141.
149 Ahmed, *Strange Encounters*, p. 107.
150 Kaplan, p. 2.
151 Gamboa, *Hotel Pekín*, p. 169.
152 Mariano Siskind, *Cosmopolitan Desires: Global Modernity and World Literature in Latin America* (Evanston: Northwestern University Press, 2014), p. 6.
153 Lisle, p. 137.

simultaneously questioning the relevance of locations and identities bound to nationhood and instead hinting at what the transnational might allow.

This preference for the transnational emerges with particular force when Michalski discusses his origins with Li and Ming. Michalski admits to his nationality, stating: 'soy colombiano de Colombia, Sudamérica, no confundir con Colombo, Sri Lanka, ni con Columbia, Estados Unidos.'[154] Li retorts to Michalski saying:

> [...] habría que ser muy estúpido para confundir a Colombia con Colombo [...] Usted es alto, fornido, de tez blanca. Nada que ver con un srilankés, que es de piel cenicienta y estructura filiforme, producto de una ingesta calórica baja por razones culturales, caso del vegetarianismo, entre otros. Y lo de Columbia [...] es francamente ridículo [...].[155]

The novel thus suggests the effect an exchange with others can have on the subject. While Li is cultured and knowledgeable, he explains that he can distinguish Michalski through racialized features, remaining within essentialist identity structures. As Li and Michalski continue to construct 'fixed' others, the novel reveals the impossibility of resolution that emerges from their exchange.

The notion of unresolvability emerges mostly through Michalski's experience of change. His change while in China is also exemplified in that Michalski more regularly thinks of Latin America. Michalski's change seems complete towards the end of the novel as he tells his boss he wants to take a sabbatical, and as he thinks of China as a deforming structure, as a place of estrangement which has had the effect of changing him.[156] Michalski's changes materialize in his anger when his boss states, regarding future operations in China, 'Podríamos poner a todo esto un nombre chino, algo así como "Operación Viento del Este," ellos adoran ese tipo de tonterías, ¿no es así?'[157] And yet Orientalist views such as those of Michalski's boss are present throughout Michalski's utterances. In this sense, Michalski's loss of belief in the relevance of essentialist cultural knowledge leads him to critique any essentialist view. That essentialist cultural knowledge is exposed as an empty token of exchange, concretely manifested in his 'failed experience'. Ultimately, Bordewich, Ming and Li make him aware of his prejudiced views of the Chinese.

At the same time, the novel also discloses and questions the 'essentialist' identities and views of the other characters, including Li as the wise sage, by telling the reader about his relationship with his children and wife, who led him to abandon his 'traditional' views and even consider a visit to the 'West'. Not provoking a crisis, as in Michalski's case, these 'traditional' views

154 Gamboa, *Hotel Pekín*, p. 94.
155 Gamboa, *Hotel Pekín*, p. 94.
156 Gamboa, *Hotel Pekín*, p. 213.
157 Gamboa, *Hotel Pekín*, p. 147.

can coexist with more modern ways of life. Thus, the unresolved conflicts between different worldviews do not imply the disavowal of conventional positions but point to the pervading presence of stereotypes and essentialist otherness while simultaneously deconstructing China as a place of deformation, estrangement, and otherness.

As in *Los impostores*, a continuous feature of *Hotel Pekín* is the use of stereotyped descriptions. Michalski is presented as the 'typical' Latin American who 'made it' in the U.S., while Bordewich is the 'typical' journalist who travels the world, and Li is the 'typical' traditional Chinese businessman of contemporary China who has had a meteoric career and has made his fortune on his own. Multiple stereotypes regarding the Chinese emerge through Michalski's and Bordewich's utterances, such as when Bordewich advises Michalski that the Chinese are a 'proud' and 'symbolic' people with 'particularities'.[158]

In this regard, the novel calls attention to Michalski's fetishized views of China while illuminating how essentialist, stereotypical constructions are brought about. Michalski's exchanges with other characters emphasize how power imbalances inform different experiences. China's economic growth has not meant an equal distribution of capital, which is made explicit in the novel through travel. For example, through Bordewich, Michalski learns about poverty in China. The material differences that inform the distribution of power emerge as the reader learns that Li is a rich, important, and influential Chinese businessman. At the same time, Ming explains how she needs to work to support her son, reminding the reader of capitalism's permeating logic.

It is precisely through showing how difference is articulated through stereotypes and the effects of capital accumulation on people's material lives that the novel makes the reader aware of power distribution and its real, tangible effects. In other words, it is not their experience of 'China' that changes the characters' perceived identities but their experiences with others during the trip. By showing this, the novel demands an acknowledgment of those discourses of difference as fiction that are imposed on experience to make sense of reality and community. The novel does not conceptualize new notions of nationhood but suggests new subjectivities of the (Latin American) subject. These new subjectivities, situating new relationships in space and time, are further explored through the metafictional aspects of the novel.

Metafiction and intertextuality abound in the novel, constantly recalling texts and events that Gamboa had already included in his non-fictional travel account *Octubre en Pekín*.[159] For example, the story of David Crook, supposedly written by Bordewich for the magazine *Selecciones* is a reproduction of a section of Gamboa's travel account.[160] In *Octubre en Pekín*, the story is

158 Gamboa, *Hotel Pekín*, pp. 26, 83, 111.

159 Santiago Gamboa, *Octubre en Pekín* (Barcelona: Mondadori, 2001).

160 Gamboa, *Octubre en Pekín*, pp. 150–57.

introduced as told to the writer by Carl, the son of David Crook, both real historical figures. Metafiction also emerges within *Los impostores*, as Michalski goes to a Caribbean bar at the Kempinsky Hotel, where he bumps into a Russian prostitute, who reminds the reader of Chouchén's affairs.

Likewise, Bordewich replicates Gamboa's visit to Baoshan cemetery.[161] What the narrator tells us about Bordewich's visit is a third-person narration that Gamboa has already provided in the first person in his travel account. Indeed, the novel ends with Bordewich telling Michalski that he might write his story down.[162] The wholesale repetition of paragraphs across the two books leads the reader to question the material's authenticity and, thus, what is 'real' in the novel. The reader is also directed to examine the differences and borders between fiction and reality, as the 'implied' author becomes intertwined with the 'real' one. From this perspective at least, the novel seems to demand to be read as autobiography.

Indeed, Michalski's 'success in China' and the role that Chouchén ascribes to the Chinese market as a place to become famous recall Gamboa's own experience. Gamboa's first literary experiences in China were as part of a residency financed by the Spanish-Italian (at the time) publishing house Mondadori. In 2001, Mondadori asked seven young Spanish Language writers for a travelogue; the publishing house financed their stay in the city they were asked to write about. The collection, called *Año Cero*, was intended to show Spanish and Spanish-speaking Latin American visions of the world. As Estefanía Bournot states,[163] these texts are revealed as engaging with the marketing dynamics of publishing houses. Still, they also reveal the expansion of the fictional spaces that are being written about.

Within this context, Gamboa's statement: 'Yo no quiero que nadie lea un libro mío por ser latinoamericano, sino porque le gusta lo que escribo',[164] expresses a desire to belong to a literature valued for itself within a global context. And regarding his interest in China, he states:

> Después de muchos viajes, en este momento lo que más me interesa es llegar a un lugar donde todas tus referencias ya no funcionan. En China nadie sabe quién es John Lennon y ellos te miran con sorpresa si tú no sabes quién es el campeón de ping-pong. Es divertido ver que todos los iconos de nuestra cultura occidental son figuras de paja. Es un extrañamiento total y a mí eso me gusta, se aprende mucho.[165]

161 Gamboa, *Hotel Pekín*, pp. 70, 74, 79; *Octubre en Pekín*, p. 195.

162 Gamboa, *Hotel Pekín*, p. 217.

163 Bournot, p. 140.

164 Pablo Ordaz, 'La literatura latinoamericana ya ha alcanzado la mayoría de edad', *El País*, 14 May 2012 <http://cultura.elpais.com/cultura/2012/05/11/actualidad/1336761317_461722.html> [accessed 1 July 2021].

165 Ana Zarzuela and Luis García, Santiago Gamboa <http://www.literaturas.com/gamboa.htm> [accessed 1 July 2021].

It is precisely the notion of 'total estrangement' that Michalski seems to experience in *Hotel Pekín* in his exchanges with Bordewich, Li and Ming, as well as a closure that is ultimately incomplete, as the reader never learns what Michalski does with his future. From this perspective, the novel challenges any closure of identity, emphasizes interrelations and makes us question an essentialist understanding of community. Simultaneously, by situating the crisis of the Latin American subject in China, the novel exposes how internal conflicts are created and recreated by interactions with other spaces.[166] In this way, the novel reminds us that while 'the experience of cultural difference is now internal to a culture [...] it *is* implacably also a question of different others in distant lands'.[167] The novel takes a cosmopolitan stance by discussing the position of the Latin American subject in the world, the limits of national identities and new imaginings of global communities.

Through this cosmopolitan positioning, and as the characters continue to make sense of their experiences through stereotypes, the novel emphasizes that the idea of difference shapes the subject's experience. In this sense, *Los impostores* suggests a call for a new vision of cosmopolitanism, which aims, at least in theory, to address subjects' experiences in contrast to a 'traditional cosmopolitanism' in which an elite bystander travels under privileged circumstances.[168] *Hotel Pekín*, on the other hand, presents a diagnosis of the Latin American subject within a globalized context. By denying the audience closure, the novel seems to build on Bhabha's notion of hybridity as the in-between space where hegemonic and normalized practices can be rearticulated, allowing new identities to emerge.[169] From this perspective, Michalski's embracing of uncertainty might represent his experience of the *mêlée*, where unity is abandoned, and the 'being-in-common' of subject and community is revealed.

Both *Los impostores* and *Hotel Pekín* emphasize togetherness, and the impossibility for the main characters to find any real centre to their identities, revealing the denial of inequality that discourses of difference and distance conceal. The novels uncover and remind the reader of historically and culturally embedded material inequality. From this perspective, the novels reveal their awareness of Ahmed's warning: a narrative that equates geographical movement with the transgression of identity 'conceals the complex and contingent social relationships of antagonism which grant some subjects the ability to move freely at the expense of others'.[170] Recalling the dynamic and unfixed nature of the encounter as articulated by Ahmed, both *Hotel Pekín*

166 Massey, p. 183.

167 Massey, p. 194.

168 Schoene, p. 3; Hazel Smith, *The Contemporary Literature-Music Relationship: Intermedia, Voice, Technology, Cross-Cultural Exchange* (New York: Routledge, 2016), pp. 171–73, 188.

169 Bhabha, pp. 53–56, 296.

170 Ahmed, *Strange Encounters*, p. 86.

and *Los impostores* challenge the notions of geographical bearings, centre, and peripheries. This, in turn, allows for the possibility of different geographies of affect and loyalty,[171] which, as we shall now see, is precisely the arena in which Sánchez Echenique's *El ombligo del dragon* intervenes.

Mediated Histories in Ximena Sánchez Echenique's *El ombligo del dragón*

Read through Ahmed's explorations of how differences, otherness, and strangeness can become 'properties' of bodies and spaces over time, *El ombligo del dragón*[172] discloses various ways through which bodies can be read and recognized as different. Kaplan warns that an overemphasis on difference and similarity risks us losing sight of a world in which 'new subjectivities' produce new relationships with space and time. Read alongside Ahmed, this allows us to explore the pervading regimes of difference which are shown to continue to inform Mexican society. From this perspective, through its exposure of the colonial history of epistemological classifications as arbitrary, the novel discloses the dynamics that establish 'strangerness' and community in Mexico.

While Gamboa's novels are in a sense, realist novels, *El ombligo del dragón* includes indeterminate fantastical texts and interjections. It tells the story of a Mexican woman whose child, Elio, becomes a person with albinism after receiving an ivory crocodile statuette sent from China by his father, Ermilo. The woman may be Ale, a name only revealed towards the novel's end. Ermilo, a biologist, is in China studying the origins of albinism. In search of answers regarding her son's albinism, the woman visits Ermilo's parents in Acapulco. She then travels to rural China, reuniting with Ermilo, who has discovered a cure for melanoma. Ermilo is then kidnapped and taken to Hong Kong, where he is forced to give up the patent on his discovery. The end of the novel shows Ale back in Mexico, and the indeterminacy of the ending reopens questions concerning the events narrated.

The reader is reminded of the contrast between scientific and literary epistemologies throughout the text as it evokes, through its notions of classification and ordering, a type of colonial taxonomy. The novel is divided into forty-six chapters, resembling a chromosomic structure. It is organized in two sets of twenty-three chapters that share the same title format: a number followed by an 'x'. The only exception is the final chapter, '23y'. As in Julio Cortázar's *Rayuela*,[173] as Valeria Luiselli notes,[174] there are two sets of chapters. The first set of chapters is narrated by the woman and includes

171 Massey, p. 188.
172 Sánchez Echenique.
173 Julio Cortázar, *Rayuela* (Buenos Aires: Editorial Sudamericana, 1966).
174 Valeria Luiselli, '"El ombligo del dragón", de Ximena Sánchez Echenique', *Letras Libres*, November 2007 <http://www.letraslibres.com/revista/libros/el-ombligo-del-dragon-de-ximena-sanchez-echenique> [accessed 1 August 2021].

the main story, while the second set includes various types of 'texts', such as poems, games with words, and a blank page. In the first set of 'x' chapters, the story is chronological. However, events can be told in a different order within the same chapter, confusing the reader regarding the chronological sequence. In the second set of chapters, events are temporally intercalated, and it remains unclear whether what the reader has read has actually occurred. Luiselli suggests that this second set of chapters evokes blogs and scrapbooks and can be read as notes from a travel account.[175]

The scientific layout is interrupted by emotions that are not chronologically tethered, the impulsive reactions of the main character, and anachronistic elements in the story. For example, the first set of chapters includes comments in parenthesis that could be utterances of the woman narrator or of an implied author who could be the figure who has included the second set of chapters in the novel. The text continuously incorporates multiple contradiction-ridden voices and ideologies.[176] This is especially evident by the fact that the last chapter is not 23x, but 23y, representing an alteration in the chromosome's structure. However, the interruption of this 'y' at the end also evokes sex determination, as human females have two of the same sex chromosomes (xx) while males have two different sex chromosomes (xy). While it simulates sex determination, the novel simultaneously challenges systematic fixity. The two sets of chapters play a fundamental role in exposing the scientific and literary ideologies available in the novel, ultimately not allowing the methodical scientific system to hold sway. While the main storyline is chronological, the second set of 'x' chapters suggests that these may be dreams, the product of the woman's imagination, or the intervention of other 'voices' or worldviews.

Since fantastic events are not actually developed or explained, the novel shows the notion of order and classification as fictitious and imposed. As noted by Luiselli,[177] things seem to occur because of the feverish desire of the protagonist, disconcerting the reader. As the dogma of science contrasts with emotional and impulsive reactions, and as this dogma of science is never allowed to rule, the novel sheds light on what informs the woman's histories and reactions. In this sense, science and emotions are revealed as central to the woman's subjectivity. Simultaneously, it also sheds light on the distribution of power that informs her subjectivity, questioning the power that class, gender and race have historically embodied. The shift from a fixed to a haphazard notion of the subject ultimately signifies a dislocation of where the 'other' is located, acting as a critique of power imbalance. Following Massey's approach, space is thus exposed as a product of interrelationships, as the sphere of possibility for the existence of multiplicity, and as being

175 Luiselli.

176 Mikhail Bakhtin, *The Dialogic Imagination: Four Essays*, ed. by Michael Holquist (Austin: University of Texas Press, 1981), p. 272.

177 Luiselli.

always under construction.[178] Furthermore, as articulated by Ahmed,[179] the novel reminds us how strangers are constructed in the encounter and that the recognition of the stranger is an affective judgement. Indeed, this is emphasized in the novel through the figure of the child with albinism and the woman's geographical movements.

The book commences with the erratic thoughts of the woman narrator, who gradually goes on to disclose the existence of her three-week-old son and the arrival of the ivory crocodile sculpture sent by Ermilo. Because of the crocodile, the reader learns that her son has developed albinism. Through her son's albinism, the novel challenges racial distinctions and questions the 'difference' they imply, revealing its preference for nuance and indistinctiveness. His albinism is for her less a condition than a mystery to be solved, and only briefly does she reflect on the practical problems it might cause him in the future. By not believing in the fantasy of a coherent self, the novel reminds us how differences, otherness, and fetishistic strangeness may become the 'properties' of bodies and spaces over time.

Non-belief in a coherent and essential self is also recalled in the novel through its treatment of class distinctions. The woman's position within the complex power structures governed by race and gender is disclosed in her relationships with other characters. She is shown to be aware of power distribution as she states 'conque madre soltera, hija de un político, con un niño color de muerte y en una casa donde tal vez estén conspirando en mi contra'.[180] The utterance also reveals an ironic and defiant attitude, challenging the normative heterosexual nuclear family through the figure of a single mother suspicious of those around her. However, while she criticizes her parents she lives in their house. She acknowledges the social injustice that led her maid, Luz, to remain illiterate, yet she continues to rely on Luz's help to care for her son.

Yet this is not presented in simple terms; its complexity results from a contradictory first-person narrative. For example, while she explicitly criticizes classism, such as when she describes her father, her own classism is revealed through her description of her maid as 'una niña vieja',[181] infantilizing a grown-up woman. On the other hand, while sometimes limited, her defiant outlook towards racial and class structures is explicit on her trip to find Ermilo. Indeed, on her trip, racial and class borders seem suspended because of her ability to move between places. She can get a driver and a car to get to Acapulco and a boat and a sailor to sail to the middle of the sea. The reader learns that she easily acquires a visa for China. When she arrives in Dali with her travel companions, they have no problem taking a bus and

178 Massey, p. 9.

179 Sara Ahmed, 'Making Strangers', *Feminist Killjoys*, (2014) <http://feministkilljoys.com/2014/08/04/making-strangers/> [accessed 1 July 2017].

180 Sánchez Echenique, p. 54.

181 Sánchez Echenique, p. 28.

walking across swamps until finally arriving on the island where the scientists live. All of these actions seem to go smoothly with no major disruptions. When they arrive in China, language does not seem to be a barrier because an interpreter is provided, while her stated limited knowledge of English allows her to communicate with the scientists at the camp.

This idea of fluidity across borders and distance is reinforced through other characters' actions, events, and descriptions. For instance, distance is subverted by the recollection of similarities between China and Mexico, as in this e-mail from Ermilo: 'La montaña de jade verde y el lago me recuerdan un buen a México. Quién iba a creer que en este pueblo perdido de Asia iba a existir una copia de la Quebrada.'[182] However, the ability to transcend borders discloses an ironic take on the ease of global travel. Indeed, the similarities presented between countries are highly ironic, leading the reader to question how 'different' Mexico and China actually are, or whether Ermilo and the woman are simply unable to apprehend China's difference because of their biased attitudes.

From this perspective, the novel seems to acknowledge the importance that descriptions of 'place' have concerning the 'idea' of China, thus recalling a notion of 'China' as a shifting signifier. When the woman travels to China, the novel displaces the geographical location of 'China' as a place for change and instead suggests that all changes happen within the character herself. However, by providing the ivory crocodile that makes the baby albino, it is 'China' as a place of 'otherness' that causes the change. In other words, the novel does not allow any exclusive notion of hegemonic sameness or otherness to prevail. This emerges most notably in the text's presentation of the woman's awareness of power imbalance, later questioning that awareness through intertextuality and parody.

Indeed, the woman's awareness of the histories that determine encounters appears through the different topics upon which she reflects. For example, she describes herself and those who accompany her to China—Ermilo's friend and Ermilo's sister—as not 'looking Mexican'. While she explains that this is true of Ermilo because his green eyes make him look European, revealing Mexican racial systems of difference, she does not explain why she and her friends do not 'look Mexican'. Her appraisal of the class system in Mexico sheds light on the context that would make them 'different' from the traditional Mexican stereotype as she explains the different social classes in Mexican society.[183] This suggests an attitude of condemnation towards Mexican society and classism, yet she still has a mistress-servant relationship with Luz. The same things happen with her driver, whose existence she acknowledges, and yet she continues giving orders to him as if he were detached from his own subjectivity. Both relationships betoken her

182 Sánchez Echenique, p. 113.
183 Sánchez Echenique, p. 118.

middle-class status. Ahmed's naturalization of histories that render things invisible, functioning to conceal forms of social difference,[184] comes to mind. The text exposes the character's biased views, contrasting thoughts and actions, as is evident through the differences between the first and second set of chapters.

Although the woman seems aware of what informs her encounters in the first set of chapters, the reader learns about those she is unaware of in the second set of chapters. Her privileged background is exposed through her access to material objects, houses, and places, such as her visit to her parents-in-law's house in Acapulco, which has big rooms, a swimming pool, a library, a piano, and a 'vieja nana de la familia'.[185] Similarly, her background is recognizable through her knowledge of languages, like when she laughs at a misunderstanding regarding a Chinese name—Hu—and a word in English—who.[186] However, the characters' privileged backgrounds are no guarantee of knowledge concerning China, as an undefined narrator describes Ermilo as the kind of tourist to which 'los Bai del sur le resultan idénticos a los Han del norte'.[187] The unknown yet authoritative narrator denounces Ermilo's ignorance and underlines their knowledge of China. And while the woman openly reflects on the power imbalance in Mexican society, she continues to be part of the system she criticizes. As the novel reveals its awareness of the 'histories of determination', it also reminds us of the embedded practices which continue to establish regimes of difference beyond national contexts.

The woman's awareness of her own subjectivity is also available in her descriptions of Chinese cultural specificities, presenting them in a stereotypical fashion, such as when she describes herself as being like ancestral China, 'pasiva, pasiva, pasiva',[188] emptying not only herself but also China of agency. Her stereotyped views also emerge in her descriptions of China, as she states: 'Me apena decir que la vida de estas personas parece una antología de anécdotas al pie de una fotografía. Sí, para sus párpados colgantes, yo también he de provenir de una guía de viajero.'[189] While she admits that exoticism lies in the eye of the beholder, the reader can see that she is not completely aware of the racism that her words exude in using a physical feature to mark the difference between Chinese women and herself. Simultaneously, she subverts such stereotyping, equating her foreignness with the foreignness she also perceives in the Chinese. This double mirror demonstrates that subjective identification is constructed based on structures beyond our explicit awareness, again emphasizing the histories that have led her to think of China and the Chinese through such specific images.

184 Ahmed, *Strange Encounters*, pp. 3, 86.
185 Sánchez Echenique, p. 35.
186 Sánchez Echenique, p. 81.
187 Sánchez Echenique, p. 22.
188 Sánchez Echenique, p. 134.
189 Sánchez Echenique, p. 115.

From this perspective, the experience of travel to China in the novel seems to turn any notion of the 'exotic' on its head. The novel apparently critiques essentialist differentiation, as emphasized by its overt denouncements of imperialism and its classificatory systems, such as that by which Ermilo is thought to 'be European' because of the colour of his eyes. These classification systems are shown to be informed by gender and are constantly (re)created through history and the written word. A critique of imperialism is revealed in the novel, echoing the woman's awareness of what informs her position of power. For example, she speaks about an English scientist called Johnny Walker and his wife, a parody that begins with his name:

> Johny [sic] bebía demasiado whisky. Además [...] ambos compartían un exacerbado racismo contra el pueblo chino. A no ser porque éste fuera el hábitat natural del aligátor, a Johnny le hubiera gustado transportar el lago Ehrai [sic] en una avioneta para colocarlo en el British Museum. Algunos de sus colegas planeaban hacerlo con la Acrópolis. Excepto que él – <<*My poor Johnny*>>, como le decía su mujer – tenía que soportar el olor de esos cochinos.[190]

The extract introduces Walker as the ultimate imperialist scientist. The text accuses Walker of being racist, while the abusive language used to describe his working conditions as perceived by his wife reveals the utterance as ironic on several levels. In this sense, the mimicry of abusive racist language allows not only for the constructedness of the words used, but also the narrator's critique of Walker's worldview. Furthermore, the novel devalues the exclusivity of a scientific outlook on the world. Choosing a name that coincides with a whisky brand simultaneously recalls consumption patterns, shedding light on the regimes of difference established through consumption itself. Johnny not only drinks whisky but has the opportunity to drink 'too much whisky'. Ultimately, Walker is eaten alive by an albino alligator in China. That Walker received a prize from the Plinian Society in Edinburgh, the club to which Charles Darwin belonged, reminds us of the travels of European scientists to the Americas. The metafictional aspects of the novel thus emphasize the pervading elements of Enlightenment classification systems. The novel sheds light on how history is to be understood as a matter of interpretation and not an objective account. By doing this, it critiques the hegemonic structures through which certain histories have been chosen to be told, as the narrator states, 'contar esta historia y no otra, un suceso totalmente arbitrario'[191] while also describing pictures of white men, a white baby, and a Chinese woman smoking opium. As she critiques hegemonic structures, she simultaneously refers to a display of fetishized otherness.

190 Sánchez Echenique, p. 154.
191 Sánchez Echenique, p. 153.

The main narrator's critique of hegemonic structures also extends to gender differences as she tells the story of Rosalynd [sic] Franklin, explaining how her role in the discovery of the DNA double helix was usurped by James Watson and Francis Crick, who later published 'their discovery' in *Nature*.[192] As the narrator states, her colleague Maurice Wilkins showed Franklin's X-ray photograph to Watson without her permission. Her discovery is introduced in the novel through a citation from their paper, in the original English, as the novel's second epigraph. When Watson and Crick received the Nobel Prize in 1962, together with Wilkins, Franklin had already died, and the Nobel Prize was never awarded posthumously. According to the National Library of Medicine's website, it was only after people challenged Watson's caricatures of Franklin in his memoirs *The Double Helix* and that Franklin's friend Anne Sayre published a biography in rebuttal of Watson's account of Franklin that Franklin's role in the discovery became better known.[193] Read in tandem with the first epigraph—Lewis Carroll's parodic poem 'How Doth the Little Crocodile', from *Alice in Wonderland*, also quoted in English—the novel warns the reader in advance of deception and predation, describing the 'gentile smiling jaws' of the crocodile that 'welcome little fishes in'.[194] While focusing on the female subject, the text shows that power distribution organizes social forms. From this perspective, fixed classification systems and decisions based on them are shown to hold the potential to embed, conceal, and justify injustice.

The injustice embedded in fixed classification systems also appears in the narration that explains how Ermilo's discovery was stolen from him by those with more power. His kidnappers make him cede his discovery rights to a multinational pharmaceutical company in Hong Kong. Ermilo holds the knowledge, but he is unable to claim power over it because, as the narrator states, 'a pesar de que los tres podemos testificar, ninguna corte internacional ni ninguna comunidad científica apelarán a su favor'.[195] We thus find Ermilo, previously a model scientist, questioning his systematic certainties.

It is interesting to apply the studies of two female academics to the fictitious Ermilo's participation in the male enterprise of discovery: Anne McClintock[196] and Mary Louise Pratt.[197] Pratt's analysis of travel writing by Europeans about non-European parts of the world sheds light on how 'domestic subjects' of Euroimperialism were, and continue to be, created.[198]

192 Sánchez Echenique, p. 167.

193 'The Rosalind Franklin Papers: Biographical Information' <https://profiles.nlm.nih.gov/ps/retrieve/Narrative/KR/p-nid/183> [accessed 1 July 2021].

194 Lewis Carroll, *The Annotated Alice: 'Alice's Adventures in Wonderland' and 'Through the Looking-Glass'*, originally published 1865 (London: Penguin, 2001).

195 Sánchez Echenique, p. 167.

196 McClintock, p. 29.

197 Pratt, p. 204.

198 Pratt, p. 4.

Ermilo's scientific enterprise is what Pratt calls 'imperial men reinvent[ing] a moment of pure (male) origin'.[199] Within this context, Ermilo appears to be a sort of continuation of the elites of Spanish America whose identities and decisions were shaped in relation both to Europe and to non-European subjects, as was articulated in *mestizaje*. As Pratt explains, the 'liberal creole project involved founding an independent, decolonized American society and culture, while retaining European values and white supremacy'.[200] Imperialism is thus acknowledged as part of the Latin American subject's 'histories of determination', as told by the narrator's partner.

As McClintock shows, race, gender, and class were fundamental coordinates of Western modernity, coming into existence in and through each other, 'existing in intimate, reciprocal and contradictory relation'.[201] Ermilo's lack of power, as he loses the rights to his discovery, contrasts with the male scientific enterprise, further developing the complexities of what determines subject positions, shedding light on new forms of subjectivity. While Franklin lost out to her male colleagues, Ermilo, although male, lost to a big transnational pharmaceutical company. The role of a male-controlled international scientific community is denounced. Indeed, Ermilo's experience as a young Latin American subject emerges as analogous to Franklin's 'loss'. The novel thus questions imperialized, gendered, and racial epistemologies through which injustices have historically been committed. Simultaneously, it exposes how essentialism remains central to the paradoxically hybrid articulation of *mestizaje*. Indeed, the novel not only explores race and class but also explores comparative imperialism, and history, as contained in articulations of identity and community in Latin America.

As Patience Schell shows, Latin American scientific discourses have been shaped by and shared dialogue with international intellectual discourses that privilege elite European knowledge.[202] According to Schell, scientific imperialism collected and produced knowledge about other parts of the world, claiming it was objective, scientific, and definitive.[203] From this perspective, the novel can be seen to question the epistemological structures through which Latin American countries, first as colonies and later as republics, were and continue to be established. This is further emphasized as Ermilo states towards the end of the story: 'lo menos es preguntarse si existe o no China,

199 McClintock, p. 30.

200 Pratt, p. 175.

201 McClintock, p. 184.

202 Patience Schell, 'Eugenics Policy and Practice in Cuba, Puerto Rico and Mexico', in *The Oxford Handbook of the History of Eugenics*, ed. by Alison Bashford and Philippa Levine (Oxford: Oxford University Press, 2010), pp. 477–91 (p. 477); Patience Schell, *The Sociable Sciences: Darwin and His Contemporaries in Chile* (Basingstoke: Palgrave Macmillan, 2013), p. 3.

203 Schell, *The Sociable Sciences*, p. 3. See also, by Nicola Miller, *Republics of Knowledge* (New Jersey: Princeton University Press, 2020).

eso ya lo hicieron los decimonónicos.'[204] Ermilo's question interrogates the role of transnational enterprises, both of the nineteenth-century (males) who questioned the existence of China and of the contemporary transnational companies that stole his discovery.

Indeed, within the 'discoveries' of places by scientific communities, it is worth considering the figure of the crocodile featured in the novel's title, whose presence is a catalyst for events. According to Spencer J. Weinreich, the discoverers' idea of the 'New World' as an extension of the Old led new animal specimens to be thought of as within 'models of morphological normalcy', shaped on the Old World animals.[205] Indeed, he argues that the crocodile performed the cultural work of bridging the New and Old worlds well, as it indicated deeper geographical connections. Weinreich explores how this culturally and religiously significant animal could shape the discourses in which it was deployed.[206] As he shows, quoting Louise W. Lippincott:

> No clear taxonomy distinguished crocodiles from dragons or snakes – to the contrary, both dragons and crocodiles were considered "large, exotic snakes," a kinship that bestowed upon the crocodile elements of the dangerous and the fantastic.[207]

Thus, the novel not only explores the semantic field that an animal such as the crocodile can evoke but also explores the continuity of the epistemologies and histories at play during the processes of globalization which began with Columbus's expedition.

In this regard, the woman is shown to defy the versions of history to which she has access and on which she reflects. Such as when she states '¿Pero, qué pasaría si la Historia plasmada en los jarrones de flor de loto fuera un mero invento de nuestros ancestros?'[208] Her utterance recalls the multiple uses and deployment of the word 'chino', as we have seen previously. Her words reveal an idea of commonality between herself as a Mexican, and China, as the pottery mentioned simultaneously brings to mind traditional Chinese ceramics and Mexican Talavera poblana. The latter is influenced by the white and blue Ming ceramics that arrived in Mexico via the Manila Galleons trade route during the seventeenth and eighteenth centuries.[209] This articulation of a worldwide commonality is recalled in the novel with

204 Sánchez Echenique, p. 190.

205 Spencer J. Weinreich, 'Thinking with Crocodiles: An Iconic Animal at the Intersection of Early-Modern Religion and Natural Philosophy', *Early Science and Medicine*, 20.3 (2015), pp. 209–40.

206 Weinreich, p. 238.

207 Louise W. Lippincott, 'The Unnatural History of Dragons', *Philadelphia Museum of Art Bulletin*, 77.334 (1981), pp. 3–24 (p. 3).

208 Sánchez Echenique, p. 83.

209 Margaret Connors McQuade, 'Talavera Poblana: Cuatro siglos de producción y coleccionismo', *Mesoamérica*, 40 (2000), pp. 113–40.

the disappearance of 'all texts' announced on the radio.[210] As the narrator explains, people lose their minds, not knowing who they are anymore, while still acting in ways learnt from texts and following practices and traditions that are no longer relevant without the texts themselves. The constructedness of the fixity that the text provides is further emphasized by Luz's illiteracy, as she would therefore be unaffected by the disappearance of text. The novel thus reminds us that not only do written histories lead to power imbalances, but also practices, traditions, and word usage, beyond national borders.

The importance of text is also highlighted when the narrator 'plays' with the word 'Chinese' and the idea of 'China' in Mexico. She states, 'Si China fuera una mentira, entonces ya nada estaría en chino y la vida sería más sencilla. [...] Pero si los cuentos chinos fueran falsos, tampoco se habría inventado la tinta [...].'[211] The novel's challenge to official histories is also present through the play on the stereotypical ideas of what the Chinese do, such as illegally copying things, or are, such as being contemplative. In particular, 'cuentos chinos' is an expression used in Spanish to mean 'false stories'. On various occasions, terms that use the word 'China' go beyond the specific, such as when she describes her skin turning 'chinita' when listening to a song.[212] 'China' emerges as a fetishized place in the woman's descriptions: a term that can be used loosely, inhabited by contemplative people and copiers.

Yet at the same time, her utterances are revealed to be ironic as she mentions a Mexican chilli pepper resulting from la 'China poblana'.[213] The narrator plays with images and words such as 'China poblana', a traditional style of dress worn by women in Mexico, but also the name by which Catarina de San Juan, a slave of possibly Indian or Chinese origin who arrived in Mexico in the seventeenth century, is known.[214] Indeed, the myth goes that the 'china poblana' dress was popularized because of Catarina de San Juan. The potential Chinese origin of the word '*china*' is a common belief[215] that has been contested by academics such as María del Carmen Vázquez Mantecón[216] and John Charles Chasteen. Chasteen states in his introduction

210 Sánchez Echenique, p. 79.

211 Sánchez Echenique, p. 83.

212 Sánchez Echenique, p. 66.

213 Sánchez Echenique, p. 112.

214 Nicole von Germeten, 'Tatiana Seijas. Asian Slaves in Colonial Mexico: From Chinos to Indians', *The American Historical Review*, 120.4 (2015), pp. 1531–32 (pp. 1531–32); Tatiana Seijas, *Asian Slaves in Colonial Mexico* (New York: Cambridge University Press, 2015).

215 'La China Poblana en 12 comentarios', *Wikipuebla*, (2013) <http://www.wikipuebla.poblanerias.com/la-china-poblana-en-12-comentarios/> [accessed 1 July 2021].

216 María del Carmen Vázquez Mantecón, 'La china mexicana, mejor conocida como china poblana', *Anales del Instituto de Investigaciones Estéticas*, 22.77 (2000), pp. 123–50 (p. 123).

to the translation of 'La China' by José María Rivera,[217] 'although chino/china means Chinese in Spanish, the meaning of china here is from an indigenous language and has nothing to do with Asia'.[218] The novel thus recalls the hegemonic imperialism embodied by identity constructions in the Spanish colonial period in Latin America, where Asians were collected under the category of 'chinos'.[219] In its questioning of imperialistic epistemologies, the novel allows for the scrutiny of the meaning-making powers of human relations and denies fixed alterity and immutable boundaries.

The novel thus comments on classification systems as guarantors of difference, such as those that Edward Said exposes in *Orientalism*,[220] or that Gayatri Chakravorty Spivak terms 'epistemic violence'.[221] While Spivak thinks of 'epistemic violence' as the infliction of harm against subjects through discourse, Said's idea of 'otherness' builds on his observations that the 'Orient' worked in negative oppositional terms for the 'West'. Foucault's conceptualization of the power of discourse sheds significant light on my reading of *El ombligo*, as the complexity and conflicts embedded in the globalized commercial and scientific structures, as well as the epistemologies used since the 'discovery' of America, become available, and are subverted in the text. This appears explicitly in Ermilo's reflection on Columbus's arrival to the Americas:

> Baste como ejemplo el 12 de octubre de 1492. Entonces, según el calendario gregoriano, un puñado de hombres desembarca en las costas de un supuesto sito que luego se comprobará que en realidad es otro. A continuación se topa con una población – no sólo un hombre, sino una población –, se dirige a ella en buen castellano y, al no recibir respuesta, decide adueñarse de su territorio. Descubrir es, como afirma O'Gorman, hallar lo que estaba ignorado.[222]

By mentioning the Gregorian calendar, Ermilo emphasizes the European framework underlying the Spanish expedition. By not mentioning Columbus, his utterance extends responsibility and appropriation of the 'discovery' to

217 Juan de Dios Arias, *Los Mexicanos pintados por si mismos: tipos y costumbres nacionales* (Mexico City: Impr. de M. Murguia y Comp., Portal del Aguila de Oro, 1854).

218 John Charles Chasteen, *Born in Blood and Fire: Latin American Voices* (New York: W.W. Norton & Company, 2011), p. 91.

219 Seijas.

220 Edward Said, *Orientalism* (London: Penguin, 2003), p. 49.

221 Gayatri Chakravorty Spivak, 'Can the Subaltern Speak?', in *Marxism and the Interpretation of Culture*, ed. by Cary Nelson and Lawrence Grossberg (Urbana: University of Illinois Press, 1988), pp. 271–313 (pp. 280–83). Both Said and Spivak build on Michel Foucault's notion of discourse as an entity of signs which assign and communicate specific relations to, between and among objects, subjects, and statements.

222 Sánchez Echenique, p. 39.

Europe. The text also challenges scientific assumptions, stating that the place they think they arrived at will later be proved to be another. The silence of the locals sheds light on the violence of the imperial conquest. Indeed, science as practice is revealed to be ordering and naming and the intersection of the scientist's works, institutions, objects of study, and the money that funded their projects.[223] In addition, the mentioning of Mexican historian Edmundo O'Gorman, considered one of the earliest and most influential historical revisionists to the narratives of the Spanish colonial period in Latin America, critiques those same narratives. O'Gorman challenged and objected to the expressions 'discovery of America', 'encounter between two worlds', and 'cultural fusion'.[224] From this perspective, the novel reveals the continuities of the scientific epistemologies between those of the eighteenth and nineteenth centuries and those of the twentieth and twenty-first centuries.

Furthermore, insofar as the novel reflects upon the complexities of the 'discovery', it simultaneously discloses the characters' awareness of the injustices they see and experience, not only through Ermilo's denunciation of the 'discovery of America' but also through the woman's awareness of her upper-class privilege. Like Marina/Xian of Cristina Rivera Garza's *Verde Shanghai*,[225] she seems aware of the existence of some of the racial, class and gendered social constructions that inform her experiences. Like *Verde Shanghai*, the novel also shows how histories of determination in encounters can go beyond one's own awareness. Indeed, the story simultaneously reveals how their critique remains an intellectual project, as they are ultimately unable to act upon it. The characters' awareness and unawareness shed light on how it is ultimately impossible to escape the epistemological frameworks that shape a subject's experience.

The novel thus exposes the complicity between, and continuity of, scientific epistemologies and power, recalling how, during the nineteenth century, both were linked to Empire and a Western and Eurocentric notion of the world. The twentieth and twenty-first centuries, the novel reveals, are a period dominated by the transnational flow of economic globalization, embodied by the pharmaceutical company that steals Ermilo's patent. Furthermore, the theft of Ermilo's patent sheds light on the relevance of epistemology beyond the violence itself, as it is his interpretation of and control over the data which has been taken away from him.

In this sense, the emphasis on the interpretation of the data, rather than the data itself, suggests that it might actually be possible to contest epistemologies. Indeed, the novel does not focus on the figure of the albino alligator or the ivory crocodile. Instead, it focuses on what it can do, such as eating

223 Schell, *The Sociable Sciences*, pp. 2–3.

224 Edmundo O'Gorman, *El proceso de la invención de América* (Mexico City: Fondo de Cultura Económica, 1958); *México: El trauma de su historia* (Mexico City: Universidad Nacional Autónoma de México, 1977), pp. 4–5, 8–9.

225 Cristina Rivera Garza, *Verde Shanghai*, Kindle (Mexico City: Tusquets, 2011).

Walker or making a child albino. By having a Mexican protagonist travel to China, the novel discloses the mechanisms at play in epistemologies and scientific structure. It concurrently discloses the intellectual awareness of those mechanisms and the impossibility of escaping from them, allowing the reader to reflect upon the possibility of a decentred world, embodied in the idea of the exotic turned on its head, and in 'China' itself, a decentred world that allows for a new epistemology. Orientalism and an essentialist notion of 'China' are thus subverted through a redistribution of geopolitical power as knowledge is gained by, and stolen from, Mexican scientist Ermilo and his discovery. The embracing of the exotic and, furthermore, the acknowledgment of the 'exotic within', symbolized by the attachment of the mother to her son, turns the notion of the exotic on its head. Mysterious events, such as the albino transformation, serve to exoticize Mexico; in this process, the exoticness of China is equated to that of Mexico.

The novel thus discloses how injustice and scientific discourses are linked. While the novel shows the characters' awareness of injustices, illustrated by the upper-class Mexican woman's consciousness of her privilege, it also shows how her critique of injustice remains an intellectual project, as she does not act upon it. Furthermore, her unawareness is presented in parallel to the victory of globalization, as Ermilo's discovery is ultimately stolen from him. Moreover, the novel shows the continuity between old and new globalization, led by the endurance and complicity of scientific epistemologies. The figure of the double helix thus represents the problem the novel describes. As the novel is arranged scientifically, after the structure of the double helix, the text reveals how even the 'aware' implied author is also part of the problematic upholding of scientific epistemologies.

From this perspective, the novel's DNA structure leads the reader to question whether it can go beyond epistemology. Indeed, even while the novel tries to challenge fixed structures, it ultimately still conforms to the textual structure of literary narrative. In other words, no matter how aware the implied author might be of the epistemic structure, the DNA structure of the text discloses the persistence of scientific discourses and the difficulty, and maybe even impossibility, of going beyond epistemologies. Indeed, the novel shows how this problematic is inscribed in our DNA, revealing the lack of a space from where the mind can be decolonized. In postmodern style, the novel 'acknowledges the human urge to make order, while pointing out that the orders we create are just that: human constructs [...]'.[226] However, as Rosi Braidotti states, 'belief systems and their rituals are perhaps not incompatible with critical thought and practices of citizenship'.[227] In this sense, the novel recalls Braidotti's appeal for a review of the segregation of discursive fields.[228]

226 Linda Hutcheon, *A Poetics of Postmodernism: History, Theory, Fiction* (New York: Routledge, 1988), p. 41.

227 Rosi Braidotti, *The Posthuman* (Cambridge: Polity, 2013), p. 35.

228 Braidotti, *The Posthuman*, p. 43.

El ombligo del dragón emphasizes and exposes the mechanisms of inclusion and exclusion at play in 'encounters'.

It is necessary here to find a place for the albinism of the child and to consider whether it is justified to interpret his condition as exemplifying the lost cause of the scientific method. For this, I draw on Bonnie TuSmith, who explores the stereotype of the albino, considering how authors represent what she terms the 'multi-ethnic possibilities of the albino'.[229] According to her, albinism offers 'depths and nuances [...] which the tag of white American versus black ethnic has not been able to accommodate'.[230] In this sense, the child's 'becoming' albino after the sculpture's arrival challenges science, as well as recalling the fact that the discourse of *mestizaje* has also been unable to accommodate everyone. In contrast, the mother's embracing of otherness, as embodied by the albino child and 'China', towards the novel's close hints towards a more inclusive notion of community beyond the fixed borders of nation and race.

From this perspective, the novel tells us of the exhaustion of scientific classification systems imposed by a Western colonial ideology, suggesting instead a relationship not mediated by imperial histories and conquests between Mexico and China. By emphasizing the interstitial and unfixed experiences in contrast to the powerful scientific dogmas and denying agency to a fetishized notion of China, the novel sheds light on aspects that go beyond current nation-state structures. Furthermore, the novel not only questions the persistence of fixed class, race, and gender differentiations but simultaneously challenges the relevance of the nation state. Latin America, like 'China', thus becomes 'another' imagined space in a world context, ultimately interrupting essentialist understandings of 'China' and 'Latin America'. Thus, 'China' here disturbs hierarchical understandings of Latin American identity and community based on *mestizaje*. Like Derrida's notion of the supplement,[231] the role of 'China' here discloses the lack of 'China' in essentialist definitions of Latin American identity. This is epitomized in the Uruguayan Gabriel Peveroni's collection *Shanghai*,[232] which the following section discusses.

Deferring Resolution: Posthumanism and Postnationalism in Gabriel Peveroni's *Shanghai*

The collection *Shanghai* can be described as *nouvelles* within a larger novel which has yet to appear. To date, only *Shanghai* #1, *Shanghai* #2 and *Shanghai* #3, out of twelve, have been published. Peveroni then published the novel *Los*

229 Bonnie TuSmith, 'The "Inscrutable Albino" in Contemporary Ethnic Literature', *Amerasia*, 19.3 (1993), pp. 85–102 (p. 85).

230 TuSmith, p. 99.

231 Jacques Derrida, *Of Grammatology* (Baltimore: The Johns Hopkins University Press, 2016).

232 Gabriel Peveroni, *Shanghai #1. Enero 2010* (Alfaguara, 2013); *Shanghai #2. Febrero 2005* (Alfaguara, 2013); *Shanghai #3. Marzo 2007* (Alfaguara, 2014).

ojos de una ciudad china,[233] a rewriting of these first three *nouvelles*; however, it must be noted that *Los ojos de una ciudad china* has differences in terms of content and structure with *Shanghai* and a detailed analysis of these differences is beyond the scope of this book. Each *nouvelle* is assigned a month from the years 2005, 2007 and 2010 but they have not been published in chronological order regarding the storyline. Within these *nouvelles*, each chapter corresponds to a day of the month, while events themselves are introduced through different characters/narrators. While some chapters are in the first person, others are extracts from fictional essays and novels. Metafictionally layered, the novel incorporates the names of 'real' people as characters and 'characters' as 'real' people in the novel. It continuously relocates events from one place to another. Technology also plays a central role, not only because the text was published as an e-book but because all relationships are mediated by technologies which are ubiquitous in the present day.

In their portrayal of the spaces characters inhabit and move through, the *nouvelles* articulate the relations that strangers have with each other in different spaces. The texts open up ideas of home and belonging concerning the role of the nation state because it is not really present in the events. In doing this, the novel hints towards the mechanisms through which 'otherness' is constructed. Indeed, while most aspects of the novel are connected to the city of Shanghai, events cannot be pinned down to any specific location. The novel thus challenges how 'strangerness' is constructed in relation to 'others', precisely by its constant displacement of the sites of 'otherness'. The novel thus challenges the hegemonic geographies constructed around notions such as North and South or East and West, simultaneously mapping a new de-centred politics, geography, and subjectivity.

Through its fragmented texts and the relations between the characters, the *nouvelles* disclose that they (the characters) are not related to one another but that their experiences are in-common,[234] calling essential 'otherness' into question. From this perspective, and building on Rosi Braidotti's articulations of the posthuman,[235] I see the novel's elaboration on subjectivity through 'China' as a way of shedding light on contemporary forms of Latin American identity, cosmopolitanism, and community, simultaneously rearticulating subjectivity and alterity.

The coherence of the story is lost between places and events. The presence of change emphasizes and embraces the notion of unresolvability. The novel disarticulates any idea of a fixed Shanghai or China through the overwhelming information that technology makes possible. The text weakens exoticism by making everything and nothing exotic. *Shanghai #1* is set in 2010 and starts with a text in the first person by Xiaomei, an elderly Chinese woman living in Shanghai who, we discover, was raped by a Japanese soldier, Akira, during the

233 Gabriel Peveroni, *Los ojos de una ciudad china* (Montevideo: HUM, 2016).

234 Schoene, p. 181.

235 Braidotti, *The Posthuman*.

Nanjing Massacre. This we learn through the supposed transcription in the text of the novel *Los ojos de Nanjing* being read by the character Melina López, allegedly written by the character 'César Aira', and that tells the story of Akira and Xiaomei. Xiaomei speaks of telling her story to other people, including a writer called Lu Hsin. As we have seen in the first chapter of this book, Lu Hsin is a character in César Aira's *Una novela china*, and thus ironizes the presence and role of Aira in Latin America by inserting him as a character in the novel. Written in the first person, the text's epigraphs, we later learn, are written by Xiaomei and recommended by another character, Ziggy Stardust. We learn that Xiaomei's daughter died during the Tian'anmen Revolt and that Xiaomei is the grandmother of a woman called Alaia, who used to be the girlfriend of the *Shanghai* character Joy Hsieh.

In *Shanghai #1*, we also learn that Joy Hsieh has travelled to Barcelona to learn about his unknown Latin American history. The trip is made possible by Arturo Ledesma and his wife Teresa, a Chilean couple living in Shanghai. Hybridity and intertextuality occur here with the Jewish origin of the surname Ledesma and the name coinciding with that of a 'real' Chilean editor. Ledesma is an academic researching poetry and dictatorship in the Latin American Southern Cone; kidnapped and having been given up for adoption during the Chilean dictatorship, he follows clues to learn about his past. Hsieh met Ledesma when the latter heard him muttering words in Spanish and recognized his *rioplatense* accent. In Barcelona, Hsieh discovers he is one of many clones.

Brian Pujol, a Catalan journalist, recalling a more restricted identity, is the third 'narrator' in *Shanghai #1*. Once a war correspondent, he has teamed up with his former boyfriend, Igor. In Shanghai, they plan to interview, among others, María Remedi, who has also been cloned. In 2010, the reader was left with Alaia, Xiaomei, Joy Hsieh, Ziggy Stardust, Brian Pujol, Igor and Melina López in Barcelona, and while the other cloned Joys are in Barcelona, one is at Frankfurt airport. Ledesma is in Chile on his way to meet 'the author César Aira' in Buenos Aires to learn about his real origins. In *Shanghai #2* and *#3*, set in 2005 and 2007, the reader is introduced to other characters and learns how the events in 2010 have come about.

In *Shanghai #2*, we find extracts of an essay by the character Charlotte Tzara. In the prologue to her essay, an undisclosed author tells us about Tzara speaking of being contacted by Lu Hsin's nephew. He has continued writing Lu's stories which, he explains, César Aira would publish after Lu's wife translated them. Lu's wife, the narrator explains, revealing further intertextuality with *Una novela china*, was incestuously adopted. Tzara's hypotheses are that Aira's novels can be used to live out a story. She thinks that Akira embodies the Akira of the novel as a way to escape the consequences of his terrible past,[236] or that the story is written for someone to find their own story

236 Peveroni, *Shanghai #3*, loc. 393, 408.

in it, as in the case of Igor and *La trama infinita*, another novel written by the César Aira of *Shanghai*.

We later learn that Xiaomei is the daughter of a British soldier called David Jones, recalling musician David Bowie's 'real' name. The reader also learns how Xiaomei met Ziggy, who shows her he is her brother. We also find Joy Hsieh with Alaia and his friend Popil, a man obsessed with Ziggy Stardust; they go around the city making graffiti marks and posting stickers. In *Shanghai #3* Igor tells Brian about his search for Ziggy Stardust, who he thinks might result from a Raelian cloning. Ziggy, the reader knows, has already told Xiaomei he is a David Bowie clone and the first clone to exist. In metafictional style, the woman who leads the cloning programme of the 'real' Raelians is called Briggite Boisselier,[237] her name coinciding with the leader of the cloning programme in the novel. Metafiction and intertextuality, undeniably central to the novel, ironically comment on authorship and fiction. While the reader is reading extracts of novels and essays that some characters also read, the novel, through other characters, questions the authorship of those same extracts. As in the essay written by Tzara on Aira's book that a character reads, the reader is also led to question the limits of reality, something we saw in the novels analysed in the first chapter of this book.

Like *La escuela del dolor humano de Sechuán* and *Verde Shanghai*, *Shanghai* also rejects closure. Its fragmentation defies any kind of order or organized system. For example, in a dialogue between Ziggy and Xiaomei, the latter asks about Melina López, who, in the novel *Shanghai* is a real character, but, according to Ziggy, is also a fictional character of some other undisclosed texts.[238] Also, according to Ziggy, all 'real' characters in the novel are fiction. It thus becomes impossible to separate fiction from reality, with the novel playing with fiction within fiction as 'real' people in *Shanghai* are presented as characters in other texts. This confuses the reader regarding which events are, if any, 'real' in the story. However, the novel leaves this unresolved, questioning the limits between history and reality and literature and history. The same thing occurs with memories, which are intertwined with history and events, and impossible to outline without a context.

The novel's embracing of unresolvability also comes to the fore through its representations of cities, and especially of Shanghai itself. The novel tells about how 'las torres avanzan y ha llegado el día del irremediable desalojo'.[239] Ledesma tells how Xiaomei's house is going to be demolished.[240] The novel explores the rapid urban expansion in China, revealing how the landscape makes encounters seem almost miraculous. While the novel is set around Shanghai, events occur around the globe: Ledesma meets Aira

237 'The Raelian Movement' <http://www.rael.org/home> [accessed 1 August 2021]; 'Clonaid' <http://clonaid.com/page.php?18> [accessed 5 July 2016].

238 Peveroni, *Shanghai #3*, loc. 1194.

239 Peveroni, *Shanghai #1*, loc. 88.

240 Peveroni, *Shanghai #1*, loc. 212.

in Buenos Aires, Joy's clones live in Spain and Germany, and Akira dies in the Philippines. Throughout the different chapters, the reader learns about characters of diverse nationalities in various locations worldwide. The expansion of the city and the notion of the no-place seem to reveal that social organization needs to find new ways through technologies, such as the internet, which, for example, allows the character Arturo Ledesma to learn about his past or the character Joy Hsieh to meet his clones. However, as the novel shows, there are risks in learning and embracing these new ways and kinds of knowledge. Indeed, Joy Hsieh's life is put at risk precisely because he meets his clones who belong to a mafia.

The idea of objects in relation to other objects, which we also see in the fetishized construction of 'chino', is recurrent throughout the text. One of the first ways in which the 'copies' are highlighted is through the statement of Aira publishing texts written by someone else. Another way in which this is highlighted is through the idea of cloning. Indeed, the clone is presented in parallel with the notion of the copy. For example, María Remedi's reflection on copies as a paradigm of China and China as a gravitational centre of the world[241] emphasize the pervading presence of the transnational flows of globalization and neoliberal capitalism. Her reflection simultaneously forces the reader to reflect, precisely because she has her own 'copy', on the notion of what constitutes the human and the relations between them. Braidotti's critical text *The Posthuman* allows us to shed light on how the figure of the clone in *Shanghai* elaborates alternative ways of conceptualizing subjectivity, by transcending what she terms 'lethal boundaries'.[242]

In her text, Braidotti explores how the 'boundaries between the natural and the cultural categories have been displaced and to a large extent blurred by the effects of scientific and technological advances'.[243] Indeed, Braidotti, explicitly echoing Gilles Deleuze and Félix Guattari's work, argues for 'the dislocation of difference from binaries to rhizomatics' and for moving away from oppositions and towards processes.[244] A posthumanist position allows thinking of the Joys as within a reconceptualization of subjectivity which sidesteps 'the pitfalls of binary thinking'.[245] I see Joy becoming, borrowing Braidotti's words on the sheep Dolly, 'a copy made in the absence of one single original [...] [spinning the] Immaculate Conception into a biogenetic third-century version'.[246] Dolly, Joy, Ziggy and Remedi's clone 'shatter the linearity of time and exist [...] in a continuous present',[247] as the novel tells

241 Peveroni, *Shanghai #3*, loc. 80.
242 Braidotti, *The Posthuman*, p. 37.
243 Braidotti, *The Posthuman*, p. 3.
244 Braidotti, *The Posthuman*, p. 96.
245 Braidotti, *The Posthuman*, p. 86.
246 Braidotti, *The Posthuman*, p. 74.
247 Braidotti, *The Posthuman*, p. 74.

us that the ageing of clones is different in all cases, while cloning allows us to think we live forever.

Through the leading role played by Joy Hsieh, the novel defies human 'normality, normalcy and normativity'.[248] By delving into Joy's 'human nature', the novel reveals the human as a historical construct and questions the distinction between being and not being human. Furthermore, Joy, as a semantic embodiment of Latin America and China, in line with radical critiques of humanistic arrogance arising from feminist and post-colonial theory, proposes new alternatives for looking at the 'human' exploring 'masculinism, racism, white superiority, the dogma of scientific reason and other socially supported systems of dominant values'.[249] The novel exposes the complexity of notions of difference and similarity as they occur during encounters, exemplified by Joy meeting his *mafioso* brothers. Joy's conflicted awareness of being a clone alters the relevance of the possibility of originality: he does not really care about being the 'original' but knowing he is not leads him to question his subjectivity. From this perspective, the novel seems to argue towards a subjectivity which is aware of the presence of others.

This idea of 'being-with', which emerges throughout the three *nouvelles* evokes a Nancean community and Schoene's cosmopolitanism. The novel's defiant disregard for what is 'original' acknowledges the exoticism found in views and descriptions regarding Shanghai, China and a vision of the 'Orient'. However, the texts defy those visions since the 'real' places and people cannot live up to those expectations. Like the novels explored in the previous chapters, *Shanghai* challenges essentialism and deconstructs fixed notions of the 'other' by exposing the mechanism at play in the practice and (re)making of difference and otherness. The choice of Shanghai, as with China, is not random, as it is shown to embody a figure of difference and distance from Latin America. At the same time, the text simultaneously destroys any possibility of fixed differences.

Indeed, a fetishized 'China' is explored in *Shanghai* through various stereotypical derogatory images of the Chinese in Latin America: Chinese mafia, Chinese involved in the traffic of opium, the selling of shoddy products, or the expression of conservative values of the Chinese grandfather.[250] While the novel includes various stereotypical visions of China, it continuously defies those same traditional ideas about China by making Shanghai equivalent to any other city.

Indeed, as Sarah Misemer observes in another work by Peveroni, *Groenlandia* (2005), his characters use the repeating patterns of the fractal to show how the local and global intersect.[251] According to her, Peveroni's

248 Braidotti, *The Posthuman*, p. 26.

249 Braidotti, *The Posthuman*, pp. 28–29.

250 Peveroni, *Shanghai #2*, loc. 803.

251 Sarah M. Misemer, 'Gabriel Peveroni's Luna Roja: Eclipsing and Recycling Information and Meaning on the Stage', *Symposium: A Quarterly Journal in Modern*

characters demonstrate the persistence of past histories behind new technologies, or economic or social changes, shedding light on globalization. Indeed, *Shanghai* also embraces the relations between local and global processes, as well as personal and communal histories, never resolving where one starts and the other ends. This lack of purposefulness is especially evident in Xiaomei's words as she states: 'poco importaba si el relato era imperfecto, porque las historias reales siempre son imperfectas y se pierden en otras historias, tan confusas como las que creíamos principales.'[252] From this perspective, the novel stresses the notion that the subject is the effect of 'flows of encounters, interactions, affectivity and desire that one is not in charge of'.[253] According to Braidotti, a posthuman ethics challenge 'urges us to endure the principle of not-One at the in-depth structures of our subjectivity by acknowledging the ties that bind us to the multiple "others" in a vital web of complex interrelations'.[254]

Susanne Klengel and Alexandra Ortiz Wallner offer valuable input regarding this notion of conflict and community by challenging epistemologies and rethinking the notion of the South as editors of *Sur/South: Poetics and Politics of Thinking Latin America-India*.[255] In their introduction, they show how 'despite the widespread and powerful mindset of a thinking based on difference, there have recently been significant attempts to promote other, integrative and epistemic non-violent "world" concepts'.[256] Indeed, another possibility for understanding *Shanghai* (and arguably also *El ombligo del dragón*) is Enrique Dussel's 'trans-modern pluriverse' as the two books disclose a discursive positioning which attempts to go beyond Eurocentric and North American philosophical modernity.[257] Indeed, according to Silvia Rivera Cusicanqui, there can be no discourse or theory of decolonization without a decolonizing practice.[258] She shows, exemplifying with the social studies that study the Andean region, that one finds 'internal colonialism' as defined by Pablo González Casanovas in 1969—simultaneously denouncing

Literatures, 61.4 (2008), pp. 278–90; 'Tragedias tradicionales e historias de un nuevo orden global: Groenlandia de Gabriel Peveroni', *Gestos: Teoría y Práctica del Teatro Hispánico*, 23.46 (2008), pp. 65–84.

252 Peveroni, *Shanghai #3*, loc. 1183.

253 Braidotti, *The Posthuman*, p. 100.

254 Braidotti, *The Posthuman*, p. 100.

255 Susanne Klengel and Alexandra Ortiz Wallner, 'A New Poetics and Politics of Thinking Latin America / India. SUR / SOUTH and a Different Orientalism', in *Sur/South: Poetics and Politics of Thinking Latin America-India*, ed. by Susanne Klengel and Alexandra Ortiz Wallner (Madrid: Vervuert, 2016), pp. 7–26.

256 Klengel and Ortiz Wallner, p. 12.

257 Enrique Dussel, 'A New Age in the History of Philosophy: The World Dialogue Between Philosophical Traditions', *Prajñā Vihāra*, 9.1 (2008), pp. 1–22 (pp. 512–14).

258 Silvia Rivera Cusicanqui, 'Ch'ixinakax Utxiwa: A Reflection on the Practices and Discourses of Decolonization', *South Atlantic Quarterly*, 111.1 (2012), pp. 95–109 (p. 100).

his invisibility in contrast to Peruvian sociologist Adolfo Quijano, who is the recognized author of 'internal colonialism' even though he would have only used/coined the term in the nineteen-eighties.[259] This term is based on the notion that the modern world system emerged in conjunction with the Conquest of the Americas and is, therefore, simultaneously colonial.[260] According to this 'coloniality', as different people and places were configured in specific ways to meet the needs of capital, 'coloniality' normalized these particularities, which then became hegemonic.[261] Echoes of this 'coloniality' emerge in Dussel's critique of modernity and alleged universality. And yet, as Rivera Cusicanqui makes explicit and Escobar notes, these critiques are mostly on what Escobar calls the academic-intellectual level.[262] It is from this perspective that I would like here to extend Rivera Cusicanqui's thought in order to understand the role that these novels play within Latin America, considering this novel as a practice of decolonization. As a transmodern project, the novel engages with the cultures which 'have been ignored, upon the basis of their own resources, in constructive dialogue with European and North American Modernity'.[263] This emerges through *Shanghai* as it develops characters from and in different parts of the world, coming from different cultures and philosophical traditions.

The novel can thus be seen to defy the idea of fixed belonging. Indeed, in *Shanghai*, cartographic references only seem to work as guides or references. The same holds true for characters and events. While wars and dictatorships are mentioned, these are present through conflicted and unresolved personal experiences rather than national or official narratives. Not only does Xiaomei state that war conditioned her life, but the Chilean dictatorship also permeates Arturo's past. At the same time, another character tells of her father being killed by the military in Uruguay. Within this context, the past is revealed to be impossible to leave behind, constantly haunting Xiaomei's, Joy's and Arturo's actions and influencing decisions. The novel thus emphasizes personal experiences linked to trauma beyond specific dictatorships or nations. While not (yet) central to the story, the references to dictatorships and war provide a background of trauma and fear common to most of the characters.

By displacing and dislocating subjects and places and exposing the complex layers of (non)difference through the figure of the clone, metafiction, and intertextuality, the novel defies the 'great abstraction' of race, nationalism, and formal politics, which are territorially organized. Through

259 Rivera Cusicanqui, p. 103; Kiran Asher, 'Latin American Decolonial Thought, or Making the Subaltern Speak', *Geography Compass*, 7.12 (2013), pp. 832–42 (p. 834).

260 Asher, p. 834.

261 Asher, p. 834.

262 Arturo Escobar, 'Worlds and Knowledges Otherwise', *Cultural Studies*, 21.2–3 (2007), pp. 179–210.

263 Dussel, p. 20.

Schoene's compositeness, the novel crams as many storylines and clashing images into the text as possible. The novel can thus be described as postnational, not because it 'resolves, transcends, or otherwise leaves the national behind, but because it defers and delays the resolution, or dissolution, of the national because it attests to the passion and pain of the personal in its dealings with it'.[264]

In this sense, *Shanghai* questions any bounded relation to cartography and nation states by thinking of subjectivity from a relational standpoint—one beyond difference and fixed alterity. The novel acknowledges the nation as a political reality but simultaneously explores the politics and subjectivities beyond the nation itself. The clones, which coexist in different spaces, weaken the physical underpinning of places as two identical beings coexist in different spaces. *Shanghai* thus reveals the mechanisms of a practice of space while simultaneously critiquing the possibility of an essential fixity of any given space. Ultimately, the text hints at an underlying interrelatedness despite the existing identitarian and power divides.

The novel thus fits Schoene's description of compositeness as cosmopolitan representation, 'blighted by global inequality and crushed into an accident-prone mosaic of misfitting segments that push and press one on the other, yet remain worlds apart'.[265] This spacing of the inoperative community allows for community but does not endorse any essentialist understanding of it. Indeed, it reminds us of the 1989 Argentine declamation: 'la palabra Shangai, no existe, porque puede escribirse de tantas formas distintas que ni siquiera es necesario escribirla'.[266] The novel's challenge of hegemonies through the figure of the clone and its geographical diversity exposes an overall notion of new ways of thinking about identity and community as non-essentialist and in constant development.

Conclusion: Travel Beyond Movement

The characters in the four novels studied here thus think of home from beyond specific locations and the idea of 'difference'. The idea is rather constructed around subjectivities. Travel to China is shown to be an experience of estrangement, yet the characters reject otherness, instead embracing 'being-in-common'. The novels in this chapter seem to call for a Latin American identity in terms of what Braidotti has termed 'nomadic subjects', a way out of the dilemma between essentialism and poststructuralist contingency through the figure of the mobile subject. According to her, the nomad is a 'transgressive identity, whose transitory nature is precisely the

264 Brad Epps, 'Before Postnationalism: Supernationalism, Modernisme, and Catalonia', *Arizona Journal of Hispanic Cultural Studies*, 7.1 (2010), pp. 133–60 (p. 153).

265 Schoene, p. 15.

266 Martín Caparrós, 'Nuevos avances y retrocesos de la nueva novela argentina en lo que va del mes de abril', *Babel*, 2.10 (1989), pp. 43–45.

reason why s/he can make connections at all'.[267] As she explains, nomadic politics is thus a 'matter of bonding, of coalitions, of interconnections'.[268] As Alexandra Ganser[269] notes, we must remember that figures like the nomad cannot be utilized without accounting for them as sites of colonial discourses constructed by specific power relations, as Kaplan has concluded.

Braidotti's views, alongside her emphasis on the experience of what she terms 'non-Oneness, which is constitutive of the non-unitary subject',[270] echo Nancy's notion of being singular plural. While for Braidotti, the non-Oneness 'anchors the subject in an ethical bond to alterity, to the multiple and external others that are constitutive of that entity which, out of laziness and habit, we call the "self"',[271] for Nancy 'what is at stake is [...] thinking, absolutely and without reserve, beginning from the "with," as the proper essence of one whose Being is nothing other than with-one-another'.[272] According to Nancy, subjects are never atomized individuals that can exist outside any relation to those around them; they are always part of this series of relations. And it is precisely because they are part of a relation that they are a relation.[273] Considering this, the novels seem to come close to Chantal Mouffe's notion of identity, where we are in permanent contact with others and in a process of 'permanent hybridization and nomadization'.[274] According to Mouffe, if identity is based on difference, it is also based on exclusion. Thus, hybridity emphasizes the importance of others in a subject's identity, while the nomadic expresses the need of agency to move between identities.

Ultimately, *Los impostores*, *Hotel Pekín*, *El ombligo del dragon*, and *Shanghai* demand that one consider the subject in relation to others as they disclose the global as being intrinsically formed by the local. These novels thus advocate for greater specificity in the relationship between the local and the global. Rather than reflecting on China as a country itself, 'China' in these novels becomes a setting through which to explore philosophical considerations. The theme of travel relates to the judgement whereby different places in the world become equivalent, in line with a Nancean cosmopolitanism, thus challenging hegemonic structures and the bearing of sites of enunciation. As borders and

267 Rosi Braidotti, *Nomadic Subjects: Embodiment and Sexual Difference in Contemporary Feminist Theory* (New York: Columbia University Press, 1994), p. 35.

268 Braidotti, *Nomadic Subjects*, p. 35.

269 Alexandra Ganser, *Roads of Her Own: Gendered Space and Mobility in American Women's Road Narratives, 1970–2000* (Amsterdam: Rodopi, 2009), p. 176.

270 Braidotti, *The Posthuman*, p. 100.

271 Braidotti, *The Posthuman*, p. 100.

272 Nancy, *Being Singular Plural*, p. 34.

273 Paul Simpson, 'What Remains of the Intersubjective? On the Presencing of Self and Other', *Emotion, Space and Society*, 14 (2015), pp. 65–73 (pp. 67–68).

274 Chantal Mouffe, 'For a Politics of Nomadic Identity', in *Travellers' Tales: Narratives of Home and Displacement*, ed. by George Robertson (London: Routledge, 1994), pp. 102–10 (p. 110).

difference continue to shape public discourses and to generate discourses of violence, these novels seem to call for a Nancean community, 'the reality of *being-in-common* as such'.[275]

References

Ahmed, Sara, 'Making Strangers', *Feminist Killjoys*, (2014) <http://feministkilljoys.com/2014/08/04/making-strangers/> [accessed 1 July 2017]

———, *Strange Encounters: Embodied Others in Post-Coloniality* (London: Routledge, 2000)

Aínsa, Fernando, 'Nueva cartografía de la pertenencia. La pérdida del territorio en la narrativa latinoamericana', *Iberoamericana*, 14.54 (2014), pp. 111–26

Aira, César, *Una novela china* (Buenos Aires: Javier Vergara, 1987)

Ardila, Clemencia, 'Cronistas, investigadores y reporteras -policíacos- en la narrativa colombiana contemporánea', *América: Cahiers du CRICCAL*, 43.1 (2013), pp. 69–78

Ardila, Clemencia, and Grupo de Especialización en Hermenéutica Literaria Eafit, '"Los impostores" de Santiago Gamboa: El juego de la escritura', *Estudios de Literatura Colombiana*, 13 (2003), pp. 121–38

Arias, Juan de Dios, *Los Mexicanos pintados por si mismos: tipos y costumbres nacionales* (Mexico City: Impr. De M. Murguia y Comp., Portal del Aguila de Oro, 1854)

Asher, Kiran, 'Latin American Decolonial Thought, or Making the Subaltern Speak', *Geography Compass*, 7.12 (2013), pp. 832–42

Augé, Marc, *Non-Places: Introduction to an Anthropology of Supermodernity* (London: Verso, 2009)

Bakhtin, Mikhail, *The Dialogic Imagination: Four Essays*, ed. by Michael Holquist (Austin: University of Texas Press, 1981)

Bhabha, Homi K., *The Location of Culture* (Oxon: Routledge, 1994)

Borges, Jorge Luis, 'El escritor argentino y la tradición', in *Discusión*, essay originally published 1953 (Madrid: Alianza, 1976), pp. 128–37

Bournot, Estefanía, 'Rutas y encrucijadas: Cronotopos de la narrativa contemporánea latinoamericana', *Anales de Literatura Hispanoamericana*, 44 (2015), pp. 139–48

Braidotti, Rosi, *Nomadic Subjects: Embodiment and Sexual Difference in Contemporary Feminist Theory* (New York: Columbia University Press, 1994)

———, *The Posthuman* (Cambridge: Polity, 2013)

Campbell, Jan, *Arguing with the Phallus. Feminist, Queer, and Postcolonial Theory: A Psychoanalytic Contribution* (London: Zed Books, 2000)

Caparrós, Martín, 'Nuevos avances y retrocesos de la nueva novela argentina en lo que va del mes de abril', *Babel*, 2.10 (1989), pp. 43–45

Carroll, Lewis, *The Annotated Alice: 'Alice's Adventures in Wonderland' and 'Through the Looking-Glass'*, originally published 1865 (London: Penguin, 2001)

275 Nancy, *Being Singular Plural*, p. 55.

Chasteen, John Charles, *Born in Blood and Fire: Latin American Voices* (New York: W.W. Norton & Company, 2011)
Cheah, Pheng, 'The Cosmopolitical', in *The Ashgate Research Companion to Cosmopolitanism*, ed. by Maria Rovisco and Magdalena Nowicka (Farnham: Ashgate, 2011), pp. 211–24
Clifford, James, *Routes: Travel and Translation in the Late Twentieth Century* (Cambridge: Harvard University Press, 1997)
'Clonaid' <http://clonaid.com/page.php?18> [accessed 5 July 2016]
Connors McQuade, Margaret, 'Talavera Poblana: Cuatro siglos de producción y coleccionismo', *Mesoamérica*, 40 (2000), pp. 118–40
Cortázar, Julio, *Rayuela* (Buenos Aires: Editorial Sudamericana, 1966)
Dann, Graham, 'Writing out the Tourist in Space and Time', *Annals of Tourism Research*, 26.1 (1999), pp. 159–87
Deckard, Sharae, Nicholas Lawrence, Neil Lazarus, Graeme Macdonald, Upamanyu Pablo Mukherjee, Benita Parry, and others, *Combined and Uneven Development: Towards a New Theory of World-Literature* (Liverpool: Liverpool University Press, 2015)
Deleuze, Gilles, and Félix Guattari, *A Thousand Plateaus: Capitalism and Schizophrenia* (London: Athlone, 1987)
Dentith, Simon, *Parody* (London: Routledge, 2000)
Derrida, Jacques, *Of Grammatology* (Baltimore: The Johns Hopkins University Press, 2016)
———, *On Cosmopolitanism and Forgiveness* (London: Routledge, 2001)
Digou, Mike, 'Hitchcock's MacGuffin in the Works of David Mamet', *Literature-Film Quarterly*, 31.4 (2003), pp. 270–75
Dussel, Enrique, 'A New Age in the History of Philosophy: The World Dialogue Between Philosophical Traditions', *Prajñā Vihāra*, 9.1 (2008), pp. 1–22
Eco, Umberto, 'Reflections on "The Name of The Rose"', *Encounter*, (1985), pp. 7–19
———, *The Name of the Rose* (London: Vintage, 2004)
Epps, Brad, 'Before Postnationalism: Supernationalism, Modernisme, and Catalonia', *Arizona Journal of Hispanic Cultural Studies*, 7.1 (2010), pp. 133–60
Escobar, Arturo, 'Worlds and Knowledges Otherwise', *Cultural Studies*, 21.2–3 (2007), pp. 179–210
Fernández Bravo, Álvaro, 'Apropiaciones de la cultura china en la literatura sudamericana contemporánea: Contribución para un mapa tentativo a partir de obras de César Aira, Bernardo Carvalho y Siu Kam Wen', *452°F Revista de Teoría de la literatura y Literatura Comparada*, 13 (2015), pp. 50–70
Gamboa, Santiago, *Hotel Pekín* (Bogota: Editorial Planeta Colombiana, 2008)
———, *Los impostores* (Barcelona: Seix Barral, 2002)
———, *Octubre en Pekín* (Barcelona: Mondadori, 2001)
Ganser, Alexandra, *Roads of Her Own: Gendered Space and Mobility in American Women's Road Narratives, 1970–2000* (Amsterdam: Rodopi, 2009)
García García-Herreros, Catalina, 'Personajes que viajan: Una tipología del desplazamiento global en la narrativa de Santiago Gamboa' (presented at the V Congreso Europea CEISAL de Latinoamericanistas, Bruselas, Bélgica, 2007)

Germeten, Nicole von, 'Tatiana Seijas. Asian Slaves in Colonial Mexico: From Chinos to Indians', *The American Historical Review*, 120.4 (2015), pp. 1531–32

Gilbert, Helen, and Jacqueline Lo, *Performance and Cosmopolitics: Cross-Cultural Transactions in Australasia* (Basingstoke: Palgrave Macmillan, 2007)

Gombrowicz, Witold, *Ferdydurke*, trans. by Danuta Borchardt (New Haven: Yale University Press, 2000)

González Miranda, Sergio, and Cristián Ovando Santana, 'Hacia un Nuevo Pensamiento Integracionista Latinoamericano: Aproximación a una lectura de segundo orden', *Polis*, 7.21 (2008), pp. 265–85

Grewal, Inderpal, and Caren Kaplan, eds, *Scattered Hegemonies: Postmodernity and Transnational Feminist Practices* (London: University of Minnesota Press, 1994)

Hatfield, Charles, *The Limits of Identity: Politics and Poetics in Latin America* (Austin: University of Texas Press, 2015)

Holland, Patrick, and Graham Huggan, *Tourists with Typewriters: Critical Reflections on Contemporary Travel Writing* (Ann Arbor: University of Michigan Press, 1998)

Hook, Derek, 'The Racial Stereotype, Colonial Discourse, Fetishism, and Racism', *Psychoanalytic Review*, 92.5 (2005), pp. 701–34

Hoyos, Héctor, 'Orientalismo, globalización e imaginarios transpacíficos en la novela latinoamericana actual', *Cuadernos de Literatura*, 17.34 (2013), pp. 82–105

Hsieh, Yvonne Ying, *From Occupation to Revolution: China Through the Eyes of Loti, Claudel, Segalen, and Malraux (1895–1933)* (Birmingham: Summa Publications, 1996)

Hubert, Rosario, 'Rewriting Travel Literature: A Cosmopolitan Critique of Exoticism in Contemporary Latin American Fiction', in *Peripheral Transmodernities: South-to-South Intercultural Dialogues between the Luso-Hispanic World and 'the Orient'*, ed. by Ignacio López-Calvo (Newcastle upon Tyne: Cambridge Scholars Publishing, 2012), pp. 42–61

Hulme, Peter, *Cuba's Wild East: A Literary Geography of Oriente* (Liverpool: Liverpool University Press, 2011)

Hutcheon, Linda, *A Poetics of Postmodernism: History, Theory, Fiction* (New York: Routledge, 1988)

Kaplan, Caren, *Questions of Travel: Postmodern Discourses of Displacement* (London: Duke University Press, 1996)

Klengel, Susanne, and Alexandra Ortiz Wallner, 'A New Poetics and Politics of Thinking Latin America / India. SUR / SOUTH and a Different Orientalism', in *Sur/South: Poetics and Politics of Thinking Latin America-India*, ed. by Susanne Klengel and Alexandra Ortiz Wallner (Madrid: Vervuert, 2016), pp. 7–26

Kobylecka-Piwonska, Ewa, 'Ricardo Piglia, Lector de Witold Gombrowicz', *Neophilologus*, 97.2 (2012), pp. 333–47

'La China Poblana en 12 comentarios', *Wikipuebla*, (2013) <http://www.wikipuebla.poblanerias.com/la-china-poblana-en-12-comentarios/> [accessed 1 July 2021]

Lippincott, Louise W., 'The Unnatural History of Dragons', *Philadelphia Museum of Art Bulletin*, 77.334 (1981), pp. 3–24

Lisle, Debbie, *The Global Politics of Contemporary Travel Writing* (Cambridge: Cambridge University Press, 2011)

López, Kathleen, 'The Asian Presence in *Mestizo* Nations: A Response', in *Critical Terms in Caribbean and Latin American Thought*, ed. by Yolanda Martínez-San Miguel, Ben. Sifuentes-Jáuregui, and Marisa Belausteguigoitia (New York: Palgrave Macmillan, 2016), pp. 125–31

Loti, Pierre, *The Last Days of Pekin*, trans. by Myrta L. Jones (Boston: Little, Brown and Company, 1902)

Luiselli, Valeria, '"El ombligo del dragón", de Ximena Sánchez Echenique', *Letras Libres*, November 2007 <http://www.letraslibres.com/revista/libros/el-ombligo-del-dragon-de-ximena-sanchez-echenique> [accessed 1 August 2021]

Malagón, Camilo A., 'Dislocated Subjects in the Global City: Santiago Gamboa's Hotel Pekín', in *Urban Spaces in Contemporary Latin American Literature*, ed. by José Eduardo González and Timothy R. Robbins, Hispanic Urban Studies (Cham: Palgrave Macmillan, 2019), pp. 153–74 <https://doi.org/10.1007/978-3-319-92438-0_8>

Massey, Doreen, *For Space* (London: SAGE, 2005)

McClintock, Anne, *Imperial Leather: Race, Gender, and Sexuality in the Colonial Contest* (New York: Routledge, 1995)

Merriman, Peter, 'Driving Places: Marc Augé, Non-Places, and the Geographies of England's M1 Motorway', *Theory, Culture & Society*, 21.4–5 (2004), pp. 145–67

Michaux, Henri, *A Barbarian in Asia* (New York: New Directions, 2016)

Miller, Nicola, *Republics of Knowledge* (New Jersey: Princeton University Press, 2020)

Misemer, Sarah M., 'Gabriel Peveroni's Luna Roja: Eclipsing and Recycling Information and Meaning on the Stage', *Symposium: A Quarterly Journal in Modern Literatures*, 61.4 (2008), pp. 278–90

———, 'Tragedias tradicionales e historias de un nuevo orden global: Groenlandia de Gabriel Peveroni', *Gestos: Teoría y Práctica del Teatro Hispánico*, 23.46 (2008), pp. 65–84

Montt Strabucchi, Maria, Carol Chan, and María Elvira Ríos, *Chineseness in Chile: Shifting Representations during the Twenty-First Century*, Studies of the Americas (Cham: Palgrave Macmillan, 2022) <https://doi.org/10.1007/978-3-030-83966-6>

Mouffe, Chantal, 'For a Politics of Nomadic Identity', in *Travellers' Tales: Narratives of Home and Displacement*, ed. by George Robertson (London: Routledge, 1994), pp. 102–10

Nancy, Jean-Luc, *Being Singular Plural* (Stanford: Stanford University Press, 2000)

———, 'Eulogy for the Mêlée', in *The Inoperative Community* (Minneapolis: University of Minnesota Press, 1991), pp. 145–58

———, *The Inoperative Community* (Minneapolis: University of Minnesota Press, 1991)

Nicol, Bran, *The Cambridge Introduction to Postmodern Fiction* (Cambridge: Cambridge University Press, 2009)

O'Gorman, Edmundo, *El proceso de la invención de América* (Mexico City: Fondo de Cultura Económica, 1958)

———, *México: El trauma de su historia* (Mexico City: Universidad Nacional Autónoma de México, 1977)

Ordaz, Pablo, 'La literatura latinoamericana ya ha alcanzado la mayoría de edad', *El País*, 14 May 2012 <http://cultura.elpais.com/cultura/2012/05/11/actualidad/1336761317_461722.html> [accessed 1 July 2021]

Ouellet, Eric, 'Multinational Counterinsurgency: The Western Intervention in the Boxer Rebellion 1900–1901', *Small Wars & Insurgencies*, 20.3–4 (2009), pp. 507–27

Peveroni, Gabriel, *Los ojos de una ciudad china* (Montevideo: HUM, 2016)

———, *Shanghai #1. Enero 2010* (Alfaguara, 2013)

———, *Shanghai #2. Febrero 2005* (Alfaguara, 2013)

———, *Shanghai #3. Marzo 2007* (Alfaguara, 2014)

Pöppel, Hubert, 'Fuerzas centrífugas y centrípetas en Santiago Gamboa y Gonzalo España: La novela policíaca colombiana en el contexto de la glocalización', *Revista Iberoamericana*, 76.231 (2010), pp. 359–76

Prasso, Sheridan, *The Asian Mystique: Dragon Ladies, Geisha Girls, & Our Fantasies of the Exotic Orient* (London: PublicAffairs, 2006)

Pratt, Mary Louise, *Imperial Eyes: Travel Writing and Transculturation* (London: Routledge, 1992)

Ríos, María Elvira, María Montt, and Carol Chan, 'El imaginario de lo chino en las revistas magazinescas chilenas de principios del siglo XX', *Revista Rumbos TS. Un espacio crítico para la reflexión en Ciencias Sociales*, 24 (2021), pp. 129–50 <https://doi.org/10.51188/rrts.num24.434>

Rivera Cusicanqui, Silvia, 'Ch'ixinakax Utxiwa: A Reflection on the Practices and Discourses of Decolonization', *South Atlantic Quarterly*, 111.1 (2012), pp. 95–109

Rivera Garza, Cristina, *Verde Shanghai*, Kindle (Mexico City: Tusquets, 2011)

Roth, Wolff-Michael, 'In Praise of the Mêlée: Toward a New Conception of Scientific Identity and Literacy', 2007 <http://web.uvic.ca/~mroth/teaching/600-13Fall/1007/Melee.pdf> [accessed 1 March 2021]

Rovisco, Maria, and Magdalena Nowicka, 'Introduction', in *The Ashgate Research Companion to Cosmopolitanism*, ed. by Maria Rovisco and Magdalena Nowicka (Farnham: Ashgate, 2011), pp. 1–14

Rutherford, Jonathan, 'The Third Space: Interview with Homi Bhabha', in *Identity: Community, Culture, Difference*, by Jonathan Rutherford (London: Lawrence and Wishart, 1990), pp. 207–21

Said, Edward, *Orientalism* (London: Penguin, 2003)

Sánchez Echenique, Ximena, *El ombligo del dragón* (Mexico City: Tusquets, 2007)

Saravia, Daisy, *Migración china y orientalismo modernista. Análisis en la revista Variedades (1909–1919)* (Lima: Ediciones MyL, 2020)

Schell, Patience, 'Eugenics Policy and Practice in Cuba, Puerto Rico and Mexico', in *The Oxford Handbook of the History of Eugenics*, ed. by Alison Bashford and Philippa Levine (Oxford: Oxford University Press, 2010), pp. 477–91

———, *The Sociable Sciences: Darwin and his Contemporaries in Chile* (Basingstoke: Palgrave Macmillan, 2013)

Schoene, Berthold, *The Cosmopolitan Novel* (Edinburgh: Edinburgh University Press, 2011)

Seijas, Tatiana, *Asian Slaves in Colonial Mexico* (New York: Cambridge University Press, 2015)

Simpson, Paul, 'What Remains of the Intersubjective? On the Presencing of Self and Other', *Emotion, Space and Society*, 14 (2015), pp. 65–73

Siskind, Mariano, *Cosmopolitan Desires: Global Modernity and World Literature in Latin America* (Evanston: Northwestern University Press, 2014)

Smith, Hazel, *The Contemporary Literature-Music Relationship: Intermedia, Voice, Technology, Cross-Cultural Exchange* (New York: Routledge, 2016)

Spivak, Gayatri Chakravorty, 'Can the Subaltern Speak?', in *Marxism and the Interpretation of Culture*, ed. by Cary Nelson and Lawrence Grossberg (Urbana: University of Illinois Press, 1988), pp. 271–313

Stephens, Angharad Closs, *The Persistence of Nationalism: From Imagined Communities to Urban Encounters* (Abingdon: Routledge, 2013)

'The Raelian Movement' <http://www.rael.org/home> [accessed 1 August 2021]

'The Rosalind Franklin Papers: Biographical Information' <https://profiles.nlm.nih.gov/ps/retrieve/Narrative/KR/p-nid/183> [accessed 1 July 2021]

TuSmith, Bonnie, 'The "Inscrutable Albino" in Contemporary Ethnic Literature', *Amerasia*, 19.3 (1993), pp. 85–102

Vázquez Mantecón, María del Carmen, 'La china mexicana, mejor conocida como china poblana', *Anales del Instituto de Investigaciones Estéticas*, 22.77 (2000), pp. 123–50

Weinreich, Spencer J., 'Thinking with Crocodiles: An Iconic Animal at the Intersection of Early-Modern Religion and Natural Philosophy', *Early Science and Medicine*, 20.3 (2015), pp. 209–40

Werbner, Pnina, *Anthropology and the New Cosmopolitanism: Rooted, Feminist and Vernacular Perspectives* (Oxford: Berg, 2008)

Zarzuela, Ana, and Luis García, Santiago Gamboa <http://www.literaturas.com/gamboa.htm> [accessed 1 July 2021]

Epilogue

In 2020, the Argentine writer-chronicle Martín Caparrós published a book called *Sinfín*. In it, a dystopic future is presented to the reader: 天 is at the centre of it. Only late in the novel is the reader introduced to what this character represents. In *Sinfín*, there is one dominant language, and death has been overcome by life in 天. Dislocation is at the centre of the argument; the Chinese language has become one of the most used languages in the world. In the dystopic future of the novel, the 'Chinese Central Committee' dominates the world, while the book's cover reminds us of this illustration by a code-like (*Matrix*-like) format of many 天. And yet, in the dystopic future that *Sinfín* refers to, and as the narrator explains, power imbalance becomes worse: '[...] el famoso 1 por ciento apiñaba alrededor del 90 por ciento de la riqueza del mundo'.[1] Inequality and injustice are at the narrative's centre, with a journalist (a first-person narrator) exploring how the world became what it is in *Sinfín*. Indeed, *Sinfín* can be seen as an indicator of China as an undisputed protagonist in the current global context, as well as an indicator of China's importance in Latin America today.

In the last few years, Asia and China have become increasingly more relevant topics of study in Latin America. Current research has focused on case studies by country, studying historical links between the regions; the assimilation of Asian cultures in Latin America, Spain, and Portugal; how Asians in Latin America represent themselves in literature; or how Asia is seen and represented by Latin American travellers, among others. Regarding the specific case of China, most scholarly research has focused on economic relations, especially since the PRC's growing economic and geopolitical influence in Latin America. In recent years, scholarship on Chinese–Latin American relations has grown, responding to newly opened archives, new memoirs, revisionist research, and the rising economic and political exchange between both regions. This has led to a re-evaluation of the role and presence of the Chinese diaspora in Latin America and the cultural relationship

1 Martín Caparrós, *Sinfín* (Buenos Aires: Literatura Random House, 2020), p. 157.

between China and Latin America. Furthermore, because more Chinese people have arrived in Latin America as a result of the opening of the PRC since the 1980s as well as its economic acceleration and growth since the 2000s, the community has become more noticeable in the region. In this sense, and within stronger identity movements in the area, these changes expose the shifting representation of 'China' and 'Chineseness', linked to the current growing presence of Chinese people in the region.[2]

Within this context, Latin American novels where 'China' is a central part of its narrative can be shown to deconstruct China's otherness by making the reader aware that a Latin American identity or one linked to what we can refer to as 'Latin Americanness' goes beyond notions of white, indigenous, or mestizo. In other words, it establishes a dialogue with those included when we are referring to different groups of people (nations, continents, communities). In recent years, we can see a growth in novels that include the historical presence of the Chinese in Latin America, starting with *La casa del dolor ajeno* by Julián Herbert and including Antonio Gil's novel *Viaje al oeste* (Trip to the West).[3] In Chile, for example, the book *El vuelo de la luciérnaga* (The Flight of the Firefly)[4] was published in 2019, a comic book on the Chinese that fought together with the Chilean during the War of the Pacific (between Chile and Peru, 1879–1883). And while on the one hand, racism abounds, there is also a growing regular critique and criticism of it[5] as well as more nuanced, i.e., more open and less essentialist, ways of approaching the presence of Chinese people in the Americas.

Indeed, Covid-19 in Latin America brought a rise in racism, anti-Chinese, and anti-Asian violence, and sentiment,[6] reminding people that race and multiculturalism are concepts easily misused and misinterpreted, used by

2 See, for example, Monica DeHart, *Transpacific Developments: The Politics of Multiple Chinas in Central Americas* (Ithaca and London: Cornell University Press, 2021); Maria Montt Strabucchi, Carol Chan, and María Elvira Ríos, *Chineseness in Chile: Shifting Representations during the Twenty-First Century*, Studies of the Americas (Cham: Palgrave Macmillan, 2022) <https://doi.org/10.1007/978-3-030-83966-6>.

3 Forthcoming with Sangría Editores (Chile).

4 Vicente Wilson and Cristóbal Torres, *El vuelo de la luciérnaga* (Santiago: Trayecto Ediciones, 2019).

5 Montt Strabucchi, Chan, and Ríos.

6 See, for example, Carol Chan and Maria Montt Strabucchi, 'Many-Faced Orientalism: Racism and Xenophobia in a Time of the Novel Coronavirus in Chile', *Asian Ethnicity*, 22.2 (2021), pp. 374–94. <https://doi.org/10.1080/14631369.2020.1795618>; Carol Chan and Maria Montt Strabucchi, 'Emerging Pan-Asian Identities in Chile in #StopAsianHate', *British Journal of Chinese Studies*, 12.1 (2022), pp. 105–9 <https://doi.org/10.51661/bjocs.v12i1.159>; Lok Siu and Claire Chun, 'Yellow Peril and Techno-Orientalism in the Time of Covid-19: Racialized Contagion, Scientific Espionage, and Techno-Economic Warfare', *Journal of Asian American Studies*, 23.3 (2020), pp. 421–40 <https://doi.org/10.1353/jaas.2020.0033>, as well as the special issue on Covid-19 of the *Journal of Asian American Studies*.

relying on essentialist understandings of identity. It also allowed for the advancement of ideas of collaboration and cooperation beyond racialized understandings of nationalities. This coincided with China growing as an economic power and gaining leverage in the international arena. With the aftermath of the 2020 crisis, we are reminded of how easily anti-Chinese sentiment becomes used in times of crisis and how 'China' continues to be a concept used in different ways and at different times with differing meanings. It is from this perspective that this book aims to analyse how 'China' emerges as a term that redefines discourses of alterity.

As previous chapters of this book have explored, in most Latin American novels, 'China' serves as a concept through which essentialist notions of identity are critiqued. By emphasizing the constructedness of 'China' as available in the novels studied here, 'China' and its constructedness in Latin America as a theoretical concept are useful for the understanding of 'Chineseness', identity, and community in Latin America and beyond. Through a close reading of novels published in Spanish in Latin America between 1987 and 2016, this book has sought to illustrate the value of bringing together multiple genealogies for a multidimensional understanding of 'China' in Latin America. From my analysis, the novels rely on 'China' as a shifting signifier that interrupts notions of otherness in Latin America.

Drawing on psychoanalysis, philosophy, literature, and history, 'China' is used to subvert notions of difference and distance and to introduce the question of what defines identities (as seen in chapter 1). These types of novels displace 'traditional' images of the 'Orient' by acknowledging and subverting the stereotypes of 'China' as antipodal and unknown in Latin America. 'China' thus appears as a fetishized stranger, a figure that is retrieved and then destabilized through the act of narration. 'China' also interrupts Latin American definitions of community by raising the question of who is included in the nation/community (see chapter 2). In novels whose stories are linked to Chinese communities and Chinatowns in Buenos Aires and Mexico City, one can observe a critique of discourses of a racially homogeneous Latin America. The novels depict city landscapes in which the Chinese communities are revealed as constitutive and transformative of both cities' cultural, economic, and political landscapes. This demonstrates that these novels challenge and condemn essentialist conceptions of race, gender, and national identities, suggesting instead contrasting views on alterity, the state of being different or other, and community. On another level, 'China' is informed by China's economic and political role in contemporary Latin America, disclosing the changing demographic landscape of Latin America while simultaneously pointing towards the historical heterogeneity of Latin American identity, which has silenced the 'Chinese' from within discourses of *mestizaje*. In this type of novel, where events are set in Latin American spaces, and through the cultural imaginaries that resonate in Chinatowns worldwide, Chinatowns and Chinese communities in Latin America are used to expose the presence of the Chinese as part of the city's changing landscapes.

'China' can also be used as a figure through which hegemonic distinctions can be challenged in a global context (chapter 3). In novels in which the underlying theme is travel (to China), the emphasis on transnationalism and mobility make different locations somehow equivalent, thus calling for a reconsideration of community and cosmopolitanism. These types of novels make available new subjectivities that are aware of difference and power imbalances within a global context. Using Ahmed's examination of migration and estrangement narratives and Doreen Massey's notion of cultural difference being simultaneously local and global, travel to 'China' is exposed as an experience of estrangement. Focusing mostly on privileged travellers, the novels disclose forms of othering and strangerness and question hegemonic Eurocentric structures and nationally bounded epistemologies. Simultaneously, the novels show a preference for a nomadic identity, a being-in-common, thus rejecting fetishized understandings of the stranger.

The ways these works engage with 'China' overlap, and therefore it is fruitful to consider them together, as they all use 'China' to comment on Latin America. As we can see, 'China' changes as different use is made of it while still containing the capacity to disrupt fixed discourses of otherness. By exposing the different imaginings of 'China' in Latin America, my analysis thus reveals the fetishistic construction of 'China' in Latin America. From this perspective, this book argues that, through a comprehensive analysis of how 'China' is imagined in contemporary Latin American literature, 'China' is revealed as used to interrupt discourses of otherness while allowing us to rethink new understandings of identity and community.

Analysing and describing the role that a fetishized 'China' plays in articulating notions of identity and community in contemporary Latin American novels, this book suggests that 'China' can be a symbolic figure that plays a specific role in Latin America. Deployed as a fetish figure, 'China' in these novels interrupts discourses of *mestizaje*, evidenced through an analysis of the strangerness that the novels convey. Ultimately, the novels reveal their 'China' to be beyond the traditional racial access points of *mestizaje* in Latin America. In other words, the novels studied here use 'China' to resist racial essentialist constructions of Latin American identity and mestizaje and its nuances. In this sense, this book dialogues with the areas of study, research, and activism, such as Chino/Latino, Asian Latinx, or Chinese Latinx groups.

Because of the emphasis on the 'otherness' of 'China' revealed here, Sara Ahmed's theorizations on strangerness[7] become central to my understanding of how 'otherness' is employed, constructed, and critiqued in these novels. As we have seen, 'China' is made to adopt different forms of 'strangerness' in the different novels and within each text. Indeed, not only does 'strangerness' query an ontology of 'China' as other, but it simultaneously evokes and enacts

7 Sara Ahmed, *Strange Encounters: Embodied Others in Post-Coloniality* (London: Routledge, 2000).

different forms of strangerness, which include, but are not restricted to, an 'exotic', 'different', or 'distant' 'China'. Read in relation to Jean-Luc Nancy's understanding of the subject as being-with and community as inoperative,[8] Ahmed's notion of strangerness emphasizes the importance of the active process of encounter. As a Nancean reading reveals, the novels emphasize relations between people, pointing broadly to a cosmopolitan attitude that is non-essentialist.[9] 'China' thus emerges here as a literary/imaginary 'third' term that reframes Latin American discourses of alterity. Despite their nuances, the novels examined in this corpus present coinciding tropes and themes that establish recurring patterns in how 'China' is represented. The novels construct and challenge fetishized otherness through the figure of 'China', thus suggesting a regional imagination of 'China' to be available across a group of Latin American novels.

This multidimensional understanding of 'China' thus interrupts discourses where identity is considered in essentialist terms. This may occur via the use of multiple narrative voices and fragmentation (see chapter 1) or with the stereotypical 'Latin American' serve to interrupt what emerges as stereotyped and gendered notions of the 'Chinese' communities in Latin America (see chapter 2). 'China' thus appears as a supplement to a racial and cultural narrative mix of *mestizaje*: an additional element that simultaneously disturbs (and, following Derrida, supplements) the mix itself. Overall, the novels studied here both establish and interrogate the idea of China as 'other', revealing the new forms of community being imagined in Latin America.

On one level, the growing presence of 'China' in public discourses in Latin America can be seen as a result of increased economic engagement. According to Carlos Malamud, today there is a 'true rediscovery' of Latin America by China underway, sparked by an interest in energy, metals, and natural resources.[10] The impact of China's economic growth can be exemplified through the production of soybeans in Argentina, which since 1987/88 has become its major crop, displacing wheat,[11] and is now roughly half

8 Jean-Luc Nancy, *The Inoperative Community* (Minneapolis: University of Minnesota Press, 1991); *Being Singular Plural* (Stanford: Stanford University Press, 2000).

9 Berthold Schoene, *The Cosmopolitan Novel* (Edinburgh: Edinburgh University Press, 2011).

10 Carlos Daniel Malamud Rikles, 'China y América Latina: ¿qué esperan los unos de los otros?', *Anuario Asia-Pacífico*, 1 (2006), pp. 103–14 (pp. 104–5); see also, Jonathan R. Barton and Johannes Rehner, 'Neostructuralism through Strategic Transaction: The Geopolinomics of China's Dragon Doctrine for Latin America', *Political Geography*, 65 (2018), pp. 77–87 <https://doi.org/10.1016/j.polgeo.2018.05.002>; Maria Montt Strabucchi and Johannes Rehner, 'Del Galeón de Manila a la IED: Rutas de intercambio entre China y América Latina', *Asia América Latina*, 5.8 (2020), pp. 8–31 <https://doi.org/10.33177/8.3>.

11 Nicola Borregaard, 'An International Environmental Effect of the Common Agricultural Policy: Soil Erosion through Soya Bean Production in Argentina' (unpublished doctoral dissertation, University of Cambridge, 1992), p. 123.

of the total production of grain in the country,[12] precisely because of the quantities exported to China. According to the International Organization of Immigration, while not yet relevant in quantitative terms, African and Asian migration to Latin America has shown a clear growth trend since 2008.[13] This could be due to privileged entry facilities provided by Latin American states, combined with the relative improvements of their economies, labour markets, and the material/symbolic migratory barriers of developed countries.[14] As Gonzalo Paz notes for Argentina, Chinese communities have spread throughout the different cities of the country,[15] while other scholars have explored their integration and local experiences.[16] And in terms of investment, Chinese companies can be found throughout Latin America.[17]

12 Gonzalo S. Paz, 'Argentina and Asia: China's Reemergence, Argentina's Recovery', in *Reaching across the Pacific: Latin America and Asia in the New Century*, ed. by Cynthia Arnson and Jorge Heine (Washington: Woodrow Wilson International Center for Scholars, 2014), pp. 153–86 (p. 162); Eduardo Daniel Oviedo, 'Argentina and China: An Analysis of the Actors in the Soybean Trade and the Migratory Flow', *Journal of Chinese Political Science*, 20.3 (2015), pp. 243–66 (p. 244).

13 Jacqueline Mazza, 'Migration in a Mobile Age: Perspectives from China, India, and the Americas', in *Latin America and the Asian Giants*, ed. by Riordan Roett and Guadalupe Paz (Washington: Brookings Institution Press, 2016), pp. 183–204; Ezequiel Texidó and Jorge Gurrieri, 'Panorama Migratorio de América del Sur 2012', 2012 <http://publications.iom.int/system/files/pdf/panorama_migratorio_de_america_del_sur2012.pdf> [accessed 1 July 2021]; Macarena Bonhomme, '"We're a Bit Browner but We Still Belong to the White Race": Making Whiteness in the Context of South-South Migration in Chile', *Latin American and Caribbean Ethnic Studies*, 18.2 (2023), pp. 227–43 <https://doi.org/10.1080/17442222.2022.2099170>; Francisca De la Maza and Luis Eugenio Campos, 'The Irruption of Afro-Descendants in Diversity Politics: The Case of Arica in Northern Chile', *Identities*, 28.4 (2021), pp. 436–53 <https://doi.org/10.1080/1070289X.2020.1813458>; Antonia Mardones Marshall, 'Who Is Afro-Chilean? Authenticity Struggles and Boundary Making in Chile's Northern Borderland', *Ethnic and Racial Studies*, 44.1 (2021), pp. 1–23 <https://doi.org/10.1080/01419870.2020.1839667>.

14 Texidó and Gurrieri, p. 34.

15 Paz, p. 169.

16 Carol Chan, 'Imagining and Linking Latin America: Chinese Regional Mobilities and Social Networks in Chile', *Journal of Latin American Geography*, 17.2 (2018), pp. 23–45; Carol Chan, 'Permanent Migrants and Temporary Citizens: Multinational Chinese Mobilities in the Americas', *Global Networks*, 21.1 (2020), pp. 64–83 <https://doi.org/10.1111/glob.12279>; Jorge Moraga Reyes, 'Reparto comunitario y gasto agonístico: diferenciaciones y hegemonías entre antiguos y nuevos migrantes chinos en Chile', *Rumbos TS*, 17 (2018), pp. 133–52; *Race and Transnationalism in the Americas*, ed. by Benjamin Bryce and David M.K. Sheinin (Pittsburgh: University of Pittsburgh Press, 2021).

17 Andres Borquez and Carlos Bravo, 'Who Are China's Strategic Economic Partners in South America?', *Asian Education and Development Studies*, 10.3 (2021), pp. 445–56 <https://doi.org/10.1108/AEDS-09-2019-0153>; Montt Strabucchi and Rehner;

Indeed, one can notice shifts in how China is being marketed and perceived in the region,[18] as well as how discourses are being constructed by governments and the multiple actors involved in relations.[19] The presence of Chinese people and brands is also more common and growing steadily. Chinese companies in the region are ubiquitous; brands of the PRC, such as Alibaba, Chery, Didi, Huawei, Lenovo, or Mobike, are identified and used broadly.

However, on another level, the role of 'China' as presented in the novels goes beyond China's economic and geopolitical growth. Up until today, words such as 'mutual ignorance' or 'thin' are still deployed regarding knowledge about China in Latin America.[20] Notwithstanding a long history of engagement, China is still sometimes described as a 'new and unknown actor in Latin America',[21] and one can argue that there is still limited knowledge of China in general in the region, even though this is changing fast due to the growing advance of the PRC in the region as well as growing engagement between Latin America and the Asian country.[22] David Shambaugh

Miguel Pérez Ludeña, *Chinese Investments in Latin America: Opportunities for Growth and Diversification*, Production Development (Santiago: United Nations, 2017); Juan Enrique Serrano-Moreno, Diego Telias, and Francisco Urdinez, 'Deconstructing the Belt and Road Initiative in Latin America', *Asian Education and Development Studies*, 10.3 (2021), pp. 337–47 <https://doi.org/10.1108/AEDS-01-2020-0021>; Francisco Urdinez, Jan Knoerich, and Pedro Feliú Ribeiro, 'Don't Cry for Me "Argenchina": Unraveling Political Views of China through Legislative Debates in Argentina', *Journal of Chinese Political Science*, 23.2 (2018), pp. 235–56 <https://doi.org/10.1007/s11366-016-9450-y>.

18 Montt Strabucchi, Chan, and Ríos.

19 Claudia Labarca and Maria Montt Strabucchi, 'Discurso como representación de sentido en las relaciones internacionales: el caso sino-chileno', *Estudios Políticos*, 47 (2019), pp. 163–84. <http://dx.doi.org/10.22201/fcpys.24484903e.2019.47.69504>.

20 Ariel C. Armony, 'A View from Afar: How Colombia Sees China', *The China Quarterly*, 209 (2012), pp. 178–97 (p. 179); Eduardo Tzili Apango, '"Estudios sobre China desde Latinoamérica. Geopolítica, Religión e Inmigración" - Susan Chen Mok, Jorge Bartels Villanueva y Ricardo Martínez Esquivel (eds.)', *Estudios Internacionales*, 46.178 (2014), pp. 207–12 (p. 207).

21 Benjamin Creutzfeld, 'América Latina en la política exterior china; One Broad Push: Latin America in China's Foreign Policy', *Pap. Polit.*, 18.2 (2013), pp. 599–611 (pp. 599–607).

22 Among others, see *Relaciones entre Chile-China. Un enfoque integral*, ed. by Andrés Bórquez, Dorotea López, and Felipe Muñoz (Santiago: RIL Editores, 2021); Damir Galaz-Mandakovic and Jorge Moraga Reyes, 'Migración china en Tocopilla. Heterogeneidad relacional y transformaciones internas (Chile, 1884-1960)', *Revista Rumbos TS. Un espacio crítico para la reflexión en Ciencias Sociales*, 16.24 (2021), pp. 85–128. <https://doi.org/10.51188/rrts.num24.467>; María Elvira Ríos, María Montt, and Carol Chan, 'El imaginario de lo chino en las revistas magazinescas chilenas de principios del siglo XX', *Revista Rumbos TS. Un espacio crítico para la reflexión en Ciencias Sociales*, 24 (2021), pp. 129–50 <https://doi.org/10.51188/rrts.num24.434>; Chan, 'Permanent Migrants and Temporary Citizens'; Serrano-Moreno, Telias, and

has expressed that his 'impression is that there is an extremely low level of understanding among the region's people and governments about China'.[23] Ariel Armony suggests that Latin American ideas regarding China are based on an

> "imported Orientalism" which tends to be dominated by misrepresentations of Chinese society and culture [which include] a combination of timeworn images of China as "mysterious" and the projection on to China of changing beliefs and interests in the West [...].[24]

These statements reveal the ways in which China is still misrepresented or how its presence in Latin America has been silenced.[25] In this context, the novels show an awareness of the common negligence regarding the recognition of China in Latin America. Furthermore, the novels' depictions of China expose the mechanisms that produce and inform those silences, such as the generalizations that maintain hierarchical knowledge.

While recent public opinion polls depict a mildly positive opinion of China in Latin America, anti-Chinese attitudes persist in the region, as 'China's rise' has generated anxieties due to the perceived threats posed by environmental impact, migration, and the demand for natural resources.[26] In their study on Mexican perceptions of China, Romer Cornejo, Francisco Javier Haro Navejas, and José Luis León-Manríquez show how historical and contemporary views of China are primarily based on prejudice and oscillate between frustration, indifference, and envy.[27] According to them,

Urdinez; Urdinez, Knoerich, and Ribeiro; Barton and Rehner; Patricia Palma and José Ragas, 'Enclaves Sanitarios: Higiene, Epidemias y Salud en el Barrio Chino de Lima, 1880–1910', *Anuario Colombiano de Historia Social y de la Cultura*, 45.1 (2018), pp. 159–90 <https://doi.org/10.15446/achsc.v45n1.67555>; Monica DeHart, 'Chino Tico Routes and Repertoires: Cultivating Chineseness and Entrepreneurism for a New Era of Trans-Pacific Relations', *The Journal of Latin American and Caribbean Anthropology*, 23.1 (2018), pp. 74–93; José Antonio González Pizarro and others, 'Tres Problemáticas de La Inmigración China En El Norte de Chile', *Si Somos Americanos*, 20.2 (2020), pp. 91–115 <https://doi.org/10.4067/S0719-09482020000200091>.

23 David Shambaugh, *China–Europe Relations: Perceptions, Policies and Prospects* (London: Routledge, 2008), p. xii.

24 Armony, p. 179.

25 Maria Montt Strabucchi and Carol Chan, 'Questioning the Conditional Visibility of the Chinese: (Non)Normative Representations of China and Chineseness in Chilean Cultural Productions', *Journal of Chinese Overseas*, 16.1 (2020), pp. 90–116 <https://doi.org/10.1163/17932548-12341414>.

26 Ariel C. Armony and Nicolás Velásquez, 'Anti-Chinese Sentiment in Latin America: An Analysis of Online Discourse', *Journal of Chinese Political Science*, 20.3 (2015), pp. 319–46 (p. 342).

27 Romer Cornejo, Francisco Javier Haro Navejas, and José Luis León-Manríquez, 'Trade Issues and Beyond: Mexican Perceptions on Contemporary China', *Latin American Policy*, 4.1 (2013), pp. 57–75 (pp. 58, 72).

unfavourable contemporary perceptions of China in Mexico mostly spring from an uneven economic relationship with China boosted by mass media, business, and politicians. They state that 'unlike the 1910s or the 1920s, when anti-Chinese rhetoric in Mexico grew into expropriations of Chinese business and even physical aggression, contemporary conflict has mostly been symbolic'.[28] While the Chinese can be spared physical violence, in this scenario, the latter observation reflects the persistence of a different kind of aggression against the 'Chinese'. As occurred during the Covid-19 pandemic, there are many different perspectives on China and Chinese people: from exotic to techno-orientalist ideas where China is the 'future', to more sombre associations such as fear, anti-China or anti-PRC sentiments, and explicit racism.[29] As we have seen, representations of 'China' in Latin America can be profoundly exoticist and racist. For example, in her tweet, '*Más de 1.000 asistentes al evento… ¿Serán todos de 'La Cámpola' y vinieron sólo por el aloz y el petlóleo?*' former President of Argentina Cristina Fernández de Kirchner, replaced 'r' for 'l', in what has been described as a 'cartoonish Chinese accent'.[30] Her tweet elicited different kinds of reactions, many of them as essentializing and stereotyping as the original tweet, but with others openly critical and condemning.[31] Unfortunately, Kirchner's comments are not isolated, as stereotyped views of the Chinese continue to emerge daily in Latin America.[32]

And yet, according to Pew Research, there is a favourable opinion of China in Latin American nations that have become large commodity exporters to Beijing.[33] Overall, Latin American views of China are more positive than negative, although many queried offered no opinion.[34] Despite

28 Cornejo, Haro Navejas, and León-Manríquez, p. 63.

29 Montt Strabucchi, Chan, and Ríos.

30 Evan Osnos, 'Christina Kirchner's Misadventure in China', *The New Yorker*, 2 June 2015 <http://www.newyorker.com/news/daily-comment/cristina-kirchner-misadventure-china> [accessed 1 July 2021].

31 'Medios de todo el mundo criticaron a Cristina Kirchner por burlarse del acento chino', *La Nación*, 2 April 2015 <http://www.lanacion.com.ar/1765712-medios-de-todo-el-mundo-criticaron-a-cristina-kirchner-por-burlarse-del-acento-chino> [accessed 1 July 2021].

32 Ríos, Montt, and Chan; Montt Strabucchi and Chan.

33 'America's Global Image Remains More Positive than China's', *Pew Research Center's Global Attitudes Project*, (2013) <http://www.pewglobal.org/2013/07/18/americas-global-image-remains-more-positive-than-chinas/> [accessed 1 August 2021]; Pew Research Center, 'Balance of Power: U.S. vs. China', *Pew Research Center's Global Attitudes Project*, (2014) <https://www.pewresearch.org/global/2014/07/14/chapter-3-balance-of-power-u-s-vs-china/> [accessed 17 May 2022]; see also, Richard Q. Turcsányi and others, 'US-China Rivalry in the Global South? Insights from a Public Opinion Survey', *CEIAS*, 2022.

34 'Global Opposition to U.S. Surveillance and Drones, but Limited Harm to America's Image', *Pew Research Center's Global Attitudes Project*, (2014) <http://www.pewglobal.

the paratextual aspects, Kirchner's statements, or Pew Research's findings, the corpus studied in this book reveals how China's role and presence in Latin America are much more complex than being simply 'positive', 'distant', or 'unknown'. From the sceptical, anti-China, Covid-19 racism to the techno-orientalist views where 'China' is the future, 'China' emerges as a heterogenous construct—what Monica DeHart also refers to as the multiple forms of China when discussing Central America specifically. These multiple Chinas, following DeHart, include citizens of Chinese descent, diplomats, entrepreneurs, engineers, and institutions representing Taiwan and embassy officials, investors, tourists, and workers from the PRC. Within them diverse identities, politics, and practices are experienced, revealing what she describes as the 'fluid and often entangled connections and affiliations'.[35] And thus within this context, a broad poststructuralist and deconstructive approach has allowed me to show how 'China' symbolizes 'otherness' in Latin America, with racist, condescending, and admiring perspectives all at once. 'China', as a symbolic figure, becomes a site of otherness that discloses, replicates, and challenges discourses of strangerness in Latin America.

Through Ahmed's figure of the 'stranger' and Nancy's being-in-common, the novels studied in this book reveal the complexity that the term 'China' embodies. Overall, the previous chapters show how 'China' is a multifaceted signifier that is used to perform 'Chineseness', maintaining, for example, titles and covers that recall an exoticist imaginary of 'China'. The rhetorical use of 'China' may also be read as a covert parody of racist categories, contrasting race with understandings of identity. By exposing 'China' as an intersectional site of otherness in Latin America along with the multidimensional aspects of 'China', these novels make the reader think about how they imagine 'China' and how that 'China' highlights issues of race in Latin America.[36]

As a fetish, 'China' displays the multiplicity of contradictions that mark a crisis in the social meaning of historical and personal narratives of 'China'.[37] The notion of 'China' as a place of difference is thus established and simultaneously critiqued. From this perspective, the novels can be seen, on one level, to embrace the irresolution contained in the fetishistic representation of 'China' in these novels. Inhabiting the 'threshold of both personal and historical memory', fetishes mark a 'crisis in social meaning as the embodiment of an impossible irresolution'.[38] On another level, the novels themselves

org/2014/07/14/global-opposition-to-u-s-surveillance-and-drones-but-limited-harm-to-americas-image/> [accessed 1 August 2021].

35 DeHart, *Transpacific Developments: The Politics of Multiple Chinas in Central Americas.*

36 An especially relevant analysis regarding race and the racial other in Latin America is the work of Ana Paulina Lee, *Mandarin Brazil: Race, Representation, and Memory* (Stanford: Stanford University Press, 2018).

37 Anne McClintock, *Imperial Leather: Race, Gender, and Sexuality in the Colonial Contest* (New York: Routledge, 1995), p. 184.

38 McClintock, p. 184.

make use (even if involuntarily) of China as a 'fetishized stranger', engaging with the current publishing market and the growing presence of China in Latin America. However, while 'China' is shown to embody 'otherness' in Latin America by focusing on essentialism (stereotypes, racism, post-racism) and the constructedness of hegemonic discourses (stereotypes, narratives, narrators), the novels subvert the ontologizing constructedness of China as 'stranger'. Situated beyond the 'West', the West/non-West, and West/East binaries, China allows Latin Americans in the novels to stand outside themselves and examine themselves.

As Mariano Siskind argues, the differential affirmation of a disruptive cosmopolitan aesthetic identity in Latin America must be read as a 'strategic literary practice that forces its way into the realm of universality, denouncing both the hegemonic structures of Eurocentric forms of exclusion and nationalistic patterns of self-marginalization'.[39] Siskind goes on to suggest that this 'omnipotent fantasy' where cosmopolitan subjectivity can be represented on equal terms with the metropolitan cultures whose hegemonic discourse they try to undermine is 'nonetheless very effective in opening a cosmopolitan discursive space'.[40] Siskind's words here both defy the notion of cultural difference and situate Latin American literature within a global context. And within this context, analysed through Nancy's 'being singular plural' in relation to Ahmed's figure of the 'stranger', the novels have been shown to converse with currents that critique multiculturalism and question the idea of a post-racial Latin America.[41]

While the absence of the Chinese as part of a Latin American identity has led to their supplemental position within Latin American discourses of race and *mestizaje*, their inclusion within notions of Latin American hybridity may also lead to essentialist generalizations. Indeed, terms like hybridity, transculturation, or syncretism may sweep distinctions under the rug and lead to generalizations, allowing for the essentializing of Latin American identities as homogeneously hybrid and free of internal conflicts.[42] However,

39 Mariano Siskind, *Cosmopolitan Desires: Global Modernity and World Literature in Latin America* (Evanston: Northwestern University Press, 2014), p. 6.

40 Siskind, p. 7.

41 Mónica G. Moreno Figueroa and Emiko Saldívar Tanaka, '"We Are Not Racists, We Are Mexicans": Privilege, Nationalism and Post-Race Ideology in Mexico', *Critical Sociology*, 42.4–5 (2016), pp. 515–233; Alexandre Emboaba Da Costa, 'Thinking "Post-Racial" Ideology Transnationally: The Contemporary Politics of Race and Indigeneity in the Americas', *Critical Sociology*, 42.4–5 (2016), pp. 475–90.

42 Antonio Cornejo Polar, 'Mestizaje e Hibridez: Los riesgos de las metáforas', *Revista de Crítica Literaria Latinoamericana*, 24.47 (1998), pp. 7–11 (pp. 7–8); Laura Catelli, 'The Persistence of Racism in Critical Imaginaries on Latin America', in *Critical Terms in Caribbean and Latin American Thought*, ed. by Yolanda Martínez-San Miguel, Ben. Sifuentes-Jáuregui, and Marisa Belausteguigoitia (New York: Palgrave Macmillan, 2016), pp. 145–51 (p. 145).

following Charles Hatfield's critique from a more universalist position,[43] I see these novels' emphasis on the figure of 'China' as a mechanism to avoid circumventing the power difference which is contained by the idea of difference itself. These novels show that 'China' and 'Latin America' can be equivalent 'fictions', that the Chinese are part of Latin America, and that geopolitical distributions on the map are there to be questioned. The reader is led to reflect upon citizenship and agency in a global context by regarding the novels' negotiation of subjectivities beyond fixed global cartographies. These novels bring China to Latin America, calling for a Latin America that is more representative of its heterogeneous and composite nature.

A deconstruction of the processes through which China is constructed as 'fetishized stranger' reveals how any 'stranger' can be 'othered'. As Ahmed's model of 'strange encounters' suggests, 'we need to find ways of re-encountering these encounters so that they no longer hold other others in place'.[44] In line with Ahmed, I question the assumption that we can have any valid ontology of strangers, and I refuse to take for granted the stranger's status as a pre-determined figure. Because of this, the mutual marginalities of China and Latin America within a global context underline cosmopolitanism by always including the subjects of these regions in relation to each other, threatening any dualist notion. In this sense, the texts question any bounded relation to cartography and nation states by thinking of subjectivity beyond fixed alterity and from a non-hierarchical standpoint. This book acknowledges race and the nation as political realities but simultaneously explores the politics and subjectivities beyond the subject and nation itself. In this way, it reveals how the novels point towards ways out of essentialist understandings of identity and community in Latin America.

While Ahmed's theoretical approach is especially interesting because of her emphasis on the dynamic process of the encounter, Nancy's idea of the subject as being-in-common is also central to my analysis. Indeed, I argue that we need to explore the ways through which the (re)production of strangerness continues to produce 'otherness'. From this perspective, Nancy's understanding of the subject as being-in-common allows us to focus on the relationships between people and their understandings of community, which emerges as crucial in the novels studied here. Ultimately, the choice of 'China' exposes the availability in Latin America of new ideas on identity and new forms of inoperative community, which allows for community but does not endorse any essentialist understanding of it. These novels can thus be considered to form part of a corpus that denounces histories of racism against the Chinese, who continue to be relatively 'invisible' or 'unknown' in Latin

43 Charles Hatfield, *The Limits of Identity: Politics and Poetics in Latin America* (Austin: University of Texas Press, 2015).

44 Ahmed, p. 17.

America,[45] while offering new understandings of identity and community as non-essentialist and in constant development.

While the theories expose the mechanisms at work in encounters between subjects, the novels themselves out-do the theory by simultaneously hinting at the impossibility of fully expressing complex articulations of difference and essentialism, as well as the consequent discrimination and exclusion of subjects along different axes—such as race, class, or gender—and their intersections. Thus, I view the novels as using 'China' as a fetishized multidimensional term (exponentially diverse) to disclose the complexities inherent in the mechanisms of strangerness and (essentialist) otherness. The novels' interruption of *mestizaje* is thus strategic precisely because of the contradictory and multivariate meanings of 'China' in Latin America, informed, among other things, by histories of imperialism, racism, economic exchanges, and exotic imaginaries. Published at a time when people of Asian descent in the region have also begun to explore race and identity through literature, poetry, art, and politics,[46] with a growing academic body of work that deals with the role of Asian communities in Latin America, these novels stimulate thinking about Latin America in non-essentialist ways. Simultaneously, an academic body of work dealing with Asian labour migration, settlement, and the Asian role in national development has also emerged globally, and the Asian presence has been highlighted in studies of race, citizenship, and culture.[47] While *mestizaje* has endured as a salient paradigm for understanding race in Latin America, the political construction of Latin America has suppressed the presence of people of African and Asian descent while favouring the intermixing between indigenous and European.[48] And while later theorizations have aimed to go beyond the reductionism of *mestizaje*, a post-racial Latin America remains a myth.[49] A non-essentialist understanding allows for

45 Julián Herbert, *La casa del dolor ajeno* (México, D.F: Literatura Random House, 2015); Silvia Solano Rivera, 'El destino y la explotación legitimada en "Tarciso Cantón", de Tatiana Buch', *Revista Comunicación*, 25.1 (2016), pp. 31–39 (p. 38); La Jornada Morelos, 'Julián Herbert: "Pancho Villa no asesinó a los 303 chinos de Torreón en 1911"', *La Jornada Morelos*, (2016) <http://www.elclarin.cl/web/entrevistas/18622-julian-herbert-pancho-villa-no-asesino-a-los-303-chinos-de-torreon-en-1911.html> [accessed 1 July 2017].

46 Kathleen López, 'The Asian Presence in *Mestizo* Nations: A Response', in *Critical Terms in Caribbean and Latin American Thought*, ed. by Yolanda Martínez-San Miguel, Ben. Sifuentes-Jáuregui, and Marisa Belausteguigoitia (New York: Palgrave Macmillan, 2016), pp. 125–31 (p. 128).

47 Evelyn Hu-DeHart, 'Multiculturalism in Latin American Studies: Locating the "Asian" Immigrant; or, Where Are the Chinos and Turcos?', *Latin American Research Review*, 44.2 (2009), pp. 235–42; Jason Oliver Chang, 'Racial Alterity in the Mestizo Nation', *Journal of Asian American Studies*, 14.3 (2011), pp. 331–59.

48 López, p. 125.

49 Moreno Figueroa and Saldívar Tanaka.

a more comprehensive understanding of the role of people whose presence seems to have been silenced within the political constructs of Latin America.

Indeed, a transnational approach may show how national spaces are intimately connected, challenging opposition between the national and the international and allowing for new ways to think of the region.[50] Thus, the 'transnational' assumes the centrality of Latin America (and potentially any other place) in the modern world while simultaneously echoing the 'asymmetries from which global economies, politics, and epistemologies are conceived, imagined, defined'.[51] Susanne Klengel and Alexandra Ortiz Wallner note how:

> an appropriate handling of positions, theories, attitudes, opinions and statements from the "South" remains problematic as long as the theoretical location of the concrete exchange is viewed solely from the perspective of a thinking based on the concept of difference.[52]

They also show how within the 'South-South relationship there is also a *horizontality*, which leads to an articulation of *similarities* with relation to a third party'.[53] Their views are relevant to this research in that they shed light on the notion of a positioning of the 'South', i.e., not the 'West'. And yet, the emphasis on the notions of horizontality and similarities might obscure the power imbalances that inform the dynamics that these novels might reveal.

Future projects could explore the uses of a fetishized 'China' in relation to other Asian communities, as well as the meanings that a fetishized 'China' acquires when presented in other cultural manifestations and in other parts of the Americas, underlined by the transnational experience of Chinese migration to the region. For the specific case of Latin America, an analysis from the perspective of texts being written by self-identified Asian diasporas or communities perceived as minorities may reveal other ways in which otherness is being deployed and how it can be challenged and/or used strategically. Also, the scope of this project does not permit an analysis of how 'China' engages with the understanding of a fetishized 'Latin America'.

50 Pedro Iacobelli and Maria Montt Strabucchi, 'Encuentros con Asia: Una reflexión en torno a la historiografía latinoamericana desde la cuenca del océano Pacifico', *Historia 396*, 10.2 (2020), pp. 179–204; Yolanda Martínez-San Miguel, Ben. Sifuentes-Jáuregui, and Marisa Belausteguigoitia, 'Introduction', in *Critical Terms in Caribbean and Latin American Thought*, ed. by Yolanda Martínez-San Miguel, Ben. Sifuentes-Jáuregui, and Marisa Belausteguigoitia, New Directions in Latino American Cultures (Palgrave Macmillan US, 2016), pp. 1–21 <https://doi.org/10.1057/9781137547903_1>.

51 Martínez-San Miguel, Sifuentes-Jáuregui, and Belausteguigoitia, p. 2.

52 Susanne Klengel and Alexandra Ortiz Wallner, 'A New Poetics and Politics of Thinking Latin America / India. SUR / SOUTH and a Different Orientalism', in *Sur/South: Poetics and Politics of Thinking Latin America-India*, ed. by Susanne Klengel and Alexandra Ortiz Wallner (Madrid: Vervuert, 2016), pp. 7–26 (p. 12).

53 Klengel and Ortiz Wallner, p. 13.

Furthermore, the novels, taken together, show that Argentina and Mexico are the two Latin American countries publishing the most novels on China. However, there is also a growing trend throughout the Americas, something worth studying further. This may contribute to the exposure of contradictory discourses at play nationally about Latin American identity as a whole.

While the novels studied here embrace non-binary definitions, which are more open to diversity, other 'texts' may disclose alternative perspectives. Interestingly, I opened this book with an example from art. I see literature as being in dialogue with other cultural manifestations that shed light on identity formations in Latin America. Literature, I argue, can reflect the relationship between China and Latin America beyond academic, official, or seemingly objective discourses. In terms of the imagination, literature makes the reader aware of the diversity of the experiences and lives of others, remaining a 'matter of social interaction'[54] in its production, circulation, and reception. As a result, literary texts can present a vision that may uncover a fuller understanding of China's place in Latin America today. When I first began exploring the presence of China in Latin American literature, I was struck with the emergence of a corpus that engaged with China in different but resonant ways with one another. Not only do intertextual references emerge, but similar perceptions of how China is perceived in Latin America are present.

In this sense, the novels studied here allow us to change the frames through which identity, identities, and subjectivities have been defined, thus leading the reader to reflect on the identities denied to the subject. At a time when borders and differences are becoming increasingly entrenched, and we see an increasing emphasis on the concept of the 'nation' and nationalisms, further research can contribute to the exploration of strategies for non-essentialist transnational constructions of identity, the defiance of hegemonic understandings of self and other, the positioning of national cultures in relation to global discourses, and new forms of transnational and local alliances and community.

References

Ahmed, Sara, *Strange Encounters: Embodied Others in Post-Coloniality* (London: Routledge, 2000)

Armony, Ariel C., 'A View from Afar: How Colombia Sees China', *The China Quarterly*, 209 (2012), pp. 178–97

Armony, Ariel C., and Nicolás Velásquez, 'Anti-Chinese Sentiment in Latin America: An Analysis of Online Discourse', *Journal of Chinese Political Science*, 20.3 (2015), pp. 319–46

54 Rick Rylance, *Literature and the Public Good: The Literary Agenda* (Oxford: Oxford University Press, 2016), p. 105.

Barton, Jonathan R., and Johannes Rehner, 'Neostructuralism through Strategic Transaction: The Geopolinomics of China's Dragon Doctrine for Latin America', *Political Geography*, 65 (2018), pp. 77–87 <https://doi.org/10.1016/j.polgeo.2018.05.002>

Bonhomme, Macarena, '"We're a Bit Browner but We Still Belong to the White Race": Making Whiteness in the Context of South-South Migration in Chile', *Latin American and Caribbean Ethnic Studies*, 18.2 (2023), pp. 227–43 <https://doi.org/10.1080/17442222.2022.2099170>

Borquez, Andres, and Carlos Bravo, 'Who Are China's Strategic Economic Partners in South America?', *Asian Education and Development Studies*, 10.3 (2021), pp. 445–56 <https://doi.org/10.1108/AEDS-09-2019-0153>

Bórquez, Andrés, Dorotea López, and Felipe Muñoz, eds, *Relaciones entre Chile-China. Un enfoque integral* (Santiago: RIL Editores, 2021)

Borregaard, Nicola, 'An International Environmental Effect of the Common Agricultural Policy: Soil Erosion through Soya Bean Production in Argentina' (unpublished doctoral dissertation, University of Cambridge, 1992)

Bryce, Benjamin, and David M.K. Sheinin, eds, *Race and Transnationalism in the Americas* (Pittsburgh: University of Pittsburgh Press, 2021)

Caparrós, Martín, *Sinfín* (Buenos Aires: Literatura Random House, 2020)

Catelli, Laura, 'The Persistence of Racism in Critical Imaginaries on Latin America', in *Critical Terms in Caribbean and Latin American Thought*, ed. by Yolanda Martínez-San Miguel, Ben. Sifuentes-Jáuregui, and Marisa Belausteguigoitia (New York: Palgrave Macmillan, 2016), pp. 145–51

Chan, Carol, 'Imagining and Linking Latin America: Chinese Regional Mobilities and Social Networks in Chile', *Journal of Latin American Geography*, 17.2 (2018), pp. 23–45

———, 'Permanent Migrants and Temporary Citizens: Multinational Chinese Mobilities in the Americas', *Global Networks*, 21.1 (2020), pp. 64–83 <https://doi.org/10.1111/glob.12279>

———, 'Many-Faced Orientalism: Racism and Xenophobia in a Time of the Novel Coronavirus in Chile', *Asian Ethnicity*, 22.2 (2021), pp. 374–94 <https://doi.org/10.1080/14631369.2020.1795618>

Chang, Jason Oliver, 'Racial Alterity in the Mestizo Nation', *Journal of Asian American Studies*, 14.3 (2011), pp. 331–59

Cornejo Polar, Antonio, 'Mestizaje e Hibridez: Los riesgos de las metáforas', *Revista de Crítica Literaria Latinoamericana*, 24.47 (1998), pp. 7–11

Cornejo, Romer, Francisco Javier Haro Navejas, and José Luis León-Manríquez, 'Trade Issues and Beyond: Mexican Perceptions on Contemporary China', *Latin American Policy*, 4.1 (2013), pp. 57–75

Creutzfeld, Benjamin, 'América Latina en la política exterior china; One Broad Push: Latin America in China's Foreign Policy', *Pap. Polit.*, 18.2 (2013), pp. 599–611

Da Costa, Alexandre Emboaba, 'Thinking "Post-Racial" Ideology Transnationally: The Contemporary Politics of Race and Indigeneity in the Americas', *Critical Sociology*, 42.4–5 (2016), pp. 475–90

De la Maza, Francisca, and Luis Eugenio Campos, 'The Irruption of Afro-Descendants in Diversity Politics: The Case of Arica in Northern Chile', *Identities*, 28.4 (2021), pp. 436–53 <https://doi.org/10.1080/1070289X.2020.1813458>

DeHart, Monica, 'Chino Tico Routes and Repertoires: Cultivating Chineseness and Entrepreneurism for a New Era of Trans-Pacific Relations', *The Journal of Latin American and Caribbean Anthropology*, 23.1 (2018), pp. 74–93

———, *Transpacific Developments: The Politics of Multiple Chinas in Central Americas* (Ithaca and London: Cornell University Press, 2021)

Galaz-Mandakovic, Damir, and Jorge Moraga Reyes, 'Migración china en Tocopilla. Heterogeneidad relacional y transformaciones internas (Chile, 1884–1960)', *Revista Rumbos TS. Un espacio crítico para la reflexión en Ciencias Sociales*, 24 (2021), pp. 85–128 <https://doi.org/10.51188/rrts.num24.467>

González Pizarro, José Antonio, Claudio Llanos Reyes, Marcelo Lufin Varas, José Antonio González Pizarro, Claudio Llanos Reyes, and Marcelo Lufin Varas, 'Tres Problemáticas de La Inmigración China En El Norte de Chile', *Si Somos Americanos*, 20.2 (2020), pp. 91–115 <https://doi.org/10.4067/S0719-09482020000200091>

Hatfield, Charles, *The Limits of Identity: Politics and Poetics in Latin America* (Austin: University of Texas Press, 2015)

Herbert, Julián, *La casa del dolor ajeno* (México, D.F: Literatura Random House, 2015)

Hu-DeHart, Evelyn, 'Multiculturalism in Latin American Studies: Locating the "Asian" Immigrant; or, Where Are the Chinos and Turcos?', *Latin American Research Review*, 44.2 (2009), pp. 235–42

Iacobelli, Pedro, and Maria Montt Strabucchi, 'Encuentros con Asia: Una reflexión en torno a la historiografía latinoamericana desde la cuenca del océano Pacifico', *Historia 396*, 10.2 (2020), pp. 179–204

Klengel, Susanne, and Alexandra Ortiz Wallner, 'A New Poetics and Politics of Thinking Latin America / India. SUR / SOUTH and a Different Orientalism', in *Sur/South: Poetics and Politics of Thinking Latin America-India*, ed. by Susanne Klengel and Alexandra Ortiz Wallner (Madrid: Vervuert, 2016), pp. 7–26

La Jornada Morelos, 'Julián Herbert: "Pancho Villa no asesinó a los 303 chinos de Torreón en 1911"', *La Jornada Morelos*, (2016) <http://www.elclarin.cl/web/entrevistas/18622-julian-herbert-pancho-villa-no-asesino-a-los-303-chinos-de-torreon-en-1911.html> [accessed 1 July 2017]

Labarca, Claudia, and Maria Montt Strabucchi, 'Discurso como representación de sentido en las relaciones internacionales: el caso sino-chileno', *Estudios Políticos*, 47 (2019), pp. 163–84 <http://dx.doi.org/10.22201/fcpys.24484903e.2019.47.69504>

Lee, Ana Paulina, *Mandarin Brazil: Race, Representation, and Memory* (Stanford: Stanford University Press, 2018)

López, Kathleen, 'The Asian Presence in *Mestizo* Nations: A Response', in *Critical Terms in Caribbean and Latin American Thought*, ed. by Yolanda Martínez-San Miguel, Ben. Sifuentes-Jáuregui, and Marisa Belausteguigoitia (New York: Palgrave Macmillan, 2016), pp. 125–31

Malamud Rikles, Carlos Daniel, 'China y América Latina: ¿qué esperan los unos de los otros?', *Anuario Asia-Pacífico*, 1 (2006), pp. 103–14

Mardones Marshall, Antonia, 'Who Is Afro-Chilean? Authenticity Struggles and Boundary Making in Chile's Northern Borderland', *Ethnic and Racial Studies*, 44.1 (2021), pp. 1–23 <https://doi.org/10.1080/01419870.2020.1839667>

Martínez-San Miguel, Yolanda, Ben. Sifuentes-Jáuregui, and Marisa Belausteguigoitia, 'Introduction', in *Critical Terms in Caribbean and Latin American Thought*, ed. by Yolanda Martínez-San Miguel, Ben. Sifuentes-Jáuregui, and Marisa Belausteguigoitia, New Directions in Latino American Cultures (Palgrave Macmillan US, 2016), pp. 1–21 <https://doi.org/10.1057/9781137547903_1>

Mazza, Jacqueline, 'Migration in a Mobile Age: Perspectives from China, India, and the Americas', in *Latin America and the Asian Giants*, ed. by Riordan Roett and Guadalupe Paz (Washington: Brookings Institution Press, 2016), pp. 183–204

McClintock, Anne, *Imperial Leather: Race, Gender, and Sexuality in the Colonial Contest* (New York: Routledge, 1995)

'Medios de todo el mundo criticaron a Cristina Kirchner por burlarse del acento chino', *La Nación*, 2 April 2015 <http://www.lanacion.com.ar/1765712-medios-de-todo-el-mundo-criticaron-a-cristina-kirchner-por-burlarse-del-acento-chino> [accessed 1 July 2021]

Montt Strabucchi, Maria, and Carol Chan, 'Questioning the Conditional Visibility of the Chinese: (Non)Normative Representations of China and Chineseness in Chilean Cultural Productions', *Journal of Chinese Overseas*, 16.1 (2020), pp. 90–116 <https://doi.org/10.1163/17932548-12341414>

Montt Strabucchi, Maria, Carol Chan, and María Elvira Ríos, *Chineseness in Chile: Shifting Representations during the Twenty-First Century*, Studies of the Americas (Cham: Palgrave Macmillan, 2022) <https://doi.org/10.1007/978-3-030-83966-6>

Montt Strabucchi, Maria, and Johannes Rehner, 'Del Galeón de Manila a la IED: Rutas de intercambio entre China y América Latina', *Asia América Latina*, 5 (2020), pp. 8–31 <https://doi.org/10.33177/8.3>

Moraga Reyes, Jorge, 'Reparto comunitario y gasto agonístico: diferenciaciones y hegemonías entre antiguos y nuevos migrantes chinos en Chile', *Rumbos TS*, 17 (2018), pp. 133–52

Moreno Figueroa, Mónica G., and Emiko Saldívar Tanaka, '"We Are Not Racists, We Are Mexicans": Privilege, Nationalism and Post-Race Ideology in Mexico', *Critical Sociology*, 42.4–5 (2016), pp. 515–233

Nancy, Jean-Luc, *Being Singular Plural* (Stanford: Stanford University Press, 2000)

———, *The Inoperative Community* (Minneapolis: University of Minnesota Press, 1991)

Osnos, Evan, 'Christina Kirchner's Misadventure in China', *The New Yorker*, 2 June 2015 <http://www.newyorker.com/news/daily-comment/cristina-kirchner-misadventure-china> [accessed 1 July 2021]

Oviedo, Eduardo Daniel, 'Argentina and China: An Analysis of the Actors in the Soybean Trade and the Migratory Flow', *Journal of Chinese Political Science*, 20.3 (2015), pp. 243–66

Palma, Patricia, and José Ragas, 'Enclaves Sanitarios: Higiene, Epidemias y Salud en el Barrio Chino de Lima, 1880–1910', *Anuario Colombiano de Historia Social y de la Cultura*, 45.1 (2018), pp. 159–90 <https://doi.org/10.15446/achsc.v45n1.67555>

Paz, Gonzalo S., 'Argentina and Asia: China's Reemergence, Argentina's Recovery', in *Reaching across the Pacific: Latin America and Asia in the New Century*, ed. by Cynthia Arnson and Jorge Heine (Washington: Woodrow Wilson International Center for Scholars, 2014), pp. 153–86

Pérez Ludeña, Miguel, *Chinese Investments in Latin America: Opportunities for Growth and Diversification*, Production Development (Santiago: United Nations, 2017)

Pew Research Center, 'Balance of Power: U.S. vs. China', *Pew Research Center's Global Attitudes Project*, (2014) <https://www.pewresearch.org/global/2014/07/14/chapter-3-balance-of-power-u-s-vs-china/> [accessed 17 May 2022]

PewResearch, 'America's Global Image Remains More Positive than China's', *Pew Research Center's Global Attitudes Project*, (2013) <http://www.pewglobal.org/2013/07/18/americas-global-image-remains-more-positive-than-chinas/> [accessed 1 August 2021]

———, 'Global Opposition to U.S. Surveillance and Drones, but Limited Harm to America's Image', *Pew Research Center's Global Attitudes Project*, (2014) <http://www.pewglobal.org/2014/07/14/global-opposition-to-u-s-surveillance-and-drones-but-limited-harm-to-americas-image/> [accessed 1 August 2021]

Ríos, María Elvira, María Montt, and Carol Chan, 'El imaginario de lo chino en las revistas magazinescas chilenas de principios del siglo XX', *Revista Rumbos TS. Un espacio crítico para la reflexión en Ciencias Sociales*, 24 (2021), pp. 129–50 <https://doi.org/10.51188/rrts.num24.434>

Rylance, Rick, *Literature and the Public Good: The Literary Agenda* (Oxford: Oxford University Press, 2016)

Schoene, Berthold, *The Cosmopolitan Novel* (Edinburgh: Edinburgh University Press, 2011)

Serrano-Moreno, Juan Enrique, Diego Telias, and Francisco Urdinez, 'Deconstructing the Belt and Road Initiative in Latin America', *Asian Education and Development Studies*, 10.3 (2021), pp. 337–47 <https://doi.org/10.1108/AEDS-01-2020-0021>

Shambaugh, David, *China–Europe Relations: Perceptions, Policies and Prospects* (London: Routledge, 2008)

Siskind, Mariano, *Cosmopolitan Desires: Global Modernity and World Literature in Latin America* (Evanston: Northwestern University Press, 2014)

Siu, Lok, and Claire Chun, 'Yellow Peril and Techno-Orientalism in the Time of Covid-19: Racialized Contagion, Scientific Espionage, and Techno-Economic Warfare', *Journal of Asian American Studies*, 23.3 (2020), pp. 421–40 <https://doi.org/10.1353/jaas.2020.0033>

Solano Rivera, Silvia, 'El destino y la explotación legitimada en "Tarciso Cantón", de Tatiana Buch', *Revista Comunicación*, 25.1 (2016), pp. 31–39

Texidó, Ezequiel, and Jorge Gurrieri, 'Panorama Migratorio de América del Sur 2012', 2012 <http://publications.iom.int/system/files/pdf/panorama_migratorio_de_america_del_sur2012.pdf> [accessed 1 July 2021]

Turcsányi, Richard Q., Klára Dubravčíková, James Iocovezzi, Matej Šimalčík, and Kristína Kironská, 'US-China Rivalry in the Global South? Insights from a Public Opinion Survey', *CEIAS*, 2022

Tzili Apango, Eduardo, '"Estudios sobre China desde Latinoamérica. Geopolítica, Religión e Inmigración" - Susan Chen Mok, Jorge Bartels Villanueva y Ricardo Martínez Esquivel (eds.)', *Estudios Internacionales*, 46.178 (2014), pp. 207–12

Urdinez, Francisco, Jan Knoerich, and Pedro Feliú Ribeiro, 'Don't Cry for Me "Argenchina": Unraveling Political Views of China through Legislative Debates in Argentina', *Journal of Chinese Political Science*, 23.2 (2018), pp. 235–56 <https://doi.org/10.1007/s11366-016-9450-y>

Wilson, Vicente, and Cristóbal Torres, *El vuelo de la luciérnaga* (Santiago: Trayecto Ediciones, 2019)

Index

Printed and bound by CPI Group (UK) Ltd, Croydon, CR0 4YY

07/07/2026

14916210-0002